The break-up of Greater Britain

Manchester University Press

General editors: Andrew S. Thompson and Alan Lester
Founding editor: John M. MacKenzie

When the 'Studies in Imperialism' series was founded by Professor John M. MacKenzie more than thirty years ago, emphasis was laid upon the conviction that 'imperialism as a cultural phenomenon had as significant an effect on the dominant as on the subordinate societies'. With well over a hundred titles now published, this remains the prime concern of the series. Cross-disciplinary work has indeed appeared covering the full spectrum of cultural phenomena, as well as examining aspects of gender and sex, frontiers and law, science and the environment, language and literature, migration and patriotic societies, and much else. Moreover, the series has always wished to present comparative work on European and American imperialism, and particularly welcomes the submission of books in these areas. The fascination with imperialism, in all its aspects, shows no sign of abating, and this series will continue to lead the way in encouraging the widest possible range of studies in the field. 'Studies in Imperialism' is fully organic in its development, always seeking to be at the cutting edge, responding to the latest interests of scholars and the needs of this ever-expanding area of scholarship.

To buy or to find out more about the books currently available in this series, please go to:
https://manchesteruniversitypress.co.uk/series/studies-in-imperialism/

The break-up of Greater Britain

Edited by Christian D. Pedersen
and Stuart Ward

MANCHESTER UNIVERSITY PRESS

Copyright © Manchester University Press 2021

While copyright in the volume as a whole is vested in Manchester University Press, copyright in individual chapters belongs to their respective authors, and no chapter may be reproduced wholly or in part without the express permission in writing of both author and publisher.

Published by Manchester University Press
Oxford Road, Manchester M13 9PL

www.manchesteruniversitypress.co.uk

British Library Cataloguing-in-Publication Data
A catalogue record for this book is available from the British Library

ISBN 978 1 5261 4742 4 hardback
ISBN 978 1 5261 7446 8 paperback

First published 2021
Paperback published 2023

The publisher has no responsibility for the persistence or accuracy of URLs for any external or third-party internet websites referred to in this book, and does not guarantee that any content on such websites is, or will remain, accurate or appropriate.

Typeset
by Sunrise Setting Ltd, Brixham

Contents

List of figures		vii
Notes on contributors		viii
Acknowledgements		xi
Introduction: The anatomy of break-up – *Stuart Ward*		1
1	Maintaining racial boundaries: Greater Britain in the Second World War and beyond – *Wendy Webster*	22
2	Cut loose: the British in China and the aftermath of empire – *Robert Bickers*	41
3	Entangled citizens: the afterlives of empire in the Indian Citizenship Act, 1947–1955 – *Kalathmika Natarajan*	63
4	'How come England did not know me?': the 'rude awakenings' of the Windrush era – *Stuart Ward*	84
5	Indians of Durban, South Africa and the break-up of Greater Britain – *Hilary Sapire*	103
6	The birth of 'white' republics and the demise of Greater Britain: the republican referendums in South Africa and Rhodesia – *Christian D. Pedersen*	125
7	'King's men', 'Queen's rebels' and 'last outposts': Ulster and Rhodesia in an age of imperial retreat – *Donal Lowry*	147
8	The tale of two Commonwealths? The (British) Commonwealth of Nations, decolonisation and the break-up of Greater Britain – *Andrew Dilley*	172
9	Greater Britain and its decline: the view from Lambeth – *Sarah Stockwell*	192

10	From *Pax Britannica* to *Pax Americana?* The end of empire and the collapse of Australia's Cold War policy – *James Curran*	213
11	Boundaries of belonging: differential fees for overseas students in Britain, c. 1967 – *Jodi Burkett*	234
12	Persistence and privilege: mass migration from Britain to the Commonwealth, 1945–2000 – *Jean P. Smith*	252
13	'The mouse that roared': the Falklands and Gibraltar in Thatcher's (Greater) Britain – *Ezequiel Mercau*	272
14	Falling Rhodes, building bridges, finding paths: decoloniality from Cape Town to Oxford, and back – *Stephen Howe*	294
Index		311

Figures

12.1 Net migration between the United Kingdom and the empire/former empire, 1913–2000 — 255
12.2 Emigration from the United Kingdom, 1952–2000 — 256
12.3 Emigration from the United Kingdom to the empire/former empire by destination, 1946–2000 — 257

Contributors

Robert Bickers is a Professor of History at the University of Bristol. His most recent books are *China Bound: John Swire & Sons and its World, 1816–1980* (2020), and *Out of China: How the Chinese Ended the Era of Foreign Domination* (2017).

Jodi Burkett is Principal Lecturer and Subject Area Leader for History at the University of Portsmouth. She has published widely on ideas of Britishness at the end of empire, and left-wing and student anti-racist activism. Her most recent book, the edited collection *Students in Twentieth Century Britain and Ireland*, was published in 2018.

James Curran is Professor of Modern History at Sydney University and Non-resident Fellow at the United States Studies Centre. He is the co-author, with Stuart Ward, of *The Unknown Nation: Australia after Empire* (2010) and his most recent work is *Unholy Fury: Whitlam and Nixon at War* (2015). He is currently working on a history of Australia–China relations for NewSouth Press. Curran has held a Fulbright Scholarship at Georgetown University and in 2013 was Keith Cameron Chair of Australian History at University College Dublin. He is also a foreign affairs columnist for the *Australian Financial Review*.

Andrew Dilley is a Senior Lecturer in History at the University of Aberdeen. He has researched and published widely on the economics and politics of the British Empire, with a current focus on the political economy and political culture of the Commonwealth of Nations.

Stephen Howe is a Senior Research Fellow at the University of Bristol and an editor of the *Journal of Imperial and Commonwealth History*.

Donal Lowry is a Senior Member of Regent's Park College in the University of Oxford. He is a member of the Editorial Board of the *Journal of Southern*

African Studies. His recent publications include: '"Cuckoo in the Commonwealth Nest": The Irish Impact and the Commonwealth Legacy for Ireland', in R. Drayton and S. Dubow (eds), *Commonwealth History in the 21st Century* (2020); 'A "Supreme and Permanent Symbol of Executive Authority": The Crown and the Governorship of Northern Ireland in an Age of Troubles', and 'The Queen of Rhodesia versus the Queen of the United Kingdom: Conflicts of Allegiance in Rhodesia's UDI', both in H. Kumarasingham (ed.), *Viceregalism: The Crown and its Representatives in Political Crises in the Post-War Commonwealth* (2020).

Ezequiel Mercau is a Research Fellow at the Centre for War Studies in University College Dublin. He was awarded a Government of Ireland Postdoctoral Fellowship by the Irish Research Council. His research interests encompass global imperial decline and the diminishing frontiers of Britishness, especially in the context of overseas 'British' communities in the Falklands, Northern Ireland, Gibraltar and Hong Kong. He is the author of *The Falklands War* (2019).

Kalathmika Natarajan is a Teaching Fellow in South Asian History at the University of Edinburgh. She is currently working on a monograph based on her doctoral thesis that examines the afterlives of indenture in Indian diplomacy and is also involved in projects that seek to address the amnesia over caste in the study of Indian diplomacy and international relations. She has previously worked as a research associate to the editors of the *Oxford Handbook of Indian Foreign Policy* at the Centre for Policy Research, New Delhi and received a Sarai fellowship from the Centre for the Study of Developing Societies, New Delhi.

Christian D. Pedersen is Assistant Professor in Modern History at the University of Southern Denmark. His research interests include modern British history, connections between Britain and Africa, and the history of the British world. He has previously been a visiting scholar at Oxford University and the British Institute in Eastern Africa.

Hilary Sapire is an historian of Southern Africa who teaches imperial, global and African history at Birkbeck College, University of London.

Jean P. Smith works on the history of race and migration in twentieth-century Britain and the (former) British Empire. She has held appointments at the University of Leeds and King's College London, where she was a Leverhulme Trust Early Career Fellow and is currently Lecturer in British Imperial History. Her work has appeared in *War and Society, Twentieth*

Century British History, *The Journal of Imperial and Commonwealth History* and *Women's History Review*.

Sarah Stockwell is Professor of Imperial and Commonwealth History at King's College London. Her most recent books are *The British End of the British Empire* (2018) and, with Véronique Dimier, an edited collection, *The Business of Development in Post-Colonial Africa* (2020). Other recent publications relate to the Church of England and decolonisation, the subject of her contribution to this volume. As well as ongoing research on Anglicanism and the end of empire, her other current research focus is on the history of development.

Stuart Ward is Professor and Head of the Saxo Institute for History, Archaeology, Ethnology and Classics at the University of Copenhagen. He is the author of *Australia and the British Embrace: The Demise of the Imperial Ideal* (2001), and co-author with James Curran of *The Unknown Nation: Australia after Empire* (2010). He has edited *British Culture and the End of Empire* (2001) and co-edited *Australia's Empire* (2008) with Deryck M. Schreuder in the *Oxford History of the British Empire* series. He was director of the collaborative research project 'Embers of Empire: The Receding Frontiers of Post-Imperial Britain' (funded by the Velux Foundation, 2013–2018) and has recently co-edited, with Astrid Rasch, *Embers of Empire in Brexit Britain* (2019). He is currently completing a forthcoming book, *Untied Kingdom: A World History of the End of Britain*.

Wendy Webster is Professor of Modern Cultural History at the University of Huddersfield and has published widely on twentieth-century history. She is the author of *Not A Man to Match Her: The Marketing of a Prime Minister* (1990), *Imagining Home: Gender, 'Race' and National Identity* (1998), the prize-winning *Englishness and Empire* (2005), *Gendering Migration* (edited with Louise Ryan, 1998) and *Mixing It: Diversity in World War Two Britain* (2018). She has been a Visiting Fellow at Australian National University and the University of Tasmania.

Acknowledgements

This volume has its origins in a conference held at Holckenhavn Castle in Denmark in 2018, the culmination of a major collaborative research project, 'Embers of Empire' at the University of Copenhagen (2013–2018), funded by the Velux Foundation. Comprising both members of the project as well as leading specialists in the field, *The Break-up of Greater Britain* aims to shed novel light on the receding frontiers of post-imperial Britain and Britishness from a global perspective. We acknowledge the generous financial support of the Velux Foundation and the Department of History at the University of Southern Denmark, Odense.

Our sincere thanks are due to the contributors for being part of this venture as well as other participants at the conference for their moral and intellectual support, especially Kristine Kjærsgaard, Harshan Kumarasingham, Harriet Mercer, Astrid Rasch, Casper Sylvest and Nils Arne Sørensen. At Manchester University Press, Emma Brennan and Paul Clarke have been supportive and efficient from the outset, and we thank them too. We finally thank the two anonymous referees of the original book proposal and the reader of the final manuscript for their helpful and encouraging comments and remarks.

INTRODUCTION

The anatomy of break-up

Stuart Ward

In his surprise 1962 bestseller *The Anatomy of Britain*, Anthony Sampson was among the first to diagnose the post-war ailments of a nation 'confused about her purpose – with those acres of red on the map dwindling, the mission of the war dissolving, and the whole imperial mythology of battleships, governors and generals gone for ever'.[1] Sampson's guide to the intricate maze of individuals who controlled the sinews of power in 1960s Britain – from politics to business, industry, education, finance, the media and the military – furnished a portrait of collective delusion on a nationwide scale. Everywhere he looked, he encountered a 'discrepancy between Britain as she liked to appear, and Britain as she is'; a ruling caste, caught between the obsolete monuments to 'an apparently unchanged and permanent world' and the ubiquitous traces of endemic decline. Employing Yeats's aphorism 'Things fall apart; the centre cannot hold', he identified a pervasive dread that Britain 'will be to the twenty-first century what Spain was to the eighteenth'. Indeed, of all the stages in any nation's history, 'the aftermath of Empire must be the hardest'.[2]

Fifteen years later, in 1977, Tom Nairn published *The Break-up of Britain*, his opening salvo noting how 'inconceivable' such a title would have been 'only a few years ago'. Nairn's sweeping critique of Britain's 'backward' state configuration, nurturing a society in which 'bourgeois radicalism and popular mobilization were eschewed for the sake of conservative stability', was similarly harnessed to the remnants of empire. For centuries, he argued, an 'imperial state' whose 'ascendancy over its competitors in colonization accompanied the crystallization of its internal forms' had fostered a 'symbiosis' between Britain's social system and 'the country's maritime and conquering adventures'. Indeed, it was the imperial state's 'extraordinary external successes … that permitted it to survive so long', well into the post-Second World War era even as its worldwide mission came unstuck. But with the empire now relegated to the distant past, Nairn, like Sampson, could perceive how 'the loss of its critical overseas wealth and connections was bound to promote internal readjustments'. More radically, he looked forward to the prospect of wholesale social renewal in the wake of impending 'territorial disintegration' across the country, revelling in what had now become (to him at least) self-evident: 'There is no doubt that the old British state is going down', along with the empire that had underpinned its worst defects.[3]

In the fifteen years between Sampson's polemic and Nairn's prophecy, speculation about a possible connection between the end of empire and Britain's unsteady future had become increasingly commonplace. Writers, academics and columnists spanning the full bandwidth of political persuasion could agree that the entanglements of empire posed a threat (or promise, depending on the persuasion) to the integrity and long-term viability of the United Kingdom. Sampson's book appeared amid an upsurge of critical writing and social commentary that was soon dubbed the 'What's wrong with Britain?' genre – a tide of introspection and self-examination that dissected the nation's innumerable flaws. Some, like Michael Shanks's *The Stagnant Society* (1961), pondered whether Britain was poised to become 'a lotus island of easy, tolerant ways, bathed in the golden glow of an imperial sunset', or whether the spirit of 'the tough, dynamic race we have been in the past' could be recovered.[4] Others, like John Mander's *Great Britain or Little England?*, considered this rear-view gaze the crux of the problem, echoing Sampson's lament that the British people had never been properly jolted into a full appreciation of their downsized dimensions in the post-war world. While Europe's war-weary peoples had learned the hard way 'that loss of Empire is an irreversible and agonising process', Britain alone, it seemed, had been spared the necessity of a 'total national reorientation' – much to their own detriment.[5]

Enoch Powell's characteristically contrarian response was to negate the premise itself, dismissing the empire variously as a 'myth', an 'invention', 'deception', 'fantastic structure' and a 'giant farce', which had flourished in the realm of the imagination without ever materially impinging on the lives of English men and women in any profound way. That being so, its passing could be embraced not just with equanimity, but as a rare opportunity to reconnect with the unchanged essence of Englishness. According to this logic, if the empire had never carried any real meaning or significance for ordinary people, its loss could be 'no very strong argument for national decline'.[6] Yet Powell's rediscovery 'at the heart of a vanished empire, amid the fragments of demolished glory' of an England untarnished by imperial delusion was itself an exercise in dissolving the emotional bonds between the constituent elements of the United Kingdom.[7] His attempt to disaggregate the fate of empire from the viability of the nation itself merely affirmed their mutual entanglement.[8]

Scottish and Welsh separatists tended to view the matter differently, warming to the idea of a unitary Britishness on the verge of extinction. As their party membership surged throughout the 1960s and their share of the popular vote in key constituencies multiplied, causation was frequently attributed to the empire's precipitate demise. Celebrating victory at the 1966 Carmarthen by-election, Plaid Cymru's official newspaper declared that 'Post-imperialist' Britain had reached a turning point; 'bereft of the "empire on which the sun never set" and of her world-wide maritime power', the country now stood 'disillusioned in the cold grey light of unromantic dawn'.[9] Glasgow University's Harry Hanham diagnosed a similar causality when the Scottish National Party snatched the seat of Hamilton from Labour the following year: 'Now that the Empire is dead', he ventured, 'many Scots feel cramped and restricted at home ... To give themselves an opening to a wider world the Scots need some sort of outlet, and the choice appears at the moment to be between emigration and re-creating the Scottish nation at home'.[10] Such reasoning was not confined to secessionist groups but affected a wide and restless spectrum of social and political movements clamouring for reform. As Raphael Samuel recalled years later, 'for the "Progressives" of the 1960s, Empire, the British national identity itself, was something to escape from'.[11]

Variations on the theme continued into the 1970s, with Jan Morris's memorable verdict: 'Who gets satisfaction from the present state of the Union? Who is really content with this grubby wreck of old glories?'[12] Michael Hechter's 'internal colonialism' paradigm posited the 'Celtic Fringe' as the last frontier of a contracting English state that 'in common with colonialism overseas ... attempted to rule the Celtic lands for instrumental ends'.[13] With the publication of Nairn's *Break-up of Britain* in 1977, the subject entered into mainstream academic debate. Sensing the gathering momentum of what he termed the 'decline of empire thesis', Keith Webb offered a corrective in *The Growth of Nationalism in Scotland* (1977) where he questioned the extent to which growing support for Scottish separatism could plausibly be linked with imperial decline.[14] Keith Robbins joined the fray, noting how late-nineteenth-century home rulers in Scotland had used the empire as an argument *in favour* of devolved constitutional powers – hence there could be no 'inevitable corollary' between a 'common sharing in empire' and a robust centralised state.[15] But these interventions did little to dampen speculation, or to temper Welsh Historian Gwyn Williams' 1979 verdict that Britain itself had 'begun its long march out of history ... into a post-imperial fog'.[16]

These early works laid the groundwork for what would evolve into an historical axiom, widely echoed in press commentary and public debate as a self-evident proposition needing little elaboration. Linda Colley's 1992 study of the origins of a unitary Britishness was enormously influential in popularising the 'decline of empire' thesis, not least her remarks about 'today's increasingly strident calls for a break-up of Britain':

> We can understand the nature of the present crisis only if we recognize that the factors that provided for the forging of a British nation in the past have largely ceased to operate. Protestantism, that once vital cement, has now a limited influence on British culture ... Recurrent wars with the states of Continental Europe have in all likelihood come to an end ... And, crucially, both commercial supremacy and imperial hegemony have gone.[17]

Colley's deployment of a Hegelian 'other' (via Lacan and French psychoanalysis) furnished the constitutive markers against which Britons had defined themselves historically, foreshadowing a later process of inevitable fragmentation in an era when 'so many of the components of Britishness ha[d] faded'.[18] Her ideas soon became common currency in contemporary diagnoses of the British problem, ready to hand in newspaper op-eds and political commentary.[19] Yet only rarely, if ever, was the chain of causation developed beyond Colley's emphasis on a *dynamic absence* (the triangulation of empire, religion and war, all relegated to the past), as though the mere removal of Britain's external props inexorably paved the way to internal fragmentation.[20]

This template has continued to frame the problem in more recent scholarship. Krishan Kumar, for example, points to the 'missionary zeal' of an inherently expansive Britishness that had held the constituent parts of the United Kingdom together for generations but could never survive the realities of imperial retreat.[21] Again, the emphasis was on documenting the expansive zeal rather than the sequence of causation that attended its removal. Others have stressed the loss of a sense of common endeavour and shared material self-interest that for centuries had rewarded the British peoples for sinking their differences. Andrew Gamble puts the case most succinctly: 'The end of empire meant the disappearance of the project which for so long had defined Britishness and British institutions'.[22] Much seems to hinge on the dynamic properties of 'disappearance', shifting the burden of proof onto the period preceding decolonisation rather than its crucial aftermath.

All of these positions are certainly intriguing, and more than superficially persuasive. But they also share a conspicuous lack of interest in testing the argument empirically, or mounting a case based on the complex interplay between empire and metropole. The reliance on overarching meta-narratives has tended to preclude any formulation of clear criteria for historical validation. This has enabled the 'decline of empire' thesis to pervade media commentary, political debate and the scholarly literature virtually unopposed. To the extent that dissenting views have emerged, these too have tended to be intuitive rather than intensively researched. Early sceptics such as Webb and Robbins (as we have seen) were content to dismiss the underlying assumptions rather than offer a genuine alternative, and subsequent critique has unfolded along similar lines. T. M. Devine's objection that 'Mrs Thatcher has an infinitely greater claim to be the midwife of Scottish devolution than the factor of imperial decline' presumed a zero-sum game of historical causation (it could only be the one or the other), deflecting the question rather than engaging with its possibilities.[23] Even Linda Colley, apparently ill at ease with a too hasty historical consensus, felt obliged to revise and finesse her position in 2007: 'Claims that the end of Empire *must* also and desirably result in the disintegration of the UK', she cautioned, 'are driven at once by selective history and teleology'. The emphasis on 'must' suggested that it was only a partial recantation.[24]

* * *

This volume addresses the 'absence' at the heart of the equation, or rather, the other side of the equation that has consistently been overlooked in the more than half a century since the external dynamics of 'break-up' were first broached. In placing so much stress on the instrumentalities of 'disappearance', historians and political commentators have performed a remarkable disappearing act of their own, erasing any tangible imperial experience or influence from their field of vision. With only few exceptions, all of the major contributors to the 'break-up of Britain' debate have written from a metropolitan perspective, traversing the problem as a 'four nations' story of internal dislocation, even as they attribute causation to undifferentiated external factors. No meaningful connections across the empire–metropole interface have ever been elaborated, nor any deeper reflection on precisely how a declining empire might have played a part in effecting a rupture at the heart of the Union. Nor indeed has the evident absurdity of the empire's presumed 'absence' been subjected to scrutiny, as though somehow its myriad legacies and lasting entanglements literally ceased to matter once the formalities of decolonisation had run their course.

In his 2009 elegy, *The Country Formerly Known as Great Britain*, Ian Jack assembled a collection of thirty-five highly personal essays that 'turned out to be journeys into odd corners of a British civilization that is vanishing, if not quite vanished'. He added a revealing rider:

> It was never of course, confined to Britain – the empire saw to that – and in the 1980s in India and Sri Lanka, it was still possible to find people and places (the jute workers of Serampur, the Anglo-Indians of McCluskiegunge) formed by the empire's social and technical legacy. These were good vantage points from which to look back and wonder.[25]

They also provide a useful starting point for this volume; a belated acknowledgement that the end of empire was not simply an inert backdrop to the realignment of national allegiances in Britain but entailed simultaneous challenges to collective selfhood among vast constituencies of peoples and cultures around the world, all variously engaged, willingly or otherwise, in extricating themselves from the obsolete totems of empire and Britishness. In recent decades, major works of imperial and global history have brought overseas projections of British culture and identities to the fore, advancing a transnational conception of imperial Britishness arising out of trans-oceanic migrations and communications, economic and cultural exchange, institutional networks and perhaps, above all, shared emotional investments.[26] Generally, however, this work has focused on connections forged during a vaguely inscribed 'heyday' of Victorian and Edwardian imperialism, leaving aside how these fared through the decades of decolonisation and its aftermath.[27]

Indeed, for all the renewed interest in these lapsed templates of transnational British belonging, the demise of Britishness as a global civic idea remains a neglected line of enquiry. Over a remarkably short time span (little more than a few decades in the wake of the Second World War), the ideas, assumptions and networks that had sustained an uneven and imperfectly imagined British world dissolved under the weight of the empire's burdensome legacies. Although these developments have been explored in several local contexts ranging from Australia to Canada, South Africa, the Caribbean, Hong Kong and the Falkland Islands, relatively little attention has been paid to the wider mesh of interlocking British subjectivities that unravelled at empire's end.[28]

This book offers no clear resolution to the problem of how the end of empire contributed to the loosening bonds of Britishness in the United Kingdom; indeed, the metropolitan context is deliberately rendered in a minor key so as to allow much wider patterns of reorientation and realignment to emerge. Rather than frame the empire as the 'one big thing' that fractured the integrity of the United Kingdom,[29] there is valuable perspective to be gained from putting the travails of the Union into their proper perspective, as just one of any number of civic ruptures occasioned by the serial dislocations of decolonisation. Nor do the following chapters present any straightforward consensus about the nature and significance of British modes of self-representation around the world, either during the lifespan of the empire itself or the myriad adjustments that occurred in its wake. The sheer range of historical settings, social conditions and subject matter that need to be taken into consideration militates against any easy formulation of uniform attributes or shared trajectories.

One obvious difficulty is the matter of terminology. As James Vernon points out, the 'worlding' of British history is by no means a new endeavour;

indeed, it is arguably as old as the empire itself.[30] New scholarship that emerged in the 1980s under the rubric of 'empire and metropolitan culture' or, more broadly, the 'new imperial history' was largely welcomed as long overdue; the former for breaking down rigid conceptual barriers that had insulated British social and cultural history from wider imperial influences; the latter for re-energising the subject by seeking to 'unsettle' a pervasive imperial 'amnesia' and to 'grapple with the continuing hold of racialized forms of politics' in a post-imperial nation.[31] But more recent attempts to frame the subject in terms of 'Britain and the world' or a more objectified 'British World' have not been uniformly well received.[32] Partly, the suspicion arises from the resurgence of white nationalist movements across the English-speaking world that frequently elicit a family resemblance with older, empire-wide affinities (the 'Anglosphere' being one prominent reminder of the lingering ideological resonances).[33] Related to this is the concern that the new 'worldly' rubrics resonate 'uncannily with Conservative justifications of Brexit as an opportunity to "embrace the world" and once again be a "Global Britain"'.[34]

Uncanny resonances, however, are not the same as a conscious common endeavour, and it would be misleading to posit a crude instrumentality between British World historical paradigms and the resurgence of global posturing in the Brexit debate (let alone the reactionary far-right politics of white victimhood).[35] Tamson Pietsch allows for greater subtlety, identifying a 'tendency to flatten out fissures and frictions' in the relentless focus on 'Britishness', which has 'worked to obscure the ways such identities helped to normalize the practices of settler colonialism, while simultaneously sidelining issues of power, access, difference, and contest within colonial societies'.[36] But she stops short of dismissing the paradigm itself as inherently regressive.[37] Others have countered that workable concepts need to be devised in order to provide a way for historians to 'avoid using "empire"' – rather than be lumped with an imprecise blanket term that, as Miles Ogborn attests, encompasses merely one aspect (albeit a highly significant one) of all the 'thinkable connections' between Britain and the world.[38] Clearly, more is at stake than conceptual convenience, yet for all the extensive critique, no alternative formulation has secured universal endorsement.[39] Nor, for that matter, is there any broad agreement as to whether a viable subject can or should be named at all, with Rachel Bright and Andrew Dilley prominent among those convinced that 'a distinctive concept of the British world is not really needed' – nor particularly serviceable.[40]

The conceptual ambiguity also arises from what Saul Dubow terms the 'fissile multiplicity' of the British sensibilities that fell within the empire's sway.[41] Contemporaries never formulated any stable nomenclature that could capture wide divergences of perspective and experience, and it is thus unsurprising that historians have been unable to agree on a shared conceptualisation. This highlights the risk of constructing a discrete British 'world' out of the subjective (and often slippery) subjectivities of its putative membership – particularly when the question of membership itself was a prominent bone of contention.[42] But if the object is to look beyond presumptive 'worlds' to consider the 'global history of the multiple, patchy, and at times subversive uses to which vocabularies of Britishness have been put, by all actors within and beyond Britain and the British Empire', these terminological fractures and fissures become central to the undertaking – not least when it comes to explaining the unravelling of those vocabularies in the decades after 1945.[43]

In co-opting the idea of *Greater Britain* – originally coined by Charles Dilke in his 1868 travelogue and later popularised by John Seeley's *The Expansion of England* (1883) – our aim is not to trace the semantic history of one fixed iteration or a specific form of words. Dilke's term enjoyed popular currency throughout the late nineteenth and early twentieth centuries before fading from view in the 1930s and falling quickly into disuse after the Second World War. On the face of it, it might seem crudely anachronistic in the context of post-war decolonisation and beyond.[44] But as James Belich points out, focusing strictly on rhetorical form 'does not do the reality justice … Greater Britain was not just a failed idea. It had no formal shape, no federal constitution, yet it was an important economic and cultural reality'.[45] As a means of capturing a more generalised, transcontinental sweep of peoples unbounded (in theory) by the conventional constraints of geography, citizenship and separate statehood, the term invokes an entity that contemporaries would at least have recognised and understood, albeit from multiple standpoints and assorted permutations of meaning.

Duncan Bell's work has been particularly influential in reviving the term as a means of furnishing 'an adequate account of the languages through which the empire – or, more precisely, the various socio-political formations that composed the imperial system – was imagined by its inhabitants'. Much the same could be said for employing *Greater Britain* as the touchstone of a protracted *unimagining* in the decades after 1945. Bell makes a further point that is especially pertinent to conceptualising the relationship between empire and civic identity: 'While numerous scholars have argued that British identity was formed through a binary coding of difference in relation to an exotic "Other," many, perhaps even the majority, of late Victorian British theorists of empire were concerned as much (and sometimes more) with the projection and sustenance of a coherent sense of Britishness'.[46] In this scheme of things, accounting for the break-up of *Greater* Britain becomes less a matter of obsolescent 'otherness' and more an inquiry into the steadily waning expectation of global *coherence*, with consequences much wider in their implications than the fragmentation of the United Kingdom.

How wide, depends on how far we are inclined to stretch the term itself.[47] Charles Dilke's original coinage was strictly limited to the rarefied realm of race, his journey to Greater Britain tracing the movements of white settlers to those select parts of the world where, though 'climate, soil, manner of life ... had modified the blood ... in essentials, the race was always one'.[48] Seeley too espoused a thoroughly white conception of Greater Britain, devoting a sizeable portion of his energies to discounting the non-white inhabitants of British India who were completely unlike 'those tens of millions of Englishmen who live outside of the British Islands. The latter are of our own blood, and are therefore united to us by the strongest tie'.[49] J. A. Froude's *Oceana, Or England and Her Colonies* (1886) similarly insisted that 'the people at home and the people in the colonies are one people', leaving no doubt that his conception of the people extended only to 'our kindred, bone of our bone, flesh of our flesh'.[50] Bill Schwarz underlines how these three high priests of Greater Britain made the case 'for appreciating the specificity of the settler colonies ... race was what mattered'. Moreover, when imagined against the backdrop of 'the decay, degradation, and dirt of domestic England ... those living on the frontier could assume a kind of hyper-whiteness'.[51] Greater Britain did not lend itself easily to wider imperial affinities beyond its core racial tenets, and still retains something of its exclusively white-settler connotations.[52]

But there were also certain limits to the appeal of race nationalism in mid-Victorian Britain, which partly explains why the white racial overtones of Greater Britain were often couched in such strident terms. Advocates of Greater Britain were not simply positing a verifiable, self-evident entity, but engaging in fierce dispute about the empire's past shortcomings and boundless future potential. What Peter Mandler terms the 'civilisational perspective' of an earlier generation of English intellectuals proved remarkably adaptive and resilient, promoting the alternative view that race nationalism – so prevalent in Europe post-1848 – was 'an atavism from which England had providentially escaped'.[53] Metropolitan humanitarians had frequently depicted settler depredations against indigenous peoples as a deplorable affront to the principles of protestant liberalism – the work of a species of 'aberrant Briton', in Alan Lester's useful phrase. This was not lost on the settlers themselves, whose shrill protests against the outside meddling of metropolitan humanitarians often resembled 'struggles over the nature of Britishness itself' – a contest that hinged on how far non-white subjects should be included within the fold.[54]

As Andrew Thompson and others have shown, these fissures opened a space for other ethnicities within the empire's sway to develop 'their own strains of Loyalist ideology, which saw the Crown as a source of protection against the machinations of labour- and land-hungry settler politicians'.[55] The practice of petitioning the sovereign was just one way of prising open the racial exclusiveness of Greater Britain, drawing on the symbolism of Queen Victoria as the benevolent bestower of rights in a nominally colour-blind empire. Victoria's name furnished 'both of a common sense of membership in empire and alienation from it' – a 'moral compass', as Michael Belgrave terms it, against which settler encroachments could be measured and redress urgently sought.[56] Indigenous petitions were invariably couched in the elaborate language of fealty and loyalty, but they also offered an opportunity 'for masking and ventilating less than loyal feelings' (as Hilary Sapire has shown).[57] To be categorised as 'natives' was to be denied political and civil rights, hence the imperative of petitioning specifically as loyal British subjects. An early African National Congress (ANC) delegation arriving in London during the Great War was at pains to resist relegation to the inferiority of separate status: 'We have come not to ask for independence, but for an admission into British citizenship as British subjects so that we may also enjoy the free institutions which are the foundations and pillars of this magnificent Commonwealth'.[58] These modes of petitioning were not simply about submission to imperial authority, but also a means of drawing the petitioner and the authority into a 'shared moral order' (Ravi De Costa's term) that enshrined a higher morality than the closed circle of settler racism – one in which they themselves could claim inclusion as 'full human subjects'.[59]

Furnishing Greater Britain with a broader conceptual remit in this way is not simply about a more 'inclusive' history, but an interpretative challenge in its own right to place the contradictions of perennial difference squarely within its purview. The possibilities become far more apparent in shifting the focus to the post-Second World War era when the terms of inclusion and exclusion were constantly refashioned. Here, the pervasive permutations and pronounced *disconnections* long inherent in global conceptions of Britishness were greatly exacerbated by the onset of imperial decline. To tease this out requires more than glib assertions that Greater British identities were 'contested' and 'unstable', and to look instead at the terms of contestation itself which (perhaps ironically) constituted a shared stake in something larger. As Philip D. Morgan notes:

> Not everything is indeterminate and permeable, not everything is contested, not everything is fragile. Multiple and hybrid these identities may have been, but their integrity, their totality, their continuities with a past, their ability to maintain boundaries should not be underestimated. The British, for all their diffuseness, were, after all, rather unified linguistically and culturally.[60]

This is not to say that they were, indeed, 'one people', or that they bought equally and uniformly into the terms of endearment, still less that they were spared the iniquities of stark political, social and ethnic asymmetries. Indeed, the sheer variety of global 'incarnations' of British selfhood was never more apparent than in the circumstances of its protracted demise.[61] Gaining a better purchase on how these intersecting patterns of claim and counter-claim played out across multiple interlocking histories is the primary aim of this volume.

The chapters that follow traverse an assortment of national, regional and local contexts – from India, to China, Southern Africa, the Caribbean, Australia, New Zealand, the Falklands, Gibraltar, and the United Kingdom itself. The emphasis is not on any specific place, so much as a particular way of thinking about place, community and belonging at a time when these categories were undergoing rapid adjustment. They illustrate the extraordinary range of individual and collective subjectivities that were affected by the diminishing purchase of Britishness as a viable civic or ethnic identity, ranging far beyond (but also necessarily including) the stereotypical white settlers who recoiled at the serial betrayals (as they saw it) of a Britain engaged in rapid imperial retreat.

The opening chapter begins with the New Zealand Maori pilot, Porokuru Patapu Pohe, who enlisted only nine days after declaration of the Second World War and soon found himself flying sorties over Britain in 1941. In so doing, he defied an RAF regulation that 'only men who are British subjects and of pure European descent' could be accepted, a cardinal example of the racial demarcations of Britishness sidestepped by the exigencies of war. Wendy Webster examines the wartime hierarchies assigned, not only to racial difference, but also the subtle distinctions of rank among white 'colonials' that blurred the boundaries between white and non-white ethnicities throughout the empire, 'challenging the privileged position occupied by white people in the global community of Greater Britain'.

The next three chapters consider the disparities between theory and practice in the conception of Britishness as a broad, inclusive category, and the racial anomalies that these inevitably produced. Robert Bickers invokes the mixed-race world of the British in China, for whom the break-up of Greater Britain was a more abrupt affair than most, abolished by Treaty on 11 January 1943. These 'China Britons' adhered to a Britishness that was always contingent, tenuous, subject to practices of 'recognition and derecognition', and ever liable to be 'cut loose' upon changes in their personal or collective fortunes. Indeed, one reason that no integrated history of the end of Britain overseas was ever written was because 'they had little opportunity to articulate their interests corporately', little in the way of a shared imperial afterlife as they 'mostly made their way under their own steam, refashioning themselves as they could'. Distinctions of race, gender, personal wealth and social standing could produce deep discrepancies in terms of their ultimate fate, underlining how the empire (and the Greater British social imaginaries it upheld) unravelled according to widely varying timescales and social dictates.

Kalathmika Natarajan's chapter shifts the focus to independent India, where the deceptively simple exercise of drafting Indian citizenship legislation brought to light the complexities of disentangling the new nation from the sinews of British subjecthood – a task that was compounded by the open-ended terms of the 1948 British Nationality Act. The ongoing status of Indians as British subjects in the years immediately after 1947 is rarely ever broached, still less the complicated diplomatic wrangling between Britain and India over the legal and moral responsibility towards Indian peoples in diasporic settings throughout the decolonising world. In asking the simple question: 'Who is an Indian citizen?', the independent government of India was forced to come to terms with the 'complex, even paradoxical negotiation of entangled identities shaped by Empire'.

This theme is taken up in a West Indian context in Chapter 4, addressing the 'rude awakening' of the Windrush generation of post-war Caribbean migrants who were acutely aware of their British nationality, but found it was wholly unreciprocated when they encountered rampant racial prejudice in Britain. The chapter challenges the prevailing myth of the 'mother country' shattered by 'sudden proximity', arguing that such naïve accounting overlooks a much longer history of West Indian demands for equal access to the civic entitlements of being British. The apparent 'shock' of unrequited Britishness in so many personal testimonies needs to be viewed in terms of the 'congenital flaws in the fabric of imperial subjecthood' that had long been intrinsic to the idea of Greater Britain and were instrumental in its subsequent demise.

The next three chapters examine several variants of British loyalism in Africa that came under strain in this period. Starting with the Indians of South Africa's 'most Anglophone province' of Natal, Hilary Sapire traces the demise of the once-dominant entitlements of 'imperial citizenship', traditionally advanced by Indian political elites 'as a counter to the denial of these rights and to whites' exclusivist claim to Britishness'. Squeezed between a burgeoning African national consciousness and the creation of a white minority republican state, the diminished force of imperial constitutional norms posed 'discomfiting questions about belonging, affiliation, identity and subjecthood' for a minority, diasporic South Asia population.

At the pinnacle of these strained allegiances was the symbolism of the British monarchy, the subject of Christian Pedersen's chapter examining the post-war fate of this crucial 'spiritual nexus'. In the 1960s, the conflict over the role of the British Crown culminated in two republican referendums in southern Africa, initially in South Africa (1960) and subsequently in Rhodesia (1969). These marked respectively the first and second time the British monarchy was dissolved by white voters in popular referendums, serving as key bellwethers for the viability of Britishness among settler communities determined to uphold white privilege.

Donal Lowry's chapter explores the frequent analogies drawn (both at the time and since) between Rhodesia and Ulster, two loyal provinces that came to share an acute sense of alienation from Britain and a fear of metropolitan 'betrayal', as well as a growing sense of solidarity with each other. Challenging the argument, often advanced, that imperial Britishness played only a peripheral role in Ulster unionism, the chapter argues that Greater British consciousness could be at once both highly parochial and expansive, not least because ignorance of the empire in no way detracted from its symbolic value as a source of loyalist strength and resolve.

Institutions, no less than individuals, were vulnerable to the ruptures of empire's end, and none were more exposed than the Commonwealth of Nations, arguably Greater Britain's 'most practical political expression'. In the decades after 1945, the Commonwealth was subjected to unprecedented centrifugal pressures as it rapidly became a 'repository for all the UK's post-imperial relationships'. Andrew Dilley's 'tale of two Commonwealths' is the subject of Chapter 8, examining the institutional transition from an interwar Commonwealth of exclusively white members to the 'new' post-1945 Commonwealth that was completely overhauled to the point where it 'was no longer a synonym for the British connection'. The chapter seeks to reconnect the Commonwealth of institutional and political forms with the changing sentiments and significance it embodied in the eyes of contemporaries – a dimension that 'ought to be a crucial element in the story of the break-up of Greater Britain' but remains largely neglected, ironically enough, due to the very processes whereby the Commonwealth 'was reimagined in ways that divorced it from notions of global Britishness'.

A not dissimilar tale of institutional adversity and incremental change emerges in the case of the Church of England, considered in Chapter 9. Riding at the apex of the worldwide Anglican Communion, senior Anglicans registered awareness of the diminishing reach of British sentiment in the post-war era and the corresponding challenge to the Church's authority and organisation. Taking the 'view from Lambeth', Sarah Stockwell considers the connection between Anglicanism and Greater Britain in the context of Australia and New Zealand, highlighting 'anxieties about the erosion of the "Anglican-ness" of the old dominions' and particularly the prospect of 'losing ground' to Roman Catholics. Anglican elites, she argues, 'remained significantly invested in the political, social and cultural worlds of Greater Britain' in these years but were ultimately powerless to reverse the trends that undermined the pre-eminence of Anglicanism in two of its most cherished centres.

The idea of Greater Britain was sustained by multiple agencies, not least the deployment of military power and diplomatic capital. In Chapter 10, James Curran explores the implications of British military withdrawal from South East Asia, challenging the widely held view that the end of empire moment in Australia saw Canberra easily shed its British orientation, switching dependency from London to Washington. Rather, he contends that the twilight of British imperialism in the region was followed by increasing Australian doubts about American staying power in Asia at a time of rising Cold War tensions. Caught in a geopolitical bind not of its own making, the Australian government looked to the American alliance as an anchor in a post-imperial world, but it could not provide an easy substitute for the one-time verities of Greater Britain.

The movement of people was arguably the main driver of Greater British imaginaries, an element that persisted even as the imperial rationale itself foundered. Chapter 11 looks at the reception of overseas students in Britain in the aftermath of the immigration restrictions of the 1960s. The 1966 announcement of a tripling of fees for 'foreign' students (as Commonwealth students were now designated) was widely regarded as 'another step in Britain's global withdrawal from empire and from the notion of Greater Britain'. Jodi Burkett traces long-standing assumptions about Britain's place at the 'apex of an imperial University structure' that were called into question with the introduction of differential fees at a time of deep political discord over Commonwealth immigration more generally.

In Chapter 12, Jean Smith turns to the phenomenon of outward migration from the British Isles, the scale and longevity of which has generally been obscured by the intense focus on Commonwealth immigration. It is not always recognised that outward flows to the Commonwealth consistently outperformed inward migration throughout the years of decolonisation and beyond, buoyed by subsidised fares and other preferential recruiting policies practised by Australia, Canada, South Africa, New Zealand and Rhodesia. Indeed, these practices were greatly enlarged upon in the period conventionally associated with the break-up of Greater Britain, and continued into the 1970s and 1980s, perpetuating settler colonial assumptions and structures in the receiving countries. The chapter considers the paradox whereby ordinary Britons in greater numbers than ever availed themselves of the opportunity to remake their lives in the 'better-Britains' of the former empire, even as the core precepts that ordered their world were drained of legitimacy.

The last two chapters consider latter-day legacies of Greater Britain; the political live wires that continue to spark controversy into the present. Ezequiel Mercau discusses two iconic settings where the notion (and sometimes even the semantics) of Greater Britain continue to thrive: Gibraltar and the Falkland Islands. His focus is the crucial early Thatcher years, when age-old territorial disputes with Argentina and Spain erupted into open controversy. For all the outward, ostentatious displays of loyalism from the local inhabitants of these territories, the spectre of betrayal at the hands of Britain itself frequently loomed larger than the threat from irredentist neighbours. A pattern of lobbyism familiar from white settler organisations in previous decades became commonplace, appealing to the British people's residual 'greater' instincts while shielding them from the worst inclinations of their political leaders, the fundamental contours of which continue to this day.

The final chapter considers the unextinguished intensity of 'imperial history wars'; the polemical afterlife of Greater Britain waged on the terrain of university campuses, op-ed journalism, and disputed monuments and memorials. Superficially, an abundance of shared vestiges and mutual influences are to be found among the lapsed constituencies of Britain's former settler colonies (including ambivalent 'cousins' in the United States), all experiencing newly energised social and political movements addressing the legacies of racial injustice, indigenous rights and white privilege. But Stephen Howe argues that these global cross-currents equally bear witness to the greatly diminished resonance of specifically English-speaking patterns of mutual influence, and indeed that 'such interconnections have been perhaps at least as salient across Europe, all over Africa, to and from Latin America, and more'. Surveying the wide and extremely varied influences that have produced the contemporary notion of 'decoloniality', it becomes much harder to identify the imprint of Greater Britain among the intellectual legacies of the end of empire.

Much the same can be said of predominantly far-right attempts to resist these reckonings by reviving the notion of the 'Anglosphere', an idea prominently advanced on the unlikely battleground of Brexit, where Boris Johnson's promise of 'Global Britain' emerged as the only future on offer once the extractive work of leaving the European Union was finally complete. Johnson's signature post-Brexit vision of restoring Britain's global credentials was originally conceived in considerable haste, three weeks *after* his Brexit triumph of June 2016. Since then it has become something of a talisman for embattled Brexiteers, invoked at every sign of adversity to instil confidence in the uncertain world that lies beyond. But Johnson's signal failure to elaborate his ideas beyond a fleeting sound bite has only fuelled suspicion that 'Global Britain' is merely a cynical euphemism, useful for conjuring older, discredited enthusiasms but ill suited to driving any deep-seated recrudescence of affinities and passions long since relegated to the past.[62]

But to the extent that Greater Britain remains accessible as a distant rallying cry, this collection offers a sober historical perspective on the impulses that have brought such obsolete thinking once again to the fore. More than perhaps at any other time since the empire's purported 'disappearance', it is crucial to appreciate the irreversible nature of the break-up of Greater Britain – the remnants of sentiments that never wholly cohered, long since comprehensively uncoupled.

Notes

1. Sincere thanks to my co-editor, Christian Damm Pedersen, for comments and input to this introduction and his valiant efforts in coordinating the crucial production phase of this volume.
2. A. Sampson, *Anatomy of Britain* (London: Hodder and Stoughton, 1962), pp. 620–622; his comparison with eighteenth-century Spain was taken from an interview with Sir Geoffrey Crowther.
3. T. Nairn, *The Break-up of Britain: Crisis and Neo-Nationalism* (London: NLB, 1977), pp. 11, 13, 14, 20, 22, 23, 42.
4. M. Shanks, *The Stagnant Society: A Warning* (Harmondsworth: Penguin, 1961), p. 232.
5. J. Mander, *Great Britain or Little England?* (Harmondsworth: Penguin, 1963), p. 57.
6. Quoted in B. Porter, *The Absent-Minded Imperialists: Empire, Society, and Culture in Britain* (Oxford: Oxford University Press, 2004), p. 4.
7. Quoted in S. Heffer, *Like the Roman: The Life of Enoch Powell* (London: Phoenix, 1999), pp. 334–338. See also C. Schofield, *Enoch Powell and the Making of Post-Colonial Britain* (Cambridge: Cambridge University Press, 2013).
8. For more on how 'Powell's positions on both the internal configuration of the nation state and its external relations were intertwined' see L. Aqui, M. Kenny and N. Pearce, '"The Empire of England": Enoch Powell, Sovereignty and the Constitution of the Nation', *Twentieth-Century British History*, early view July 2020, https://doi.org/10.17863/CAM.53030.
9. *Welsh Nation*, August 1966.
10. H. J. Hanham, *Scottish Nationalism* (London: Faber, 1969), p. 212. See also J. Ø. Nielsen and S. Ward, '"Cramped and Restricted at Home"? Scottish Separatism at Empire's End', *Transactions of the Royal Historical Society*, 25 (December 2015), pp. 159–185.
11. R. Samuel, *Island Stories: Unravelling Britain* (London: Verso, 1998), p. 83.
12. Quoted in K. Robbins, '"This Grubby Wreck of Old Glories": The United Kingdom and the End of the British Empire', *Journal of Contemporary History*, 15:1 (1980), pp. 81–95, at p. 83.
13. M. Hechter, *Internal Colonialism: The Celtic Fringe in British National Development, 1536–1966* (London: Routledge and Kegan Paul, 1975), p. 342; Hechter did not necessarily assume that 'decolonisation' would inevitably follow. He ventured that the 'prospects for achieving … equality for individuals of Celtic social origins in the United Kingdom seem relatively good', but left open the possibility that 'the Celts themselves may be more willing to identify with England as immigration from Asia, Africa and the West Indies proceeds', pp. 350–351.
14. K. Webb, *The Growth of Nationalism in Scotland* (Glasgow: Molendinar Press, 1977), p. 87.
15. Robbins, 'Grubby Wreck of Old Glories', p. 87.
16. G. A. Williams, *The Welsh in their History* (London: Croom Helm, 1982), p. 190. The chapter cited: 'When was Wales', was a reprint of his BBC Wales

Annual Radio Lecture broadcast on 12 November 1979. Williams, however, did not present a straightforward 'devolutionary' history, but rather suggested that 'We Welsh look like being the Last of the British ... [having] emerg[ed] into history from the wreck of Roman Britain as highly self-conscious heirs of the British' (p. 192).

17 L. Colley, *Britons: Forging the Nation, 1707–1837* (New Haven: Yale University Press, 1992), p. 383.

18 Colley, *Britons: Forging the Nation*, p. 395. See also Colley, 'Britishness and Otherness: An Argument', *Journal of British Studies*, 31 (1992), pp. 309–329.

19 A 1995 editorial in *The Times*, for example, reproduced Colley's maxim almost word for word: '…with the Empire lost, the Royal Family weakened, the Church no longer so potent and the threat of war a dimming memory, it is not surprising that Scots now question the benefits of Union and the absence of a parliament', *The Times*, 27 May 1995. For Colley's influence on press commentary see J. Ø. Nielsen and S. Ward, 'Three Referenda and a By-Election: The Shadow of Empire in Devolutionary Politics', in B. S. Glass and J. M. MacKenzie (eds), *Scotland, Empire and Decolonisation in the Twentieth Century* (Manchester: Manchester University Press, 2015), pp. 200–222.

20 To be fair, Colley's ambition was to unearth the eighteenth-century origins of Britishness, not to offer a sophisticated appraisal of its twentieth-century demise. But her work nevertheless gained traction in the febrile atmosphere of 1990s devolutionary politics.

21 K. Kumar, *The Making of English National Identity* (Cambridge: Cambridge University Press, 2003).

22 A. Gamble, 'A Union of Historic Compromise', in M. Perryman (ed.), *Imagined Nation: England after Britain* (London: Lawrence and Wishart, 2008), p. 38.

23 T. M. Devine, 'The Break-up of Britain? Scotland and the End of Empire', *Transactions of the Royal Historical Society*, 16 (2006), pp. 163–180, at pp. 163, 166. See also similar remarks in his *To the Ends of the Earth: Scotland's Global Diaspora, 1750–2010* (London: Penguin, 2011), pp. 251–269. Others have taken their lead from Devine, such as Richard Finlay who cites him as authority for the claim that 'the decline of the empire did not lead to a diminution in British identity north of the border …'. R. Finlay, 'National Identity, Union and Empire', in J. M. MacKenzie and T. M. Devine (eds), *Scotland and the British Empire* (Oxford: Oxford University Press, 2011), p. 315. For a critique of Devine see Nielsen and Ward, 'Three Referenda and a By-Election', pp. 217–219.

24 L. Colley, 'Does Britishness Still Matter in the Twenty-First Century – and How Much and How Well Do the Politicians Care', *The Political Quarterly*, 78:1 (2007), pp. 21–31, at p. 28.

25 I. Jack, *The Country Formerly Known as Great Britain: Writings, 1989–2009* (London: Jonathan Cape, 2009), p. xiii.

26 A. Lester, *Imperial Networks: Creating Identities in Nineteenth-Century South Africa and Britain* (London: Routledge, 2001); J. Belich, *Replenishing the Earth: The Settler Revolution and the Rise of the Anglo-World, 1783–1939* (Oxford: Oxford University Press, 2009); J. Darwin, *The Empire-Project: The Rise and*

Fall of the British World-System, 1830–1970 (Cambridge: Cambridge University Press, 2009); T. Pietsch, *Empire of Scholars: Universities, Networks and the British Academic World, 1850–1939* (Manchester: Manchester University Press, 2013); S. J. Potter, *News and the British World: The Emergence of an Imperial Press System* (Oxford: Oxford University Press, 2003); S. J. Potter, *Broadcasting Empire: The BBC and the British World, 1922–1970* (Oxford: Oxford University Press, 2012); R. Bickers (ed.), *Settlers and Expatriates: Britons over the Seas* (Oxford: Oxford University Press, 2010); G. B. Magee and A. S. Thompson, *Empire and Globalisation: Networks of People, Goods and Capital in the British World, c. 1850–1914* (Cambridge: Cambridge University Press, 2010); T. M. Devine, *To the Ends of the Earth: Scotland's Global Diaspora 1750–2010* (London: Allen Lane, 2011); K. Fedorowich and A. S. Thompson (eds), *Empire, Migration and Identity in the British World* (Manchester: Manchester University Press, 2013); and D. Thackeray, *Forging a British World of Trade: Culture, Ethnicity, and Market in the Empire-Commonwealth, 1880–1975* (Oxford: Oxford University Press, 2019).

27 There are exceptions, see for example A. G. Hopkins, *American Empire: A Global History* (Princeton: Princeton University Press, 2018) who devotes a major portion of his work to what he terms 'postcolonial globalization'; see also B. Schwarz, *The White Man's World: Memories of Empire, Vol. I* (Oxford: Oxford University Press, 2011).

28 J. Curran and S. Ward, *The Unknown Nation: Australia after Empire* (Carlton, Vic.: Melbourne University Press, 2010); J. E. Igartua, *The Other Quiet Revolution: National Identities in English Canada, 1945–71* (Vancouver: University of British Columbia Press, 2006); J. Lambert, 'An Unknown People: Reconstructing British South African Identity', *Journal of Imperial and Commonwealth History*, 37:4 (2009), pp. 599–617; A. Spry-Rush, *Bonds of Empire: West Indians and Britishness from Victoria to Decolonization* (Oxford: Oxford University Press, 2011); E. Mercau, *The Falklands War: An Imperial History* (Cambridge: Cambridge University Press, 2019); C. Mark, 'Decolonising Britishness? The 1981 British Nationality Act and the Identity Crisis of Hong Kong Elites', *Journal of Imperial and Commonwealth History*, 48:3 (2019), pp. 565–590.

29 The phrase is borrowed from R. Price, 'One Big Thing: Britain, Its Empire, and Their Imperial Culture', *Journal of British Studies*, 45 (July 2006), pp. 602–627.

30 See Vernon's contribution to T. Sasson, J. Vernon, M. Ogborn, P. Satia and C. Hall, 'Britain and the World: A New Field?', *Journal of British Studies*, 57 (October 2018), pp. 677–708, at p. 686.

31 Referring to Pocock's seminal, 'British History: A Plea for a New Subject', *Journal of Modern History*, 47:4 (December 1975), pp. 601–621. See Vernon in Sasson et al., 'Britain and the World', pp. 687–688. David Armitage has also taken Pocock to task for the 'long, withdrawing roar of empire' that 'could be heard behind this plea … in the voice of an aggrieved and abandoned New Zealander'. D. Armitage, 'Great Britain: A Useful Category of Historical Analysis?', *American Historical Review*, 104:2 (April 1999), pp. 427–445, at p. 431. For Pocock's undisguised unction at being so described see his reply: 'The New British History in Atlantic Perspective: An Antipodean Commentary', in the same issue, pp. 490–500.

32 Key works advancing the 'British World' paradigm include C. Bridge and K. Fedorowich (eds), *The British World: Diaspora, Culture and Identity* (London and New York: Routledge, 2003); P. Buckner and R. Douglas Francis (eds), *Rediscovering the British World* (Calgary: University of Calgary Press, 2005); K. Darian-Smith, S. Macintyre and P. Grimshaw (eds), *Britishness Abroad: Transnational Movements and Imperial Cultures* (Melbourne: Melbourne University Press, 2007); B. Crosbie and M. Hampton (eds), *The Cultural Construction of the British World* (Manchester: Manchester University Press, 2015).

33 D. Geary, C. Schofield and J. Sutton (eds), *Global White Nationalism: From Apartheid to Trump* (Manchester: Manchester University Press, 2020). See also M. Kenny and N. Pearce, *Shadows of Empire: The Anglosphere in British Politics* (Cambridge: Polity Press, 2018); A. Mycock and B. Wellings (eds), *The Anglosphere: Continuity, Dissonance and Location* (Oxford: Oxford University Press, 2019).

34 See Priya Satia's contribution to Sasson et al., 'Britain and the World', p. 695. See also B. Wellings, *English Nationalism, Brexit and the Anglosphere: Wider Still and Wider* (Manchester: Manchester University Press, 2019).

35 Vernon seems to imply something along these lines in charging 'British World historians' with reconstituting a history where white men 'once again take centre stage in their self-appointed role as guardians of the world'. He stops short of making the charge stick to the work of specific British World historians, which is far more varied and nuanced – and indeed useful – than the caricature allows. See Vernon in Sasson et al., 'Britain and the World', pp. 689–690.

36 T. Pietsch, 'Rethinking the British World', *Journal of British Studies*, 52 (April 2013), pp. 441–463, at p. 446.

37 Indeed, she adopts the rubric herself in *Empire of Scholars: Universities, Networks and the British Academic World, 1850–1939* (Manchester: Manchester University Press, 2015).

38 Miles Ogborn's contribution in Sasson et al., 'Britain and the World', p. 682. Ogborn's contribution was couched largely (but by no means solely) in defence of his choice of title for *Global Lives: Britain and the World, 1550–1800* (Cambridge: Cambridge University Press, 2008).

39 Pietsch proposes that instead of focusing on 'a British World conceived as a whole', or the space it occupied as a 'fixed entity', it would be more fruitful to look at 'the imagined, material, and local British *worlds*' that reflected everyday lived experience. See Pietsch, 'Rethinking the British World', pp. 441, 445, 447. Vernon, for his part, states a preference for 'a global history of Britain', entailing a focus on 'how Britain was transformed from the outside in by processes and structures that were always already transnational or global in scale', see Vernon in Sasson et al., 'Britain and the World', p. 691. Neither approach has (as yet) seized the conceptual high ground. See for example Bright and Dilley's verdict on Pietsch: 'the pluralization of the term … in and of itself cannot salvage the concept'. R. K. Bright and A. Dilley, 'After the British World', *The Historical Journal*, 60:2 (2017), pp. 547–568, at p. 558.

40 Bright and Dilley, 'After the British World', p. 560.

41 S. Dubow, 'How British was the British World? The Case of South Africa', *Journal of Imperial and Commonwealth History*, 37:1 (2009), pp. 1–27, at p. 14.
42 Bright and Dilley, 'After the British World', p. 568.
43 The formulation is Bright and Dilley's, which they further describe as the 'only object worth pursuing' across the broad, uneven, nebulous terrain of British world studies: 'After the British World', p. 566.
44 C. W. Dilke, *Greater Britain: A Record of Travel in English-Speaking Countries During 1866 and 1867* (London: Macmillan, 1868); J. R. Seeley, *The Expansion of England: Two Courses of Lectures* (London: Macmillan, 1883).
45 Belich, *Replenishing the Earth*, pp. 456–460.
46 D. Bell, *The Idea of Greater Britain: Empire and the Future of World Order, 1860–1900* (Princeton: Princeton University Press, 2007), p. 24.
47 There is no shortage of voices of caution in this regard. Saul Dubow issues a warning about producing history that 'is merely a dressed up form of the old imperial history, or worse, that … recalls the racially inflected nineteenth-century vision of "Greater Britain."' See Dubow, 'How British Was the British World?', p. 2. Bright and Dilley rule out the term explicitly as one that 'conceptually can only be used at a specific historical juncture in the late nineteenth and early twentieth centuries', p. 562.
48 Dilke, *Greater Britain*, pp. vii–viii.
49 Seeley, *Expansion of England*, pp. 11, 301–302.
50 Quoted in Schwarz, *White Man's World*, p. 79.
51 Schwarz, *White Man's World*, pp. 83, 73, 79–80.
52 This is the frame of reference adopted by Bell, for example, in *The Idea of Greater Britain*.
53 P. Mandler, 'Race and Nation in Mid-Victorian Thought', in S. Collini, R. Whatmore and B. Young (eds), *History, Religion and Culture: Intellectual History 1750–1950* (Cambridge: Cambridge University Press, 2000), pp. 224–244, at p. 230.
54 A. Lester, 'British Settler Discourse and the Circuits of Empire', *History Workshop Journal*, 54 (2002), pp. 25–48, at pp. 25, 33, 39. See also Lester, *Imperial Networks*.
55 A. S. Thompson, 'The Languages of Loyalism in Southern Africa, c. 1870–1939', *English Historical Review*, cxviii (2003), pp. 617–650, at p. 635. See also D. Lowry, 'The Crown, Empire Loyalism and the Assimilation of non-British White Subjects in the British World: An Argument Against "Ethnic Determinism"', in Bridge and Fedorowich, *British World*.
56 M. Belgrave, '"We Rejoice to Honour the Queen, for She is a Good Woman, who Cares for the Maori Race": Loyalty and Protest in Maori Politics in Nineteenth-Century New Zealand', in S. Carter and M. Nugent (eds), *Mistress of Everything: Queen Victoria in Indigenous Worlds* (Manchester: Manchester University Press, 2016), pp. 54–77, at pp. 56, 73.
57 H. Sapire, 'Ambiguities of Loyalism: The Prince of Wales in India and Africa, 1921-2 and 25', *History Workshop Journal*, 73:1 (2012), pp. 37–65, at p. 39.
58 Quoted in P. Walshe, *The Rise of African Nationalism in South Africa: The African National Congress, 1912-52* (Berkeley: University of California Press, 1971), p. 64.

59 R. de Costa, 'Identity, Authority, and the Moral Worlds of Indigenous Petitions', *Comparative Studies in Society and History*, 48:3 (2006), pp. 669–698, at pp. 670, 673, 680.
60 P. D. Morgan, 'Encounters between British and "Indigenous" Peoples, c. 1500–1800', in M. Daunton and R. Halpern (eds) *Empire and Others: British Encounters with Indigenous Peoples, 1600–1850* (London: UCL Press, 1999), p. 49.
61 'Incarnations' is borrowed from Bright and Dilley, 'After the British World', p. 566.
62 See, in particular, S. Ward and A. Rasch, 'Greater Britain, Global Britain', in Ward and Rasch (eds), *Embers of Empire in Brexit Britain* (London: Bloomsbury, 2019), pp. 2–3; D. Reynolds, *Island Stories: Britain and its History in the Age of Brexit* (London: William Collins, 2019).

1

Maintaining racial boundaries: Greater Britain in the Second World War and beyond

Wendy Webster

Porokuru Patapu Pohe enlisted in the Royal New Zealand Air Force in September 1940, sailed for Britain in 1941 and became the first Maori pilot in the Royal Air Force (RAF). Pohe applied to join on 12 September 1939 – only nine days after New Zealand declared war on Germany. A question on his application form asked whether he was 'of pure European descent' and he wrote 'no'. Under the question about the nationality of his parents, he gave both as New Zealander and added that his father was 'Maori' and his mother 'half-caste Maori'.[1]

The regulation that Pohe encountered on his application form drew on the wording of an RAF regulation in force at the outbreak of war: 'only men who are British subjects and of pure European descent are accepted for enlistment or commission … and they must be the sons of parents both of whom have British nationality'.[2] There were similar instructions to candidates in the British army.[3] These regulations did not envisage the recruitment of women. They had been suspended during the First World War but were reinstated when the war was over. They demonstrated a racial definition of who counted as British. Men could be British subjects but unless they were judged to belong in the racial category 'pure European' they were insufficiently British to serve in its armed forces.

This chapter traces the history of racial definitions of Britishness, assumptions of white superiority and the maintenance of racial boundaries that characterised many wartime policies and practices in the British Empire. Pressure for change came from organisations such as the League of Coloured Peoples and the Maori War Effort Organisation, and there were some concessions to their campaigns. The government of New Zealand conceded the principle of Maori control and leadership of their war-related activities.[4] But there was no guarantee that these concessions would outlast the war.

The chapter also considers the complex hierarchy that assigned different positions and different status in a ranking of different groups. Racial difference was seen as marking out the distinction between a colonial empire under British rule and the self-governing Dominions – regarded as white men's countries even though they included South Africa with a black majority population and indigenous populations in Canada, Australia and New Zealand. There was also a ranking within the colonial empire with India at the apex.

The chapter demonstrates that racism runs like a deep scar through the history of the British Empire during the Second World War and beyond. A racial hierarchy was evident not only in official thinking but also in people's experiences and feelings about the subordinate or superior places assigned to them. In the context of a war fought against a racist Nazi regime, there was increasing emphasis in propaganda on a 'people's empire' of friendliness, free of racial discrimination.[5] This was the public face of empire that concealed what was said in private government discussions. There was often a wide gulf between this propaganda and the wartime experiences of people of colour. When the war was over, many racial boundaries and racial definitions of Britishness remained in place.

Togetherness and racial boundaries

There is no way of knowing what Porokuru Pohe felt about the question of whether he was of 'pure European descent', but Dudley Thompson remembers his response. Thompson decided to join the RAF after picking up a copy of *Mein Kampf* in a dentist's waiting room in Kingston, Jamaica. His reading of Hitler's 'vicious vituperation against Jews and Negroes' made him want to prove Hitler wrong, inspiring a vision of himself 'up there in a Spitfire ... and I'm going to meet some German – and I'm going to *show* him that I'm not an anthropoid'.[6] But when Thompson arrived in Britain to join the RAF, he encountered the question of whether he was of 'pure European descent'.

> I wrote 'Yes', because some of my friends had been turned down because they were not. And they were told so. There was a difficulty, particularly in the early stages of the war, getting in if you were coloured. I thought this was bad, really bad; this was stupid; this was prejudice, really wrong. So I said 'Yes', because I wanted to fight – I wanted to fight against *that*.[7]

At the beginning of the war, the phrase 'of pure European descent' ran through policies of recruitment to the armed forces applied across the Commonwealth. It featured in the Canadian as well as the New Zealand Air Force regulations. Regulations for the Royal Canadian Navy added a gloss to this phrase – applicants must be 'of the White Race'.[8] In Australia, a meeting of chiefs of staff in February 1940 stated that 'eligibility to enlist or to serve is subject to the condition that a person must be of pure or of substantially European origin or descent'.[9] In South Africa, black and coloured South Africans were recruited to the armed forces but were confined to non-combatant roles where their only weapons were assegais and knobkerries and they were prohibited from bearing firearms.[10] There were also racial restrictions on combatant roles in Australia. An official attempting to clarify rules for the recruitment of indigenous people wrote in 1941, 'A full blooded aboriginal is … required to render only non-combatant service, but a half-caste could be required to perform combatant duties if the medical authorities considered that he was of substantially European origin or descent'.[11] Early in the war, a booklet issued to RAF personnel in Britain before they went to overseas theatres 'directed that segregation should be practised by white personnel'.[12] Many of these policies were subsequently suspended for the duration of the war.

In Britain, the League of Coloured Peoples campaigned against the regulation on 'pure European descent' and in Trinidad there were demonstrations against it.[13] In October 1939, the British government announced that this regulation was suspended 'during the present emergency', and extended eligibility for voluntary enlistment and for the granting of emergency commissions to British subjects – from the empire or from Britain – who were not of 'pure European descent'.[14] As the announcement made clear, the suspension was an emergency measure and only applied to people living in Britain. It prompted a scathing comment from George Padmore, the Trinidadian writer and journalist. In a piece in *The Crisis* – the official magazine of the National Association of the Advancement of Coloured People in America – he wrote:

> It is one of the greatest ironies of history that, thanks to the notorious race-baiter, Adolf Hitler, England the greatest upholder of racial segregation among colonial powers, has been forced to discard the Color Bar in the Royal Air Force in order to save herself.[15]

Dudley Thompson's view that racism did not belong only to Hitler's Germany found many echoes from people of colour in the empire. In August 1941, the *Nigerian Eastern Mail* asked, 'What purpose does it serve to remind us that Hitler regards us as semi-apes if the Empire for which we are ready to suffer and die … can tolerate racial discrimination against us?'[16] In Natal, a leading article in a black newspaper commented:

> What is needed is not mere drugging of the non-European with assurances that this is his war. The exhortations and assurances are sounding very hollow when … eight million Bantu are denied the citizen's duty to work in the manufacture of war equipment for his country's fighting forces for no reason other than that he has a dark skin.[17]

In India, Mohandas Gandhi also commented on the hollow ring of Allied words. After Britain and the United States declared their war aims in the Atlantic Charter at a meeting in August 1941, he wrote to President Roosevelt to enlist his support in a proposal that Britain should unreservedly and immediately withdraw its rule in India:

> I venture to think that the Allied declaration; that the Allies are fighting to make the world safe for freedom of the individual and for democracy sounds hollow so long as India, and for that matter Africa, are exploited by Great Britain, and America has the Negro problem in her own home.[18]

Imperial propaganda made no mention of exploitation or colour bars. It was designed not only to deflect criticism in the empire but also to counter opposition to British imperialism in America and Nazi propaganda which portrayed the British Empire as oppressive. According to a Postal Censorship report in 1941 on letters sent to Britain from America, Nazi propaganda strengthened American opposition. The report concluded: 'Few people in England have any conception of the reality of the Empire bogey in the American mind and elsewhere. The Nazi radio keeps at it all the time, and upon this topic it is effective'.[19]

Propaganda branded Britain and its empire against Nazi Germany as a 'people's empire' of freedom and togetherness, not of oppression and brutality. The message was conveyed in West Africa through a leaflet quoting the Nazi Minister of Labour's view that 'a German is higher above an African than an African is above an ape' and showing Nazi storm troopers beating and shooting Africans. In contrast, the portrayal of Britain featured justice, education and health care through the figures of a black judge, teacher, nurse and policeman.[20] This 'people's empire' of welfare and development was conveyed throughout the empire in King George VI's broadcast on Empire Day 1940: 'There is a word that our enemies use against us – Imperialism. By it they mean the spirit of domination, the lust of Conquest'. But he countered: 'Our one object has always been peace – peace in which our institutions may be developed, the condition of our peoples improved'.[21]

When women were shown in propaganda on a 'people's empire', they were usually white. But coverage of women serving in the forces and doing war work – in Australia, Britain, Canada, New Zealand and South Africa – was limited. The Ministry of Information and the Colonial Office acted to ensure that there was coverage of non-white contributions to the war effort and this also focused on men. *Maximum Effort* (1944) – a documentary targeted mainly at an audience in New Zealand – was characteristic of this gendering. The film incorporated a Maori man into its narrative of an RAF aircrew, also comprising Canadians and English, flying an air raid over Germany, but represented New Zealand women's contribution to the war effort through the story of a white woman married to a crew member, who lost her life in an industrial accident back home.[22]

West Indies Calling (1943), sponsored by the Ministry of Information, portrayed a friendly empire of togetherness but was unusual in showing black women's involvement in the war effort.[23] Their arrival in Britain had been publicised in a *Picture Post* article that claimed 'the coloured girls come over not to be segregated but to join the ATS [Auxiliary Territorial Service] in a state of equality with all its white members'.[24] But a 'state of equality' was very far from what the War Office envisaged in discussions on their recruitment. As late as March 1943, it was prepared to 'accept any suitable European women from the Colonies for enrolment into the ATS' but emphasised that 'this applies to European women only and ... we cannot agree to accept coloured women for service in this country'. Later in 1943, and only under pressure from the Colonial Office, the War Office conceded that a limited number of black women from the Caribbean could be enlisted.[25]

The effectiveness of propaganda varied in different locations in the British Empire. The fall of colonies in South and South East Asia to Japanese forces from December 1941 – Hong Kong, Singapore, Malaya and Burma – produced some uneasiness about colonial policy in Britain, but their impact on ideas about the British Empire in South East and South Asia was immeasurable. The demise of white racial and imperial prestige was highly visible on the streets of Singapore in February 1942, where white imperial soldiers, now Japanese prisoners of war and subject to ritual humiliation, were transformed into street sweepers. The demise of white imperial prestige was also visible on the streets of India where white imperial soldiers and civilians arriving from Burma as refugees were ragged and starving. There followed allegations of racial discrimination in evacuations from these colonies, with preferential treatment of Europeans and Anglo-Indians. These were better known in India than in much of the empire where they were not widely reported. In Britain, an article in the *News Chronicle* in April 1942 on allegations of racial discrimination in the evacuation from Burma was dismissed by the Secretary for India, Leo Amery, as 'misleading'.[26]

The history of imperial violence was entirely missing from the wartime image of a benign and peace-loving British Empire but the violent repression of the Quit India movement in the aftermath of the arrest of the leadership of the Indian National Congress in August 1942 added significantly to this history. The RAF was brought in to machine-gun protestors from the air, and it was British statistics which showed that, by mid-September, police firing on rioters and clashes with troops had caused 658 Indian deaths and 'large numbers' of injuries. This compared with eleven troops killed and seven injured.[27] An emergency Whipping Act, introduced in August, enabled whipping to be inflicted on anybody convicted of rioting.[28] More than 100,000 people were imprisoned.

The government of India prohibited the printing or publication of news about the Quit India movement or measures taken by the government against it.[29] Hindu-owned newspapers ceased publication in protest.[30] In Britain, violent repression was justified by Churchill, speaking in Parliament, who claimed that the Congress Party was unrepresentative of the Indian majority, and attributed rioting to 'hooligans and agitators' and 'lawless elements'.[31] British newsreels and newspapers followed suit, like Churchill, attributing the demonstrations to hooligans and agitators, who were unrepresentative of 'India's Millions'.[32] In Australia, the *Sydney Morning Herald* reported that the action taken had been 'preventive and not punitive' and that Congress leaders 'had already forfeited the sympathy of well-wishers abroad'.[33]

In 1943, the Bengal famine caused the death of up to four million Indians. The impact of the famine was felt across India and by Indian soldiers serving overseas who received painful news from their families. Censorship reports on letters from the Eighth Army in Italy recorded of Indian soldiers there, 'The famine that has occurred in parts of India has caused deep anxiety to many men whose homes are in affected areas'.[34] General Wavell, Viceroy of India, wrote to London that the famine was 'one of the greatest disasters that has befallen any people under British rule and damage to our reputation both among Indians and foreigners in India is incalculable'.[35] Earlier, the Governor of Bengal, writing to the Viceroy, urged efforts to minimise the impact of the news. He advised, 'effective propaganda to counteract the present unhelpful tales of horror in the Press which manifests itself largely in photographs which might have been taken in Calcutta at any time during the last 10 years'.[36] This advice appeared to acknowledge that hunger and starvation had been common experiences in Calcutta before the war.

As Andrew Muldoon has demonstrated, encounters with poverty and famine undermined the image of a benevolent British Empire for British soldiers serving in India. A report on their morale noted their 'open criticism of the Government' as well as their efforts to feed Indians from their own rations. Many were shocked at Indian poverty. Some sympathised with Indian nationalism. A British soldier declared himself 'all in favour of giving India her freedom' if Indian troops were 'an example of her qualities'. Others regarded the imperial project as anachronistic. But British soldiers held many conflicting views. Angela Bolton, a British nurse serving in India, wrote in her diary that 'service people out from the United Kingdom, after an initial interest in Indians as individuals, adopted the prevalent attitude of indifference'. In January 1944, officials reported that famine had lost its news value and that 'most soldiers show indifference to India and her politics'.[37] One British soldier wrote in a letter, 'There is only one thing wrong with India and that is that it is above sea level'.[38]

British concerns to justify the violent repression of the Quit India movement were in the context of American opposition to British imperialism. As early as June 1942, preparations were made for propaganda in the event of a protest movement. The Home Department of the Government of India advised the Secretary of State for India, 'one matter that we consider of prime importance is that public opinion in England and even more in America should be prepared well in advance for any strong action we may eventually decide to take', and that there should be emphasis on the danger to the American war effort and to the safety of American troops in India of British withdrawal from India.[39] This theme was taken up in August 1942, when Stafford Cripps wrote in the *New York Times* warning of the danger of British withdrawal from India to 'the life and safety of every European, American and Chinese soldier and civilian'.[40]

Attempts to keep their American ally sweet also meant that governments in the empire refrained from criticism of the racial segregation of the American armed forces throughout the war. But popular opinion had little interest in keeping America sweet. Criticism of racial discrimination practised by American armed forces came particularly from people who saw this at first hand. In Australia, when Banjo Clarke was attacked by a white American in a dance hall, he records that two white women hit the American soldier and he heard one of them say, 'This dirty Yank threw our Aboriginal friend out down the stairs ... He might get away with doing that in America, but he can't in Australia'.[41] Sonja Davies, the New Zealand trade unionist and peace campaigner records:

> One of the disturbing things about Americans was their racial prejudice, particularly among those from the southern states. Their attitude to their own black troops was bad enough, but when they extended it to New Zealand Maoris, I and many others saw red. Fights often broke out in bars and cafes between pakeha [white] New Zealanders and American troops.

Davies also witnessed the Battle of Manners Street in April 1943 in Wellington, New Zealand which began at the Allied Services Club 'sparked off by an unwise remark by an American ... about New Zealand Maoris' and which developed into 'a free-for-all with hundreds ... of willing participants'.[42] There were no reports of the Battle of Manners Street in the New Zealand press.

In Britain, criticism of white American attitudes to black GIs also boosted an image of tolerance and true democracy against the racism attributed to white Americans. According to BBC listener research, 'The attitude of white American troops to their coloured compatriots was mentioned only to be condemned and used as evidence against the reality of American democracy'.[43] In an incident reported from the Eastern Region, 'British soldiers were taken to task by those from America for fraternising with the Negroes. The British replied that as both black and white troops had come 3,000 miles to help us win the war they saw no reason to draw distinctions between one type of American and another'.[44] The American military supplied the British government with a report on a number of incidents where 'British personnel ... interfered in disputes between white and coloured US troops', siding with black GIs against white American authorities. In one case where American military police were arresting a black soldier, 'a group of civilians gathered and were heard to make such remarks as "They don't like the blacks", "Why don't they leave the blacks alone" and so on, until the civilians were moved on by the civil police'. In another case, 'British civilians interfered between American white officers and a negro driver. They took the part of the driver both verbally and by laying hands on the American officers to get them away from the driver'.[45]

At the Colonial Office, there was some criticism of American segregation, but this was not made public. A range of moves to keep the empire sweet included a request to the BBC to invite the black conductor Rudolph Dunbar to conduct the BBC orchestra. Such a performance, the Colonial Office wrote, would 'create a good impression among the West Indians and many people of African descent throughout the Colonial Empire'.[46] When an application from Peter Thomas to join the RAF arrived at the Colonial Office, forwarded by the Chief Secretary of the Government of Nigeria, Thomas went on to become the first West African to qualify as a pilot and to be commissioned. The Chief Secretary had pointed out that Thomas's father was one of the 'leading lights from the African community in Lagos' and his acceptance would 'have excellent publicity value in Nigeria'.[47] The potential for 'excellent publicity value' was exploited in a documentary made by the Colonial Film Unit, sponsored by the Ministry of Information and intended for an African audience. *Africa's Fighting Men* (1943) ended with shots of Thomas shaking hands with a white officer.[48] A range of other wartime documentaries and newsreels celebrated the contribution of men of colour to the imperial war effort.

The public celebration of a 'people's empire' in government-sponsored films conflicted with the private views expressed by the government in confidential documents. In 1942, the War Cabinet noted 'the serious social consequences which might arise from the demobilisation in this country of any appreciable numbers of certain classes of coloured men who are serving in His Majesty's Forces'. It also noted that those from British colonies could not be deported if they proved to be 'undesirable', since they were British subjects with a right of settlement, and that overt discrimination, in the form of a colour bar, could not be accepted. In this context, covert discrimination was recommended:

> The only course open to us is to recommend very strongly that service departments should do all they possibly can by administrative action to reduce to a minimum the opportunities these men might have of being demobilised in this country. The concentration of these men in separate units, the restriction of their service to theatres of war overseas, and the repatriation of men in complete units would do much to prevent a serious social problem arising.[49]

The discrepancy between what government policymakers recorded here privately and the public messages of wartime propaganda could scarcely have been wider.

Letters written by white soldiers offer some evidence that people from the British Empire did work and come together across differences of race and ethnicity in wartime, particularly in the armed forces. Reports from censors quoted a Canadian soldier serving in the Eighth Army in Italy, 'This is the first time we've been with the Indians and I can think of nothing worse than having to compete with those boys'.[50] A British soldier in Italy echoed this, 'We were very sorry to leave the Indians, who must rank with the best troops in the world'.[51] Another wrote, 'No doubt you have seen in the papers what grand work the Indians are doing here ... They are grand fellows and I'm proud to be serving in the Div with them'. Another British soldier wrote, 'The Kiwis and Maori from New Zealand stand out as being grand chaps, they share everything they've got and their good will is enormous'.[52]

There are few memories of camaraderie in the personal narratives of non-white soldiers. Waruhiu Itote who joined the Kenyan African Rifles in 1942 remembers:

> In 1944, we returned to India from the Kalewa battlefront [Burma]. I took back with me many lasting memories. Among the shells and bullets there had been no pride, no air of superiority from our European comrades-in-arms. We drank the same tea, used the same water and lavatories, and shared the same jokes. There were no racial insults, no references to 'niggers', 'baboons' and so on. The white heat of battle had blistered all that away and left only our common humanity and our common fate, either death or survival.

But this memory was of facing common danger on the battlefield. Outside the field of combat, Itote experienced racial segregation: 'We shared the same chances of death and salvation, but used separate messes and separate lavatories'.[53] Togetherness was only for the heat of battle, for facing death.

Togetherness between women and men that crossed differences of race was regarded very differently from any male camaraderie, especially when it involved physical contact. According to Lilian Pert, a white British nurse in India, this was the reason for the dusty answer she received from senior military officers about a proposal to encourage more British women to volunteer for work in Indian hospitals, 'By the tone of their remarks [I] might almost have made an improper suggestion by saying that English women should nurse Indian soldiers!!'[54] Fears about sexual crossings of racial divides in the empire were fuelled by the perception that they would undermine the authority of whites, and particularly the authority of white men.

The history of the British Empire involved a wide range of interracial sexual relationships between white men and non-white women, but the focus of imperial anxieties about interracial sex was always on white women. The British Board of Film Censors banned representations of interracial sexual relationships, but only relationships between black men and white women, not white men and black women.[55] Wartime propaganda generally avoided showing white women with non-white men, although *West Indies Calling* included a sequence of interracial dancing. Interracial dancing was also generally acceptable to the significant strand of wartime popular opinion in Britain that championed mixing across racial difference. But the proximity of white and black bodies was expected to be strictly confined to the dance floor. Interracial sex and marriage attracted considerable uneasiness and much outright hostility, particularly from white men.[56] If mixing between white women and non-white men brought fear of the collapse of the boundaries between colonisers and colonised, black and white, it was particularly through the breaching of this internal frontier that such a collapse was imagined.

Racial hierarchies

An early wartime poster on the imperial war effort showed an imperial community united under the fluttering Union flag of Britishness. It portrayed a male community and arranged them in a racial hierarchy. Africans and Indians bring up the rear behind white men representing Australia, Britain, Canada, New Zealand and South Africa – the core constituencies of Greater Britain. Titled 'Together', the poster was designed to show a 'people's empire' united across differences of race and ethnicity, but the image suggested how far a racial hierarchy was embedded in official thinking. The same image was later titled 'British Commonwealth of Nations'. The term 'Commonwealth' was generally reserved for the self-governing Dominions, but the poster's title – if not its image – stretched this meaning to include the Indians and Africans portrayed, suggesting that they belonged to the Commonwealth as much as the white figures and that their countries enjoyed the same status as the Dominions.

The term 'Dominions' had been introduced in 1907 for the self-governing settler colonies who regarded the term 'colony' as inappropriate because of its associations with inferiority and subordination.[57] This distinction between Dominions and colonies was not widely understood in Britain. A Survey of Public Opinion on Colonial Affairs in 1948 found that only 25 per cent of those questioned could name it correctly.[58] A number of letters by British soldiers in the Eighth Army referred to Canadians and New Zealanders who were fighting alongside them as 'colonials'.[59] Those addressed as 'colonials' were offended by this label. A Canadian stationed at the radio school at RAF Cranwell wrote home, 'We're not liked here [which] makes us wonder why the hell we ever came … our w o [Warrant Officer] here gave us a lecture first morn[ing] [and] called us a bunch of rotten Colonials'.[60] Errol Crapp, an Australian navigator in Bomber Command, wrote in his wartime diary:

> For being late on parade owing to very-late serving of breakfast at the mess, we N.Z. [New Zealander], Canadian and Australian pilot-officers were severely reprimanded by an RAF 'wingless wonder' Flight Lieut who said that so far he has had decent officers under him. I mention this as this R.A.F. attitude of being a step above the 'Colonials' is apparent wherever you go.[61]

The label 'colonials' may have caused offence not only because of its assumption of British superiority at the apex of the imperial hierarchy, but also because it collapsed the boundaries between people of white ethnicity in the Dominions and people of non-white ethnicity in the colonial empire – challenging the privileged position occupied by white people in the global community of Greater Britain.

In wartime propaganda the meaning of the term 'Commonwealth' became increasingly elastic as the war progressed, blurring the distinction between self-governing Dominions and the colonial empire. The commentaries in wartime films such as *India Marches* (1941) and *West Indies Calling* referred to them as members of the Commonwealth.[62] BBC audience research found that this blurring went down well with audiences in Britain: 'in response to questions about the meanings of the terms "British Empire" and "British Commonwealth of Nations" most people regarded them as geographically synonymous, but much preferred the term "British Commonwealth of Nations" because of its more democratic implications and "freedom from imperialistic associations"'.[63] After the fall of British colonies to Japanese forces, the image of togetherness in propaganda was increasingly joined by the idea of 'partnership', emphasising not only unity but also equality across racial and ethnic differences against a common enemy.

Officials at the War Office had no expectation of equality across racial differences. In 1944, when they offered the use of the Caribbean regiment for deployment in Asia, they warned the Commander-in-Chief in India, that 'the men are extremely colour conscious and expect to be treated as white troops'.[64] Unequal treatment included pay and promotion. The pay of South

African soldiers was organised on a racial hierarchy where those serving in the Coloured Cape Corps received half the white rate and black Africans received two-thirds of the coloured rate.[65] In Africa, a Ghanaian soldier commented, 'A British soldier the same rank as one may receive seven shillings a day. I receive two and nine pence. We knew through the pay voucher. I once worked with the office people, that's how I knew'. At the bottom of the hierarchy, African privates were paid a shilling a day.[66] In Australia, nearly one thousand Torres Strait Islanders joined the war effort between 1942 and 1945 and received a third of the pay of white Australian soldiers. In 1943, they went on strike, demanding equal pay.[67]

Promotions were shaped by concerns about black officers having the power of command over white men. When a West Indian signalman sought a commission, the War Office recommended that he should be considered only for command over 'an African Transport unit or Labour corps' and that it was not advisable for him to 'hold any command over British soldiers'.[68] One RAF participant in discussions on reinstatement of the 'pure European descent' regulation as the war was ending wrote:

> [W]e all know that to have a coloured officer in command of whites just does *not* work – certainly not where Dominion troops are concerned … this coloured question is one which must be taken very slowly and possibly in 100 or 200 years we will think nothing of having a black commander in charge of white troops.[69]

These views were not lost on those who served. Dudley Thompson records of the RAF: 'If an individual went for a board, recommended for a commission or promotion, all sorts of spurious arguments were put, like: "Oh, we know that it's going to be difficult to have men of colour as officers over other people"'.[70] Kofi Gendi who enlisted in the Gold Coast regiment remembers, 'You never saw a white private soldier – because he might have had to take orders from a black NCO (non-commissioned officer)'.[71] In the South African forces, non-European NCOs could only command men in the non-European Army services, not Europeans in the Defence Force.[72] Frank Sexwale who served in the South African Native Military Corps commented:

> Relationships between the South African officers and their men were master–servant. It broke our spirit. If you are not armed then the white man is a superior and you are an inferior person … It became so painful that in later years I was reluctant to talk about it. It was nothing to be proud about, being a soldier under the South African government. We were never soldiers, in fact – we were just black civilians in uniform.[73]

Fighting in the imperial armed forces involved many experiences of colonial subjugation through policies and practices that sustained racial boundaries. In 1941, Winston Churchill made it clear that these boundaries were not about to be dismantled. The joint eight-point declaration of Anglo–American war aims in the Atlantic Charter of 1941 included the declaration that both nations would 'respect the right of all peoples to choose the government under which they will live'. In Britain, propagandists were instructed not to make too much of it. Clement Atlee, leader of the British Labour Party and Deputy Prime Minister in the wartime National Government, speaking to the West African Students Union told them that the Charter 'will be equally applicable to all races, including Asiatics and Africans ... We in the Labour party have always demanded that the freedom which we claim for ourselves shall be extended to all'.[74] But Churchill took a very different view. Speaking in Parliament in September, he stated:

> At the Atlantic meeting, we had in mind, primarily, the restoration of the sovereignty, self-government and national life of the States and nations of Europe now under the Nazi yoke ... So that is quite a separate problem from the progressive evolution of self-governing institutions in the regions and peoples which owe allegiance to the British Crown.[75]

Churchill's speech gave the lie to propaganda that incorporated colonial peoples into a Commonwealth of self-governing nations. The colonies were not self-governing. They were in 'progressive evolution' towards self-government at some unspecified future date. The declaration in the Atlantic Charter that 'all peoples' had the right to choose the government under which they lived did not apply to them. Churchill denied to colonised peoples the universal rights proclaimed in the Charter. Universal rights belonged only to Europeans.

When the war was over

Across the Commonwealth in the aftermath of war, policies on immigration and emigration were designed to exclude British subjects of colour as far as possible. In Australia, the 'White Australia' policy was widely known and featured regularly in the Australian press, usually with an upper-case W and A. *The Sydney Morning Herald* claimed in 1949 that 'the belief of the Australian people in the necessity of a White Australia policy is probably as intense as ever it was'.[76] In Canada, Prime Minister William Mackenzie King, speaking in the Canadian House of Commons in 1947, reaffirmed pre-war policy: 'There will, I am sure, be general agreement with the view that the people of Canada do not wish, as a result of mass immigration, to make a fundamental alteration in the character of our population'.[77] In New Zealand, the Immigration Restriction Amendment Act of 1920 remained the basis of post-war policy. Under this Act, 'the admission of persons who are not of British birth and parentage and wholly of European race and colour' was controlled 'by means of the individual permit system' – entry by application only.[78]

Britain's attempts at exclusion were covert. Both the post-war Labour government and subsequent Conservative government ruled out legislation to restrict the immigration of British subjects of colour, but both set up secret committees to review measures which could be taken to do so.[79] These committees recommended informal methods to discourage black and Asian migrants, through encouraging colonial governments to restrict the issue of passports and other travel documents and publicising the difficulties potential migrants would face in Britain.[80] The Conservative government's secret committee noted in 1956 that 'coloured immigration has become an ominous problem which cannot now be ignored'.[81]

Both Australia and New Zealand encouraged the migration of white British through Free and Assisted Passages schemes. Arthur Calwell, Australia's Minister of Immigration and a champion of the 'White Australia' policy, stated: 'It is my hope that for every foreign migrant there will be ten people from the UK'.[82] Calwell appeared on British newsreels in 1947 urging Britons to emigrate and telling them, 'Australia believes that the world's finest export always has been and always will be men and women of British stock. We want men and women with courage and enterprise'.[83] In an arrangement made by Britain and Australia in 1945 it was agreed that Polish people who had served in the war with the British forces and were living in Britain should be eligible for emigration to Australia under the Free and Assisted Passages scheme, but that West Indians who had served in the war would not be eligible.[84] This agreement meant that black British subjects were excluded, while white people who were officially aliens were granted honorary Britishness to enable them to participate in the scheme.

The New Zealand government wanted to specify that only people 'of wholly European race' were eligible for its Assisted Passages schemes. It was advised by the British government that 'the rejection of a coloured applicant after interview without any reason being given' would avoid making such open acknowledgement of a colour bar.[85] In Britain, an RAF participant in the 1945 discussion on whether to reinstate a colour bar in recruitment suggested covert discrimination that would operate in a similar way through an 'unwritten rule':

> I felt we certainly cannot tell candidates to their faces that their colour is a bar to a normal career ... Therefore on paper coloured troops will be eligible for entry to the Services, but the process of selection will eliminate them. The applications of this unwritten rule will require great tact and diplomacy.[86]

In the Australia forces, the colour bar was reinstated when the war was over.[87] Recruitment advertisements for cadetships in 1946 and 1947 demonstrate that it was also reinstated in the British army.[88] Dudley Thompson, reflecting on wartime British policy, talked of 'running battles between the Colonial Office and the War Office, and it was the Colonial Office that was largely carrying the ball for us'.[89] As the war was ending, the War Office wanted to reinstate the 'pure European descent' rule, but the Colonial Office championed an end to the colour bar regarding it as 'flatly contrary to avowed colonial policy'.[90] In 1948, it was finally removed in all the British armed services. It is impossible to know how far they applied the 'unwritten rule' after 1948.

When the war was over, white women continued to be the focus of anxieties about interracial sexual relationships. These received extensive publicity when Seretse Khama's marriage to a white British woman prompted the British Labour government to refuse to recognise him as Chief of the Bangwato in Bechuanaland and to banish him. There was wide condemnation of this decision in the colonial empire. There were also protests in Britain and suggestions that the government had bowed to pressure from South Africa where mixed marriages were made illegal in 1949.[91] Despite these protests, British hostility to interracial marriages continued. A Gallup poll in 1958 found that 71 per cent of its respondents opposed them. In the same year, the *Daily Telegraph* suggested, 'what most of us instinctively recoil from is miscegenation'.[92] The focus on white women was evident in a question that was recurrent in the British media in the 1950s, 'Would you let your daughter marry a Negro?' Such a question was never asked of sons.[93] In Australia, Calwell argued in support of the 'White Australia' policy: 'The average Australian parents rearing children wanted to see their land as free from the evils of miscegenation as it was when they were growing up'.[94]

In 1953, an article in the *Sunday Times* described Queen Elizabeth's coronation tour of the empire and Commonwealth as 'a sign of the strange unity-in-diversity that characterises the modern Commonwealth, its family oneness, though it is scattered across the globe'.[95] The piece was titled 'Family Feelings'. Government discussions of colonial immigration in coronation year took a different view of 'family oneness':

> [I]t may well be argued that a large coloured community as a noticeable feature of our social life would weaken the sentimental attachment of the older self-governing countries to the UK. Such a community is certainly no part of the concept of England or Britain to which people of British stock throughout the Commonwealth are attached.[96]

This was an argument which confined family belonging and attachments to a white community. 'Family oneness' was threatened by British subjects of colour. 'Family feelings' did not cross racial divides. British subjects of colour did not count as British under immigration policies in Australia, Canada,

New Zealand and South Africa while British governments attempted covertly to keep their numbers down. When Australia and New Zealand actively recruited British migrants through assisted passages schemes, British subjects of colour did not count as British. The wartime slogan of 'togetherness' was always a thin façade behind which many policies and practices across the British Empire maintained racial boundaries and assumptions of white superiority. The view of 'family oneness' produced in government discussions in coronation year and its racial definition of Britishness remained a cornerstone of much policymaking when the war was over.

Notes

1 I am grateful to Kawana Pohe for permission to use this material about his brother.
2 The National Archives, London (TNA), AIR 10/965.
3 D. Killingray, 'Race and Rank in the British Army in the Twentieth Century', *Ethnic and Racial Studies*, 10:3 (1987), pp. 276–290, at p. 280.
4 C. Orange, 'An Exercise in Maori Autonomy: The Rise and Demise of the Maori War Effort Organization', in J. Binney (ed.), *The Shaping of History: Essays from the New Zealand Journal of History* (Wellington: Bridget Williams Books, 2001), pp. 62–77.
5 For the *'people's empire'* see W. Webster, *Englishness and Empire, 1939–1965* (Oxford: Oxford University Press, 2005), Chs 2 and 3.
6 C. Somerville, *Our War: How the British Commonwealth Fought the Second World War* (London: Weidenfeld and Nicolson, 1998), pp. 65–66.
7 Ibid., p. 152.
8 R. Scott Sheffield, '"Of Pure European Descent and of the White Race": Recruitment Policy and Aboriginal Canadians, 1939–1945', *Canadian Military History*, 5:1 (1996), pp. 8–15, at p. 9.
9 R. Scott Sheffield and N. Riseman, *Indigenous Peoples and the Second World War: The Politics, Experiences and Legacies of War in the US, Canada, Australia and New Zealand* (Cambridge: Cambridge University Press, 2019), p. 65.
10 L. Grundlingh, 'The Recruitment of South African Blacks for Participation in the Second World War', in D. Killingray and R. Rathbone (eds), *Africa and the Second World War* (Basingstoke: Macmillan, 1986), p. 191.
11 Scott Sheffield and Riseman, *Indigenous Peoples and the Second World War*, p. 80.
12 TNA, CO 537/1224, 'Colour Discrimination in the UK'.
13 Somerville, *Our War*, p. 58.
14 *The Times*, 19 October 1939.
15 *The Crisis*, March 1941, p. 82.
16 K. Jeffery, 'The Second World War', in J. Brown and Wm. Roger Louis (eds), *The Oxford History of the British Empire*, Vol. IV: *The Twentieth Century* (Oxford: Oxford University Press, 1999), p. 314.

17 Grundlingh, 'The Recruitment of South African Blacks', p. 190.
18 M. K. Gandhi to Franklin D. Roosevelt, 1 July 1942, US National Archives Catalog, https://catalog.archives.gov/id/7065056.
19 TNA, CO 875 11/13, 'Digest of Material Based on Incoming Letters from US', April 1941.
20 Somerville, *Our War*, pp. 66–67.
21 *Daily Express*, 25 May 1940.
22 *Maximum Effort* (Michael Hankinson, 1944).
23 *West Indies Calling* (John Page, 1943).
24 'West Indian Girls Join the ATS', *Picture Post*, 4 December 1943.
25 B. Bousquet and C. Douglas, *West Indian Women at War: British Racism in World War II* (London: Lawrence & Wishart, 1991), pp. 148–161.
26 H. Tinker, 'A Forgotten Long March: The Indian Exodus from Burma, 1942', *Journal of Southeast Asian Studies*, 6:1 (1975), pp. 1–15, at p. 14.
27 *The Times*, 26 September 1942; *The Times*, 17 September 1942.
28 *The Times*, 16 August 1942.
29 *Manawatu Standard*, 10 August 1942; *Manchester Guardian*, 10 August 1942.
30 Commander-in Chief, India to War Office, 18 August 1942, www.cvce.eu/en/obj/telegram_from_the_commander_in_chief_in_india_concerning_the_riots_in_india_18_august_1942-en-490b3938-428d-4548-a887-2fce18964b5b.html (accessed 3 July 2019).
31 *The Times*, 11 September 1942.
32 'The Trouble in India', *Pathe Gazette*, 3 September 1942; *Daily Express*, 12 August 1942.
33 *Sydney Morning Herald*, 10 August 1942.
34 TNA, WO 204/1038, Appreciation and Censorship Report No 35 for period 16–31 December 43.
35 Y. Khan, *The Raj at War: A Peoples' History of India's Second World War* (London: Bodley Head, 2015), p. 213.
36 Ibid., p. 208.
37 A. Muldoon, '"India is a Fine Country after All": The Cultivation of Military Morale in Colonial India', in A. Jackson, Y. Khan and G. Singh (eds), *An Imperial World at War: Aspects of the British Empire's War Experience, 1939–1945* (Abingdon: Routledge, 2017), pp. 181–183.
38 B. Henriques, *Fratres: Club Boys in Uniform, An Anthology* (London: Secker and Warburg, 1951), p. 44.
39 India Office Records, IOR/L/PJ/7/5405, 'Congress and the War', July–September 1942, https://blogs.bl.uk/untoldlives/2013/05/political-propaganda-and-the-quit-india-movement.html (accessed 14 July 2019).
40 *Manchester Guardian*, 24 August 1942.
41 Scott Sheffield and Riseman, *Indigenous Peoples and the Second World War*, p. 166.
42 S. Davies, *Bread and Roses* (Auckland: David Bateman, 1993), pp. 54–55.
43 BBC, Written Archives Centre (WAC), R9/9/7, BBC Listener Research Report on the changes in the state of British Public Opinion on the USA during 1942 and 1943, 7 February 1944.

44 TNA, INF 1/292, Home Intelligence Weekly Report, no. 94, 23 July 1942.
45 TNA, PREM 4/26/9, Secretary of State for War to Prime Minister, 21 October 1943.
46 BBC, WAC, Noel Sabine to BBC, 15 July 1942, Rudolph Dunbar contributor file.
47 R. Lambo, 'Achtung! The Black Prince: West Africans in the Royal Air Force, 1939–1946', in D. Killingray (ed.), *Africans in Britain* (London: Routledge, 2012), pp. 145–163, at p. 150.
48 *Africa's Fighting Men* (Colonial Film Unit, 1943).
49 TNA, AIR 20/9051, 'Demobilisation and Resettlement, Extract from War Cabinet paper', 16 November 1942.
50 TNA, WO 204/10381, Appreciation and Censorship report no 34, 16 November–15 December 1943.
51 TNA, WO 204/10381, Appreciation and Censorship report no 37, 16–31 January 1944.
52 TNA, WO 204/10381, Appreciation and Censorship Report no 51, 16–31 August 1944.
53 W. Worger, N. Clark and E. Alpers, *Africa and the West: A Documentary History, Vol. 2* (Oxford: Oxford University Press, 2001), pp. 79, 81.
54 Khan, *The Raj at War*, p. 251.
55 J. Robertson, *The British Board of Film Censors: Film Censorship in Britain, 1896–1950* (London: Croom Helm, 1985), p. 60.
56 W. Webster, '"Fit to Fight, Fit to Mix": Sexual Patriotism in Second World War Britain', *Women's History Review*, 22:4 (2013), pp. 607–624.
57 S. R. Mehrotra, 'On the Use of the Term "Commonwealth"', *Journal of Commonwealth Political Studies*, 2 (1963), pp. 1–16.
58 G. K. Evans, *Public Opinion on Colonial Affairs*, June 1948 (London: HMSO, 1948), p. 2.
59 TNA, WO 204/10381.
60 C. Stacey and B. Wilson, *The Half Million: The Canadians in Britain, 1939–1946* (Toronto: University of Toronto Press, 1987), p. 58.
61 H. Nelson, *Chased by the Sun: The Australians in Bomber Command in World War II* (Crows Nest: Allen and Unwin, 2006), p. 57.
62 *India Marches* (Bombay Talkies, 1941); *West Indies Calling* (John Page, 1943).
63 BBC, WAC, R9/9/7, Audience Research Special Reports no. 7, 1943.
64 F. Furedi, 'The Demobilized Soldier and the Blow to White Prestige', in D. Killingray and D. Omissi (eds), *Guardians of Empire: The Armed Forces of the Colonial Powers, 1700–1964* (Manchester, Manchester University Press), p. 188.
65 K. Grundy, *Soldiers Without Politics: Blacks in the South African Armed Forces* (Berkeley: University of California Press, 1983), p. 83.
66 A. Israel, 'Measuring the War Experience: Ghanaian Soldiers in World War II', *The Journal of Modern African Studies*, 25:1 (1987), pp. 159–168, at pp. 161–162.
67 Scott Sheffield and Riseman, *Indigenous Peoples and the Second World War*, pp. 152, 220–221.
68 Somerville, *Our War*, pp. 184–185.
69 TNA, AIR 2/13437, Minute Sheet, 27 August 1945. Emphasis in the original.

70 Somerville, *Our War*, p. 184.
71 Ibid., p. 228.
72 Grundy, *Soldiers Without Politics*, p. 83.
73 Somerville, *Our War*, pp. 189–190
74 J. Bew, *Citizen Clem: A Biography of Attlee* (London: Riverrun, 2017), p. 271.
75 *Hansard*, House of Commons Debates, 9 September 1941, vol. 374 c. 69.
76 *Sydney Morning Herald*, 19 March 1949.
77 Canada, House of Commons Debates, 1 May 1947, 2646, http://parl.canadiana.ca/view/oop.debates_HOC2003_03/656?r=0&s=1 (accessed 21 July 2019).
78 Dominion Population Committee Report, 1946, https://paperspast.natlib.govt.nz/parliamentary/AJHR1946-I.2.5.3.12/0 (accessed 21 July 2019).
79 K. Malik, *The Meaning of Race: Race, History and Culture in Western Society* (Basingstoke: Macmillan, 1996), p. 20.
80 I. Spencer, *British Immigration Policy since 1939: The Making of Multi-Racial Britain* (Abingdon: Routledge, 1997), pp. 25–33; R. Hansen, *Citizenship and Immigration in Post-War Britain* (Oxford: Oxford University Press, 2000), p. 59.
81 TNA, CAB 129/81/45, Cabinet Committee, Colonial Immigrants, 22 June 1956.
82 R. T. Appleyard, *British Emigration to Australia* (London: Weidenfeld & Nicolson, 1964), p. 34.
83 'Wot, no Babies!', *British Paramount News*, 10 July 1947.
84 K. Paul, '"British Subjects and British Stock": Labour's Postwar Imperialism', *Journal of British Studies*, 35 (1995), pp. 233–276, at p. 252.
85 Ibid., pp. 251–252.
86 TNA, AIR 2/13437, Minute Sheet, 23 August 1945.
87 Scott Sheffield and Riseman, *Indigenous Peoples and the Second World War*, p. 288.
88 *Manchester Guardian*, 28 August 1946; 29 November 1946; 11 June 1947.
89 Somerville, *Our War*, p. 184.
90 TNA, AIR 2/13437.
91 S. Williams, 'The Media and the Exile of Seretse Khama', in C. Kaul (ed.), *The Media and the British Empire* (Basingstoke: Palgrave Macmillan, 2006), pp. 70–87.
92 *Daily Telegraph*, 2 September 1958.
93 T. Philpott, 'Would You Let Your Daughter Marry a Negro?', *Picture Post*, 30 October 1954; *Daily Express*, 18 July 1956.
94 *Newcastle Morning Herald and Miners' Advocate*, 2 December 1949.
95 *Sunday Times*, 27 December 1953.
96 B. Carter, C. Harris and S. Joshi, 'The Racialization of Black Immigration', in K. Owusu (ed.), *Black British Society and Culture: A Text Reader* (London: Routledge, 2000), p. 36.

2

Cut loose: the British in China and the aftermath of empire

Robert Bickers

We might start with three men who died in Canada, far from the China that shaped their lives. Kenneth Morison Bourne was born in Canton (Guangzhou) in 1893, where his father was British vice-consul. The family lived on the pleasant island of Shameen, its seventy-four acres housing two foreign-controlled administrations, one British, one French, its buildings set among lawns and banyan trees, its trim riverbanks separating it from the surrounding suburbs of the Chinese city. John James Carney, by contrast, had been born in British Columbia in 1894, to a family of Irish descent. Menahem Hayward was born in Bombay in 1887; orphaned, he was brought up by a great aunt in Hong Kong, and then from 1894 in Shanghai by her son, who worked for the firm David Sassoon & Co. A farmer's son who trained as a teacher, Carney, like Bourne, served in France in the First World War. Bourne, however, was a product of Clifton College and Sandhurst. Both men went to work in Shanghai, each spending most of the interwar years as British subjects working for the semi-autonomous administration that ran the city's International Settlement; Carney joined its police, then switched to the Public Health Department. Bourne entered the police force as an officer cadet, and from 1938 onwards led it.[1] Hayward's youth is more obscure, but he joined his uncle's firm, working for it in Shanghai until 1949, and in the late 1930s running his own manufacturing firm. Class, religion, career trajectory and social connections distinguish these three lives, but they were all China Britons, registered as such at the Consulate-General (on payment of a small fee, duly noted with a stamp in their British passports), and thereby formally 'recognised' as such by officials.[2]

So too were their wives and children: Jim Carney married Dora Sanders, a South African-born journalist; Bourne wed a consul's daughter, Marion Royston Porter; Hayward married Stella David, born in Hilla, Iraq, the daughter of the Shamash (beadle) of Shanghai's Shearith-Israel Synagogue who had arrived in the city sometime before 1915. Between them they had twelve children, all these events duly registered by British consular officials. The term 'China Britons' also embraced: Karta Singh Sangha, a Punjabi Sikh who lived and worked in Shanghai from 1920–1960; Angelina Archer, born in Hong Kong in 1881 to an African American father and Macanese mother (but a British subject by birth in the colony), who lived in Peking from the mid-1920s until her death in 1959; Bertie Hayton-Fleet, born in St Petersburg to a Scottish family prominent in the Russia trade, a journalist and businessman, who died in Shanghai in 1942, leaving his Russian widow Natalia Andreevna his British nationality; Bombay-born Isaac Silas Hardoon, a clerk in the banking arm of the trading firm E. D. Sassoon & Co. in Hong Kong for some thirty years up to 1946. All were British subjects, none had lived in Britain, barring two who had schooled there. China Britons too were the tens of thousands who came from the British Isles, and who might be more usually assumed to make up these China communities. Some came to start careers, some to start afresh, some for short-term postings, others following family traditions, some by chance.

Theirs was a diverse and capacious world, which encompassed British-owned enterprises of sorts – shipping, foodstuffs, mining, utilities, trading houses – schools, churches, newspapers, municipal administrations, traditions and histories, literature and a patois. While it was sometimes characterised as a coastal world (and 'China coast' became a shorthand for it), and while it was geographically mostly located in China's riverine and coastal cities, it spread across China. Parts of it were deeply embedded in China's economy, infrastructure and society. It would be impossible to easily disentangle and withdraw it, argued its defenders in the face of Chinese nationalist drives to restore China's ragged sovereignty. Yet this British world was abolished on 11 January 1943, a century after it came into being in the aftermath of the 1839–1842 conflict known as the 'Opium War'. That day Britain and the Republic of China signed a treaty for 'The Relinquishment of Extra Territorial Rights in China and the Regulation of Related Matters'. When it came into effect four months later it nullified the foundations of the position the British had secured in China in treaties and through precedence since 1842, and little provision was made for British residents and their interests.

Well into the interwar period the British had held a commanding position in China's modern economy; now it was fatally weakened. In this chapter I will outline the shape and reach of this presence, its practical and rhetorical entanglement in the wider 'Greater British' world, its trajectory after January 1943, and its legacies. These were complex and would return, as we shall see, as a matter of controversy in the early twenty-first century, in a case study of what was characterised as 'British identity theft' by two of those involved. This emotionally charged episode indicated for some how far the state's understanding of British subjecthood had hardened, and for others that the plural realities of empire had been forgotten after its end. But I will argue instead that it shows how such pragmatic accommodations to difference had mostly in fact been contingent, had served their purpose, and were now simply seen as history, even though they remained a lived experience for those concerned. And what made it more complex and fraught was all the rhetorical work and performance that had been undertaken at the time, that tied this world together, and tied its participants into it, with words and notions of what it was to be British.[3]

This withdrawal from a position of strength was surely one of the easiest retreats from empire that metropolitan British officials ever had to oversee. Neither in London nor in the Chinese treaty ports could British interests affect these developments in any way at all. In fact, by the end of December 1941, when Hong Kong fell to the Japanese, nearly all British assets in China were in enemy hands. After its defenders surrendered, British interests in the Crown Colony were seized by the Japanese, and British subjects (excepting on the whole those who were ethnically Chinese, South Asian, or Portuguese – by which was meant Luso-Asian Eurasians, or Macanese) were, with a few exceptions, incarcerated in prisoner of war or internment camps.[4] In occupied China, where they were mostly at first left at liberty, Japanese firms were appointed to administer British enterprises. By the time the 1943 treaty was being negotiated, British subjects including Baghdadis, and many who were British by marriage (but not all) were also about to be moved into a network of internment camps. There was little opportunity for lobbying. They became aware of what had been agreed; all they could do was hope that it might be undone, or that some cause might arise in the interval between intention and implementation that would save them.

For their part, while diplomats could comfortably work for once on a major policy development without being pestered, and without having to consult, their standing in the eyes of the Chinese interlocutors had never been flimsier. The collapse of colonial British Asia in the face of the Japanese onslaught shocked and outraged the National Government. Thus wrong-footed, British negotiators had little ability to lobby to retain anything, signing away privileges they had stubbornly refused to consider abandoning for decades. American pressure and the independent tempo and objectives of its negotiations were also critical.[5] Both sides committed themselves to negotiating a new framework for commercial relations, and to settle matters relating to property ownership and concession employees, but nothing ever came of the former, and very little of the latter. After 1945, even if the Chinese government had been able to consider tolerating such claims in a post-war atmosphere characterised by heightened nationalism, its finances, and the communist insurgency, prevented this.

Despite Chinese and US opposition, the British managed to reoccupy Hong Kong on the initiative of its interned senior administrator, who left the camp shortly after the surrender and confidently declared the resumption of

British rule in what was arguably one of the last moments in which the classic 'man on the spot' forced an issue on the imperial periphery.[6] The post-war position of British interests in the rest of China, however, was degraded, or precarious, or simply never restored. Many confiscated allied assets had been transferred to the collaborationist regime in the summer of 1943, which meant that those, alongside interests still in Japanese hands at the end of the war, were subject to national government enemy property policy. More pragmatically, nationalist agencies and personnel simply seized enemy property for their own use. Re-establishing title could prove difficult. Some failed, such as the Shanghai Race Club, which owned an extensive site, and whose race meets had played a central role in the accumulation of social capital by city grandees and their challengers.[7]

Pride and arrogance aside (and there was much of both), what had been at stake? One 1949 estimate of the value of British investment in China estimated it as totalling between £110m–£300m (something like £3.9bn–£10.7bn at 2019 prices).[8] Hong Kong was worth £150m (£5.34bn).[9] Put another way, in 1936, the last full year of peace, trade with China accounted for 1.7 per cent of total British overseas trade. It might seem, then, an imperial outlier. For many of those involved, the value of their investment in China formed the totality of their interests, although there were significant exceptions, including such multinationals as ICI, British American Tobacco, Lever Brothers, the Calico Printers Association, and the Asiatic Petroleum Company (a subsidiary of Royal Dutch Shell). But it had also involved some 28,000 Britons personally vested in China; what became of them?

To understand that story more fully, it will help first to consider the nature of the British presence in more detail. A window onto it is provided by the 6 July 1937 edition of one of the 10,400-circulation copies of the Shanghai newspaper, *North-China Daily News*. This was the day before an accidental exchange of fire between Chinese and Japanese troops near Peking set in motion a full-scale Japanese invasion. Established as a weekly in 1850, the paper catered to a diverse readership, including Anglophone Chinese, but it was a British-owned company, registered as such in Hong Kong (as British companies in China were required to do), with a British editor. In its pages that day can be found a presentation of a networked city and a networked community. British-owned firms were among the shipping companies advertising schedules that linked Shanghai to the rest of China, to Asia, Europe, North America and the Antipodes. On those British-officered ships British subjects travelled to and from other Chinese ports, to vacation in Japan, or in resorts that echoed hill stations in colonial Asia or Africa, or they sailed 'home' on long leave – P&O's RMS *Carthage* was sailing that day for London – or to holidays across the Pacific or in New Zealand ('healthy and cheap'), booking passages at Thomas Cook's. As British shipping left and entered

Shanghai's harbour that day it passed two Royal Navy vessels anchored there. *North-China Daily News* readers listened to BBC broadcasts from Daventry, caught up with news of all kinds from Britain, and its territories, checked their investments in Malayan rubber companies, or subscribed to a local Coronation Memorial Bond. British investment from India in Shanghai real estate was represented in advertisements for E. D. Sassoon's Bundside Cathay Hotel, and nightclub, Ciro's. Both were closely associated with the firm's chairman, race club stalwart Sir Victor Sassoon who, it was reported, had donated an outdoor dance floor for the Shanghai Yacht Club's coronation dinner and dance. In these pages the British in China were assumed to live in their concerns partly in Britain ('home') and in the wider empire (that British home over the seas), but the community was confident in its own identity and the worth of its own quotidian round which was recorded in full. There was no Shanghai cringe. These are the mundane fragments of individual and communal life that constituted a coherent and authentic British world that existed in this Chinese city, and across others.

Copies of that day's *North-China Daily News* will have been delivered to the north China headquarters on the French Concession bund of Butterfield & Swire.[10] That month the company had branches in nineteen Chinese cities, and two in Japan. As well as insurance agencies, it managed the China Navigation Company, which operated fifty-seven steamers on coastal routes, on the Yangzi River, and in joint venture operations; servicing these was an extensive infrastructure of wharves and warehouses. British shipping accounted for around 20 per cent of tonnage in Chinese waters but conveyed around 42 per cent of cargo in 1930. China Navigation held a significant share of this traffic and operated as a feeder for the Liverpool-based Blue Funnel line (Ocean Steam Ship Company), for whom Swire acted as agents, and which was the most prominent British shipping company operating to Asia.[11] Butterfield & Swire's Hong Kong headquarters also managed a sizeable sugar refinery, and a busy dockyard. The company was looking into commercial aviation, operated a paint factory in Shanghai, and marketed its 'British' sugar across South East Asia, India, and British East Africa. The firm's London-based owners, John Swire & Sons, had sent thousands of men out to China and Hong Kong since its first agents had arrived in the summer of 1866; mercantile assistants and ancillary staff joined Butterfield & Swire, mariners passed through its fleet, the refinery and the dockyard recruited heavily, especially in Scotland. They often married on leave at 'home', and brought wives out to join them, and the hope of opportunity encouraged chain migration through family or community networks.

The Swire company interests were almost wholly focused on China and Hong Kong, but its owners were in London, and it therefore had some freedom of manoeuvre, as had E. D. Sassoon. This was not the case for many of the smaller British enterprises that can be found mentioned in the *North-China Daily News*, or the Kailan Mining Company, firmly stuck to its coal concession in north China. At the other end of the scale in 1937, Bertie Hayton-Fleet operated at Harbin: a trading company, Hayton Fleet & Co., commercial agents, an Anglo-American store, publishing ventures, and as a stringer for the *Morning Post* in London, and *North-China Daily News*, having also at one point run a British school there and for a long time a daily evening paper, the *Harbin Observer*. That paper's offices flew the Union Jack at the heart of the city's business district.[12] Like many others, Hayton-Fleet was flexible in what he undertook, and underpinning his activities was the legal protection for his ventures of his British status. Angelina Archer was involved in the little-recorded world of cabarets (nightclubs) in Peking; Ranjit Singh Sangha served as a watchman for the Chinese Maritime Customs service in Shanghai, investing his earnings in property in Shanghai that he then rented out. In their different ways, each relied just as much as the Kailan Mining Company on their British status, and the legal protection that gave their interests.

Outside Hong Kong, significant numbers of Britons worked for the municipal administrations that ran the British-controlled concessions in Tianjin and Shameen, but in greatest part for the British-dominated International Settlement's Shanghai Municipal Council (SMC).[13] They were policemen, like Bourne, or worked in public health, like Carney, but also as teachers, accountants, in public works, as architects, in hospitals, and in its secretariat. The SMC governed the core of the world's fourth-largest city using British local government norms. Britons held positions in the Chinese state administration as well, in the Post Office and the Salt Gabelle, but principally in the Maritime Customs, which had been led by British nationals since its inception in 1854. Half of its recruits from that year until 1949, were foreign nationals, and half of those again were British subjects: five and a half thousand men. The foreign staff of the customs was diverse in composition, but Britons were numerically the largest before 1941. China might be just one port of call in a career. Among the men recruited by Swire as sugar inspectors were a rancher from Southern Rhodesia, an upcountry agent of the Siam Forest Company, a Canadian farmer, and a member of the British South African Police. During the interwar depression, speculative applications arrived at the headquarters of the customs service from across the world. I have tracked one Shanghai draper back to Quebec then to Devon, and from China onwards to Melbourne, then Auckland, bankruptcy after bankruptcy propelling him to flight and to fail again somewhere else.

While a steady stream of young British men sailed to Asia from British ports to join Butterfield & Swire or the customs, the Shanghai police or British American Tobacco, those identified as British subjects in China included (but were not restricted to): Dominions subjects, including Chinese Australians; Anglophone Macanese born in Hong Kong; the Baghdadis, who either came from Bombay or from elsewhere in the Baghdadi diaspora (Hayward's uncle was born in Aden), and who were in large part drawn to work with the Sassoon firms, which had been active in China since they secured the treaties; British Chinese subjects from South East Asia, or Hong Kong (although there could be disputes over their status in China outside Hong Kong); British Indian subjects like Sangha; and people of mixed heritage (usually of British fathers and Asian mothers).[14] Consular records capture their births, marriages and deaths; consuls oversaw the administration of probates, and registered property transfers. This was only ever as efficient as the stuff of people can be. Menahem Hayward was hardly alone in neglecting to register the births of his first three children, but after making a statutory declaration and presenting documents to prove his right to British status, the Secretary of State gave permission in 1929, as it would to others who had through 'carelessness', 'neglect', 'forgetfulness' or 'inadvertence' failed to register their children. The files abound with claims for retrospective registration. 'I had no suspicion that my national status was other than that of a British subject', pleaded Valdemar Zimmerman in 1930, born in Singapore to a Palestine-born father, when after five years of registration at the Shanghai consulate-general he was deemed ineligible. Bombay-born Hannah Levy's former husband was an Iraqi national and she had thereby lost her British nationality, but her 'children were educated in British schools and have adopted English habits and customs and English is their mother tongue'. Both were successful in their claims. Occasionally the registers record excision, and formal derecognition, even after death.[15]

The 1931 peak of c. 28,000 British subjects in China and Hong Kong (including 8,000 servicemen), undercounted the total (not least because at that point all those born in the colony of Hong Kong were British subjects). There was a steady turnover. In 1921 it was estimated that the average length of residence in Hong Kong was barely five years, but there were many exceptions. More and more Britons spent longer and longer in China, some in retirement, but generally from China they returned 'home' or moved on. Shanghai's monthly *China Journal* was rich in advertising for pleasant climes in which to retire, and Vancouver Island's temperate climate had attracted a noticeable colony.[16] The opportunities in view from the China coast were expansive, not constricted. Roads from work in China did not lead back, as it were, to Cheltenham, or other haunts of the retired colonial British.[17]

Four factors underpinned this British presence: law, force, rhetoric and a smooth integration into wider global networks of British power and imperial life and mobility. Extraterritoriality, that is exemption from Chinese jurisdiction, had been secured in the mid-nineteenth-century treaties and conventions. Britons and their enterprises were subject to a British Supreme Court in Shanghai. Extraterritoriality was vested in individuals and their property. Logically, the China Britons claimed, it applied also to their employees. All that they touched was charmed. The canny and (for a consideration) the crooked, might extend their reach to cover property that was not theirs, and not British. Consuls worked to rebuff the claims of individuals whose British status or bona fides they doubted. The abolition of extraterritoriality had been developing as a nationalist objective in China since the early 1910s (but had always generated controversy). It had survived the first ten years of the resolutely nationalistic national government established by the Guomindang in 1927 by virtue simply of the existential crisis posed by the Japanese assault on China. Pragmatism trumped ideology – until the fall of British Asia.

Consular jurisdiction was part of the portfolio of privileges that provided the foundations of the British presence, which included urban districts ceded to the British state in which Britons might live and work (concessions), inland navigation rights for shipping, and a right, embedded in treaty, that a Briton would head the Maritime Customs service as long as British trade predominated. Some concessions had been abandoned after 1927 and there had been a notable diminution of foreign dominance in the customs, but a Briton still headed the service. British medical and educational establishments accepted Chinese demands that they register under Chinese law. After 1928, the Shanghai Municipal Council accommodated (a minority of) Chinese councillors.[18] Looking to a future in which extraterritoriality might end, firms such as John Swire & Sons looked to ways in which they could continue to operate through new alliances with Chinese interests. But still, on 6 July 1937 Britons were required by law to register annually at their consulate and were subject to British-administered justice. Many, like the *Harbin Observer* flew the flag to make their status clear (the puppet state of Manzhouguo had accepted the treaty obligations of its predecessor sovereign), others painted it on their buildings.

When law had failed, force had prevailed. The two Royal Navy vessels in Shanghai's harbour on 6 July 1937 were part of a much larger China Station. HMS *Tern* was one of several specially designed Yangzi river gunboats; the sloop HMS *Grimsby* was visiting from Hong Kong, the navy's regional headquarters. The colony hosted the Commander-in-Chief of British forces in China, including garrisons in Tianjin and Shanghai. The British had been to war in China three times, but military power was more routinely threatened, or implicit. Flying the flag – in the harbour at Shanghai in July 1937 – formed the substance of its daily round. The first line of defence, after concession police forces, lay in the China Britons themselves, who in large numbers joined militia units that were overseen by the British China command: the Shanghai Volunteer Corps (SVC), the Tientsin British Volunteer Corps, and the Hong Kong Defence Corps. Jim Carney served for a dozen years drilling and parading alongside traders and bankers, drapers and printers – and Hayward's eldest son, an insurance agent – who were mobilised regularly in times of disorder or war. The SVC was a multinational force, with units staffed on national lines (or publicly unspoken social or racial ones). It supported the police, when needed, and both were supported by local garrisons, and by the reservoir of force at Hong Kong. Around one and a half thousand men in the Hong Kong Volunteers took part in the colony's defence in 1941; nearly 300 died in battle or captivity.

Force could clear streets but could not resolve a crisis. That required metropolitan support and acknowledgment that these China outposts were authentic sites of British interest. Like others across the British world, China Britons knew that they could not take this for granted: they had to talk, and to perform. As well as a business lobbying group based in London (the China Association), private connections, and trying to set the agenda about British China policy and interests in the metropolitan press, Britons in China made it very clear whenever they could that they indeed were very much just that: Britons. In London, in his journalism and in books, the *North-China Daily News*'s former editor O. M. Green, pushed the British China story. And while their monuments and memorials commemorated local grandees, they also marked their identification with British norms of commemoration (in subject, in style, and in choice of designer), and with the national story: British communities across China erected memorials after 1918 to their two hundred wartime dead.[19] More routine was the making of young Britons that went on in their schools and churches, youth organisations and on sports fields. Empire Day, the King's Birthday, and coronations were marked by ceremonies, speeches, bazaars, subscription lists and all the rhythmic ritual of loyalty, dinner and dancing included. They believed themselves to be living and working entirely in the mainstream of a greater British life and they expected those outside China to believe that too. For some China Britons, the Baghdadis for example, this 'aspirational patriotism' was even more important and pronounced.[20] They faced a double task: consolidation of their inclusion within the British communities in China and playing their part in strengthening the recognition of those communities as constituents of the greater British world.

Structurally, China Britons seemed to have no cause to doubt this. They were fully integrated into circuits of British power, capital, culture and commerce. The Swire companies, for example, were spatially bound to Hong Kong and China, but their businesses depended on the interface with Blue Funnel, itself integrated into wider South East Asian networks, its key route flagged by British defence planners as a strategic priority, while Swire sugar could be found in India and Kenya.²¹ E. D. Sassoon, registered in London after 1920, had invested profits from its prominent role in the opium trade into cotton mills in Bombay, and then redirected these into significant holdings of Shanghai property. In this way this Britain in China was firmly integrated into global networks of all kinds: imperial defence and intelligence networks and those too of anti-colonial activists, as well as Zionism – Hayward's uncle co-founded Shanghai's Zionist monthly *Israel's Messenger* – religious and educational networks, and scouting. It was a site in global professional circuits, of engineers and technicians, and cultural circuits of musicians and performers. Its learned and professional journals contributed to the body of Anglophone knowledge and science.

And as the RMS *Carthage*'s Shanghai passengers made their six-week journey to London they were joined on board by, among others: a naval draughtsman, and the wife and family of a colonial administrative officer at Hong Kong; a captain in the Inniskilling Fusiliers and a planter at Singapore; an engineer working in Siam and a federated Malay States Police officer at Penang; a prominent composer and a banker working in Burma at Colombo; the Bishop of Assam and a mill manager at Bombay; a soldier and his family at Aden ('Government 3rd Class'); officers from the Cairo Fire Brigade and Palestine Police at Port Said; a civil servant and two children's nurses at Malta.²² The journey west firmly brought China Britons fully into the flows of men, women and children that coursed back and forth along the highways of British power and empire.

That soldier's class of travel pointed to the need to remember the functional realities of social class. This Britain in China was characterised by both metropolitan practices of social distinction, and by understandings of race, including anti-Semitism, however much Hannah Levy's children 'adopted English habits and customs'. Schools, masonic lodges and social clubs were among the sites where social standing was marked out as clearly as if also labelled 'Government third class'; others were separated by reason of faith. As Chiara Betta has noted, a 1908 survey of the treaty port world had profiled Baghdadi firms among 'The Oriental Mercantile Community' in its section on Hong Kong, and that ambivalence was not absent in Shanghai.²³ The Shanghai British social order intersected with the performance of official precedence by consuls and council grandees, and was more explicit in Hong Kong, with its governor and practices that surrounded him, than in the other China communities, but a way was always found to perform elitism (in the *pukka* Light Horse of the SVC, for example). Bourne would have had to accept that he shared his formal British status in China with Archer, Hayward and Hardoon, and that a man such as Harrow School-educated Sir Victor Sassoon had to be given the due his social standing and wealth demanded. Sassoon was, after all, a man who could provide a dance floor for the Yacht Club in his own performance of empire loyalty, but Bourne would not actually have recognised these men to be British, not British like him.

Abandonment in 1943 was a shock, but defence planners had long drawn the imperial front line at Singapore: Hong Kong was expected to fall; the military presence north of that had mostly been withdrawn by the autumn of 1941. The British position in China had steadily unravelled since the war broke out on 7 July 1937. The Japanese scraped away at the autonomy of the settlement, and in Tianjin they blockaded the British concession. A large-scale evacuation of British families to Hong Kong took place in August 1937, and while the majority would drift back after the fighting moved on and away from the city, some stayed or moved on home, or to Australia.[24] As the conflict in Europe deepened, and as China Britons left to join up, British subjects in key positions, such as the police force, were actively discouraged from doing so, so as not to precipitate a Japanese seizure of the settlement through the simple act of providing their replacements.

Dora Carney sailed to Hong Kong in the 1937 evacuation (as did the Hayward family; Bourne's wife and sons were on vacation in north China, and stayed there), and although the family returned, Jim Carney resigned in July 1939 and they moved back to Canada. The Haywards returned, but in the meantime their house had been stripped bare by looters and badly damaged.[25] Bourne took long leave in August 1941, also taking his family to Canada. Overseas when the war commenced, he was replaced in February 1942 by a Japanese national, who oversaw a force in which most allied staff would continue to serve until early spring 1943 when their services were terminated, and they and their families were interned. Carney resumed his Canadian life after nearly two decades, switching back to a Canadian passport, trained as a vet, returned to British Columbia and worked in government until retirement. He died in 1976. Bourne's war was more peripatetic, but his life and work were smoothed by the network of well-placed and well-connected contacts he had made at Clifton College, in the army, in the police and through family: his brother held senior roles in the Indian government; a cousin was a 'Taipan in P&O'; his father-in-law was a consul. Bourne spent the war and post-war years in British intelligence agencies, first in Washington DC, then for MI6 in India, and MI5 in Singapore and in India where he became the first British 'Security Liaison Officer' to the post-independence government of India before returning to Canada in 1948.[26] It was a 'vast clean white country', he later wrote, describing his 'relief' on arrival: 'after the Far East and India the clean air and the white people are a tonic'. At that point Bourne, who had only ever schooled or spent leave in Britain, decided to stay in Canada for good. 'I held the view that England was going to get more difficult for youngsters during the turnover from empire to a highly industrialised small island, and from a feudal to a social government'. He had spent a decade in Asia as British power collapsed – he was in New Delhi at the transfer of power in 1947 – here in Canada was a prospect of stability, when the centre too was in flux. Bourne died in Ontario in 1968.[27]

These were but two stories of this 'turnover from empire' from among thousands of tales of the exodus from China. The British left the China coast, and with them, over a roughly fifteen-year period after August 1937, went all but a few members of the polyglot communities of foreign nationals who lived in China. They left, like Carney or Bourne, of their own accord (but pushed by increasingly unstable times), they were deported, or they were evacuated. Unlike the two men and their families, over 15,000 allied nationals were interned by the Japanese from different points after Pearl Harbor in camps in east and north China, and in Hong Kong. The Haywards and Hardoons were interned; so too was Natalia Hayton-Fleet. On their release, the greater number would be repatriated to allow them to recuperate, and many did not return. Hayward resumed working in Shanghai for David Sassoon. His youngest son Jack was sent to school in England in 1946, sailing on a repatriation ship with 1,200 other Britons, while another joined a large cohort of students from a rabbinic school who went to study in the United States in 1947.[28] Ill on release, suffering badly from the privations of internment in Hong Kong, Isaac Hardoon was taken to New Zealand for medical treatment, then moved to Bombay where he died in January 1946. His wife and daughter had been repatriated to Bombay, 'stranded, penniless', as his wife reported, homeless, 'ashamed of living in such a condition'. One son returned to Hong Kong to work, the rest of the family built new lives in Bombay.[29]

Many more of the British left as China's post-war nationalism reduced the range of opportunities there for foreign nationals, and they went as the unfolding civil war turned into defeat and then rout of the National Government in the summer of 1949 at the hands of the communists. Iconic photographs of the aftermath of the fall of Shanghai by Sam Tata and Henri Cartier-Bresson caught Europeans and Americans in the act of departure, boarding the SS *General Gordon* in October that year, heading across the Pacific. On its previous voyage on the eve of the communist arrival, it had carried Menahem Hayward, his wife and three of their daughters, heading to resettle in British Columbia, where Hayward died in 1962. Over a twenty-year period, Isaac Hardoon's widow and most of his children eventually moved to Britain. Natalia Hayton-Fleet moved to Britain with their son in 1951. Angelina Archer's death in a Peking slum in 1959 was duly captured in the British consular register. Hoping to find some way to realise the value of his property, Sangha, now an Indian citizen, stayed until 1960, when he gave up. Widows and their children, or those abandoned by their British husbands, formed a significant proportion of the rump British presence in Chinese cities. Britons who stayed on after 1949 in China had found that over the next five years the new regime's steadily tightening grip on China's society and economy constricted the ability of foreign-owned enterprises to function. Few of these were appropriated; instead, life was made so difficult for them that their owners decided to withdraw. This often proved difficult – it had taken Howard Hayward a year when he left in May 1950, but by May 1957 only fourteen British companies remained in Shanghai, half of them subsidiaries of E. D. Sassoon & Co, and two of those were dormant, while one had just been confiscated. The remaining Sassoon assets were surrendered in 1958, but its Harbin-born Russian manager was unable to leave until September 1963.[30]

Tracing the movement of those flowing out from China is a matter of luck, rather than science. There are few obvious sources to track men and women whose world was dissolved, and who moved onwards largely on highly individual trajectories. Two cadres of employees prove a partial exception: police and customs. In the immediate aftermath of the war, some of the formerly interned men of the Shanghai Municipal Police found work in allied administrations in Germany and in former Italian colonies. Forty served temporarily in the colonial police force at Hong Kong, while its own men recuperated, and former detectives found work in South East Asia war crimes units. But for these men, and others established in their careers, restarting could prove difficult. The experience of the former chief inspector who initially started afresh as a petrol pump attendant was not an unusual one. A fifth of those released from internment had found their way to Australia by 1957, when at least a dozen were in Hong Kong.[31] Dick Foster-Hall was the London-based 'Non-Resident Secretary' of the Chinese Maritime Customs Service from 1942 to 1946, his work largely concerned with personnel and welfare matters, and the fate and the history of the service remained of keen interest to him after he retired and joined an insurance firm in Hong Kong. There in 1953 he bought an address book, penning on its flyleaf the words 'Chinese Customs Retired Employees'.[32] From Ashdowne to Zanadvoroff he noted addresses, occupations, and the odd personal detail, in a hand that got shakier over the years. The addresses attest to the dispersal of these men across the globe: London; Auckland then Perth; 'Master China Coast SS *Inchulver*'; Ritz Hotel, Kowloon; Sussex; Salt Spring Island, British Columbia; Los Angeles; Jos, Nigeria ('Sec. Tin Mines'); Dorset; Bath; Fremantle, Western Australia; Queensland; East Lothian; Streatham; Rangoon (d. 1954); S. Rhodesia; 'China Coast SS *Kwang Tung*'; Perth Yacht Club; Khulna, E. Pakistan.

Some of these were new careers as addresses shifted from Britain to postings overseas, then back presumably to retirement, some to houses named for their Asian pasts: 'Kuling', 'Meishan', 'Korea House'. Foster-Hall punctiliously recorded their deaths, striking through their addresses in Scotland, in Hong Kong, in Sydney. Some had clearly entered colonial services, but these were relatively few in number, and mostly only temporary, for those who found their careers cut short in China found it difficult to find new billets, especially those that might match their former stations. The post-war work in China of the United Nations Relief and Rehabilitation Administration employed a good number – a quarter of its British staff had worked in China – part of a wider international pattern of the evolution of colonial projects into international humanitarian ones.

As the listings in Foster-Hall's address book suggest, a number did not go far, and they stayed on the China coast. Hong Kong is more routinely understood as the destination for hundreds of thousands of Chinese, and as a redoubt for overseas Chinese driven out by 'hostile environments' in postcolonial South East Asia and Thailand.[33] Its persistence as a Chinese treaty port has been overshadowed by its Cold War history, but it continued into the 1960s to have all the character of one, as well as the British Crown Colony that it remained until 1997 (and which was arguably accentuated as men and women came into the administration whose Colonial Service positions in Africa or elsewhere in Asia had terminated at independence). In Foster-Hall's address book, but also in the administration's company records, and its newspapers, you can track the fate of the evacuated presence from the rest of China: Ciro's Ltd, dissolved 1950; Shanghai Properties Ltd, dissolved 1951, as was Sassoon's Cathay Hotels; Tientsin Land Investment Company, dissolved, 1953; Tientsin Club, 1954; Shanghai Race Club Stables, 1955; Tientsin Press, 1957; Shanghai Pharmacy, 1958; Shameen Estates, 1960; Hankow Dispensary, 1962; the Shanghai Club, 1963.[34] Obituaries and funeral reports pepper the Hong Kong press headed 'former Shanghai resident', or 'old Tientsin resident', and the lists of those attending record names familiar from any reading of the *North-China Daily News*. A 'China Coast' retirement home for English-speakers 'who have no home or relatives to go back to' was established in 1979.[35] Entropy, ageing and death were not the only stories. There were some successful business relocations, and there was successful reorientation – such as by the Swire companies – and there was some reinvention. But the registers of companies and cemeteries tell the most prominent story.

There was little by way of any organised afterlife outside Hong Kong. Cut loose by the British state, and by the violence of events, these China Britons mostly made their way under their own steam, refashioning themselves as they could. They did this alone; there was no body that resettled them beyond the British administration in Hong Kong that repatriated those in need in the autumn of 1945, or after the communist victory, and which gave them one-way tickets.[36] As they dispersed, they had little opportunity to articulate their interests corporately, or even their history. Diplomatic files hold claims from individuals for redress, and these were largely dealt with as such, family archives too: 'Madame Chiang Kai-shek directs me to acknowledge receipt of your letter', begins one such, '... and to inform you that it has been passed on to the Mayor of Shanghai'. 'Duly received', wrote the Mayor, and your claims have been substantiated, but they cannot be paid yet.[37] The China Association was a trade body, and these interests and claims were beyond its purview. So, all that performance captured in the pages of the *North-China Daily News* blew away in the cold winds of post-war change.

When 215 men assembled in Hong Kong in April 1954 for the centenary dinner of the Shanghai Volunteer Corps it was an exception that reinforced the point. The sight of Arnhold, Sir John Kinloch, Cumine, da Silva and Chang sitting down together demonstrated how rarely this had actually happened before, if ever, in Shanghai. In their defeat, they acted as if the SMC's motto, 'Omnia Juncta In Uno' – all together in one – had actually been true at the time, when class, race, and nation had ensured that it never had been.[38] It was easier for the four-dozen veterans who Dick Foster-Hall gathered in July the same year for a centenary celebration of the founding of the customs service, for its service 'ethos' had explicitly required it. Foster-Hall and his last chief worked to place in newspapers of record the achievements, as they saw them, of the service, which was now reimagined as something quite modern:

> Long before the League of Nations or the United Nations Organisation was dreamed of, the Chinese Customs Service demonstrated that men of all nationalities, with the most varied racial, religious, and social backgrounds, could work together harmoniously and efficiently.

So was the degradation of China's sovereignty recast.[39] Former Shanghai policemen based in Sydney organised a veterans' group in 1955. Although largely a social organisation, it did pursue the question of 'payments to ex-internees' through 'London', with the UN 'on behalf of those non British born members of our Assoc'.[40]

These were ephemeral moments, although the police group prefigured in that interest in payments to ex-internees, and especially the 'non-British born', the only formal organisation that acted to represent the interests of China Coast Britons. This was the Association of British Civilian Internees – Far Eastern Region (ABCIFER), formed in 1994 to lobby for a formal apology and compensation from the Japanese government, and that failing, for the British government to compensate internees. Ex-police, and ex-customs, could be found among its members who quickly reached a thousand in number, but it drew more widely than that by far in its membership. Half of its members lived in Britain; tellingly, a quarter were in Australia, 150 in the

United States and 120 in Canada.⁴¹ The complexities of the dispute that would eventually unfold as a result of this lobbying highlight both the variegated composition of the British communities in Asia in December 1941, and how that diversity had since been shucked off and disowned.

The sight of elderly men and women demonstrating on the streets of London – the oldest was ninety – and garnering supportive headlines in the national press, especially during the state visit of the Japanese Emperor in May 1998, embarrassed British politicians. But it was only in November 2000 that the government announced a scheme for an ex-gratia payment of £10,000 that would be made 'to each of the surviving members of the British groups who were held prisoner by the Japanese during the Second World War'.⁴² No more precise definition of eligibility than this was provided even in official scheme guidance for applicants.⁴³ After March 2001, when thousands of payments had already been made, it became apparent that it had later been decided by officials that eligibility should be based on the 1981 British Nationality Act, which thereby meant that it would be restricted to 'British subjects … born in the UK or [who] had a parent or grandparent' born in the United Kingdom. This became identified as a 'bloodlink' rule. Almost half the claims of civilian internees were rejected on these grounds. However, British subjects had been identified for internment on the basis of their recognised status at the time. Some produced the British passports that they held then, complete, of course, with consulate registration stamps. They had been British enough, they pointed out, to have been interned by the Japanese (who had, nonetheless, subdivided the British into 'United Kingdom, Eurasian, Jewish'); and they had 'by their actions regularly asserted their British nationality' it was pointed out at ABCIFER's 2001 annual general meeting.⁴⁴ They felt betrayed and belittled; they were perplexed and deeply hurt.

ABCIFER mounted unsuccessful legal challenges to the decision. More successful, eventually, was a complaint to the Parliamentary Ombudsman about maladministration brought by Jack Hayward, Menahem Hayward's younger son, whose family history meant that his claim had been rejected. In February 2006 a further refinement of the criteria was announced that rendered eligible those who could demonstrate at least twenty years' residence in the United Kingdom between 1945 and 2000. This again, of course, ignored the reality of the pattern of diaspora of the China Britons, and of the historic global mobility of the British, if not the global nature of British identity, as this generation understood it, and had lived it. Meanwhile, a related legal challenge was brought against the Ministry of Defence by one of Isaac Hardoon's daughters, Diana Elias, whose initial compensation claim had also been rejected, as had those of her siblings while her sisters-in-law who met the criteria were successful. Elias argued that the 'bloodlink rule' amounted to racial discrimination, and the courts ruled that this had, indirectly, been the outcome of the way that the process had been designed. 'I was born British', she was reported as saying, 'I have always been British. My grandparents were British. My father was British and so was my mother'.⁴⁵ It did not matter where she was born, she argued, nor that she had only moved to Britain to live in 1972, after living and working in Bombay. A third change in government policy in January 2007 heralded the award of £4,000 compensation for 'injury to feelings' of those whose claims had been rejected by the 'bloodlink' criteria. These rejections, nonetheless, still stood (although Elias and Hayward had both qualified under the twenty-year rule). This again led to inconsistencies and inequities, and a further formal complaint that was upheld by the Parliamentary Ombudsman in 2011. Eventually, all but a small number received one of these payments, although the subject of the 2011 complaint died before the decision was reached.

The state had made its point, shoddily. British civil servants in 2001 clearly could not and would not conceive of a legal British status that included, as it did, Archer, Bourne, Carney, Hardoon, Hayton-Fleet, Haward and Sangha. They were, as ABCIFER's newsletter put it that year, 'adamant that they can and will redefine who was British in 1941/5'. As Jack Hayward wrote, in that period 'imperial Great Britain had not yet shrunk to the dimensions of a Little Britain' as expressed in the 'bloodlink' policy. What was actually tested in this episode was the imagined, and performed, authentic, 'Greater British identity' captured in the *North-China Daily News* of 6 July 1937, in Foster-Hall's address book, and by the Japanese and, although this was never pointed out, by the nationalism of both the Guomindang's National Government, and of the People's Republic after 1949.⁴⁶ Distinction still mattered of course; we might not be surprised that the Parliamentary Ombudsman found a compelling witness in Jack Hayward, Fellow of the British Academy, and sometime Professor of Politics in the University of Oxford. Hayward had argued that:

> By upbringing, culture and values I have always felt wholly British, even before being 'repatriated'– yes, repatriated – to Britain early in 1946. To be informed, by implication, that I belonged to a lesser breed without the law, a law not applicable at the relevant time, was an intolerable insult, which called for an official public apology.

But Hayward missed a crucial point, in that these communities actively made Britons, although this had never been the aim, and that these Britons had also made themselves, transforming Baghdadis, for example, into Britons through their performance of what he described himself as 'aspirational patriotism', the ways they had 'asserted their British nationality', those 'English habits and customs', the Anglophilia of his parents that decided one of his names for him, Ernest, in homage to Oscar Wilde's *The Importance of Being*

Earnest. Moreover, this was a contingent process, and always a provisional arrangement. It was a function of the way that British power came to be exercised in China, and by those who found ways to make it work for them, working opportunely in the shadow of the treaties and the gunboats. The British state made Britons at the margins and at the heart of empire, until the Commonwealth Immigration Act of 1962, and its subsequent refinements. The expansive moment had passed, argued Hayward, but there had never really been one. The position of the Baghdadis, for example, had never been secure, neither in China nor in other British territories into which 'Oriental' business enterprises like the Sassoon companies had moved. Almost exactly a century earlier, the same plaints as Hayward's, the phrasing almost identical, came into British consular offices in China from Anglophone Baghdadis whose long-established recognition had been rescinded, their feelings grossly injured.[47] The ambiguities of their position in British eyes remained thereafter. Where they could be disowned, they were, but where their status and wealth suggested otherwise, as it did for Sir Victor Sassoon, then they were tolerated, and recognised, as British. Theirs was a particular story, but others too among the China Britons faced their own particular version of this same story of recognition and derecognition, and of being cut loose, and being cut out, as they were dispersed after the polities and communities in which they had lived, battered by war and nationalism, withered away.

The Ministry of Defence, Jack Hayward wrote, refused 'to acknowledge that I was (and am) a Briton without prefix or suffix'. Even so, in 1941, while the Hayward family indisputably held British nationality, it seems to me unlikely that Kenneth Bourne would actually have seen Menahem Hayward as being as British as he was, or as 'white'. Without, it seems, realising it, these twenty-first-century civil servants simply and crudely re-operationalised the distinctions that had always been there, and that their predecessors had worked with, even as consular staff in Shanghai or Tianjin stamped passports to confirm payment of registration fees, signed birth and marriage certificates, retrospectively regularised status, and acted to protect the interests of all these China Britons. The prefix was silent; now it was given voice, unabashedly, and to those concerned and to many observing, shockingly and insultingly, but it had always been there, it was always on the tip of the colonial tongue.

Notes

1 Bourne: Shanghai Municipal Archives (hereafter SMA), U102–3-825, 'K. M. Bourne'; 'Memoirs of Kenneth Morison Bourne', private collection; Carney: D. S. Carney, *Foreign Devils had Light Eyes: A Memoir of Shanghai 1933–1939* (Toronto: Dorset Publishing, 1980); SMA. U 1–16–3234, 'John James Carney';

Hayward: National Archives, Kew (hereafter TNA), FO 671/488, Foreign Office to Acting Consul-General Shanghai, No. 58, 26 April 1929 and enclosures; J. Hayward and R. Bridge, 'British Identity Theft: An Official Far Eastern Fiasco', unpublished MS, 2010. I am grateful to the Hayward family for allowing me to see this MS, and to Edward Page for his assistance. For background, this essay draws extensively from my books: R. Bickers, *Britain in China: Community, Culture, & Colonialism, 1900–1949* (Manchester: Manchester University Press, 1999), and *Empire made Me: An Englishman Adrift in Shanghai* (London: Allen Lane, 2003); biographical information is sourced via Ancestry. com unless otherwise cited.

2   Despite his Canadian birth, Carney travelled with a British passport, certainly in 1933. His choice of formal nationality was fluid.
3   Hayward and Bridge, 'British Identity Theft'.
4   On the Anglophone Macanese of Hong Kong see: C. Chan, *The Macanese Diaspora in British Hong Kong: A Century of Transimperial Drifting* (Amsterdam: Amsterdam University Press, 2021).
5   K. C. Chan Lau, 'The Abrogation of British Extraterritoriality in China 1942–43: A study of Anglo-American-Chinese relations', *Modern Asian Studies*, 11:2 (1977), pp. 257–291.
6   See P. Snow, *The Fall of Hong Kong* (New Haven: Yale University Press, 2004), pp. 205–260.
7   Profitably, too: see N. J. Chang, *Yiguo shiwu de zhuanyi: Jindai Shanghai de paoma, pao gou yu huili qiusai* (*Cultural Translation: Horse Racing, Greyhound Racing and Jai Alai in Modern Shanghai*) (Taipei: Institute of Modern History, Academia Sinica, 2019) and J. Carter, *Champions Day: The End of Old Shanghai* (New York: W. W. Norton, 2020).
8   Calculated via Measuringwealth.com.
9   D. Clayton, *Imperialism Revisited: Political and Economic Relations between Britain and China, 1950–54* (Basingstoke: Macmillan, 1997), p. 8.
10 Throughout this essay, unless otherwise noted, detail on the Swire companies is drawn from R. Bickers, *China Bound: John Swire & Sons and its World, 1816–1980* (London: Bloomsbury, 2020).
11 C. F. Remer, *Foreign Investments in China* (New York: Macmillan, 1933), p. 373; M. Falkus, *The Blue Funnel Legend: A History of the Ocean Steam Ship Company, 1865–1973* (London: Palgrave Macmillan, 1990).
12 As Hayton-Fleet probably himself noted when writing as 'Our own Correspondent', *North-China Herald*, 5 February 1936, p. 214; other details from *The Directory & Chronicle of China, Japan, Korea … 1937* (Hong Kong: Hongkong Daily Press, 1937), p. A104.
13 See I. Jackson, *Shaping Modern Shanghai: Colonialism in China's Global City* (Cambridge: Cambridge University Press, 2017).
14 Some case studies include: C. Betta, 'From Orientals to Imagined Britons: Baghdadi Jews in Shanghai', *Modern Asian Studies*, 37:4 (2003), pp. 999–1023; S. Loy-Wilson, *Australians in Shanghai: Race, Rights and Nation in Treaty Port China* (Abingdon: Routledge, 2007); M. J. Meyer, *From the Rivers of Babylon*

to the Whangpoo: A Century of Sephardi Jewish Life in Shanghai* (Lanham: University Press of America, 2003). Families from the Ottoman Jewish diaspora were variously designated in contemporary British references as Turks, or 'Baghdadis', 'Bombay Jews', or simply 'Jews'; here I shall use the term Baghdadi. See also S. Abrevaya Stein, *Extraterritorial Dreams: European Citizenship, Sephardi Jews, and the Ottoman Twentieth Century* (Chicago: University of Chicago Press, 2016). On the resulting complexities of consular jurisdiction and nationality, see A. Thompson, 'The British State at the Margins of Empire: Extraterritoriality and Governance in Treaty Port China, 1842–1927' (PhD Dissertation, University of Bristol, 2018).

15 Hayward: Foreign Office to Acting Consul-General Shanghai, No. 58, 26 April 1929; Zimmerman, 'Statutory declaration', 15 September 1933; 'Humble Petition of Hannah Levy', 15 January 1931, all in TNA, FO 671/466. Posthumous derecognition: see R. Bickers, 'Legal Fiction: Extraterritoriality as an Instrument of British Power in China in the long nineteenth century', in D. M. Brunero and B. P. Farrell (eds), *Empire in Asia: A New Global History. Volume Two: The Long Nineteenth Century* (London: Bloomsbury Academic, 2018), pp. 64–65.

16 See J. F. Bosher, 'Vancouver Island in the Empire', *Journal of Imperial & Commonwealth History*, 33:3 (2005), pp. 349–368.

17 E. Buettner, '"We Don't Grow Coffee and Bananas in Clapham Junction You Know!": Imperial Britons Back Home', in R. Bickers (ed.), *Settlers and Expatriates: Britons Over the Seas* (Oxford: Oxford University Press, 2010), pp. 302–328.

18 On these reforms see Jackson, *Shaping Modern Shanghai*.

19 S. Hammond (ed.), *The China War Book: Being a Register of Britons and their Allies on Service from China …* (Shanghai: Patriotic League of Britons Overseas, 1917).

20 Hayward and Bridge, 'British Identity Theft', Ch. 3, p. 9. For a study of these processes in the context of Hong Kong see V. Kong, 'Multiracial Britons: Britishness, Diasporas, and Cosmopolitanism in Interwar Hong Kong' (PhD Dissertation, University of Bristol, 2019).

21 G. Huff and G. Huff, 'The Shipping Conference System, Empire and Local Protest in Singapore, 1910–1911', *Journal of Imperial & Commonwealth History*, 46:1 (2018), pp. 69–82.

22 RMS *Carthage*, passenger list, 12 August 1937: TNA, BT 26/1127, via Ancestry.com.

23 A. Wright (Chief Editor), *Twentieth Century Impressions of Hongkong, Shanghai, and other Treaty Ports of China* (London: Lloyds Greater Britain Publishing Company, 1908), p. 224; Betta, 'From Orientals to Imagined Britons', p. 1009.

24 V. Kong, '"Hong Kong is my Home": The 1940 Evacuation and Hong Kong-Britons', *Journal of Imperial and Commonwealth History*, 47:3 (2018), pp. 542–567.

25 Enclosure in Consul-General Shanghai to Consul-General for Japan, 8 March 1938, TNA, FO 671/555.

26 C. J. Murphy, '"Constituting a Problem in Themselves": Countering Covert Chinese Activity in India: The Life and Death of the Chinese Intelligence Section, 1944–46', *Journal of Imperial and Commonwealth History*, 44:6 (2016), pp. 928–951; Bourne, 'Memoirs'.

27 Bourne, 'Memoirs', pp. 103–104.
28 'New school principal brings Oriental background to Dade', *Miami Herald*, 16 August 1968, p. 56.
29 Public Record Office, Hong Kong, HKRS41-1-1559, 'The Late Mr. Isaack Hardoon …'.
30 Consulate-General Shanghai to Foreign Office, 10 May 1957: TNA, FO 371/127353; *Hongkong Standard*, 14 September 1963.
31 Shanghai Police Association circulars, 1955–1957, copies in author's collection.
32 On Foster-Hall see B. E. Foster-Hall, *The Chinese Maritime Customs: An International Service, 1854–1950* (Bristol: Chinese Maritime Customs Project Occasional Papers No. 6, 2015), pp. 45–49; address book: Tita & Gerry Hayward Collection, University of Bristol, Special Collections.
33 L. Madokoro, *Elusive Refuge: Chinese Migrants in the Cold War* (Cambridge, MA: Harvard University Press, 2016); Chi-Kwan Mark, 'The "Problem of People": British Colonials, Cold War Powers, and the Chinese Refugees in Hong Kong, 1949–62', *Modern Asian Studies*, 41:6 (2007), pp. 1145–1181.
34 See records in Public Record Office, Hong Kong, Series HKRS95-1, 'Files Relating to the Voluntary Liquidation of Companies'.
35 *South China Morning Post*, 23 September 1984, p. 14.
36 Four years later, it was still trying to clarify liability for the cost, in an interdepartmental squabble recorded in: TNA, CO 129/607/4, 'Repatriation of Ex-internees: Financial Responsibility for Passages: 1949 Feb. 2–Dec. 29'.
37 Pearl L. Chen to John Crighton, 8 September 1947, and K. C. Wu to Crighton, 20 October 1947, private collection. 'My father got nothing', his daughter wrote on the letter.
38 *South China Morning Post*, 3 April 1954, p. 6; 'Shanghai Volunteer Corps, Centenary Dinner, held at the Royal Hongkong Yacht Club on Friday 2nd April 1954', souvenir programme, private collection.
39 *South China Morning Post*, 12 July 1954, p. 7, 14 July 1954, p. 7; *The Times*, 12 July 1954, p. 9, letter and editorial.
40 Shanghai Police Association circular, February 1957.
41 Hayward and Bridge, 'British Identity Theft', Ch. 3, p. 5. ABCIFER's membership reports retained the dead, as they passed away. Across the thirteen years of its campaign, more than half of its original members died: *Bamboo Wireless, passim*.
42 Hayward and Bridge, 'British Identity Theft', provides a richly detailed insider account. The clearest published overview of the controversy can be found in HC 1462 *Defending the Indefensible: A report by the Parliamentary Ombudsman on an Investigation of a Complaint about the Ministry of Defence and the Service Personnel & Veterans Agency* (London: HMSO, 2011); see also: J. Lunn, *Ex-Gratia Payment for Far East POWs and Civilian Internees*, Standard Notes. (London: House of Commons Library, 2009); and Public Administration Select Committee, '*A Debt of Honour': The Ex-Gratia Scheme for British Groups Interned by the Japanese During the Second World War. Fourth Report Session 2005–2006, HC324, 12 July 2005* (London: House of Commons). For the broader context see F. Yap, 'Voices and Silences of Memory: Civilian Internees

of the Japanese in British Asia during the Second World War', *Journal of British Studies*, 50 (2011), pp. 917–940.
43 *Ex-Gratia Payment for British Groups Who Were Held Prisoner by the Japanese During World War Two. Notes for Guidance.* War Pensions Agency Leaflet 12 (c. 2000–2001).
44 *Bamboo Wireless*, No. 23 (July 2001), p. 7: this was ABCIFER's newsletter.
45 Quoted in *The Observer*, 8 October 2006, p. 5.
46 'Memorandum by Professor Jack Hayward', November 2005, Written Evidence, Public Administration Select Committee, *A Debt of Honour. First Report of Session 2005–2006, HC735, 19 January 2005* (London: House of Commons), Ev21; E. C. Page, 'Jack Hayward', *Biographical Memoirs of Fellows of the British Academy*, XVIII, pp. 63–91.
47 Stein, *Extraterritorial Dreams*, pp. 97–117.

3

Entangled citizens: the afterlives of empire in the Indian Citizenship Act, 1947–1955

Kalathmika Natarajan

In June 1954, an exasperated official from the British embassy in Washington DC sought clarification regarding three questions that were frequently asked by several bureaucrats ranging from State Department officials to staff at the New Zealand embassy.

> Is a man born in India a British subject?
> How is such a man a 'subject' if India is a republic?
> Is such a man treated as an alien in the United Kingdom?

Forwarding the message to officials at the Commonwealth Relations Office (CRO) in London, D. J. C. Crawley ventured his guesses: 'The answers to the three questions ... are probably "yes", "just one of those illogical things" and "no".'[1] This deceptively succinct exchange is an important indicator of both the complexity of negotiating identities shaped by the empire and the bureaucratic haze of interpreting overlapping citizenship frameworks after India's declaration of independence in August 1947.

Indian officials, for their part, were concerned with defining the answer to another succinct question: 'Who is an Indian citizen?' This seemingly simple question was a great dilemma for Indian officials as they set out to draft a framework for Indian citizenship, a process that took more than eight years to complete and remained a subject of debate long afterwards. The making of this 'eternal file'[2], as one Indian diplomat called it, was in no small part due to the intricacies of reconciling Indian citizenship legislation with the provisions of the 1948 British Nationality Act (BNA) which delineated Indians as British subjects or Commonwealth citizens after independence. The BNA represented a firm assertion of continued British leadership in the Empire/Commonwealth and a remarkable attempt to project a sense of global Britishness in a post-war world marked by imperial implosion.

This chapter focuses on the making of the Indian Citizenship Act of 1955 in the context of the break-up of Greater Britain. While conventional understandings of Indian citizenship view this process either solely in terms of Partition or as a mechanism through which the Indian state distanced its overseas diaspora, I interpret Indian citizenship as the product of a complex, even paradoxical, negotiation of entangled identities shaped by empire, a process largely informed by the widespread crises of citizenship encountered by overseas Indians in the 1940s and 1950s. Indeed, the BNA had long-standing consequences for those Indians resident in Commonwealth countries and British colonial territories, producing what I term 'entangled citizens': overseas Indians who were potentially eligible for multiple claims to citizenship and yet whose claims were often contested by all the countries involved. The difficulty of unravelling these claims was exemplified by the pervasive confusion over what terminologies to use to describe these persons: were they 'Indians', 'overseas Indians', 'British subjects', 'Commonwealth citizens' or 'citizens of the United Kingdom and Colonies' – or indeed perhaps something else altogether? As one British official noted, the complexity of defining such a legal status and implementing unwieldy citizenship frameworks was akin to opening a Pandora's box.[3]

My focus on the centrality of overseas Indians to the making of Indian citizenship is an effort to go beyond binary narratives of the Indian state's inclusion or exclusion of its diaspora at the stroke of independence and instead trace the afterlives of the empire that defined the Indian state's complex yet continual engagement with its overseas communities. This was a process through which India sought to ensure that its overseas communities had citizenship rights – not necessarily *Indian* citizenship. This policy was very much in line with India's call for reciprocal rights and citizenship within the Commonwealth, precisely aimed at ensuring the availability of some form of citizenship framework for its overseas communities that were increasingly facing crises of citizenship and potential statelessness. Indeed, at much the same time as the government of India was pondering over Commonwealth membership, it was also negotiating with the governments of Burma and Ceylon, that had both framed citizenship legislation explicitly designed to exclude Indians. Such crises were instrumental in shaping both India's increasing inclination towards Commonwealth membership and its call for 'reciprocity of citizenship' as the basis.

'Reciprocity' had been a strikingly persistent term underpinning India's demands at imperial conferences for the fair treatment of Indians across the British Empire. It also had a significant postcolonial resonance, not just in terms of Commonwealth membership, but very much also in terms of Indian citizenship legislation. India sought to utilise its newly sovereign status to call the bluff of the Commonwealth 'family' discourse, attempting to address the precarious status of overseas Indians in British colonial territories and Commonwealth nations at much the same time that the 1948 BNA delineated multiple possibilities of citizenship that would impact them. The BNA provided for British subject status to be derived through the 'gateway' of local citizenship – be it the 'Citizenship of the United Kingdom and Colonies', intertwining the metropole and the colonies within one citizenship framework, or the Citizenship of Independent Commonwealth Countries. For India, the provisions of the BNA meant that once Indian citizenship legislation had been passed, Indian citizens would thereby also become British subjects or Commonwealth citizens, a term introduced after Indian concerns about being termed 'British subjects' after independence. Until the Indian Citizenship Act was passed in 1955, Indians were technically 'British subjects without citizenship' – a remarkable interim period fraught with numerous legal complexities.

It is worth emphasising that the 'Pandora's box' opened up by the BNA was particularly problematic in the case of overseas Indians resident in the entangled realm of British colonial territories and Commonwealth countries. These overseas Indians could potentially fall into any of the following categories: Indian citizens, citizens of the newly minted category of 'United Kingdom and Colonies' (UKC) or temporary British subjects without citizenship. This last option was regarded by British officials as the definitive problem in the case of overseas Indians; if they, as 'temporary British subjects without citizenship', were not included in India's citizenship framework, they would have to be either automatically included into the framework of UKC citizens – a possibility that London dreaded – or left stateless.

The BNA's provision to seemingly open the floodgates for immigration from across the empire has been the subject of much debate. As Randall Hansen points out, British subject status had existed long before the BNA and, given the historically low rates of colonial migration to Britain itself, policymakers were not given to expect the influx that followed after 1948.[4] Moreover, the legislation was less about the question of migration and more about British attempts to wrest back the initiative after Canada's radical changes to the common code through its citizenship legislation.[5] That is, this attempt to reaffirm British subject status as 'a globally intertwined fellowship'[6] while recognising national frameworks of citizenship was a means 'to redress the fading image of Britain's imperial legacy through the institutionalization of a transracial, transregional citizenship category that bolstered the perception of imperial and Commonwealth uniformity'.[7] More broadly, it signalled a reaffirmation of the United Kingdom's intention to serve as a hub for a globe-spanning community of Greater Britain.

While there is vast literature on the 1948 BNA, there is comparatively less focus on its impact on Indian citizenship or the fact that the BNA guaranteed Indians the right to travel to, live and work in the United Kingdom, a remarkable contrast to the widespread discrimination and immigration restrictions encountered by Indians in virtually every other part of the world.[8] With the exception of Hugh Tinker's work, the BNA's far-ranging consequences for the contours of South Asian citizenship frameworks have only recently received some attention.[9] While Deborah Sutton and Joya Chatterji briefly mention both the 1948 British Nationality Act and the 1955 Indian Citizenship Act in their work, they do not focus on the ways in which drafting Indian citizenship legislation in lieu of the provisions of the BNA impacted the citizenship status of overseas Indians.[10]

It is Sarah Ansari's work that clearly showcases the 'bureaucratic tangle' of reconciling the BNA with citizenship legislation formulated in India and Pakistan.[11] While her focus is more on Pakistani citizenship legislation (which preceded the 1955 Indian Citizenship Act by four years) and the complexities encountered by the British missions in dealing with 'potential Pakistani' citizens abroad, she demonstrates the ways in which the British sought to avoid being what they called 'a dustbin for the refuse discarded by' India and Pakistan.[12] Drawing on this, I explore the making of the 1955 Indian Citizenship Act and its negotiation of the BNA, showing the ways in which widespread crises of citizenship and statelessness encountered by overseas Indian communities impacted the contours of Indian citizenship.

Deliberating citizenship and the issue of overseas communities

The British retreat from South Asia and India's independence in August 1947 heralded the negotiation of Indian citizenship provisions, a process that necessarily meant engaging with the status of overseas Indian communities whose identity and mobility had been shaped by empire. While a legal framework pertaining to citizenship in detail would take much longer to come into effect, draft provisions were to be included in the Indian Constitution and were discussed by the Indian Constituent Assembly in April 1947.[13] These debates touched on the fundamental question of granting citizenship by virtue of birth within the Union (*jus solis*), as opposed to the basis of descent (*jus sanguinis*). This was essentially framed as a clash between a racialised idea of citizenship (*jus sanguinis*) and an apparently more civilised and democratic one (*jus solis*). For proponents of citizenship by birth, such a framework was more suited to the international context within which Indian citizenship was being formulated. That is, such expansive notions of citizenship were considerably shaped by the position of overseas Indians who were waging many an uphill battle vis-á-vis citizenship.[14] The status of Indians in South Africa – an issue that India had taken to the UN General Assembly in 1946 – was seen as exemplifying the stakes in this debate. As Sardar Patel argued, given that 'we claim for Indians born there, South African nationality ... it is not right for us to take a narrow view'.[15] The status of overseas Indians was central even to those sceptical of the citizenship-by-birth framework; as K. N. Katju noted, the citizenship of children born outside India to Indian parents had to be accounted for. Mediating the citizenship of these children beyond the borders of India should have been, in Katju's view, a significant responsibility of Indian diplomats.[16]

A lack of consensus over the citizenship provisions led to the postponement of the debate, and by the time the Indian Constituent Assembly reconvened later in 1947, the Partition of India and Pakistan had been formally announced. This was a definitive event in the making of Indian citizenship.[17] Even as the context of Partition clearly informed the new amendments to the draft citizenship provisions presented in August 1949, one change in particular was aimed at addressing the complex status of overseas Indians. Extending Indian citizenship to those 'persons who or whose parents or whose grandparents were born in India as defined in the Government of India Act, 1935, who are ordinarily residing in any territory outside India' did not enable automatic access to citizenship but required that overseas Indians register themselves as Indian citizens through the diplomatic and consular representatives of India.[18] As Prime Minister Jawaharlal Nehru asserted in the Constituent Assembly, this was an attempt to address the prickly issue of the exact status and nationality of overseas Indians:

> We have millions of people in foreign parts and other countries. Some of those may be taken to be foreign nationals, although they are Indians in origin. Others still consider themselves to some extent as Indians and yet they have also got some kind of local nationality too, like for instance, in Malaya, Singapore, Fiji and Mauritius. If you deprive them of their local nationality, they become aliens there. So ... you will see that in this resolution we have tried to provide for them for the time being, leaving the choice to them and also leaving it to our Consul Generals there to register their names.[19]

Meanwhile, deliberations were further complicated by the presence of white British subjects in India whose status was affected by the end of empire. India's provisions of citizenship by birth were greeted with panic by a number of white Britons born in India who feared that this would make them Indian citizens at the cost of their British citizenship. The Commonwealth Relations Office and the Indian High Commission in London received dozens of letters ranging from the anxious to the angry, with enquiries from these white Britons about their citizenship status or that of their children born in India. Often affirming that they were of 'pure British blood' untouched by their birth and/or stay in India, or describing their military service for the empire, these letter-writers enquired about the procedures that would have to be followed to 'regain' British nationality. As one angry letter noted, 'I fought in the First World War. I gather in spite of this that I am now an enemy alien or something approaching it because I was born in India. I should like this blot on my escutcheon removed as soon as possible.'[20] These white Britons viewed new national and postcolonial conceptions of citizenship as a threat and therefore clung to notions of Greater Britain as a racialised community bound by blood and tradition.

It is imperative to read Indian debates on citizenship within the wider crises of citizenship-making in Asia that marked decolonisation. The year 1948 alone marked the framing of three nationality and citizenship laws that would have significant repercussions on overseas Indians. While Ceylon and Burma both legislated exclusionary citizenship acts that year, the 1948 BNA was perhaps the only legislation providing Indians with some semblance of an equal status by recognising them as British subjects or Commonwealth citizens.[21] The making of Indian citizenship thus meant that Indian officials had to engage with these provisions of the BNA that impacted both overseas Indians and those domiciled in India. Indeed, the BNA would affect the case of Indians in Burma and Ceylon too, shaping their status as citizens caught between various possibilities of citizenship, while staring down the barrel of statelessness. The Ceylon Citizenship Act was also responding to the BNA by providing 'local citizenship' for its citizens who would thereby also be eligible for 'Commonwealth citizenship'. Indians who did not qualify for citizenship in Ceylon would thus be rendered stateless if provisions were not made for their inclusion as Indian citizens. As British officials feared, this would in turn make them eligible for citizenship of the United Kingdom and Colonies. On the other hand, the citizenship status of Indians in Burma was further complicated by Burma's exit from the Commonwealth in 1948 – making these Indians 'foreigners' who were ineligible for Commonwealth citizenship status.[22] Thus, the making of Indian citizenship legislation *by default* meant negotiating the simultaneous unravelling and disentanglement of identities and nationalities during decolonisation.

Drafting the 1955 Indian Citizenship Act

While there is significant literature on Indian citizenship vis-à-vis the making of the constitution and the impact of Partition, the 1955 Indian Citizenship Act itself is not the subject of much study. Where scholars have dealt with the provisions of the 1955 Act, this is almost always in comparison with the later amendments made in the context of 'illegal immigrants' in the 1980s.[23] Anupama Roy recognises the period between 1950 (when the constitutional provisions regarding citizenship came into effect) and 1955, when the Citizenship Act was adopted, as a 'liminal space' creating 'awkward', 'transitional' and 'aspiring' citizens. However, she views this solely from the lens of Partition and movement across the India–Pakistan borders.[24] Moreover, she does not ask *why* it was that such a liminal space was created or why the Indian Citizenship Act took so long to come into effect. As I will show, this delay was very much due to the struggle to disentangle identities shaped by empire and reconcile the Indian Citizenship Act with the provisions of the BNA.

Having failed to devise a precise legal framework for the provision of Indian citizenship two years after independence, Indian ministers and officials increasingly stressed the urgency of the matter. On 18 August 1949, K. V. K. Sundaram, Secretary of the Ministry of Law, circulated a draft Indian citizenship bill to the ministries of External Affairs, Home and Law, urging that 'no time should be lost in finalizing' such an important piece of legislation.[25] Sundaram's draft was faithful in its reiteration of 'reciprocity of citizenship' that underpinned India's membership of the Commonwealth. Closely following the 'important provisions of the British Nationality Act 1948', his draft declared that every person who 'under this act is a citizen of India or who under the citizenship law in force in any Commonwealth country is a citizen of that country' would be recognised in India as having the status of a Commonwealth citizen. Provision was also made for the government of India to recognise the citizenship law of any Commonwealth country, through a declaration in the *Gazette of India*, as suitable for terms of 'reciprocity' – a clause mainly aimed at South Africa and Pakistan.[26]

These provisions of the draft bill received a guarded response from the ministries of external affairs and home affairs who were sceptical about the extent to which ideas of Commonwealth citizenship could be accommodated in Indian citizenship legislation.[27] The flurry of notes, memos and letters in the file on Indian citizenship are all united in their confusion about what exactly the conveniently hazy term 'Commonwealth citizenship' meant and what, if anything, it might have to do with that oft-used term 'reciprocity'. Was Commonwealth citizenship nothing more than a synonym for the common British subject status shared by countries of the Commonwealth, as per the BNA? Or could it be a means through which each Commonwealth nation offered the other citizenship through terms of reciprocity? As we will see, Indian officials defined the terms of Commonwealth citizenship in various ways: placing citizens of Commonwealth countries on par with 'nationals', granting them Indian citizenship itself, or, at the very least, not regarding them as foreigners. While Sundaram's draft was more on the lines of the first option, further deliberations with officials led to a rather different conception.

Indian officials railed against the hollow promises of 'reciprocity' within the Commonwealth, arguing that 'excepting in the UK, in no other dominion or colony of the Commonwealth are Indians treated with complete equality or treated on par with nationals'.[28] As Secretary General Sir G. S. Bajpai argued, this had not only created public 'resentment in India against the concept of a Commonwealth citizenship ... such citizenship would, to Indian citizens, be of no value'.[29] By 1951, the draft citizenship bill was more thorough in defining 'Commonwealth citizens' as neither aliens nor on a par with Indian citizens. As an internal note pointed out, India could 'hardly be expected to accord national treatment in respect of entry into this country to persons belonging to territories from which Indians have been excluded in view of migration regulations'.[30] Most importantly, the new version did not recognise the status of Indians themselves as 'Commonwealth citizens', arguing that 'even the nominal recognition' of Indians as possessing a 'common' British subject or Commonwealth citizen status might 'make it difficult for Government to restrict the entry of British business ... without raising a cry of unfair discrimination'.[31]

Even as Indian bureaucrats prevaricated over these provisions of Commonwealth citizenship, the delay in passing legislation had a tremendous impact on the status of Indians across the world.[32] Arguing that this was in essence 'the impinging of Indian citizenship law on Indians abroad', one official called for the draft bill to be circulated for comments from diplomatic representatives in countries with large Indian populations.[33] The draft bill was therefore circulated to the Indian missions in British colonies and Dominions, notably East Africa, Malaya, Fiji, Ceylon, South Africa, Burma, the West Indies and Mauritius. The representative in South Africa noted that they had 'discouraged' Indians from registering as Indian citizens, given that there was no time limit to register as Indian citizens and it would be to their advantage to do so later on when they settled in India or gave up domicile in South Africa.[34] R. T. Chari, the High Commissioner in Ceylon argued that if Indians in Ceylon registered for Indian citizenship, this might result in their host country denying its citizenship to them, leading to 'a large number of them seeking registration as Indian citizens for the sole object of obtaining passport facilities and without any intention of reverting to Indian domicile'.[35] There was also some concern expressed by Apa Pant, the High Commissioner in East Africa, that those Indians 'disloyal to India' might register themselves as citizens of the United Kingdom and Colonies by claiming to be stateless.[36]

By 1951, a draft incorporating some of these insights was circulated to British officials who had long been enquiring about the status of the Indian Citizenship Act. The British response was on expected lines; the Secretary of State for Commonwealth Relations, Patrick Gordon-Walker, noted that India's bill neither recognised Indians as Commonwealth citizens nor recognised citizens of Commonwealth countries as Commonwealth citizens for 'all purposes in Indian law'.³⁷ Gordon-Walker argued that it was due to India's suggestion that the term 'Commonwealth citizen' had been adopted in the BNA and it was therefore curious that India had not recognised its own citizens as such. Chiding bureaucrats who had denied any bilateral dialogue regarding Commonwealth citizenship, Nehru pointed out that this had in fact been discussed in the Commonwealth meetings of 1948 and 1949:

> I am concerned ... because of certain *rather vague* understandings arrived at between me and the UK gov[ernmen]t. They were not binding in any way but they cannot be brushed aside. The understanding was that there should be some kind of Commonwealth citizenship (to which India should be a party) ... that this should be on a reciprocal basis with each Commonwealth country ... Commonwealth citizenship (*sic*) to be something between nationality and the status of an alien.³⁸

This intervention by Nehru led to a revised draft with a clause providing that the 'Central Government may, by order notified in the Official Gazette, make provisions *on basis of reciprocity for the conferment of all or any of the rights of a citizen of India* on the citizens of a Commonwealth country', a clause modelled after the BNA and moving somewhat closer to Sundaram's initial draft.³⁹ Indian citizens were, however, still not recognised as Commonwealth citizens. Indian Commonwealth Secretary, Subimal Dutt, argued that in suggesting the change from 'British subject' to 'Commonwealth citizen', India had merely called for a change in terminology more suited to a postcolonial context, rather than make a 'permanent commitment' for formal Commonwealth citizenship status.⁴⁰

These exchanges created dissonance between the bureaucratic apparatus in Delhi and the Indian High Commission in London – palpable in High Commissioner Krishna Menon's consistent arguments for broadening the scope of Commonwealth citizenship, 'not merely to confer any or all the rights of a citizen of India but also (Indian) citizenship itself'.⁴¹ This was unacceptable back in Delhi, with officials asserting that the revised draft would nevertheless 'enable a Commonwealth citizen without being a "citizen of India" to enjoy all or any of the rights of a citizen of India on a reciprocal basis'.⁴² The Indian Citizenship Act thus reiterated the status of the Commonwealth citizen as an intermediate category: neither foreign nor Indian, although they could, on a reciprocal basis, obtain the rights of a citizen of India. Unlike Pakistan, India would not acknowledge its citizens as 'Commonwealth citizens' in its Citizenship Act, even though other countries recognised them as such. Indeed, 'implicit' recognition of this condition was regarded as sufficient; after all, 'for us, Indian citizenship is the highest imaginable status'.⁴³ Such a terminological debate over the status of Indians as

'Commonwealth citizens' or 'British subjects' had significant consequences, especially for long-settled overseas Indian communities and migrants.

Britain, India and the haze of entanglement

The example of S. N. Chaudhuri, a traveller on board the *SS United States* in 1954, exemplifies the everyday experiences of those negotiating the entangled status of Indians and the complications caused by attempts to implement an overarching legal Britishness. As the ship neared Southampton, the port of disembarkation, passengers on board were asked to line up in two queues: 'British subjects' and 'other nationalities'. Chaudhuri dutifully joined the latter and refused to move to the queue for British subjects as he was an Indian citizen. In the altercation that followed, the officer on board too stood his ground, asserting that Chaudhuri was a British subject by virtue of being an Indian citizen and would therefore be better off doing as he was told.[44] This minor incident was nonetheless the subject of diplomatic correspondence between Indian, British and American officials, a testament to both the pervasive haze over Chaudhuri's legal status and the difficulties of negotiating changing terminologies of citizenship and subject status within the Commonwealth. Even though CRO officials noted that the officer was only trying to help Chaudhuri avail himself of the advantages of a British subject, entitling him, 'to land without visas or other restrictive documents', to stay as long as he wished, and to take up employment without restrictions, they conceded that the term 'Commonwealth citizen' should be used more widely in order to avoid such misunderstandings.[45]

This was not the first time that there had been protests about the continual usage of the term 'British subject' in the United Kingdom. Nor were Indians the only ones bringing up such cases; British officials recounted many an instance of such issues raised by citizens of Ceylon, Ireland and South Africa. Yet CRO officials seeking to popularise the term 'Commonwealth citizens' were waging a losing battle. When the issue of replacing the term 'British subject' in notices displayed at ports was taken to Southampton, the same port where Chaudhuri had protested, 'the reactions of the official were so explosive (his actual remarks are unmentionable) that the matter was dropped'.[46] More mentionably, Home Office officials nevertheless refused to change the notices at immigration points, stating that there was 'no reason why an Indian citizen, if he insists, should not join the "non-British" queue and assert his independence at the cost of being delayed'.[47]

The unease among the British that came with abandoning old imperial standards no doubt manifested itself in an increasing reluctance to adopt often confusing new terminologies: as E. L. Sykes of the British High

Commission in Delhi signed off in a letter about Chaudhuri's case: 'how much simpler life must have been when the "British Empire" constituted of Colonies whose occupants were 'British subjects!'[48] Sykes also complained that the 'powers that be' in Britain seemed befuddled by the new terms pertaining to citizenship, suggesting that making the term 'Commonwealth citizen' more widespread might 'make their pronouncements more accurate and easy to understand'.[49] British officials were, however, not the only ones caught in this haze of complex new citizenship frameworks. For Indian officials seeking to disentangle identities shaped by empire, confusion over the terminologies and legal status of Indians, even the very question of defining an Indian citizen, and the 'vague' nature of the Commonwealth relationship, was all-pervasive. This uncertainty was reflected in the various, often contradictory, statements regarding India's relationship with its overseas community and would also be especially evident in diplomatic negotiations with Britain to declare and reciprocally 'recognise' each other's citizenship legislation. This was essential for delineating the responsibility of Britain and India over 'Indians' who could be Indian citizens or citizens of the United Kingdom and Colonies.

Even the most vociferous critics of the discrimination encountered by Indians across British colonies and Dominions were in agreement that the situation in Britain itself was entirely different. As Sir Bajpai noted, there was 'complete equality' in the legal status and treatment of Indians in Britain, on par with citizens of the United Kingdom and Colonies as per the BNA.[50] Indeed in November 1949, the British government had passed the India Consequential Provision Act, a 'holding act' that ensured the continuation of all laws in force vis-à-vis India until the Indian government enacted new legislation to replace them. As the British Secretary of State for Commonwealth Relations, Philip Noel-Baker, pointed out in Parliament, this also meant that Indians in Britain would 'continue to have in this country the same rights and privileges as they have today'.[51] Yet, terms of reciprocity with Britain were very much a double-edged sword; while Indian officials worried that reciprocity would open the floodgates for British capital into India,[52] they were nonetheless also concerned that refusing reciprocal treatment would adversely affect the status of Indians in the United Kingdom.[53] Moreover, how could there be 'reciprocity of citizenship' when there was no 'British citizenship' as such but a more cumbersome 'Citizenship of the United Kingdom and Colonies', including the colonies where Indians were often discriminated against?

Reconciling the citizenship frameworks of the BNA and Indian Citizenship Act was thus essential to delineating the status of Indians, especially those in British colonial territories, and the 'moral responsibility' of India or Britain over them. This was not going to be an easy process, given that

British officials were still providing passports and other consular facilities for Indians in regions where India did not as yet have diplomatic representation. Indeed, as one internal British memo caustically noted, this was an extraordinary circumstance where Indian officials themselves reiterated the status of Indians as 'British subjects' in UK law when convenient, asking them to 'ensure that British consular officers protect them as such'.[54] British officials were, however, increasingly reluctant to perform such work – a response that was not so much due to India's limited provision for Commonwealth citizenship, but more a result of what they deemed to be an inadequate draft citizenship legislation that did not substantially account for overseas Indians.[55]

British concerns stemmed from the fact that the draft legislation did not permit the automatic acquisition of Indian citizenship by 'persons of Indian origin or birth resident outside India', and asked instead that overseas Indians register for citizenship at Indian consulates and diplomatic missions in their countries of residence. Moreover, the draft did not confer citizenship on those born *before* 26 January 1950, leaving these persons under the purview of existing provisions for citizenship in the Indian constitution, provisions that British officials had long regarded as insufficient for the purposes of 'declaring' the Indian legislation under the BNA.[56] That is, officials feared that 'declaring' or recognising the Indian Act 'to be an enactment making provision for citizenship' under the BNA, would mean that all 'potential Indians' resident in British colonial territories and Commonwealth regions who were not included in India's citizenship legislation, would automatically have to be 'mopped up' as United Kingdom and Colonies citizens.[57]

British officials viewed the Indian legislation's provision of citizenship by registration as a calculated move through which Indian officials could only choose those 'regarded as likely to make good citizens', and to 'take those people they want and reject those they don't'.[58] Yet, this provision of registration served other important purposes for overseas Indians too; as one official presciently noted, this was also 'intended to warn the Ceylon government that there would not be an automatic incorporation of masses of overseas Indians as citizens of India'.[59] This was therefore a careful clause drafted at a time when repatriation had been increasingly propagated by governments in Burma, Ceylon, Malaya and South Africa as a means of permanently excluding long-resident Indian populations.[60] Thus while it is indeed the case that the clause of registration allowed Indian officials to carefully discriminate in choosing the 'right kind' of Indian citizen, this was only one aspect of the state's nuanced engagement with overseas Indians.[61] Urging these Indians to take up the citizenship of the countries of residence if available to them, Indian officials nevertheless assured them that doing so would not harm their right to acquire Indian citizenship in the future, if they so desired.[62]

Entangled citizens 75

The Indian state's relationship with its overseas communities thus involved walking a very fine line and taking even seemingly contradictory positions. This was evident in India's response to the Malayan government over its decision to 'banish' certain 'undesirable Indians'. Claiming that these persons were not Indian citizens, the Indian government refused to acknowledge their alleged right to 'return' to India. And yet, as Jean Walker, a British High Commission official in New Delhi noted angrily, 'While refusing to acknowledge these "banishees" as Indian citizens, the Indian authorities are nevertheless demanding certain things – transfer to more suitable gaols – on their behalf!'[63] Walker reiterated that this was fairly typical of the Indian government's engagement with overseas Indians: 'this ... serves as an example of the trouble we and the authorities in any colony where there is a large number of Indians, have when it comes to attempting to determine Indian citizenship'.[64] Such seemingly paradoxical actions can be better explained if we view the Indian state's actions as attempts to ensure that *Indians across the world had citizenship rights*. The goal was not necessarily to grant them *Indian* citizenship – although that option could be available in the future, at least on paper, if they were denied citizenship elsewhere. The Indian state's frequent exhortations calling on overseas Indians to identify with their countries of residence must therefore be understood in this context, in a scenario deeply impacted by the crises of citizenship and statelessness encountered by Indians who were often forcibly repatriated from countries such as Ceylon, Malaya, South Africa and Burma where they had long resided. As Nehru noted in 1953:

> We are concerned with the fate of hundreds and thousands of these people who, though no longer citizens and nationals of India, were in the past connected with India, about whom we have various agreements and assurances and the like, and therefore we have a certain responsibility with regard to them, although they are not our nationals.[65]

The question of India and Britain's responsibility over Indian communities in British colonial territories and the Commonwealth was the subject of considerable discussion between British and Indian officials deliberating over the Indian citizenship legislation. As Fateh Singh noted in a meeting with H. E. Davies, the 'Indian government's policy was to enable as many as possible of those who were India's responsibility to be registered' although it was likely that many would still be left without citizenship.[66] In Singh's view, those excluded from Indian citizenship for a variety of reasons would nevertheless have the option of being eligible for United Kingdom and Colonies and other citizenships. Of the three main categories of overseas Indians without citizenship – those living in British colonies, those living in foreign countries, and those living in Commonwealth countries such as Pakistan, South Africa and Ceylon – Singh argued that the first category was 'obviously' the responsibility of the British. Davies concurred, although he was somewhat more sceptical of Singh's suggestion that while most overseas Indians living in foreign countries would register as Indian citizens, Britain 'ought not to mind accepting the few who are left over'.[67]

Yet it was the prospect of becoming responsible for those living in Commonwealth countries that most worried the British. The stark position of Indians in these countries was becoming illustrative of British fears that they might be considered responsible for the 'left over' Indians not covered by the citizenship provisions of India. While they resisted declaring the Indian Act due to such concerns, British officials nevertheless reiterated that this should not impact India's recognition of the BNA for the purposes of reciprocity. That is, while India would have to declare the BNA in order to provide for equal rights to United Kingdom and Colonies citizens, Indian citizens in Britain – owing to their status as British subjects under the BNA – would receive equal rights regardless of the Indian Act being declared as citizenship legislation for the purposes of the BNA. As D. W. H. Wickson of the CRO angrily noted, Singh did not seem to realise that 'registration (as Indian citizens) does not appeal to many persons of Indian race for whom India should morally be responsible'. Wickson anticipated this to be a great problem for British officials:

> in the majority of cases Indians in foreign countries seem to prefer to remain British subjects without citizenship (and hold a UK passport) rather than register as Indian citizens. There will certainly be more than a few left over … The glib suggestion that we should mop up all the Indians who fail to acquire Indian citizenship as a quid pro quo for Indian declaration of the British Nationality Act, is staggering.[68]

The Indian Citizenship Act and relevant citizenship provisions in the Constitution therefore faced much the same fate as Pakistan's citizenship legislation – British officials fearing responsibility for 'left over' citizens did not move to declare these Citizenship Acts.[69] This of course meant that India would not recognise the BNA and refused reciprocity for United Kingdom and Colonies citizens, arguing additionally that while Indians did not face discrimination within the United Kingdom itself, they faced considerable inequities in British colonial territories.[70]

Britain and India's decision to not declare each other's citizenship law had several consequences, especially for Indians who had acquired United Kingdom and Colonies citizenship and later also wanted to register for Indian citizenship. Such a possibility for dual nationality would have existed if the Indian Act had been recognised by Britain. In one instance in

1959, A. K. Ray of the Ministry of External Affairs regretfully informed Indian-origin United Kingdom and Colonies citizens who had applied for Indian citizenship that they could not be treated differently from other non-Indian United Kingdom and Colonies citizens who were not allowed to register as Indian citizens, since the Indian act was not yet recognised under British law. Instead, Ray reiterated that Indians with access to citizenship in their countries of residence ought to identify themselves with these countries.[71]

With the Indian Citizenship Act coming into effect in December 1955, a flurry of applications and requests made their way to British and Indian officials. Bureaucrats had to interpret these cases not just in the context of the new legislation, but in terms of the makeshift arrangements that had defined the status of many Indians across the world until then. Thus, varying bureaucratic interpretations of Indian citizenship would be put to the test in determining the status of overseas Indians, whose incredible, entangled personal lives and histories were mapped onto their applications.

The case of Kathilal Sankaran Krishnan, an Indian-origin United Kingdom and Colonies citizen resident in Singapore, is instructive in this regard.[72] Approaching officials of the UK High Commission in Colombo during a visit to Ceylon, Krishnan sought their help in enabling his two sons – who had lived in Ceylon for some years – to join him in Singapore. The sons were born in British India in 1945 and 1947 and were regarded by Indian officials in Colombo as having lost their claim to Indian citizenship when their father opted to register as a United Kingdom and Colonies citizen in Singapore in 1954. A. N. G. Bone, a sympathetic official in the UK High Commission in Colombo wrote to his counterpart in Singapore worrying that 'it can be argued that by conferring UK citizenship on the father without warning him of the consequences, we have some responsibility for his minor children having become stateless'.[73] Bone was well aware of the complexities of getting travel documents for the sons, given the concurrence required from officials in Singapore and London, as well as the near certainty that Ceylon officials would not provide such documents for boys of Indian origin. Krishnan had gone so far as to tell Bone that he would make his own arrangements to get the boys into Singapore – 'I suspect via Malaya by a somewhat devious route or dubious practice', Bone noted – as long as High Commission officials agreed to provide travel documents. Bone reluctantly suggested that the 'possible cutting of the Gordian's knot would perhaps be achieved by the registration of these boys as UKCs under 7(1)'.[74] This was however unacceptable for CRO officials who contested the Indian claim that these boys were ineligible for Indian citizenship. Officials in London argued that while Krishnan had indeed lost his Indian citizenship by registering as a citizen of the United Kingdom and Colonies, as per the 1955 Indian

Citizenship Act, this loss of citizenship did not extend to his minor children born in India.[75]

The archival paper trail on the Krishnans does not extend beyond this, although one can consider some of the possibilities that remained. Perhaps Mr Krishnan's sons were granted some form of temporary travel document, perhaps Indian officials accepted the CRO interpretation, enabling the family to migrate to Singapore – the father, a United Kingdom and Colonies citizen, and the sons, Indian citizens. Perhaps, more worryingly, the minors remained stateless. Even in a clearly concerned letter in support of the case, Bone nevertheless signalled the oddity of Krishnan's status as a United Kingdom and Colonies citizen. Krishnan, he pointed out, 'speaks little, if any, English through the medium of a friend of his who speaks far too much!' Neither could Bone resist gesturing to the peculiarity of Krishnan's vocabulary (and indeed his United Kingdom and Colonies status), describing his full name thus: 'Mr Kathilal Sankaran Krishnan (Kazhimbram) ... the latter is his "native place".'[76] One can only imagine the poignancy of this 'native place' in rural Kerala for a man whose life criss-crossed India, Ceylon, Singapore, the United Kingdom and still stared at the prospect of statelessness for his children.

Conclusion

The 'eternal' making of Indian citizenship legislation was perhaps inevitable, given the enormous scale of the task undertaken to unravel multiple claims of identity and citizenship shaped by empire. Indeed, although officials frequently flagged concerns that the general public might find it difficult to understand these provisions for citizenship, their internal correspondence makes it amply clear that these bureaucrats were themselves often befuddled by the vast scale and complexities of implementing the law on citizenship. Divergent understandings of the law's practical application to different cases persisted not just between British and Indian officials, but just as much between Indian officials – in some ways facilitating the convenient suggestion that individual bureaucrats should decide each case 'by its merits' as a means of reconciling contrasting interpretations of the citizenship law. The haze within which these issues were mired is most clearly evident in the widespread confusion over the status of Indians as British subjects after independence – in part due to the deliberate policy of Indian officials to avoid any focus on this emotive topic but very much also due to the overwhelming complexity of the numerous provisions of the BNA.

In parliamentary debates especially, many prominent ministers frequently denied that Indians were British subjects. When asked during a debate on the citizenship bill if the BNA conferred British subject status to Indians,

B. N. Datar, deputy Home Minister, claimed that the BNA was not applicable to India and there was 'no question of Indians being British subjects or citizens of the United Kingdom and Colonies', while the Home Minister, Govind Ballabh Pant, claimed that Indians were not British subjects since they did not take any oath of allegiance to the Crown.[77] Responding to an uproar in parliament about a junior UK minister's reference to Indians as 'British subjects', Nehru himself claimed that this 'was not correct of course ... nobody in the wide world who has any knowledge of the facts considers any Indian as a British subject'.[78] Yet this was, of course, not the case.

The fact that Indians were British subjects under the BNA considerably impacted their status and produced them as entangled citizens; Indians navigating overlapping citizenship frameworks variously found that they were eligible for Indian citizenship, potentially even qualifying for dual nationality, but were almost just as likely to be told that they did not qualify within any citizenship rubric. Far from being a decisive strategy whereby the government of India defined Indian citizenship as territorially bounded with no space for its diaspora, the drafting of Indian citizenship was a messy, even paradoxical, process that was anything *but* a clean break between the Indian state and its overseas Indian communities. Not only were overseas Indians eligible to register for Indian citizenship, the Indian state was closely involved in engaging with the British government and other Commonwealth countries regarding their legal status. The Indian state's seemingly contradictory stance towards its overseas communities can be better understood in the context of the widespread crises of citizenship encountered by Indians in countries such as Ceylon, Burma and Malaya immediately after Indian independence. Framed within this scenario, India's citizenship policy was more concerned with preventing the statelessness, discrimination and forced repatriation of overseas Indians from their countries of settlement than necessarily granting them Indian citizenship. That is, Indian citizenship would be provided as a last resort if Indians were denied citizenship of their 'host countries' – the latter more likely to protect them against discrimination. As the Indian Home Secretary pointed out in a letter:

> I agree that persons of Indian origin residing in other countries should be encouraged to acquire Indian citizenship by registration. If however they have permanently settled in other countries and there is no bar to their being recognised as citizens of such countries, it would be in their interest to acquire the status of citizenship there so that they may enjoy full rights and privileges available to other citizens of such countries.[79]

But as the afterlives of empire that produced these entanglements vividly illustrate, the task of differentiating between 'origins', 'interests' and 'citizens' was rarely so clear-cut.

Notes

1. The National Archives at Kew (TNA hereafter), DO35/6387, D. J. C. Crawley to R. C. Ormerod, 'Indian citizenship legislation', 11 June 1954.
2. National Archives of India, New Delhi (NAI hereafter), 45–1/49-UK, Y. D. Gundevia to Subimal Dutt, 'Indian Citizenship Bill – Consideration Of', 16 January 1951.
3. TNA, DO35/10294, A. N. G. Bone to E. R. G. Kidd, 'Indian Citizenship Act: renunciation and automatic loss of Indian citizenship', 19 November 1959.
4. R. Hansen, 'The Politics of Citizenship in 1940s Britain: The British Nationality Act', *Twentieth Century British History*, 10:1 (1999), pp. 67–95. Hugh Tinker makes a similar point in *Separate and Unequal: India and Indians in the British Commonwealth, 1920–1950* (London: C. Hurst & Co, 1976), p. 356.
5. See J. Mann, 'The Evolution of Commonwealth Citizenship, 1945–48 in Canada, Britain and Australia', *Comparative Politics*, 50:3 (2012), pp. 293–313.
6. See S. Ward, *Untied Kingdom: A World History of the End of Britain* (Cambridge University Press, forthcoming).
7. K. H. Perry, *London is the Place for Me. Black Britons, Citizenship, and the Politics of Race* (New York: Oxford University Press, 2015), p. 58.
8. A range of useful perspectives on the 1948 British Nationality Act include A. Mycock, 'British Citizenship and the Legacy of Empires', *Parliamentary Affairs*, 63:2 (2010), pp. 339–355; K. Paul, '"British Subjects" and "British Stock": Labour's Postwar Imperialism', *Journal of British Studies*, 34:2 (1995), pp. 233–276; Hansen, 'Politics of Citizenship in 1940s Britain'; S. Ansari, 'Subjects or Citizens? India, Pakistan and the 1948 British Nationality Act', *Journal of Imperial and Commonwealth History*, 41:2 (2013), pp. 285–312; R. Karatani, *Defining British Citizenship: Empire, Commonwealth and Modern Britain* (London: Frank Cass, 2003).
9. While Tinker's account offers valuable material regarding the status of Indians in British colonies between 1920–1950 and the significance of the BNA, it only briefly refers to the 1955 Indian Citizenship Act.
10. See D. Sutton, 'Divided and Uncertain Loyalties', *Interventions*, 9:2 (2007), pp. 276–288, at p. 282; and D. Sutton, 'Imagined Sovereignty and the Indian Subject: Partition and Politics beyond the Nation, 1948–1960', *Contemporary South Asia*, 19:4 (2011), pp. 409–425. Also see J. Chatterji, 'From Imperial Subjects to National Citizens: South Asians and the International Migration Regime since 1947', in J. Chatterji and D. Washbrook (eds), *Routledge Handbook of the South Asian Diaspora* (New York: Routledge, 2013), pp. 183–197; and J. Chatterji, 'South Asian Histories of Citizenship, 1946–1970', *The Historical Journal*, 55:4 (2012), pp. 1049–1071.
11. Ansari, 'Subjects or Citizens?', p. 292.
12. Ibid., p. 295.
13. For these debates, see Constituent Assembly of India (CAI hereafter), Vol. 3, 28 April–2 May 1947, http://cadindia.clpr.org.in/constitution_assembly_debates/volume/3 (accessed 23 May 2021).
14. Statement by Alladi Krishnaswamy Aiyar, CAI, Vol. 3, 29 April 1947, http://cadindia.clpr.org.in/constitution_assembly_debates/volume/3/1947-04-29 (accessed 23 May 2021).

15 Statement by Sardar Vallabhbhai Patel, CAI, Vol. 3, 29 April 1947, http://cadindia.clpr.org.in/constitution_assembly_debates/volume/3/1947-04-29 (accessed 23 May 2021).
16 Statement by Kailash Nath Katju, CAI, Vol. 3, 29 April 1947, http://cadindia.clpr.org.in/constitution_assembly_debates/volume/3/1947-04-29 (accessed 23 May 2021).
17 N. G. Jayal, 'Citizenship', in S. Choudhry, M. Khosla and P. B. Mehta (eds), *The Oxford Handbook of the Indian Constitution* (New York: Oxford University Press, 2016), p. 163.
18 See B. R. Ambedkar, *Dr Babasaheb Ambedkar: Writings and Speeches*, vol. 13 (New Delhi: Dr Ambedkar Foundation, 2014), p. 808.
19 Speech in the Constituent Assembly, 12 August 1949, *Selected Works of Jawaharlal Nehru* (SWJN hereafter), Second Series, vol. 12 (New Delhi: Jawaharlal Nehru Memorial Fund, 1991), p. 165.
20 British Library (BL hereafter), India Office Records (IOR hereafter), L/PJ/7/15042, W. H. Marshall to the CRO, 'Persons to whom Political Dept. Memo on registration as United Kingdom Citizens of persons born in India has been sent on enquiry', 29 September 1949.
21 See L. Varadarajan, *The Domestic Abroad: Diasporas in International Relations* (New York: Oxford University Press, 2010), pp. 67–69. While Varadarajan discusses the legislation of Ceylon and Burma, she does not mention the BNA.
22 See Tinker, *Separate and Unequal*, p. 344.
23 See N. G. Jayal, *Citizenship and its Discontents: An Indian History* (Cambridge, MA and London: Harvard University Press, 2013), p. 63; and Jayal, 'Citizenship', pp. 163–168. Also see A. Roy, *Mapping Citizenship in India* (New Delhi: Oxford University Press, 2010), Ch. 1; K. Sadiq, *Paper Citizens: How Illegal Immigrants Acquire Citizenship in Developing Countries* (Oxford: Oxford University Press, 2008); and A. Roy, 'Between Encompassment and Closure: The "Migrant" and the Citizen in India', *Contributions to Indian Sociology*, 42: 2 (2008), pp. 226–230.
24 Roy, *Mapping Citizenship in India*, Ch. 1.
25 NAI, 45–1/49–UK, K. V. K. Sundaram to S. Dutt, 18 August 1949.
26 Further discussions also paved the way for Ireland to be treated as a Commonwealth country on terms of reciprocity. NAI, 45–1/49–UK.
27 NAI, 45–1/49–UK, handwritten note by P. N. Haksar, 19 January 1951.
28 NAI, 45–1/49–UK, P. N. Haksar's reply to S. Dutt, 29 May 1951.
29 NAI, 45–1/49–UK, G. S. Bajpai's reply to revised citizenship draft, 3 March 1951.
30 NAI, 45–1/49–UK, 'Internal note for Cabinet', 24 February 1951.
31 NAI, 45–1/49–UK, Ministry of Home Affairs, Note for Cabinet, undated.
32 NAI, 45–1/49–UK, R. K. Nehru's letter to J. Nehru, 2 July 1952.
33 NAI, 45–1/49–UK, note by R. T. Chari, 14 April 1952.
34 NAI, 45–1/49–UK, letter from Indian High Commission in South Africa, 2 July 1952.
35 NAI, 45–1/49–UK, R. T. Chari, 'A Minute on the Indian Citizenship Bill', 19 July 1952.
36 NAI, 45–1/49–UK, letter from Apa Pant, Indian HC in East Africa, 4 September 1952.

37 NAI, 45–1/49–UK, P. Gordon-Walker to V. K. Krishna Menon, 9 May 1951.
38 NAI, 45–1/49–UK, handwritten minute by Nehru, 29 May 1951. Italics added.
39 NAI, 45–1/49–UK, telegram from Nehru to Menon, 19 August 1951. Italics added.
40 NAI, 45–1/49–UK, S. Dutt, 'MEA Summary', 2 June 1951.
41 NAI, 45–1/49–UK, telegram from Menon to Nehru, 26 August 1951.
42 NAI, 45–1/49–UK, S. Dutt to Menon, 23 September 1951.
43 NAI, 45–1/49–UK, K. N. Katju's reply to HM (Home), 16 May 1952.
44 TNA, DO35/10303, letter from Apa Pant, New Delhi to Sheldon Mills, US embassy, '"British Subject" – Objections by Citizens Commonwealth Countries', 10 June 1954.
45 TNA, DO35/10303, J. K. Walker, 22 June 1954.
46 TNA, DO35/10303, D. W. H. Wickson to D. M. R. Skinner, 7 November 1956.
47 TNA, DO35/10303, E. N. Kent to Wickson, 7 February 1955.
48 TNA, DO35/10303, E. L. Sykes to T. Eliot Weil, US embassy, 5 July 1954.
49 TNA, DO35/10303, E. L. Sykes to F. A. K. Harrison, 6 July 1954.
50 NAI, 45–1/49–UK, G. S. Bajpai's reply to revised citizenship draft, 3 March 1951.
51 Remarks of P. Noel-Baker. 'Orders of the Day: India (Consequential Provision) Bill', *Hansard*, vol. 470 cc. 1541–1570, 5 December 1949, https://api.parliament.uk/historic-hansard/commons/1949/dec/05/india-consequential-provision-bill (accessed 23 May 2021).
52 NAI, 45–1/49–UK, memo by M. A. Husain, 29 May 1950.
53 NAI, 45–1/49–UK, S. Dutt, 2 March 1951.
54 TNA, DO35/10303, undated note marked T. D. O'L.
55 TNA, DO35/6386, E. J. Emery to A. F. Morley of the CRO, 'Indian citizenship legislation', 9 December 1953.
56 TNA, DO35/6386, H. E. Davies to F. A. K. Harrison, 6 May 1955.
57 TNA, DO35/6386, telegram from CRO to UK High Commissioners in India and Pakistan, 6 August 1955. Also see the full text of article 32(8) of the BNA, www.legislation.gov.uk/ukpga/1948/56/pdfs/ukpga_19480056_en.pdf (accessed 23 May 2021).
58 TNA, DO35/6387, J. Walker to D. W. H. Wickson, 'Indian citizenship legislation', 25 October 1954.
59 TNA, DO35/6386, note by H. E. Davies, 12 May 1955.
60 Vineet Thakur refers to South Africa's increasing preference for repatriation of Indians, see V. Thakur, 'An Asian Drama: The Asian Relations Conference, 1947', *International History Review*, 41:3 (2019), pp. 673–695.
61 NAI, letter from S. Dutt to all heads and missions of Indian representatives abroad, 'The Citizenship Rules, 1956', 21 June 1960.
62 NAI, letter from A. K. Ray, Undersecretary of MEA to Priti Singh, 'The Citizenship Rules, 1956', 1 August 1959.
63 TNA, DO35/6387, Jean Walker to D. W. H. Wickson, 25 October 1954.
64 Ibid.
65 See Appendix 1, Ministry of External Affairs annual report for the year 1953–54, https://mealib.nic.in/?pdf2480 (accessed 23 May 2021).

66 TNA, DO35/6386, H. E. Davies' report of his meeting with Fateh Singh, 20 August 1955.
67 Ibid.
68 TNA, DO35/6386, note by D. W. H. Wickson, 26 August 1955.
69 See Ansari for more detail on the 'inadequacies' of the Pakistani Act and its impact on 'potential Pakistanis'. Ansari, 'Subjects or Citizens?', pp. 299–312.
70 TNA, DO35/6386, H. E. Davies' report of his meeting with Fateh Singh, 20 August 1955.
71 NAI, A. K. Ray to Prithi Singh, 'The Citizenship Rules', 1 August 1959.
72 TNA, DO35/10294, A. N. G. Bone to E. R. G. Kidd, 19 November 1959.
73 Ibid.
74 Ibid.
75 TNA, DO35/10294, telegram from CRO to A. N. G. Bone, 30 November 1959.
76 TNA, DO35/10294, A. N. G. Bone to E. R. G. Kidd, 19 November 1959.
77 Quoted in 'Citizenship Bill referred to joint select body: Special treatment for refugees', *Hindustan Times*, 10 August 1955.
78 Ward, *Untied Kingdom*.
79 NAI, note by Home Secretary, 'The Citizenship Rules', 14 August 1957.

4

'How come England did not know me?': the 'rude awakenings' of the Windrush era

Stuart Ward

The disembarkation of MV *Empire Windrush* at London's Tilbury docks on 22 June 1948 is so emblazoned onto popular historical consciousness that its meaning and significance are often taken for granted. It comes to us virtually ready-made with a rich visual archive; the hopeful arrivals in their Sunday best, returning wartime recruits, aspirational young scholars raised on a diet of Dickens and Thackeray, able-bodied workers in search of a better deal in the 'mother country'. Such is their familiarity that the images have become blurred by their iconic depiction. The dockside figure of Trinidadian calypso sensation 'Lord Kitchener' serenading Pathé News with his impromptu rendering of 'London is the Place for Me' appears to capture the wide-eyed expectation of the 'Windrush generation', their claim to belonging as uncomplicated as the £28 passage to Britain itself.[1] The subsequent experience of social alienation and material hardship – the pervasive racism, the institutional barriers to opportunity and consequent disillusionment – has come to occupy a special niche in British popular culture. Novels, films, documentaries, television series, oral histories, radio programmes and successive 'Windrush' anniversaries have shaped these experiences into a pathos of unrequited Britishness. In the words of Andrea Levy's fictionalised protagonist Gilbert Joseph in *Small Island* (2004): 'Let me ask the Mother Country just this one simple question: how come England did not know me'?[2]

Such has been the emphasis on the *Empire Windrush* that objections are sometimes raised to its definitive status as the wellspring of multiracial Britain. It is said that Windrush presents a 'deficient and myopic accounting', which not only disavows the long history of Black Britain reaching back five centuries, but also screens out the significant African and Asian presence alongside the new post-war arrivals from the West Indies.[3] The relentless focus on a single ship as emblematic of an entire 'generation' also renders the sojourners as a 'homogenized and unreal mass', effacing the very history of hyper-mobility their presence is meant to evoke.[4] The contemporary press publicity surrounding the vessel suggested something fleeting and ephemeral rather than epoch-making, with little to indicate that it would later provide the touchstone of multicultural Britain.[5] The government officials charged with processing the passenger list were confident that the episode was 'not likely to be repeated' – and for a time these expectations were borne out by the arrival statistics, which declined to a mere 'trickle' until well into the 1950s.[6] But for the purposes of mapping the myriad connections between the end of empire and the break-up of Greater Britain, the Windrush moment remains cardinal. The significance of the newcomers lies, not in their over-freighted passage per se (in this they were by no means pioneers) but in the anomalies of imperial belonging that their arrival brought to a head.

The shock of alienation has become a ubiquitous theme in scholarly treatment of the Windrush arrivals, placing particular emphasis on the 'myth of the mother country … shattered' by the experience of sudden proximity.[7] In *Lovers and Strangers*, historian Clair Wills assembles the key elements of what has become the conventional Windrush narrative:

> West Indian immigrants had been brought up to believe they were guaranteed a welcome in the 'mother country'. It may have been hard to leave home, but migrating was simply making good on a promise that had long been made to them as citizens of the Empire.

With the passing of the 1948 British Nationality Act, she continues, the post-war Labour Government 'seemed intent on writing out the contract in black and white', guaranteeing equal citizenship to all subjects of the empire regardless of geographical and racial boundaries. Home Secretary James Chuter Ede had acknowledged widespread misgivings that 'it would be a bad thing to give the coloured races of the Empire the idea that, in some way or other, they are the equals of people in this country' but went out of his way to stress that 'the Government does not subscribe to that view'. Having spelt it out so clearly, Wills asks, 'why should "the coloured races of the Empire" have disbelieved him'?[8]

Focusing on the thwarted promise of imperial citizenship in this way can work to oversimplify the complex motivations and affiliations that produced the Windrush era. Stephen Howe notes the long-standing habit of treating West Indian affirmations of British identity 'as a simple mistake, a dream from which there was, on exposure to attitudes in Britain itself, a rude awakening'.[9] Such naïve readings take too much at face value; the idea of Greater Britain as an undifferentiated 'contract' fanning out across the globe; guileless West Indian subjects blithely buying into its terms; the encounter with racial prejudice in Britain running counter to all prior expectation. Understanding the social and political conditions that fashioned black West Indian conceptions of Britishness was once a neglected area of study, certainly when compared with the former colonies of white settlement. But it is now well established that imperial Britishness was never the exclusive preserve of white settlers, and that it could mean 'different things to different people all over the world'.[10] Bill Schwarz has remarked on how, of all the subjects of the non-white empire, 'the West Indian nations were closest to the mother country: in language, religion, schooling, literature, sport'. But though 'pride in these affinities to Britain ran deep', such sentiments at all times 'vied with vernacular, blacker, fluid cultures which constituted the traces … of a long history of racial mixing'.[11] In other words, for all its evident iniquities, Britishness was a 'capacious category' that could be made meaningful and useful in diverse social, cultural and racial contexts.[12] Moreover, these divergent registers were not at all difficult for contemporaries to discern or decode. Yet the tendency to depict the Windrush era arrivals as afflicted by a species of false consciousness continues to pervade multiple genres – historical, literary, even the oral testimony of the migrants themselves.

This chapter examines the myth of the 'rude awakening' as part of a much longer encounter, played out across the generations on both sides of the Atlantic. As countless West Indian sojourners through the ages could readily attest, the discrepancies between the theory and practice of universal British subjecthood were by no means a novelty in June 1948.[13] But it was the unprecedented scale and, more crucially, the timing of the encounter marked by the appearance of 492 West Indians at the mouth of the Thames that prompted patterns of public and political response out of all proportion to their numerical significance. Viewed in this light, the Windrush moment was not simply about the barriers of social and political exclusion in Britain, suddenly and unapologetically disabusing 'loyal' black Britons of their former affinities. Rather the 'rude awakening' was itself a well-established feature of West Indian protest and critique, containing elements of continuity as well as rupture. It forms part of a much longer history, of insistent demands for equal rights and entitlements from within the British fold that are crucial to tracing the receding frontiers of Greater Britain in the wake of the *Empire Windrush*.

'Stripped of the most vital part of their being': oral testimony

In her collection of personal testimonies of West Indian migrants who came to Britain in the 1950s and 1960s, Z. Nia Reynolds paints a familiar portrait of an illusion 'shattered' for those 'who, instead of encountering a welcoming matriarch, discovered instead a twisted stepmother; the antithesis of any maternal ideal they had imagined'. It is the dramatic contrast between colonial expectations 'so perfectly conditioned' prior to departure and the subsequent 'frosty reception' on arrival that frames the entire encounter in terms of a 'massive culture shock' and an overdue 'wake up call'.[14] A broadly similar pattern of existential rift and re-examination was identified by Mike and Trevor Phillips in their pioneering survey of the memories and impressions of post-war Caribbean migrants:

> Back in the Caribbean the migrants had been brought up to perceive British power as part of the natural order of things, but they had also believed that British citizenship made them part of the show. After a few months in Britain it was impossible to maintain that illusion. The first clue about their status was the widespread ignorance about the Caribbean ... This was a revelation demonstrating British indifference to the constitutional bargain which had formed a cornerstone of Caribbean identity. More importantly, it was a sign of the process by which the Caribbeans would come to feel deprived, stripped of the most vital part of their being.[15]

There are, of course, obvious reasons why the word 'disappointed' occurs repeatedly in West Indian memoirs of the passage to post-war Britain, as David Olusoga rightly affirms. But these feelings did not arise solely or uniformly from the fact that Britain was 'the nation they had been told was their "mother country"'.[16] Disillusionment could have multiple wellsprings: the cold, the fog, the stark social inequalities and the dashed expectation that 'England was paved with gold'.[17] Many envisaged 'England would be a beautiful place, like a palace', only to be disabused by the endless rows of belching chimneys and the 'buildings all looking so much like factories'.[18] The oral testimony in Reynolds' collection does furnish expectations of a 'guaranteed welcome' conditioned by years of imperial ritual, pageantry and education curricula. The anonymous 'Edna' from Jamaica, for example, recalled how 'back home, on certain days, we usually marched with our flags and sang "God save the King", and things like that. So, when I came here in 1962, it was a bit of a shock ... the prejudice was very, very strong, and still is today'.[19] But many of Reynolds' witnesses also convey a sense that the pervasive racial prejudice and bitter everyday experience of discrimination could be deeply shocking regardless of prior social conditioning. Gloria Browne had received ample warning from relatives who 'had sent to tell me what it was like but it still did not sink in until I got here and then it was a shock'.[20] Others were less taken aback, such as Doreen Phillips whose 'experience in Guyana, under British rule' left her with few illusions: 'We had a lot of English people, so we knew there were prejudices then with the whites, because they had the best house, the best jobs and everything'.[21]

Understanding how these accounts cohered around a shared narrative of 'rude awakenings' requires closer attention to the wider setting that shaped the contemporary perceptions and subsequent recollections of the migrants themselves. Astrid Rasch has shown how the memory of travelling to the heart of empire in the 1940s and 1950s could merge with the changing social and political climate of post-war decolonisation, as successive sojourners 'wrote themselves into a "collective story" in the making'. That is to say, in describing the encounter, individuals would 'couch their recollected feelings of exclusion in a vocabulary emerging from an end of empire context'.[22] The emphasis on emancipation, of an emotional parting of the ways with a malign mother figure and the attendant urgency of revising older assumptions about collective selfhood, all spoke to these wider concerns. So, too, did the theme of a pan-West Indian consciousness forged in the face of shared adversity in the mother country – epitomised by George Lamming's oft-quoted aphorism that 'most West Indians of my generation were born in England'.[23]

One influential early account that brought structure and meaning to the West Indian encounter with the metropole was Donald Hinds' *Journey to an Illusion* (1966) – the very title invoking the collective shock of misrecognition.[24] Hinds had arrived from Jamaica in 1955, raised on a diet of English classics and the genteel offerings of Gainsborough Studios, but he was immediately unsettled by the everyday markers of racial difference. He cited the 1958 riots in Nottingham and Notting Hill as a key catalyst for self-examination. But it was especially the racially motivated murder of the Antiguan carpenter Kelso Cochrane in May 1959 that called his British affinities into question. 'After Cochrane's death', he recalled in an interview fifty years later, 'we had to rethink everything; we had to revise our faith in the Union Jack'.[25] It was then that Hinds began to write for the *West Indian Gazette and Afro-Asian Caribbean News*, the Brixton-based monthly established in the spring of 1958 by the radical Trinidadian exile, Claudia Jones. At a time when West Indian aspirations for equal treatment as British subjects were routinely punctured, the *Gazette* offered a creative outlet for a generation relying increasingly on their own cultural resources.[26] Hinds recalled how it was in this 'climate of expectations dashed' that the first London Carnival was launched in 1959, partly as a response to the Notting Hill disturbances but also as an expression of an emergent Caribbean consciousness.[27]

Journey to an Illusion combined the author's personal experience with a compilation of memoirs from his fellow migrants: 'those of us colonial born and bred, who did not understand the meaning of imperialism, who moved towards the mirage'.[28] Lamming's influence is evident throughout, not least his famous depiction of the transatlantic voyage as a 'journey to an expectation'.[29] But where Lamming wrote of a 'perplexing', 'enigmatic' encounter with England as the 'gaiety of reprieve which we felt on our departure … gave way to apprehension', for Hinds it was a case of wholesale disenchantment;

the 'myth of the mother country' exploded. The opening chapter set the scene with a string of eyewitness accounts of the moment when the scales fell from the newcomers' eyes:

Lloyd: you know, back home if you knew an English family and you mostly did, there wasn't any prejudice. But when you get here, wham! It really hits you ...

Ken: I most emphatically had no [prior] evidence that the English were good old-fashioned bigots at heart, shrinking from race mixture ...

Devon: Britain was always there. You were aware of her presence. You felt her, you could even smell her, but you could not see her ... If we should ever get to Britain, we should not expect the fatted calf, but every Englishman would recognize Britain's favourite colonials. Who said that? We probably told ourselves that, but the godlike presence of Britain, always unseen yet seeing, agreed.[30]

This furnished the backdrop to Hinds' conviction that 'the West Indian was deceived about his country's relationship with the "mother country"'. The accumulated myths of Greater British selfhood, the entitlements conferred by the possession of a British passport, the shared history and cultural inheritance that placed them 'on a par with the Englishman', had all been 'swallowed hook, line and sinker by West Indians'. It was only 'as things got tougher and tougher' in Britain, Hinds maintained, that the 'migrants began to believe less and less in the validity' of their British birthright. If coming to Britain was the 'climax' of a journey begun in childhood, he surmised, the 'denouement' soon followed: the 'sudden realization that all the years of coaching could offer little to his being at home in Britain'.[31]

These serial epiphanies were central to Hinds' critique of the structures of colonial racism, providing a pathway to emancipation. Some of his respondents even declared themselves 'grateful to the English. Grateful for rejecting me in order to discover myself'.[32] But their testimonies also contained multiple countercurrents that painted a more nuanced picture of a gradual, halting, fitful encounter – one that clearly preceded the jolt of arrival in Britain. For all the emphasis on the sudden shock of racial prejudice, their childhood memories of the Caribbean abounded with prior experiences of a colonial society where it was 'inevitable that colour [was] more important than the brain'; of learning 'very early to associate being white with being wealthy'. When most of the doctors, judges, lawyers and Legislative Councillors in the colonial Caribbean were 'white or nearly so', it became 'obvious to a little black boy that authority [was] 95 per cent white'.[33] These individual portraits collectively depict a rigidly racialised West Indian world where 'the white people, mainly of British origin, lived apart, fortified behind that wall of reserve we have come to associate with the English. They had ammunition and Alsatian dogs. They were secure'.[34] The distinctions of race did not stop there but permeated the entire socio-economic system. Entire families could be 'split into factions' in a culture of patronage and favour that reserved 'the topmost jobs for the fairest of colour'.[35] The British, for their part, 'took little notice' of these distinctions of class and complexion; 'They lumped us all together. We were all coloured and that was good enough, or bad enough, or justifiable enough for our overlords'.[36]

Even the voyage to Britain itself could invite reflection on the rampant structural inequalities that invested it with so much promise of social mobility. One eyewitness recounted the travails of a friend obliged to share a cabin with twenty-three others:

> The thought of this recalled to us the horrors of the Middle Passage which brought our ancestors from the African coast to the Caribbean and slavery. However, the voyage from the Caribbean was the final leg of the triangle of sea routes which made the wealth of London, Marseilles, Bristol, Bordeaux, Cadiz, Seville and Lisbon. Europe's chickens were coming home to roost![37]

That such instinctive awareness of the proximity of past 'horrors' could coexist (often in the same individual testimony) with naïve expectations of British benevolence seems incongruous, suggesting that West Indians were not so much unwitting targets of an elaborate deception as unsuspecting protagonists in a wider rhetorical struggle. At least one of Hinds' interviewees disavowed any sense of ever having been misled, stating plainly that he had only ever 'used the term "mother country" in a sarcastic sense', and that although many may have 'thought of Britain as some kind of home, some place with which they have some deep connexion … frankly I don't think I have felt this way all along'.[38] This too could have been informed by hindsight; it is more likely that the majority of Windrush arrivals hovered precariously between an ingrained knowledge of racial injustice born of everyday experience, and the prospect of escape from the confinements of the colonial Caribbean to a more open metropolitan alternative that might deliver on the promise of a colour-blind Britishness. That so much tacit prior knowledge was accompanied by apparent naivety was thus not necessarily the paradox it at first seems. One of Hinds' witnesses described the mindset in terms of 'limping … along the road to whiteness', applying only for positions vacant befitting a black migrant, all the while 'fearing not so much prejudice as the discovery of its existence'.[39]

'Familiar forms and repetitions': historical antecedents

To describe Donald Hinds' rude awakening as 'mythical' is not to say that it wasn't 'true', or that it only became so with the benefit of hindsight. Nor is it to ignore the pervasive social conditioning that structured the emotional journeys of the Windrush era. It is simply to acknowledge the complexity of factors, filters and influences that are inevitably in play whenever a single story is fashioned out of many. Bill Schwarz usefully approaches this in terms of 'an accumulation of individual experiences' that over time were subtly 'worked into a collective story of mythic properties, whose familiar forms and repetitions we can still hear today'. The unique moment when the migrant entered the world that had shaped his or her self-understanding effected a transformation, unleashing an 'array of perplexed, painful musings of the unhomeliness of the imagined homeland'.[40] He dates the beginning of these 'accumulations' from the 1940s, and undoubtedly it was the Windrush era that brought a critical mass of 'perplexed' new arrivals to bear. But they did not emerge out of a void.[41] Perhaps unbeknown to themselves, Hinds and other early chroniclers were tapping into much older traditions of West Indian disaffection and dissent, seeking amends for historic wrongs by exposing the sham of equality within the British fold. The yawning gap between the theoretical entitlements of Greater Britain and the reality of everyday racial exclusion had been a mainstay of West Indian protest for more than a century – a gap that could effectively be exploited by dramatising long-nurtured expectations suddenly, indeed 'rudely', dispelled.

These strategies had their origins at least as far back as the 1830s, when the public celebration of emancipation from the plantation owners became enmeshed with the veneration of Queen Victoria (often seen as having personally bestowed the gift of abolition).[42] From the mid-nineteenth century, West Indian campaigns for political empowerment and racial equality frequently became associated with affirmations of black Britishness that were all the more rhetorically potent for their evident lack of reciprocity. Advocates of reform from the leader of Jamaica's 1865 Rebellion, Paul Bogle, to Trinidad's turn-of-the-century pan-Africanist Henry Sylvester Williams, anchored their arguments in British rights and liberties that flowed from membership of an imperial body politic. On issues ranging from land redistribution to wage reform to political representation, vocal exclamations of British 'loyalty' provided compelling grounds that their claims ought to be listened to (regardless of their immediate success or otherwise).[43] Indeed it was the frequent denial of civil liberties that both crystallised and amplified West Indian demands for active participation in shaping the meaning of British subjecthood. As Lara Putnam observes, 'if a good portion of the men who ran the empire presumed "British subjects of colour" to be categorically excluded from citizenship, a good portion of those subjects never doubted that citizenship was theirs'.[44]

What portion, precisely, and how far their claim to British selfhood permeated the many regional and social substrata of a highly dispersed and richly diversified Caribbean population is difficult to discern. In her detailed study of the civic rites of empire in the British Caribbean, Anne Spry Rush is notably circumspect, limiting her remit to the realm of 'middle class respectability'. Taking this approach, the emergence of Caribbean modes of British self-representation appears more as a matter of socio-economic advancement than political activism – its effects most clearly felt among educated, status conscious, urban-based, 'white-collar' West Indians. Rush justifies her framework in straightforward terms: 'Caribbean peoples who were trying to get ahead in their colonial society were more likely to be exposed to pro-British propaganda for longer periods of time'.[45] Thus she catalogues a steady stream of loyalist British sentiment in education curricula, public broadcasting, Empire Day celebrations and the official pageantry of royal jubilees that invited West Indians into a world of 'shared values' with their fellow subjects overseas.

Yet for all her emphasis on 'exposure' to imperial influences, Rush is also at pains to point out that middle-class West Indians were not simply brainwashed into being British but were themselves actively engaged in its social formation, harnessing imperial networks of belonging to their own circumstances and to further their own ends.[46] Kennetta Hammond Perry similarly views the idea of Britain as a 'mother country' as a potential political asset 'strategically *selected* and appropriated by colonial subjects to make claims to political rights, economic aid, and access to routes of social mobility'.[47] Indeed, if historians are agreed on one thing, it is that Caribbean Britishness 'was not merely *imposed* but actively fashioned and worked for', and that this process was 'neither mutually exclusive nor fundamentally contradictory' with more local (or indeed pan-African) identifications and affinities.[48]

But while individuals had no difficulty reconciling their Britishness with other cultural affiliations, the middle-class embrace of a shared British respectability invariably entailed a certain distancing from fellow West Indians less fortunate than themselves. Marcus Garvey once observed how black Jamaicans at the base of the social structure were 'trampled on by all the shades above', and this surely contributed to wide discrepancies in terms of access to, and identification with, the benefits of Britishness.[49] In his famous account of the social sinews of empire in Trinidad, C. L. R. James was remarkably frank in describing his grandfather's pathway out of poverty to a prestigious position 'normally held by white men' on a sugar estate:

> This meant that my grandfather had raised himself above the mass of poverty, dirt, ignorance and vice which in those far-off days surrounded the islands of black lower-middle class respectability like a sea ever threatening to engulf them ... The need for distance ... was compounded of self-defence and fear. My grandfather went to church every Sunday morning at eleven o'clock

wearing in the broiling sun a frock-coat, striped trousers and top-hat, with his walking stick in hand, surrounded by his family, the underwear of the women crackling with starch. Respectability was not an ideal, it was an armour.[50]

This suggests at the very least that West Indian Britishness was a fraught and fragmented affair, combining elements of cultural appropriation, rights advocacy, social mobility and a tenacious hold on respectability. In this respect, it was arguably not so different from equally fractured identity formations in Australia, New Zealand, Canada and elsewhere in the imperial world where local rivalries and vested interests also profoundly skewed and fractured the social and ideological bent of being British.

But in one crucial respect the West Indian example clearly stands out on its own – namely the question of race and the possibility of a mutually resonant black Britishness. Racial barriers to mobility within the empire served as a constant reminder that to be black was to be anything but British. Indeed, white spokesmen in the Dominions invoked their racially restrictive immigration laws with a stridency and stringency arising out of the need to preserve the 'British character' of their societies.[51] Even more fundamental was the disconnect between West Indian understandings of imperial community and those emanating from metropolitan Britain. Virtually all of the major late-nineteenth-century theorists of imperial fraternity tended to bypass the Caribbean entirely (or include only the descendants of the white planter oligarchy in their remit). Charles Dilke himself was quite clear in delimiting his Greater Britain concept to 'the English-speaking, white inhabited, and self-governed lands' of the empire, and others tended to follow suit.[52] Although J. R. Seeley's 1883 magnum opus included the West Indies as one of the four 'great groups of territory' that comprised Greater Britain (the others being Australasia, Canada and the Cape) he nevertheless defined these as areas inhabited 'either chiefly or to a large extent by Englishmen'.[53] Though devoting a large portion of his study to explaining why India could never be counted among this 'ethnographic unity', he could not even accord black West Indians the dignity of reasoned grounds for exclusion.[54] In predicting that 'in not much more than half a century' the combined population of the British at home and 'beyond the sea ... will be much more than 100 millions', he referred solely and exclusively to a scattered legion of white subjects.[55]

Of all the early high priests of Greater Britain, only J. A. Froude gave the Caribbean more than a second glance, devoting an entire volume to *The English in the West Indies* (1888). But as the title clearly intimated, his purpose was to assimilate the West Indian islands into the Anglo-Saxon world he lauded so lavishly in *Oceana* two years earlier. Just as the settler colonies were 'part of ourselves', so too the British West Indies could only prosper if the racially inferior black population of 'docile, good-tempered excellent and faithful servants' were properly subsumed within the Greater British orbit.⁵⁶ 'Those beautiful West Indian islands were intended to be homes for the overflowing numbers of our own race', he lamented, 'and the few that have gone there have been crowded out by the blacks'. He recognised that the proportion of whites could no longer be substantially increased, but insisted it was not too late to restore a sense of mutual responsibility and common cause between the 'English planters' and 'their countrymen at home'. If only England could 'let it be known' that '[she] regards the West Indies as essentially one with herself', the white oligarchs would 'resume their natural position, and respect and order will come back' – to the benefit of all, not least the disenfranchised black majority:

> Out of the now half-organic fragments will yet be formed one living Imperial power, with a new era of beneficence and usefulness to mankind. The English people are spread far and wide. The sea is their dominion and their land is the finest portion of the globe.⁵⁷

One could easily dismiss such grandiloquence as the inconsequential hankerings of a gentleman entering his seventies, but it was shortly after the book was published that Froude was offered the Regius Chair of Modern History at Oxford University. His authoritative bearing underscored the distance between English and black West Indian notions of a shared British subjecthood. As Catherine Hall notes, Froude visited the Caribbean at a time of widespread talk of a self-governing West Indian Federation – which accounts for the note of urgency in his appeal for the restoration of England's influence and his conviction that 'the only true West Indian was a white West Indian'.⁵⁸

Froude's intervention did not go unchallenged. Most famously, it stirred the black Trinidadian Schoolmaster, John Jacob Thomas, to pen his immortal rebuttal: *Froudacity: West Indian Fables by James Anthony Froude* (1889). Thomas's excoriation of Froude's 'ghastly imaginings', savouring 'only too much of the slave pen and the auction block' is rightly regarded as a formative work of West Indian intellectual self-determination.⁵⁹ Particularly salient were his reflections on Froude's use of the pronoun 'us' as a proxy for white planter interests:

> His US, between whom and the negro subjects of Great Britain the gulf of colour lies, comprises, as he himself owns, an outnumbered ... and not over-creditable little clique of Anglo-Saxon lineage ... He invokes the whole prestige of the Anglo-Saxon race in favour of the untenable pretensions of a few *blasés* of that race, and that to the social and political detriment of tens of thousands of black fellow-subjects.⁶⁰

Thomas was far from the only West Indian to take exception to Froude. The Barbadian Liberal, N. Darnell Davis, also responded with *Mr Froude's Negrophobia* (1888), likening Froude's actual knowledge of the West Indies to that of a 'Cook's Tourist'.⁶¹ As Theodore Koditschek notes, these critics were 'no less concerned about the place of the West Indies in Greater Britain than was Froude'; it was the latter's exclusively white vision that they set out to correct, rather than the abstract ideal itself.⁶²

In exposing the 'gulf of colour' barricading West Indian Britons from their fellow subjects in the white empire, Thomas would have many successors. Countless West Indian volunteers in the Great War experienced firsthand the inferior status of black colonial troops when it came to pay, rank, military function and even the patriotic songs they were permitted to sing.⁶³ In the interwar years, the Grenadian editor T. A. Marryshow drew on Thomas's metaphor to deplore the 'wide and unbridgeable gulf' between the theory and actuality of shared subjecthood, which inevitably appeared whenever a West Indian sought to 'put his claim to the test'.⁶⁴ Even the test cricketer Learie Constantine – an accomplished exponent of the quintessential imperial game – was not exempt from these prejudices, his virtues often extolled in the most baldly racial terms. The leading interwar cricket writer Neville Cardus drew on the literary conventions of high imperial adventure to describe a 'savage' player possessed by a 'fury of primitive onslaught', 'violently destructive ... a panther on the kill, sinuous, stealthy, strong but unburdened. The batmanship of the jungle'. The reader was left in no doubt that here was no specimen of Greater Britain:

> When we see Constantine bowl or bat or field, we know he is not an English player, not an Australian player, not a South African player. We know that his cuts and drives, his whirling fast balls, his leaping and clutchings and dartings – we know they are the consequences of impulses born in the blood, a blood heated by the sun and influenced by an environment and a way of life much more natural than ours; impulses not common to the psychology of the over-civilised places of the earth. His cricket is racial.⁶⁵

In the fashion of Froude's 'us', Cardus placed Constantine outside the circle of the 'we' who sees, the 'we' who knows – bearing witness to the asymmetrical configuration of the British–West Indian nexus.⁶⁶ Despite generations of West Indian declarations of, and indeed insistence upon, a stake in British networks of belonging, very little of this seems to have penetrated the incomprehension and ignorance of metropolitan Britain.⁶⁷ For all Constantine's skill and success on the playing field, his grasp of imperial idiom and the intricacies of English social norms, his 'blood' placed him at one remove.

Puncturing the 'conception of remoteness'

These same blinkers go a long way to explaining why the symbol of MV *Empire Windrush* is so routinely misrepresented as the opening of a new dialogue rather than the culmination of a much older one.[68] 'Welcome sons of Empire' was the *Evening Standard*'s fulsome greeting, displaying the gaping fascination that might have been reserved for visitors from another galaxy.[69] This was the view from the metropole that persists to this day, framing the moment as a radical new departure and stamping the migrants themselves with an indelible novelty. As Stuart Hall recalled in his posthumously published memoir: 'Written out of the story – forgotten, disavowed, misrecognized – were the prolonged historical entanglements between the Caribbean and Britain'.[70]

It was not how the encounter was generally reported in the West Indies where the weight of decades of dashed expectations produced a ready awareness of the continuities. The *Barbados Advocate* acknowledged 'a certain amount of racial friction' surrounding the approaching vessel and called for 'careful handling and much thought if West Indians are not to be made to feel that they are the unwanted members of the British Empire'.[71] The London correspondent of the Jamaican *Daily Gleaner* sounded a note of foreboding that 'such a large body of men' should converge on the imperial capital at once. 'Speaking as a West Indian … I would like to express the hope that nothing of the kind will be repeated under similar conditions'.[72] Meanwhile the *Trinidad Guardian* seemed even more perturbed, declaring that 'the whole affair should be a warning to people in the West Indies that they cannot expect to go to the Mother Country whenever the whim takes them'.[73] Such trepidation was part of a longer tradition, drawing on an intrinsic understanding of the limited entitlements and racial contingencies of West Indian Britishness. The black Trinidadian clergyman M. E. Farquhar predicted 'difficulties as complicated as they are far reaching' as he reflected on the profound changes since the days when Britain was a 'closed book' to all but the tiniest minority of migrants:

> The visits of West Indian cricketers to England; two great wars, furnishing the opportunity of acquaintance with England to a comparatively large number of West Indians, together with a marked rise in the economic level of the middle classes, have combined to alter the conception of this remoteness. Now people can talk casually about going to England as they would not have done 25 years ago even with respect to going to a place like Barbados … It is when these diverse facts are related together that this mass emigration assumes its proper symbol and threatens a portent.[74]

The implication seemed clear. It was only the centuries of distance and isolation from Britain's shores that had allowed West Indian Britishness to operate on its own terms, largely insulated from direct metropolitan scrutiny. Now that this 'remoteness' had been breached, a new era of uncertainty could be apprehended.

There is also ample evidence that the voyagers themselves were under no illusion about their likely reception in England. According to one passenger's testimony, rumours circulated on board that a British warship shadowing the *Empire Windrush* 'might blow us out of the water' in the mid-Atlantic 'because there was some people didn't want black people coming to England'.[75] The first journalists to board the ship at Tilbury eagerly reported the 'first question' on the migrants' lips: 'What do British people think of our coming here?' (which Jamaica's *Daily Gleaner* co-opted for its front-page splash the following day). It hardly savoured of confidence in a 'guaranteed welcome'. One cohort of new arrivals instinctively baulked at their designation as 'refugees' in a London morning newspaper. '"Refugee" is wrong', they insisted, 'We are British and give our support to the Mother Country of all that is British'.[76] Even prior to disembarkation, these purported 'pioneers' were faithfully rehearsing the taut structures of a long and turbulent encounter.

Viewed in these terms, the rude awakenings of the Windrush era were not simply a case of prior colonial 'conditioning' dashed by cold rejection on arrival. Donald Hinds seemed fully aware of the contingencies even as he promulgated the myth: 'When a migrant makes up his mind that he is going to Britain, he hardly expects to find an earthly paradise … [but] he believes he ought to be accepted, and his being a British subject is reason enough'.[77] The operative word here is 'ought', conveying something of earlier struggles for racial justice and recognition. For centuries, the idea of Greater Britain had incorporated any number of precarious accommodations across the vastly dispersed constituencies where it nominally held sway, but these became far more difficult to sustain in the face of mutual misrecognition on such a massive scale. One final testimony in Hinds' collection bears out this crucial element of metropolitan and Caribbean British worlds colliding:

> I was totally unprepared for the sudden change that had taken possession of me since I arrived at Plymouth. I began to dread the coming of the next morning when I would look from my window and see a white man sweeping the streets … Now I was seeing my colonial society in a terrible light. I had never hoped to challenge the whites in Jamaica for a job. I realized in the confusion of the crowded station that I was starting on a desperate phase of life. If the white man was sweeping the streets, then any job I asked for would mean a challenge to him. I was not one of the 'mother country's' children. I was one of her black children. That was to be my first lesson on arriving in Britain.[78]

To return to Gilbert Joseph's query, 'How come England did not know me?'; the answer lies in the congenital flaws in the fabric of imperial subjecthood itself. As Lara Putnam avers, by 1948 'men and women in the British Caribbean had been grappling explicitly with these tensions for a full generation'.

While many would later record their personal shock, alienation and apparently sudden realisation that their Britishness was not fully reciprocated, these reactions themselves were deeply embedded in a much longer history where unrequited loyalty was part and parcel of Caribbean claims to British belonging. In short, West Indians had long since developed their own vernacular of imperial citizenship 'as an ideal continually betrayed'.[79] What was pioneering about the Windrush moment is that the conversation had relocated to the heart of metropolitan Britain. The effect was to expose long-standing inequalities and inconsistencies hardwired into the conception of Greater Britain, as it succumbed to the twin pressures of decolonisation and a new global mobility.

Notes

1. British Pathé, 'Pathé reporter meets', www.youtube.com/watch?v=QDH4I-BeZF-M (accessed 21 November 2020).
2. A. Levy, *Small Island* (London: Headline, 2004), p. 141.
3. K. H. Perry, *London is the Place for Me: Black Britons, Citizenship and the Politics of Race* (Oxford: Oxford University Press, 2016), p. 14; B. Hesse, 'Diasporicity' in Hesse (ed.), *Un/settled Multiculturalisms* (London: Zed Books, 2000), pp. 97–99. See especially Tony Kushner's extended critique of the reductive and distorting Windrush mythology, which he argues was 'rediscovered' some forty years after the event for largely contemporary purposes. See T. Kushner, *The Battle of Britishness: Migrant Journeys, 1685 to the Present* (Manchester: Manchester University Press, 2012), Ch. 7.
4. M. Mead, '*Empire Windrush*: The Cultural Memory of an Imaginary Arrival', *Journal of Postcolonial Writing*, 45:2 (2009), pp. 137–149, at pp. 137–138.
5. M. Phillips and T. Phillips, *Windrush: The Irresistible Rise of Multiracial Britain* (London: Harper Collins, 1998), p. 79.
6. The Home Office was aware of reports that the *Windrush* might be the harbinger of things to come but commented that the 'grounds for this fear are not clear'. A. W. Peterson (Assistant Private Secretary to the Prime Minister) to F. L. T. Graham-Harrison (Home Office), 5 July 1948, in S. R. Ashton and D. Killingray (eds), *The West Indies: British Documents on the End of Empire*, Series B, vol. 6 (London: The Stationery Office, 1999), p. 6. Labour's Colonial Secretary, Arthur Creech Jones, assured Parliament that it was 'very unlikely that a similar event to this will occur again in the West Indies', Debates (Commons), Vol. 452, 16 June 1948, col. 422; P. Fryer, *Staying Power: The History of Black People in Britain* (London: Pluto Press, 1984), p. 372.
7. E. Thomas-Hope, 'Hopes and Reality in the West Indian Migration to Britain', *Oral History*, 8:1 (1980), pp. 35–42, at p. 40.
8. C. Wills, *Lovers and Strangers: An Immigrant History of Post-War Britain* (London: Penguin, 2018), pp. 3–4.

9 S. Howe, 'C. L. R. James: Visions of History, Visions of Britain', in B. Schwarz (ed.), *West Indian Intellectuals in Britain* (Manchester: Manchester University Press, 2003) p. 161.

10 D. Killingray, '"A Good West Indian, a Good African, and, In Short, a Good Britisher": Black and British in a Colour-Conscious Empire, 1760–1950', *Journal of Imperial and Commonwealth History*, 36:3 (2008), pp. 363–381, at p. 364.

11 B. Schwarz, 'Introduction: Crossing the Seas', in Schwarz (ed.), *West Indian Intellectuals*, p. 7.

12 B. Schwarz, '"Shivering in the Noonday Sun": The British World and the Dynamics of "Nativisation"', in K. Darian-Smith, S. Macintyre and P. Grimshaw (eds), *Britishness Abroad: Transnational Movements and Imperial Cultures* (Melbourne: Melbourne University Press, 2007), p. 232.

13 W. James, 'The Black Experience in Twentieth-Century Britain', in P. D. Morgan and S. Hawkins (eds), *Black Experience and the Empire* (Oxford: Oxford University Press, 2004), p. 378.

14 Z. Nia Reynolds (ed.), *When I Came to England: An Oral History of Life in 1950s and 1960s Britain* (London: Black Stock, 2001), p. 1.

15 Phillips and Phillips, *Windrush*, p. 99.

16 D. Olusoga, *Black and British: A Forgotten History* (London: Pan Books, 2017) p. 503.

17 The 'rumour ... that it was paved with gold' appears in several testimonies in Reynolds' collection, see for example Tom Evans and Rennie Miller in Reynolds, *When I Came to England*, pp. 71, 76.

18 M. Charlery and N. Macfarlane in Reynolds, *When I Came to England*, pp. 127, 132.

19 Ibid., p. 68–69.

20 Ibid., p. 35.

21 Ibid., p. 25.

22 A. Rasch, 'Autobiography after Empire: Individual and Collective Memory in Dialogue' (PhD Thesis, University of Copenhagen, 2016), pp. 94, 106.

23 G. Lamming, *The Pleasures of Exile* (London: Michael Joseph, 1960), p. 214. 'The idea of Federation', writes Mary Chamberlain, 'was born in the transnational belongings and dreams of West Indians overseas and soon acquired status as a kind of mythical homeland'. M. Chamberlain, *Empire and Nation-Building in the Caribbean: Barbados, 1937–66* (Manchester: Manchester University Press, 2010), pp. 184–185. Elisabeth Wallace also noted 'the saying' in the 1970s that 'the Federation and West Indian nationhood were conceived in London and Toronto rather than in the Caribbean'. E. Wallace, *The British Caribbean: From the Decline of Colonialism to the End of Federation* (Toronto: University of Toronto Press, 1977), p. 225.

24 D. Hinds, *Journey to an Illusion: The West Indian in Britain* (London: Heinemann, 1966). Nearly fifty years later, Hinds would choose a similar device in the title of his 2014 novel *Mother Country: In the Wake of a Dream* (London: Hansib, 2014) – which he dedicated to his wife, and the fact that 'the spell is now broken!'

25 Interview in I. Thomson, 'Scotland Yard: The Jamaican—British Encounter', *Nation*, 11 March 2011.
26 B. Schwarz, 'Claudia Jones and *The West Indian Gazette*: Reflections on the Emergence of Post-Colonial Britain', *Twentieth Century British History*, 14:3 (2003), pp. 264–285, at p. 270.
27 D. Hinds, 'The *West Indian Gazette*: Claudia Jones and the Black Press in Britain', *Race and Class*, 50:1 (2008), pp. 88–97, at p. 92.
28 The description is from a 1992 letter to his grandson, Liam James Marcelle, published in the 2001 edition. See D. Hinds, *Journey to an Illusion: The West Indian in Britain* (London: Bogle-L'Ouverture, 2001, 1st edn, 1966), p. xvii.
29 The title of the last chapter in G. Lamming, *The Pleasures of Exile* (London: Michael Joseph, 1960).
30 Hinds, *Journey to an Illusion*, pp. xx, 2–3, 14.
31 Ibid., pp. 157, 159.
32 Ibid., p. 5.
33 Ibid., pp. 19, 11, 12.
34 Ibid., p. 13.
35 Ibid., p. 19.
36 Ibid., p. 21.
37 Ibid., p. 34.
38 Ibid., p. 161.
39 Ibid., p. 2.
40 Schwarz, 'Introduction: Crossing the Seas', p. 8.
41 For more on West Indian and African demands for a more meaningful imperial citizenship after 1918, see M. Matera, *Black London: The Imperial Metropolis and Decolonization in the Twentieth Century* (Oakland, CA: University of California Press, 2015).
42 See A. S. Rush, *Bonds of Empire: West Indian and Britishness from Victoria to Decolonization* (Oxford: Oxford University Press, 2011), Ch. 2.
43 Perry, *London is the Place for Me*, pp. 26, 37.
44 L. Putnam, 'Citizenship from the Margins: Vernacular Theories of Rights and the State from the Interwar Caribbean', *Journal of British Studies*, 53:1 (2014), pp. 162–191, at p. 172.
45 Rush, *Bonds of Empire*, pp. 9–10. The size of the group thus 'exposed' remains somewhat vague, although the implication at times is that it was not necessarily a large-scale social phenomenon. At one point for example, Rush notes that impact was greatest among 'the small percentage' of the black population who attended both primary and secondary school. Elsewhere she seems less constrained, arguing that devotion to the royal family had a wider social base. 'Indications are', she notes cautiously, 'that a good many Jamaicans, at least, felt real affection for their monarchs' and that this admiration was 'genuine'. Ibid., p. 46, 61, 66.
46 Ibid., pp. 6, 10.
47 Perry, *London is the Place for Me*, p. 61.
48 Howe, 'C. L. R. James', p. 158; Perry, *London is the Place for Me*, pp. 35, 39; Rush, *Bonds of Empire*, p. 10.

49 Quote from 1916 in H. Johnson, 'The Black Experience in the British Caribbean in the Twentieth Century', in Morgan and Hawkins (eds), *Black Experience*, p. 320.
50 C. L. R. James, *Beyond a Boundary* (Durham: Duke University Press, 2013, 1st edn, 1963), pp. 7–8.
51 M. Lake and H. Reynolds, *Drawing the Global Colour Line: White Men's Countries and the International Challenge of Racial Equality* (Cambridge: Cambridge University Press, 2008); R. A. Huttenbuck, 'The British Empire as a "White Man's Country": Racial Attitudes and Immigration Legislation in the Colonies of White Settlement', *Journal of British Studies*, 13:1 (1973), pp. 108–137.
52 Quoted in D. Bell, *The Idea of Greater Britain: Empire and the Future of World Order, 1860–1900* (Princeton: Princeton University Press, 2007), p. 8. Dilke later lamented that this conception had been overtaken in popular usage to exclude the United States, see C. W. Dilke, *Problems of Greater Britain* (London: Macmillan, 1890).
53 J. R. Seeley, *The Expansion of England: Two Courses of Lectures* (London: Macmillan, 1891, 1st edn, 1883), p. 10.
54 Ibid., pp. 11, 301–302.
55 Ibid., p. 12.
56 J. A. Froude, *The English in the West Indies* (London: Longmans, Green, and Co., 1888), p. 287.
57 Ibid., pp. 364–365.
58 C. Hall, 'What is a West Indian?', in Schwarz (ed.), *West Indian Intellectuals in Britain*, p. 46.
59 J. J. Thomas, *Froudacity: West Indian Fables by James Anthony Froude* (Philadelphia: Gebbie and Co, 1890), pp. 9, 125; See Schwarz, 'Introduction', p. 4; and Hall, 'What is a West Indian', pp. 46–47.
60 Thomas, *Froudacity*, pp. 128–129.
61 N. Darnell Davis, 'Mr. Froude's Negrophobia: or Don Quixote as Cook's Tourist', *Timehri: Journal of the Royal Agricultural and Commercial Society of British Guiana* 2, new series (1888), pp. 85–129.
62 See T. Koditschek, *Liberalism, Imperialism, and the Historical Imagination: Nineteenth-Century Visions of a Greater Britain* (Cambridge: Cambridge University Press, 2011), pp. 200–202.
63 Winston James recounts an episode from August 1916 when members of the British West Indies Regiment were reprimanded in Alexandria for singing 'Rule Britannia' by white soldiers demanding to know 'who gave you niggers authority to sing that?' See James, 'Black Experience in Twentieth-Century Britain', p. 354.
64 Quoted in Putnam, 'Citizenship from the Margins', p. 180.
65 Quoted in A. Bateman, *Cricket, Literature and Culture: Symbolising the Nation, Destabilising Empire* (London: Routledge, 2009), pp. 162, 164.
66 Howe, 'C. L. R. James', p. 161.
67 This is not to dismiss the myriad other, more subtle, ways that the colonial Caribbean interacted with imperial subjectivities in the metropole, see generally C. Hall, *Civilising Subjects: Metropole and Colony in the English Imagination, 1830–67* (Chicago: University of Chicago Press, 2002).

68 Putnam, 'Citizenship from the Margins', pp. 188–189.
69 *Evening Standard*, 22 June 1948.
70 S. Hall (with B. Schwarz), *Familiar Stranger: A Life between Two Islands* (London: Allen Lane, 2017), p. 12.
71 *Barbados Advocate*, 25 June 1948.
72 W. A. S. Hardy, quoted in the *Daily Gleaner*, 'West Indian "Inrush" Regretted', 27 June 1948. Hardy, a black Jamaican journalist resident in London since the 1930s, went on to record the experiences of ordinary West Indians in England in the Colonial Service radio series, *Biography of an Exile*. See Rush, *Bonds of Empire*, p. 188.
73 *Trinidad Guardian*, 20 June 1948.
74 M. E. Farquhar, 'Candid comments', *Trinidad Guardian Weekly*, 27 June 1948.
75 Vince Reid, testimony in Phillips and Phillips, *Windrush*, p. 64.
76 *Evening Standard*, 22 June 1948.
77 Hinds, *Journey to an Illusion*, p. 32.
78 Ibid., p. 47.
79 Putnam, 'Citizenship from the Margins', p. 164.

5

Indians of Durban, South Africa and the break-up of Greater Britain

Hilary Sapire

On the night of 9 December 1962, the Durban offices of A. S. 'Khosaan' Kajee, a prominent Indian businessman and leader of the conservative Natal Indian Organisation (NIO) were bombed. As recalled by one of the saboteurs who returned to Alice Street the next day to inspect the damage, 'It was a very successful operation. I ... found the office totally smashed. The safe of the owner was also destroyed. There was a lot of publicity given to the destruction of this office by the forces of MK'.[1] The attack, the second attempt on Kajee's premises, was part of a wave of sabotage operations that took place following the arrest in August of Nelson Mandela, South Africa's 'Black Pimpernel' and co-founder of the newly formed armed wing of the African National Congress (ANC), Umkhonto we Sizwe, also known as 'MK'. Undertaken by a group of Natal-based Indian operatives, the bombing took place at night when there was no risk to human life. As such it was one of the many instances of 'symbolic sabotage' of government installations, power lines, telephone cables, railway lines, or offices of 'collaborators' working within the apartheid departments of Indian, African and Coloured Affairs that characterised the opening phase of the ANC-led armed struggle.[2] 'What happened [to Kajee] was symbolic', explained Debanathan Perumal, one of the saboteurs, 'We did not want him personally'. Identified as a government 'stooge', Kajee had earned particular opprobrium because he was the only Indian invitee who had agreed to participate in the installation ceremony of the South African President on the day the republic was proclaimed on 31 May 1961. In so doing, Dr Monty Naicker, President of the Natal Indian Congress (NIC), later remarked, Kajee had made himself a 'marked man in Indian circles'.[3]

As leader of the NIO that had formed in 1947 in opposition to the 'radicalised' NIC, Kajee stood at one end of the Indian political spectrum, while the young saboteurs (Debanathan Perumal, Natoo Babenia, Ebrahim Ismail Ebrahim, Sonny Singh) stood at the other. Legatee of the 'moderate' political tradition of Durban's Indians that originated in the empire loyalism of the merchant-led NIC in nineteenth-century colonial Natal, Kajee's politics of conciliation was roundly rejected by the youthful saboteurs. In turning to violence too, these representatives of a new generation of radical and progressive Indian activists were announcing the obsolescence of the civil protest, due to brutal state repression, that the NIC had embraced through the 1950s in partnership with their white, coloured and African Congress counterparts.[4] Kajee and the MK operatives also presented polarised responses to the creation of a republic by Prime Minister Dr H. F. Verwoerd after a whites-only referendum and the departure of South Africa from the Commonwealth, which were two defining events – along with British Prime Minister Harold Macmillan's 'Wind of Change' speech of February 1960 – in the wider history of decolonisation and the break-up of Greater Britain.[5] Setting a precedent for Southern Rhodesia which declared itself a republic in 1970 as a means of ensuring white minority rule, as Christian Pedersen reminds us in this volume, it was the first time the British monarchy had been rejected by whites by a popular, albeit racially restricted vote. Significantly, South Africa and Rhodesia were following a trend whereby recently decolonised African states transitioned rapidly from monarchical to republican status, beginning with Ghana in 1960 and ending with Gambia in 1970. Unlike the experience of the white minority states, those processes were, by the end, actively encouraged by British officials anxious to pre-empt any embarrassment to the Queen by African republican assertions.[6] The present chapter complements new writings that highlight the significance of monarchy in the history of Britain's decolonisation – 'the institution that ultimately symbolised the British Empire and presided over its dissolution'[7] – and the place of republicanism in anti-colonial Indian nationalist political thought. It offers a perspective on these phenomena from the vantage point of a minority, diasporic South Asian population in the Indian Ocean city of Durban in South Africa's most Anglophone province.[8] It juxtaposes the varying Indian responses to the creation of a white minority republican state and the country's unmooring from the Commonwealth against those of white English-speaking 'Natalians' for whom 'King, Flag and Empire' were sacrosanct, and explores the discomfiting questions about belonging, affiliation, identity and subjecthood that were provoked for Indians by the constitutional changes of 1961. In so doing, it brings into closer association the literature on the break-up of Greater Britain with a South African historiography which identifies 1960–1961 as the critical generative moment for the turn to armed resistance by the ANC and its allies, and the creation of political machinery abroad to sustain an external movement in the years of exile and play its part in the establishment of a global anti-apartheid movement.

Durban's Indians, imperial monarchy and popular monarchism, 1860–1949

Durban's Indian population of 231,385 in 1960 descended from indentured labourers, primarily from the Hindi-speaking Gangetic plains and south Indian coast who had been brought to work on the sugar plantations, mines and railways of Natal a hundred years previously, and the 'passengers' who came voluntarily a decade later as traders and businessmen, largely Gujarati Muslims and a handful of Hindu merchants from northern India. Following the end of the system of indenture in 1911, many moved to Durban and its fringes, a process in which they came to outnumber rapidly urbanising isiZulu-speaking Africans, and a white citizenry that jealously guarded its economic privileges and exclusivity. By mid-1949 they numbered 123,165, comprising 'the largest colony of Indians in the Southern Hemisphere outside India'.[9] Wintering in Durban in the late 1950s, the travel writer Jan Morris (like many visitors from abroad) was especially struck by the Indian character of the city with its mosques, domed temples, incense and gongs: 'you might very well be in Madras or Bombay', she wrote.[10]

As the South African Indians' 'capital', Durban, like Bombay and Madras, nurtured an elite political culture, which from the nineteenth century was dominated by moderate leaders – largely from the merchant elite – for whom empire loyalism was the central creed. Rooted in pre-and post-uprising India, this loyalism encompassed an ideology of 'rights' and 'entitlements' that was shared with African *amarespectables* (Christianised, educated) and 'big coloureds' in which the British Crown figured symbolically as a source of protection and succour against white settler rapacity and racial exclusion. For the NIC, when it was established in 1894, loyalism offered a means of expressing the aspirations of 'British Indians' in Natal, claiming the extension of the rights of British citizens. This doctrine of imperial equality was based on the Queen's Proclamation of 1858 which asserted the equality of all British subjects – 'our "Magna Carta"', proclaimed Mohandas Karamchand Gandhi, the NIC's most illustrious founding figure. He would invoke the Queen's words on behalf of Indians who had been excluded from the franchise in Natal and declared that they were 'proud to be under the British Crown because they think that England will prove India's deliverer'.[11] Repeatedly raised as a counter to the denial of these rights and to whites' exclusivist claim to Britishness, it was a loyalism that was similarly exclusive. Elite spokesmen like Gandhi campaigned for equal rights for 'Indians' insisting on separating their strivings from those of coloured and African 'sons of the soil', even if the 'friendliest' of relationships between the 'two races' could be established.[12] Notwithstanding the repeated failures of petitioning the Crown and British governments, deputations to Britain, sacrifices made in the empire's wars, and declarations of loyalty to the throne, the idea of an imperial monarch embodying personal rule and the implicit promise of constitutional remedy long remained compelling for Indian elites. Especially in the face of visceral anti-Indianism from whites demanding repatriation and restrictive controls on Indian trading and residence, members of the Congress and other organisations proclaimed their fidelity to Crown and Empire well into the 1930s.

South African Indian loyalism – that overlaid caste, religious and linguistic differences – was also intertwined with close links to and imaginative engagement with India and its nationalist aspirations. Reliance on the intercession of the government of India – often in the persons of prominent Indian Liberals who served as 'agents-general' from the late 1920s to mediate between Indian South Africans and the Union government in Pretoria – went along with associations with nationalist figures, from Sarojini Naidoo to Jawaharlal Nehru. The latter offered an alternative source of political and moral authority to those of the agents-general and the government of India, especially as the nationalist movement in India moved into its non-cooperation and confrontationist phases. Significantly, they urged South African Indians to join forces with other 'non-Europeans' in their campaigns for equality, an injunction that was not taken up with conviction until the late 1940s. Moreover, whereas the Indian National Congress (INC) and Indian nationalist leaders turned decisively against the imperial monarchy after the First World War – illustrated in the Gandhi-led opposition to the royal visit of the Prince of Wales in 1921 and 1922, and in the boycott of the 1937 coronation – the loyalist framework, however tarnished, remained dominant in Natal.

It was at events such as coronations, births and deaths of royal figures, jubilees and royal visits that this loyalism was especially prominent and these in turn served as occasions for explicit questioning about the constitutional role of the monarchy in the press and public fora – whether it was entirely symbolic, or whether the sovereign had the constitutional capacity and will to intercede in South African affairs. In the absence of political rights and representation in Natal, moreover, public royal functions with their elaborate rituals of loyal addresses and gift-giving presented opportunities for the performance of civility and respectability and, thereby, as demonstrations of Indian elites' worthiness of political inclusion. Even those who did not fully subscribe to the loyalist creed used the publicity of royal events and exaggerated language of monarchical fidelity to draw attention to the contradictions between the implied promise of imperial citizenship and the realities of Indians' political exclusion in South Africa. The segregated celebrations organised by the city authorities for Indians, whether it was for the coronation of 1911 or the ceremonies to welcome the Prince of

Wales to Durban in 1925, led Indian spokesmen to claim that the separate and inferior events were emblematic of their subordinate and unequal status. It was more than 'dinner party equality' that Indians demanded, explained Manilal Gandhi, editor of *Indian Opinion* and son of the Mahatma, when Indians were excluded from a civic banquet for the Prince of Wales in 1925. It was 'a principle of equality in the eye of the law' that was at stake.[13]

By the 1920s and 1930s, royal visits had become increasingly contentious as the loyalist idiom frayed in the face of further bouts of intense anti-Indianism. The visits to South Africa of the sons of King George V – the princes Edward and George – in 1925 and 1934 prompted agonised debates about participating in demeaning segregated ceremonies, anticipating the even more passionate responses to the royal visit of 1947.[14] Well up to the late 1940s, the culture of loyalism and the ritual veneration of the Crown were promoted by Indian agents-general who officiated and presented loyal addresses at royal and other civic celebrations. They also promoted a politics of conciliation and elite alliance-building with white liberals whom they entertained at the luxurious 'Orient Club' in the hope that they might lobby the authorities on their behalf.[15]

It was the 'top-heavy' character of the Congress, with its reputation for having 'no roots in the masses of Indians, [being] representative only of the merchant classes, and pro-imperialistic' that, along with its politics of compromise, led to the take-over of its leadership in 1945, by a younger generation of Indian activists.[16] Some of them – such as the future NIC President, 'Monty' Naicker – were educated in Britain and drew inspiration from the resurgent nationalist movement in India, anti-colonialism and the international left. The NIC was also influenced by the entry into organised politics of trade unionists, who tapped into local Indian working-class militancy, the revival of the Communist Party of South Africa and the emergence of a Non-European United Front (NEUM) that campaigned 'for the co-operation of Native, Indian and Coloured races ... against the colour bar'.[17] A broad church of Gandhi-ists, socialists and trade unionists, professionals and labour activists displaced the 'Old Guard' of merchant leaders, and with this, upended the familiar framework of imperial loyalty. Whereas 'moderate' politician, A. I. Kajee who was NIC leader until 1945, had only a decade earlier proudly accepted the King George VI coronation medal, young leaders rejected their elders' faith in the imperial connection and the Crown as a remedy for political disabilities.[18] In a speech that got him imprisoned in 1941, young radical, Dawood Seedat, voiced this rejection of the language of duty to King and country: 'We have got no more time for Kings and Emperors ... The King is not fit to be Emperor of India ... The British Empire ... drains all the wealth out of India and keeps millions of our people in suffering, starvation, sickness, illiteracy and without homes'. These phrases were repeated at many Indian meetings.[19]

Growing scepticism over the moderates' reliance on the imperial tie represented a repudiation of the underlying politics of compromise and gradualism. Especially from the war years, Indian South African radicals demanded a common franchise, the removal of the colour bar, free and compulsory education, and, however ambivalently, a widening of the struggle to include *all* black South Africans. Armed with this egalitarian programme, 'Durban's turbulent Indian tub-thumpers' embraced a politics of confrontation that culminated in the Passive Resistance Campaign (PRC) of 1946 to 1948, the most concerted political action by Indian South Africans since Gandhi's departure. To further these ends, the leaders of the Indian Congress signed the historic 'Doctors' Pact' with the ANC President, Dr A. B. Xuma, during the royal visit of 1947, to form a new multiracial alliance against white supremacy.[20]

The 1947 royal visit, following the PRC and the condemnation of South Africa's policies towards Indians in the inaugural meeting of the United Nations General Assembly the previous year, was especially contentious in Natal. Prime Minister Jan Smuts hoped to use the soft power of the royal visit to galvanise vital white Natalian electoral support against a resurgent Afrikaner nationalist movement for the following year's election. Rumours of an Indian boycott – supported by Gandhi from India – threatened to scupper the royal tour in Natal, and to compound the humiliation caused to Smuts personally by the Indian delegation at the United Nations. The royal visit provoked contradictory and passionate responses from Durban's Indians upon whose loyalties and affinities powerful and contradictory calls were made. The increasingly rancorous conflict between 'moderates' (favouring Indian participation in the associated ceremonies) and 'radicals' of the NIC (who campaigned for a total Indian boycott) came to a head during the royal tour. Despite the popularity of the NIC, Indians did not heed the boycott call of the radicals; a crowd of 65,000 people gathered to pay homage to the royal family when they came to Durban on 22 March 1947 at an event presided over by 'moderate' A. I. Kajee and supported by a wide range of organisations – from sporting clubs to the Hindu Tamil Institute and Indian Scouts Association, many of which had also supported passive resistance.

There were several reasons why Indians turned out in such great numbers to greet the royal visitors in Durban and elsewhere in Natal, some of which, undoubtedly arose from genuinely warm feelings for the monarchy. What is striking for our purposes, however, is that the language of the proponents of the boycott was the language of feeling and in keeping with the rhetoric of loyalism – of betrayed trust, mixed with Gandhist tropes, with an emphasis on mourning, dignity and *izzat* (honour). It was the source of 'profound grief', the NIC pointed out, that participation in the celebrations was impossible. Indeed, with the exception of the Communist Party and the Trotskyist NEUM, the pro-boycott stance on the royal visit was not couched in anti-monarchist or republican terms, but as the familiar loyalist refrain of betrayed hopes. In contrast, in exhorting the public to participate in the ceremonies, the language of the moderates was unvarnished and apparently unsentimental; boycotting would not 'redound to our credit', argued the leader of the national Congress body, while P. R. Pather, the veteran moderate politician maintained that boycotting was 'futile' because the King was 'above politics'. Indeed, much of the debate about participation centred on the question of whether the King should be seen as complicit in Indians' racial oppression in South Africa given that the legislation was passed in his name, making a boycott a legitimate expression of their discontent. Such debates about the monarchy's capacity to bring about the redress of wrongs or whether his position was 'entirely symbolic' would recur in the discourses about South Africa's transition to a republic in 1961 and its likely effects on Indians.[21]

One of the consequences of the failure of the boycott was that it brought the political divisions between moderates and radicals to a head, and emboldened the moderates to establish a rival organisation, the NIO. In his inaugural speech as its president, Hajee A. S. Kajee explicitly called for 'a spirit of moderation and conciliation in all matters affecting our political and social status in this country ... Realism and objectivity should be our watch words'. Counterposing this approach against the 'militant activities' in the country, he claimed that the latter 'do not recognise the fundamental principle that negotiations between human beings are subject to compromises which are desirable so long as they are honourable'.[22] It was this preference for compromise, its exclusiveness, and its less democratic modes of organisation that earned the NIO the opprobrium of a Congress newly receptive to political alliances beyond its Indian constituency. The NIO would discover over the next decade, however, that the incoming National Party government that considered Indian South Africans 'unassimilable' was even less amenable to the politics of suasion than its predecessors. With a government more purposive in its drive to push through a radical segregationist programme of racial exclusion, as two historians have put it, 'a politics of purge' had displaced 'the imperial nods to inclusion'.[23]

If the royal visit of 1947 marked the swansong of loyalism (leaving intact the pragmatic politics of elite-brokering and conciliation favoured by moderates), a new decade of mass defiance, apartheid social engineering, and the dilution of the formerly dominant white Anglophone political culture made elite-led 'black loyalism' redundant. The years immediately following the royal visit – the most 'dangerous' for the Crown and Commonwealth – ushered in significant changes to both institutions. The demands of newly independent India to become a republic within the Commonwealth had compelled both to reinvent themselves in accordance with the egalitarian ethos of an age of decolonisation. No longer an exclusive club of white Dominions, an uncompromising anti-colonial tone was set by the new African and Asian members. The British monarch was no longer the focus of a supposed 'common allegiance' of member states, but a more loosely defined 'Head of the Commonwealth'.[24] Indian nationalists, key players in this transition, had always envisaged India's attainment of freedom as inextricably bound up with the struggles for equality for Indians 'overseas' and, on becoming a republic, reaffirmed this commitment. As Rajah Maharaj Singh, Governor of Bombay, expressed it: 'Our joy will be shared nowhere more in South Africa ... you are the flesh of our flesh and bones of our bones, we cannot forget you and your suffering'.[25] However, as Nehru insisted, and this was consistent with his view since 1927, Indian South Africans needed to ally themselves with, and subordinate their cause to, that of the majority African population. Mindful of the devastating racial pogrom of Durban in January 1949 in which Indians were targeted with retaliatory violence by Africans, he specified that 'we do not wish Indians to have any special interest at the cost of Africans anywhere. We have impressed upon them to cooperate with Africans in gaining their freedom'.[26]

Notwithstanding these power realignments in South Africa and the world, there were intimations especially at the time of the coronation of the new Queen, Elizabeth II, in 1953 that there were vestigial remains of loyalist discourse, and they could be repurposed to rhetorically contrast the sovereign independence of India and the subjection of Indians in South Africa under apartheid. Just before the coronation, for example, the *Indian Opinion* called on Indian South Africans to take pride in the fact that, for the first time, India would celebrate 'not as British Empire's hand-maid but as a free and independent nation. As part of India, Indians throughout South Africa and the world will pay homage to the Queen'. Reprising the language of the royal visit of 1947, the leader article contrasted the 'peculiarly unhappy position of not being able to express our joy outwardly ... because of treatment as semi-human beings'. Another columnist declared that Indians 'were second to none in our loyalty to and deep affection', even though the Queen was 'utterly helpless' to assuage the 'woes' of 'non-Europeans'. Moreover, he or she railed, it was still not possible for 'all the people irrespective of their colour' to come together to hail her and participate equally in the jubilation.[27]

However 'helpless' the Queen may have appeared, it was also 'on this joyous occasion of the Coronation' that she was appealed to directly to intercede with the South African government in another version of loyalist plaint, reminiscent of the appeals made to Queen Victoria by indigenous and diasporic subjects to a female monarch, as a literal and metaphorical mother. A group of women and their children travelling from Kampala had been refused permission to disembark by immigration officials in Durban and rejoin their families. Writing on their behalf, Mrs J. C. Gheewalla asked the Queen 'to use your Majesty's authority to help us to join our husbands ... We know your Majesty, as a wife and mother, will appreciate the suffering this will bring to our children and families and we pray that you may use your good offices as Queen of the commonwealth to prevent this'.[28] The NIC also telegraphed Nehru, in London for the Coronation, to urge Prime Minister D. F. Malan to intercede. Neither request succeeded in shifting the government's decision.[29]

Rejecting the republic, 1960–1961

The culture of loyalism was certainly submerged during the 1950s. The planned convalescent visit of the King to Natal for 1952 did not take place as he died just as arrangements were finalised, and there were no further royal visits to South Africa during the apartheid years. Moreover, given the intransigence of the National Party, the moderates who had previously championed loyalism were rendered impotent by their tactics.[30] They were also effaced for the decade by the mass-based multiracial opposition to apartheid of the Congress Alliance and by the emergence of new political alternatives.[31] Under the leadership of Monty Naicker, the NIC played its part in the iconic Congress Alliance campaigns – the Defiance Campaign of 1952 and the Congress of the People of 1955 which produced the 'Freedom Charter'. NIC activists participated in a wide range of joint protests and boycotts.[32] The close partnership between Naicker and Albert Luthuli, the ANC's President General, symbolised what Jon Soske calls a new 'aesthetic of Afro–Asian cooperation', mirroring, locally, the spirit of Bandung.[33] Despite the disruptions caused by arrests leading to the 1956–1961 'Treason Trial', Congress activism quickened in the last years of the decade, not least because of the start of Group Areas removals in Durban from 1958. This prompted the rallies, schools and shop closures and the 'biggest political demonstration ever staged by the Indian community'. A 'Freedom Fair' was held at the iconic meeting place, Curries Fountain, in December and January 1959–1960. Yet in the wake of a final NIC rally in 1961, writes Surendra Bhana, the 'flame flickered and died'.[34]

In part, the last flurry of activism was in response to major policy shifts directed at Indians from 1960 onwards. In a volte-face, the government abandoned its policies of repatriation in 1960, the centenary year of the arrival of indentured Indian labour in Natal. In so doing, they finally recognised the permanence of Indians in the country, albeit within the rubric of apartheid and the policy of 'separate development'. An Asian Affairs division under the Minister of the Interior was set up, becoming the Department of Indian Affairs in 1961. As Prime Minister H. F. Verwoerd informed a party congress in Natal, because of his predecessor's failed repatriation policy, Indians would henceforth develop as an independent ethnic group in their 'own areas' along the same lines as 'homelands' for Africans and Coloureds.[35] In accordance with this policy, the government had earlier advertised plans for the establishment of a segregated Indian university on Salisbury Island.[36] These announcements, along with Group Areas removals, provided some common ground for the conservative NIO and Congress.[37] Despite the mutual antagonisms and ideological differences, there was some rapprochement between the two in these febrile years. From joint participation on the centenary committee formed to commemorate the arrival of Indians in South Africa, to campaigns against Group Areas and segregation in higher education, common initiatives were taken. As Hilda Kuper pointed out, the shared awareness of their vulnerability as a vote-less minority made it necessary for leaders to minimise differences and present a united front. Equally, she noted, a generational shift was taking place, whereby some formerly radical congressmen had become more conservative in private, and amenable to compromise by the end of the decade.[38] All organisations, moreover, were hamstrung by government intransigence and the brutal repression of dissent, resulting in the NIC having to sometimes adopt tactics 'that would have been approved by its NIO rival'.[39] While the NIO under A. S. Moolla was more ready to contemplate participating in new structures provided by the state, and preferred to broker better deals for Indians at Group Areas hearings rather than wholly oppose removals, their rhetoric about the injustices of government policy chimed in with those of their NIC rivals.[40] Echoing the uncompromising language of NIC president Monty Naicker, but not going as far as to demand 'universal suffrage', for example, the Conservative leader P. R. Pather declared his refusal to countenance moves to 'detach them [Indians] from the general population of the country'.[41]

The years 1960 to 1961 were climactic for South Africa, as they were for Greater Britain. British Prime Minister Harold Macmillan's epoch-making 'Wind of Change' speech in the South African Parliament was followed in quick succession on 21 March 1960 by the massacre of protesting Africans at Sharpeville, the Langa uprisings, the declaration of a state of emergency, and the banning of the ANC and Pan African Congress (PAC) which resulted in international condemnation. For the first time, Britain condemned apartheid at the UN. In fulfilment of Prime Minister Verwoerd's promise in

January, a republican referendum was held in October and, by a slim majority, white South Africans elected to become a republic. At the Commonwealth Prime Ministers' Conference in London in the following March, Verwoerd withdrew the application to be part of the Commonwealth as a republic, refusing to comply with the requirements insisted upon by the Afro–Asian members to sign up to principles that would have compromised his apartheid policies. Verwoerd returned to South Africa claiming victory and was given a hero's welcome from his supporters. With the country in a febrile state, South Africa's exclusion from the Commonwealth was, as Saul Dubow puts it, the 'culminating episode of eighteen months of feverish social tumult'.[42]

From the outset, it was intended that African, coloured and Indian South Africans would have no say in the decision about South Africa's constitutional future. Responding to a question from an African medical student why 'non-whites' could not participate in the referendum, a nationalist MP bluntly explained that 'the republic issue is one that Whites had to settle among themselves'. They could not permit coloured people to 'be their arbitrators'.[43] Piling insult upon injury, the cabinet called on South Africans to celebrate the inauguration of the republic on 31 May 1961 in an 'atmosphere of reverence'. Invitations to the ceremony were sent to the Indian conservatives, A. S. Kajee and P. R. Pather, along with hand-picked coloured representatives and nine compliant African chiefs. Commemorative medals and flags were sent to schools to be distributed to children on the day, and meat and 'kaffir beer' prepared for distribution in the African townships of Pretoria.

As Hyam and Henshaw point out, black South African responses to the declaration of a republic and the departure of South Africa from the Commonwealth were contradictory.[44] The PAC dismissed the republican issue as of no relevance to Africans, while the ANC hoped to capitalise on the widespread hostility to the republic to garner support for a national convention to create a non-racial constitution. Simultaneously, members of both the ANC and South African Communist Party, following the Sharpeville massacre continued preparing for armed resistance, leading some historians to argue that Nelson Mandela was pursuing a 'dual agenda' at this moment, enunciating both the language of mass action and consultation while preparing for armed resistance.[45] Following a conclave of the ANC in Orlando, Soweto, in December 1960, an All-In African Conference was held in Pietermaritzburg, at which the ANC called on all Congress partners and allies to support a call for a fully representative non-racial national convention. Failing the Government responding positively, a three-day 'stay at home' would be held between 29 and 31 May in protest against the declaration of the republic on 31 May. Taking up the 'clarion call', the NIC issued thousands of leaflets exhorting the Indian public – businessmen, workers, professionals, bus-owners, market gardeners, sportsmen and others – to 'Defeat Apartheid Republic' and 'Demand a National Convention'. As Monty Naicker expressed it in one of the leaflets: 'The era of the ox wagon as represented by the Broederbond Republic is finally at an end'. Shopkeepers were requested to observe a complete *hartal* (cessation of business) and school pupils and teachers were enjoined to reject flags and medals which were no more than 'emblems of oppression'.[46] When it became known that A. S. Kajee had accepted the invitation to the inaugural ceremony in Pretoria, Naicker condemned his decision: 'No Indian, in full possession of all his faculties, can participate in the celebrations, even in the event of merely attending the State function. Let South Africa and South Africans understand that Mr Kajee is acting as an individual from individual motives'.[47] It was at this moment that Kajee came clearly into the sights of the saboteurs of December 1962.

Explaining his support for the planned action, Naicker pointed out that there were few other alternatives available to make the government and white population 'see the way we feel'. Other than mass meetings and processions, only a general strike would achieve this.[48] Such was the ferment within Indian communities that Congress officials claimed to be overwhelmed with the 'tremendous political awakening amongst the Indian masses', reporting that in almost every area of Indian residence, new branches were 'springing up'.[49] Feverish organisation took place in a context of intensified police raids on homes, trade union and NIC offices.[50] The government prepared a formidable show of force to deter and disorganise protesters on the first day of the proposed strike, with Saracen tanks patrolling townships, helicopters hovering overhead and troops posted at crossroads.[51] As the *Post* observed, on the eve of the declaration of the republic the country was 'a place of fear'.[52]

Although the stay-away was called off prematurely by Mandela and was pronounced as only a 'qualified success', it is notable that Indians in Natal had rallied significantly to the call.[53] Over half (50 to 60 per cent) of Durban's Indian workers stayed out of work.[54] All Indian shops and businesses in Durban observed the call for a *hartal* and, despite offers of police protection, stayed closed for the full three-day period. Indian markets were shut, Indian-owned cinemas cancelled all programmes and Grey Street, the Indian centre of commercial activity, was deserted.[55] One estimate suggested that 80 per cent of schoolchildren were not at school. Principals of most Indian schools in Natal packed away unwanted flags and meals and sent them back to Pretoria.[56]

In explaining the perception that the action had failed – a view propounded in the white press and radio – *Drum* newspaper offered various reasons ranging from the psychological effects of intimidation to deliberately misleading news coverage of the stay-away's effect. But a key point it made was that the call had failed to catch the imagination of those not 'politically inclined'. *Contact* similarly suggested that the idea was 'too big' to succeed, and that the objectives did not strike a chord. 'The Republic', it argued, was 'too abstract an objective, a National Convention too academic'.[57] Given the relative success of the stay-away among Indians in Natal, it would appear that the idea of 'The Republic' was not too abstract to grasp, even if it carried several different meanings and associations.

'True Voice of Natal'?

Reflecting on the effects of the creation of the republic, the *Post* noted that 'it would be silly to pretend that the mass of the Non-White people have had any joy in its coming into being'.[58] The extensive support for the stay-away from Durban's Indians suggested that the call indeed tapped into, and provided a focus for, popular discontent. Attitudes towards the ending of the monarchical constitutional arrangement, and the severance of the Commonwealth connection as one of the sources of this discontent, clearly varied, as did those towards a republic from which Indians had been excluded. As the writer and former passive resister, Pat Poovalingham pointed out, 'genuine sadness' at the demise of the monarchical connection coexisted with anger at Indians' exclusion from the referendum and at the 'impertinence' of a government expecting them to rejoice at the republic's proclamation.[59]

By 1961, many of the certainties of even the most ardent of 'black loyalists' and proponents of kingship (imperial and indigenous), African and Indian alike, were threadbare. ANC President Albert Luthuli, for example, who had praised the royal families for offering a focus of national unity in 1933, and in 1947, had delivered the loyal address to King George VI at the Zululand *indaba* during the royal visit, declared in 1961 that 'only a republican form of government would meet the broad needs of the majority'. He went on to say that he would wish to see it existing within the Commonwealth as well as forming 'other alliances or unities in Africa or outside'.[60] With India setting the trend, decolonising states were emerging from the grip of empire as sovereign, democratic republics by the 1960s. Although Monty Naicker was not explicit about a republican state being the desired end of South Africans' struggle for democracy, he certainly embraced the sovereign democratic republican state that was created in 'our great motherland India' with much enthusiasm, celebrating that it was no longer ruled from Downing Street.[61] The bunting-festooned streets of Durban, and crowds wearing coloured emblems with the republic flag for Republic Day festivities, moreover, suggested that India's new status was wholeheartedly embraced.[62] Thus it was not the republican form of state that created offence, but the *raison d'être* of this particular republic, established with the aim 'To Unite and Keep South Africa White' as one of the referendum slogans proclaimed. Its predicted character directly conflicted with the NIC's aspirations for a free, democratic republic.[63] In his address for the NIC conference in March 1961, Naicker said that the government was 'foisting on the people of this country an Afrikaner caste rule under a tribal Republic which has not the support of the vast majority of the people of South Africa'.[64] Invoking both the retrogressive 'tribal' paradigm of apartheid separate development and the 'Broederbond Republic' blueprint of 1942 with its fascistic connotations, Naicker captured a visceral and shared distaste for a most unvirtuous republic.[65]

Certainly, not all Indians were indifferent to monarchy. But it was also difficult to identify with the country's most ardent white monarchists, their close neighbours, Natalian whites. The latter had voted overwhelmingly against the establishment of the republic and conducted a very 'British' campaign that was laced with fears of loss of their cultural heritage in a Verwoerdian republic, and of being cast adrift, without the Commonwealth, in a hostile and dangerous world.[66] Yet, as Luthuli pointed out, the Britishness affected by white Natalians went hand in hand with extreme racial exclusivism and hostility; they had 'more than merely participated in our oppression'. They were responsible for some of the most damaging laws, he said, singling out the Group Areas Act which had been inspired by their 'anti-Asiatic' agitation of the early 1940s.[67] The United Party leader of Natal who 'winced' at replacing the monarchy with a republic had simultaneously concurred with nationalists in the 'severe subjection' of 'Non-Whites'. In contrast, Luthuli averred that the 'true voice of Natal' was 'when one speaks for all Natalians – Black, White and Brown'.[68] Indian columnists reprised the theme of Natalian hypocrisy; while acknowledging the role of a minority of white liberals and progressives, they conjured a picture of whites who might 'fume and fret' about the disappearance of monarchist traces, who were yet no different in their views about 'the place of Indians in South Africa'.[69] Indeed, one writer predicted that given the unlikelihood of changes in white attitudes, Indians were not likely to be worse off in a republic.[70] 'Republic or Monarchy', wrote Poovalingham, Indians were all too aware that their plight was 'determined by the prejudices of South African Whites'.[71]

Noting that it was immaterial to 'non-Europeans' whether South Africa remained in the Commonwealth, cynicism was also directed against Britain by some writers, especially prior to South Africa's exit from the Commonwealth. Whether it was the memory of the British Liberal Government approving the 1910 constitution or of 'successive Governments under the

British Monarchy that supported the suppression of the non-White people', a writer for the *Indian Opinion* expressed scepticism about the likelihood of any reaction from the United Kingdom for which trading links with South Africa were paramount.⁷² Once South Africa did leave, however, others worried that previous inhibitions imposed by the Commonwealth would disappear, and that in a situation of instability to the north of the republic, repression would be likely to intensify and plans speeded up to impose a 'totalitarian blueprint'.⁷³ From this perspective, there was no 'need for any shedding of tears … for the loss of the British connection'.⁷⁴

Others took a more positive view of the Commonwealth as either a 'protector' of 'non-European' interests or as a valuable ally in a multi-fronted battle against apartheid. It was the latter re-imagining that lay behind the campaign of lobbying Commonwealth member states by the London-based South African United Front (SAUF) to request them to take steps to exclude South Africa from the Commonwealth prior to the Commonwealth Prime Ministers' meeting in London.⁷⁵ Once the 'walk out' had taken place, *Drum* claimed it as the SAUF's 'greatest victory' and placed great hopes in a 'more vigorous' new Commonwealth; the old idea of a 'club' whose members only met for 'friendly chats' was 'dead and done with', it announced triumphally.⁷⁶ Indeed, notwithstanding cynicism about Britain's unreliable record, many in African and Indian circles insisted on the value of the Commonwealth. Paul Mosaka, president of the African Chamber of Commerce who had been active in the campaign for a national convention, was ambivalent about South Africa's withdrawal, and asserted the value of the Commonwealth connection, pointing out that it had not only been 'part and parcel of the African way of life in his Christian and educational upbringing', but supplied an invaluable link between the 'Afro–Asian' group and the Western powers so necessary to maintain the world balance of powers. For some older African leaders, as Mosaka's response suggests, in addition to enthusiasm for the 'new, transformed Commonwealth' there was an emotional response to Britain and the Commonwealth that arose from their British education and religious lives. Many 'leaders of Non-White opinion' told the *Golden City Post* of their determination to bring South Africa back into the Commonwealth. Luthuli described it as 'the family fold',⁷⁷ and Oliver Tambo would later maintain that black South Africans had never left the Commonwealth.⁷⁸ The Britishness with which these individuals identified was a far cry from that claimed by conservative white Natalians; theirs was of the egalitarian, inclusive variety, increasingly associated with London's metropolitan liberal and left-wing supporters of anti-colonial causes and African leaders of newly independent states with whom a growing exile cohort became closely associated.⁷⁹

If Indian hopes were still invested in the better nature of British and Western liberalism, as demonstrated during the royal visit of 1947, the monarchy did exercise some hold on their affections. Pat Poovalingham described a complicated sense of loss associated with the end of a South African monarchy. In part, he explained, this was because the imperial monarchy had been incorporated into a deeply rooted political imaginary for which kingship and notions of dynastic sovereignty were fundamental principles. Queen Victoria had merely replaced indigenous monarchs, and for Poovalingham, it was thus unsurprising that South African Indians retained 'a traditional respect – in many cases even an affection for the monarchy'. Likewise, the coloured poet James Matthews identified a 'sentimentality for the monarchy' and popularity of the royal family as personalities, and especially among the elderly, quixotic hopes that the monarch had only to command, and the laws of South Africa would be changed'. Thus, the very word 'republic', Matthews wrote, had 'become an abomination for the Coloured people. The intellectual and labourer, housewife and grandmother are united in their dislike for South Africa's new republican status'.[80]

Conclusions

As John Lambert notes, white Natalians accommodated themselves to republican rule, their preoccupations with 'economics and security' trumped their anxieties about culture and identity. Their rapid adjustment to the new order was facilitated in part by Britain's failure to support their desire for secession. Moreover, mindful of the threats to white settlers elsewhere in British Africa, it had become evident that Natalians could not depend on British support, once Britain had joined in with international criticism of South Africa's treatment of Indians.[81] This sense of abandonment made it easier to embrace the republic, even if Natalians continued to take comfort in nostalgia and symbols of Britishness. By contrast, Natal's Indians were excluded from the start from the republic, one in which freedoms and civil rights were, if anything, even further restricted than previously. But, like their white neighbours, they were also in the processes of 'becoming South African'.[82] For progressives, left-wingers and members of the Congress Alliance, becoming South African, especially from the 1940s was increasingly expressed in the identification with other 'non-Europeans' and their common struggles against racial equality, even if affiliations and ties with the Indian 'motherland' remained firm. This identification, especially with the African majority, had been promoted by Indian nationalists from the Asian subcontinent but acquired its own impetus in the political ferment from the late 1930s, taking formal expression in 1947 with the 'Doctors Pact'.[83] Nehru encouraged this identification through the succeeding decade, and once again, after the Commonwealth Prime Ministers' meeting of 1961, said that his key advice to Indians was to cooperate with Africans 'as they were nationals of South Africa, not of India'.[84]

For Pat Poovalingham, having played his part in the NIC's passive resistance movement in the 1940s, it was only when he joined what he considered the only truly non-racial party, the Liberal Party in the following decade, that he first felt he 'became a South African'. Previously, he had been an 'Indian South African'.[85] Equally, those Conservatives who embraced an attenuated version of loyalism claimed rights as South Africans. And it was often at occasions for celebrating the monarchical and British connection that they explicitly asserted such claims. At Durban's official celebrations in the City Hall to commemorate India's independence in 1950, for example, A. M. Moolla lavishly praised the Commonwealth's 'rule of justice which has given man self-respect and freedom from want' while proclaiming: 'We Indians born in South Africa belong to South Africa. We are here for better or for worse'. In similar vein, P. R. Pather proposed a toast to the 'Land of our Birth and Adoption' reminding his audience that it was Indians who had helped develop the 'Garden Colony' of Natal: 'South Africa is our home, where we want to live in harmony'.[86] A decade later, Pather would insist once more that 'the Indian would continue to regard himself as a fully-fledged South African who owed allegiance to no other country'.[87]

Ironically, just as the majority of Indians adjusted to the South Africa of the 1960s, a small but influential group of Indian activists went into exile, joining fellow Indian South African émigrés who had left earlier for Britain as students or political exiles. For many, the choice of London was an obvious one given their Anglophone education, and the widespread adoption of English as a lingua franca that reflected processes of cultural assimilation that had taken place. As Pauline Podbrey recalled when she and her husband H. A. Naidoo, a member of the Central Committee of the Communist Party of South Africa went into exile in 1951, the choice of Britain as a destination was an immediate one. 'I am far closer to Britain than I am to India', 'H. A.' confessed to her, 'I find I have more in common with the British than I do with the Indian Indians, culturally, socially, and in every way. I doubt whether I'd fit in in India.'[88] Emphasising his identification with British political values, Kader Asmal, who went to the United Kingdom to study in 1959 reflected years later upon this affinity; he had 'thought of England as a counter to the South Africa we were living through at that time – a kind of symbol of freedom'.[89] Greater Britain may have been in the process of breaking up, but its liberal and radical traditions, if no longer its monarchical and imperial symbolism, retained a powerful hold on the imaginations of South Africans seeking their own emancipation well into the end of the last century.

Notes

1 B. Pillay, 'How MK Grew', *Dawn. Journal of Umkhonto we Sizwe, Souvenir Issue. 25th Anniversary of MK* (no date), pp. 20–21. In the same issue, see also E. I. Ebrahim, 'Though We Had No AK47's nor Revolvers', pp. 14–15.
2 T. Simpson, *Umkhonto we Sizwe: The ANC's Armed Struggle* (Cape Town: Penguin, 2016); S. Stevens, 'The Turn to Sabotage by the Congress Movement in South Africa', *Past and Present*, 245 (2019), pp. 221–255. The turn to violence in 1961 created moral quandaries for leading NIC figures such as Dr 'Monty' Naicker, as it did for Albert Luthuli, the President General of the ANC. As Varsha Lalla suggests, for a minority of Indian activists, sabotage represented an extension of passive resistance: 'Being Indian, Being MK: An Exploration of the Experience and Ethnic Identities of Indian South African Umkhonto we Sizwe Members' (MA dissertation, Rhodes University, 2011).
3 A. Desai and G. Vahed, *Monty Naicker: between Reason and Treason* (Pietermaritzburg: Shuter, 2010), p. 375; *Indian Opinion*, 2 June 1961.
4 See Chapters 5–6 of J. Soske, *Internal Frontiers: African Nationalism and the Indian Diaspora in Twentieth-Century South Africa* (Athens, OH: Ohio University Press, 2017); and G. Vahed, '"Gagged and Trussed Rather Securely by the Law": The 1952 Defiance Campaign in Natal', *Journal of Natal and Zulu History*, 31 (2013), pp. 68–89 on alliance politics in Natal in the 1950s.
5 S. Ward, 'Run before the Tempest. The "Wind of Change" and the British World', *Geschichte und Gesellschaft*, 37 (2011), pp. 198–219.
6 D. Kenrick, 'Settler Soul-Searching and Sovereign Independence: The Monarchy in Rhodesia, 1965–1970', *Journal of Southern African Studies*, 44:6 (2018), pp. 1077–1094; P. Murphy, *Monarchy and the End of Empire. The House of Windsor, the British Government, and the Postwar Commonwealth* (Oxford: Oxford University Press, 2013), pp. 88–90.
7 H. Kumarasingham, 'A New Monarchy for a New Commonwealth? Monarchy and the Consequences of Republican India', in R. Aldrich and C. McCreery (eds), *Crowns and Colonies: European Monarchies and Overseas Empires* (Manchester: Manchester University Press, 2015), p. 284.
8 Murphy, *Monarchy and the End of Empire*; Kumarasingham, 'A New Monarchy'; S. Purushotham, 'Jawaharlal Nehru, Indian Republicanism, and the Commonwealth', in S. Dubow and R. Drayton (eds), *Commonwealth History in the Twenty-First Century* (London: Palgrave Macmillan, 2020); M. Taylor, 'Epilogue', *Empress. Queen Victoria and India* (New Haven and London: Yale University Press, 2018); M. K. Ramgotra, 'Postcolonial Republicanism and the Revival of a Paradigm', *The Good Society*, 26:1 (2017), pp. 34–54.
9 Soske, *Internal Frontiers*, p. 46; G. Vahed, 'The Making of an Indian Identity in Durban, 1914–1949' (PhD Thesis, Indiana University, 1995); *Indian Views*, 26 March 1947; *A Survey of Race Relations in South Africa Compiled by Muriel Horrell* (Johannesburg: SAIRR, 1962), p. 83.
10 J. Morris, *South African Winter* (London: Faber and Faber, 1958, republished 2008), pp. 106–109. Equally striking was the high pitch of racial tension: 'The

fibres of the city are coarsened by mistrust – between black and white and brown, between Briton and Afrikaner and African and Indian'.
11 A. Desai and G. Vahed, *The South African Gandhi: Stretcher Bearer of Empire* (Stanford: Stanford University Press, 2016), p. 35; Taylor, *Empress*, pp. 270–271.
12 E. S. Reddy, 'Pandit Nehru and the Unity of the Oppressed People of South Africa', p. 2, www.sahistory.org.za/archive/pandit-nehru-and-unity-oppressed-people-south-africa-es-reddy (accessed 23 November 2019); Desai and Vahed, *South African Gandhi*, pp. 121–122 and 297–298.
13 *Indian Opinion*, 17 June 1911; *Indian Opinion*, 8 May 1925.
14 H. Sapire, 'The 1947 Royal Tour in Smuts' Raj: South African Indian Reponses', in R. Aldrich and C. McCreery (eds), *Royals on Tour: Politics, Pageantry and Colonialism* (Manchester: Manchester University Press, 2018), pp. 250–270.
15 Vahed, 'Making of an Indian Identity in Durban', pp. 225–226.
16 This characterisation of Congress is Goolam Gool's who became a leading figure in the Non-European Unity Movement. R. R. Edgar (ed.), *An African American in South Africa. The Travel Notes of Ralph J Bunche 28 September 1937–1 January 1938* (Athens, OH: Ohio University Press, 1992), p. 301.
17 E. S. Reddy, 'Pandit Nehru and the Unity of the Oppressed People'.
18 B. D. Sannyansi, *Abdulla Ismail Kajee* (Adarsh-Nager, Ajmer, India, 1941), pp. 49–50, http://scnc.ukzn.ac.za/doc/B/Ks/Kajees/Sannyasi,_BD_Abdulla_Ismail_Kajee.pdf (accessed 3 April 2018).
19 Desai and Vahed, *Monty Naicker*, p. 106.
20 Durham University Library, Baring Papers, Baring to Machtig, 21 November 1944; Soske, *Internal Frontiers*, Ch. 2.
21 Sapire, 'The 1947 Royal Tour'.
22 University of the Witwatersrand, Historical Papers Research Archive, AD 1710 Hassim Seedat Collection, 1905–1961, *South African Indian Conference, 13–14 March 1948* – Presidential Address Delivered by Hajee A. S. Kajee at the opening of the conference at Durban, 13 March 1948.
23 G. Vahed and T. Waetjen, 'Shifting Grounds: A. I. Kajee and the Political Quandary of "Moderates" in the Search for an Islamic School Site in Durban, 1943–1948', *South African Historical Journal*, 67: 3 (2015), pp. 316–334, at p. 334; H. Kuper, *Indian People in Natal* (Pietermaritzburg: Natal University Press, 1960), pp. 49–79.
24 Murphy, *Monarchy and the End of Empire*, pp. 40–48; Purushotham, 'Jawaharlal Nehru'; Kumarasingham, 'New Monarchy'.
25 *India Views*, 1 February 1950.
26 *Leader*, 2 April 1949.
27 *Indian Opinion*, 29 May 1953; *Indian Opinion*, 15 May 1953.
28 *Times*, 2 June 1953.
29 C. Schofield, *Enoch Powell and the Making of Postcolonial Britain* (Cambridge: Cambridge University Press, 2013), p. 105.
30 A. Desai, *Arise Ye Coolies. Apartheid and the Indian 1960–1995* (Johannesburg: Impact Africa Publishing, 1996), p. 27. In 1968, the moderates, P. R.

Pather and A. S. Moolla, took up positions in the government-created South African Indian Council (SAIC).
31 Some Natal Indians joined the Liberal Party, while many younger activists joined the Natal Indian Youth Congress or found a political home in the NEUM.
32 S. Bhana, *Gandhi's Legacy: The Natal Indian Congress, 1894–1994* (Pietermaritzburg: UKNZ Press, 1997), pp. 80–87; R. E. Johnson, 'Indians and Apartheid in South Africa: The Failure of Resistance' (PhD Dissertation, University of Massachusetts, 1973), p. 91.
33 Soske, *Internal Frontiers*, Chs 5–6. The 1955 Bandung Conference was the first major gathering of heads of state of recently decolonised African and Asian countries.
34 Bhana, *Gandhi's Legacy*, p. 115; Johnson, 'Indians and Apartheid', p. 145; Desai and Vahed, *Monty Naicker*, pp. 332–333.
35 *The Times*, 25 August 1961.
36 *New Age*, 16 February 1961.
37 The Group Areas Act of 1950 aimed to eliminate mixed neighbourhoods in favour of racially segregated areas designated for each 'racial' group.
38 Kuper, *Indian People*, pp. 49–56.
39 Johnson, 'Indians and Apartheid', p. 45; Kuper, *Indian People*, p. 55.
40 Desai, *Arise Ye Coolies*, p. 23; *Survey of Race Relations*, p. 30; Desai and Vahed, *Monty Naicker*, pp. 368–398; 'Presidential Address to the Twenty-Third Conference of the South African Indian Congress, Durban, September 3, 1961', in E. S. Reddy and F. Meer (eds), *Monty Speaks. Speeches of Dr G. M. (Monty) Naicker. 1945–1963* (Durban: Madiba Publishers, 1991), pp. 113–118; Bhana, *Gandhi's Legacy*, p. 104.
41 *The Times*, 25 August 1961.
42 S. Dubow, 'Macmillan, Verwoerd and the 1960 "Wind of Change" Speech', *The Historical Journal*, 54:4 (2011), pp. 1087–1114, at p. 1088.
43 *Rand Daily Mail*, 26 August 1960.
44 R. Hyam and P. Henshaw, *The Lion and the Springbok: Britain and South Africa since the Boer War* (Cambridge: Cambridge University Press, 2003), pp. 301–303.
45 S. Dubow, 'Were There Political Alternatives in the Wake of the Sharpeville-Langa Violence in South Africa, 1960?', *Journal of African History*, 56:1 (2015), pp. 119–142, at p. 138; Stevens, 'The Turn to Sabotage'.
46 'Indian South Africans Timeline, 1960–1969', www.sahistory.org.za/article/indian-south-africans-timeline-1960-1980 (accessed 23 November 2019).
47 *Indian Opinion*, 2 June 1961; *New Age*, 1 June 1961; Desai and Vahed, *Monty Naicker*, pp. 374–375.
48 *Drum*, May 1961.
49 *New Age*, 19 May 1961.
50 *New Age*, 27 April 1961.
51 A. Sampson, *Mandela: The Authorised Biography* (London: HarperCollins, 1999), pp. 147–148.
52 *Golden City Post*, 7 May 1961.
53 *New Age*, 18 May 1961.
54 *Survey of Race Relations*, p. 38.

55 *New Age*, 8 June 1961.
56 *Drum*, July 1961; *The Times*, 1 June 1961; *New Age*, 8 June 1961.
57 *Contact*, 1 June 1961.
58 *Post*, 6 June 1961.
59 *Rand Daily Mail*, 2 June 1961.
60 *Drum*, December 1961.
61 Institute of Commonwealth Studies, University of London, Papers of the African National Congress, ANC ICSS1/26 Presidential Speech, NIC Provincial Conference, 29–30 May 1948.
62 *Indian Opinion*, 13 January 1950; *Indian Views*, 1 February 1950.
63 *Golden City Post*, 12 February 1960.
64 'Presidential Address to the Thirteenth Annual Conference of the Natal Indian Congress, Pietermaritzburg, March 3, 1961', in Reddy and Meer (eds), *Monty Speaks*, www.sahistory.org.za/sites/default/files/NAICKER-SPEECHES-BOOK.pdf (accessed 25 June 2018).
65 *Rand Daily Mail*, 2 June 1961; *Golden City Post*, 6 June 1961.
66 B. J. Liebenberg and S. Burridge Spies, *South Africa in the Twentieth Century* (Pretoria: J. L. Van Schaick Academic, 1993), pp. 372–373.
67 *Golden City Post*, 12 February 1961.
68 Ibid.
69 *Indian Opinion*, 2 December 1961 and 14 October 1960.
70 *Survey of Race Relations*, p. 9.
71 *Rand Daily Mail*, 2 June 1961; *Indian Views*, 24 March 1961; *Indian Opinion*, 2 December 1960.
72 *Indian Opinion*, 14 October 1960; 3 March 1961; *Survey of Race Relations*, p. 9.
73 *Indian Views*, 24 March 1961.
74 *Indian Opinion*, 14 October 1960.
75 Formed at the behest of Kwame Nkrumah of Ghana, the SAUF was a short-lived externally based alliance of the Southern African liberation movements. A. Lissoni, 'The South African Liberation Movements in Exile, c. 1945–1970' (PhD thesis, University of London, 2008), pp. 109–112.
76 *Drum*, April 1961.
77 *Golden City Post*, 19 March 1960.
78 Sampson, *Mandela*, p. 145.
79 Lissoni, 'South African Liberation Movements', Chs 1–2.
80 *Rand Daily Mail*, 2 June 1961.
81 J. Lambert, '"The Last Outpost": The Natalians, South Africa, and the British Empire', in R. Bickers (ed.), *Settlers and Expatriates: Britons over the Seas* (Oxford: Oxford University Press, 2010), pp. 172–174.
82 R. Mesthrie, 'Language Shift, Cultural Change and Identity Retention: Indian South Africa in the 1960s and beyond', *South African Historical Journal*, 57 (2007), pp. 134–152.
83 P. Raman, '"Being an Indian Communist the South African Way": The Influence of Indians in the South African Communist Party 1934–1952' (PhD Thesis, University of London, 2003).
84 *Golden City Post*, 2 April 1961.

85 Peter Alexander, Interview with Pat Poovalingham, Durban, 19 June 1991.
86 *Indian Opinion*, 1 February 1950.
87 *The Times*, 25 August 1961.
88 P. Podbrey, *White Girl in Search of the Party* (Pietermaritzburg: Hadeda Books, 1993), pp. 144–145.
89 Asmal founded the Irish Anti-Apartheid Movement. H. Bernstein, *The Rift: The Exile Experience of South Africans* (London: Jonathan Cape, 1994), p. 248.

6

The birth of 'white' republics and the demise of Greater Britain: the republican referendums in South Africa and Rhodesia

Christian D. Pedersen

From the late nineteenth century, the British monarch was the constitutional head and cultural symbol of Greater Britain, a spiritual nexus providing unity and identity to a worldwide community of Britons. In *Britons*, Linda Colley identified the monarchy as central to the process through which the British defined themselves as a single people in the first place, while John MacKenzie, in his study of the imperial impact factor in Britain, described how popular monarchism and imperial patriotism had formed a 'core ideology' in British society and culture which persisted until the 1960s.[1] Moreover, to the champions of the idea of Greater Britain, the person of the monarch embodied communal values essential for 'linking together the colonial populations and the "mother country"'.[2] In the overseas settler colonies, as Mark McKenna has shown, monarchy represented 'the cultural guardian angel for the exiled colonial' and 'the pinnacle of racial identity'.[3] The history of the monarchy as a symbol of Britishness is fundamentally a global and imperial story.

While the monarchy's role as the symbolic head of an imperial family of loyal subjects is well established, the question of how and why monarchism failed to resonate in so many parts of the empire after 1945 has received much less attention.[4] This chapter argues that the struggles between republicanism and monarchism ought to play a more prominent role in histories of the end of empire and the break-up of Greater Britain. With the advent of decolonisation, republicanism emerged as a disruptive force that swept the British imperial world. The global proliferation of the republican form of government was arguably one of the main political and constitutional legacies of post-war decolonisation. By the 1960s this republican tide seemed irreversible, a sign of changing outlooks and new constitutional preferences. The new republican winds left no region unaffected; attitudes to the monarchy were reassessed everywhere, striking at the root of global British identities along the way.

This chapter sheds light on how monarchism and republicanism were perceived by primarily white anglophones during the republican referendums in South Africa and Rhodesia in the 1960s, which, in both cases, led to the scrapping of the monarchy. It illustrates the ways in which this republican question was caught up in the processes of decolonisation, the rise of white nationalisms and the demise of Greater Britain. In doing so, the chapter suggests that the transition from monarchy to republic was more than a constitutional watershed, because it had dramatic consequences for the ways in which white English-speakers in South Africa and Rhodesia saw themselves and their place in the Greater British world.

The republican question came at a time when multiple communities of British descendants across the globe were beginning to reconsider their relationship with Britain and the British Crown.[5] This meant that southern African debates were part of broader global conversations over constitutional designs in the decolonising world. By the 1960s, even the core constituents of Greater Britain were affected by the onset of republicanism. In Canada, for instance, Prime Minister Lester Pearson considered the possibility of changing the role of the monarchy or abandoning it altogether. According to the British High Commission in Ottawa a growing number of Canadians viewed the monarchy as 'a relic of British imperialism' and increasingly felt that the country deserved its own head of state. This was meant as a demonstration of post-imperial Canada's new sense of nationhood, and a response to the spectre of separatism in French-speaking Quebec. When Queen Elizabeth II visited in 1964, she was booed by large crowds in Quebec. Yet even among English Canadians, fewer thought affectionately of the Queen, and looked upon Britain in more pragmatic terms.[6] In Australia, another loyal bastion of settler Britishness, an incipient republicanism also emerged in the 1960s. In an age of imperial decline, some intellectuals no longer saw the monarchy as an appropriate symbol for an independent and modern Australia; a rhetoric of new nationalism supplanted older narratives of empire loyalty. The royal family became an object of satire in the media, as the pomp and circumstance surrounding monarchy grew increasingly remote and outdated. The younger generation no longer revered the royal family in quite the same way. In 1967 Prince Philip shocked Melbourne reporters when he suggested that Australia should dispense with the Crown and become a republic if it felt it was getting a raw deal from the monarchy.[7] Devoted monarchists and 'Commonwealth men' such as Sir Robert Menzies despaired about the 'dreadful stain of republicanism' which had swept away a vital object of unity and cohesion in the decolonising British world.[8]

Other powerful reminders of the increasingly contested nature of the British Crown came from within the United Kingdom itself. In England, the Queen was by no means unpopular, but sceptics argued that the end of empire diminished the role and significance of the monarchy, while others felt her title as the Head of the Commonwealth had limited value. Writer Colin MacInnes dismissed it outright as 'a last ditch claim of English neo-imperialism, trying to preserve an illusion of past splendours and authority that have vanished'.[9] Across the Irish Sea, in Northern Ireland, the Queen was more a symbol of militant Protestantism, as Ulster erupted into a battleground between republican nationalists and ultra-loyalists with the arrival of British troops in 1969 to settle a violent conflict that would continue for decades. Many had hoped the Queen's 1966 royal visit to Belfast would be a healing tonic but, instead, historic tensions were brought to the surface.[10]

In Asia and Africa, the link between anti-colonialism and republicanism was more straightforward, with a pronounced trend towards a republican form of government. In most ex-colonies the Crown symbolised imperial domination and foreign rule.[11] Ghana and the Gambia chose the route of direct democracy, calling referendums in 1960 and 1970 respectively to secure majorities in favour of scrapping the monarchy and investing the new presidential office with immense powers.[12] Generally however most newly independent African countries were keen to cut the formal bonds of monarchy and colonial rule without consulting the people in a formal referendum – a tendency that, from 1962 onwards, was positively encouraged by Whitehall officials with a view to protecting the prestige of the British Crown against the unpredictability of African politics.[13]

In white-ruled southern Africa, debates about monarchism and republicanism were part of this global process, culminating in two bruising referendums called respectively by the prime ministers of Afrikaner-dominated South Africa (1960) and the rebel state of Rhodesia (1969). These events marked the first and second time the British monarchy was dissolved by whites by popular vote and, as such, signalled bad tidings for the future of Britishness as a global civic idea. In these contexts, the chapter argues, republicanism served as a tool to entrench white domination and thereby wrong-foot the logic of decolonisation. To white republicans in both countries, constitutional change signalled national liberation, mental decolonisation and the birth of new white nations. To white anti-republicans, however, the onward march of republicanism reinforced a sense of belonging to a global community of the British peoples. Thus, the decline of loyalty to the Crown and the creation of 'white' republics was part of a process of redefining settler communities for a post-imperial age. But the demise of the concept of Greater Britain left an ideological vacuum for disaffected whites which could not be easily filled.[14]

'To unite and keep South Africa white': the republican referendum in 1960

In October 1960, an all-white South African electorate voted in favour of cutting the country's ties to the British monarchy. The referendum was won by a very narrow margin (52 per cent majority) and revealed deep-seated tensions in South Africa's white communities about constitutional issues and political principles.[15] During the first fifty years of the history of the Union, English-speaking South Africans remained largely loyal to the idea of empire and the Crown.[16] Their pride in being subjects of the monarchy provided a key marker of who they were. The significance of loyalism had a particular salience in southern Africa where relatively small populations of British migrants and their descendants were outnumbered by indigenous peoples and, in the case of South Africa, by another white minority, the Afrikaners, who saw themselves as the continent's first anti-colonial republican movement.[17] The 1960 referendum was called by Hendrik Verwoerd, Prime Minister and leader of the National Party (NP), in a bid to realise a republican ideal that had long been a defining aspect of Afrikaner nationalism.[18] By the late 1950s, however, the NP was reformulating its ideology, increasingly emphasising white unity and republicanism in place of Afrikaner ethnic communion. In his first statement to the country after his election as party leader, Verwoerd declared that he looked forward to the day of English–Afrikaans cooperation, joined together by a common patriotism, and becoming 'one people with two languages'.[19] Verwoerd's construction of a new inclusive white national identity was fuelled by internal resistance to apartheid, which, in turn, was spurred on by the decolonisation process in the rest of Africa. With the rise of militant black opposition, anxious whites were confronted by radical alternative visions of South African nationhood. In addition, British Prime Minister Harold Macmillan's Cape Town speech in 1960 and the public outcry over the Sharpeville massacre gave the impression that Britain was abandoning fellow white communities and aligning the Queen and the Commonwealth with black political aspirations. In his reply to Macmillan's 'wind of change' speech, Verwoerd had presented apartheid as a mode of decolonisation, extending increased rights and responsibilities to Africans in the reserves.[20] Verwoerd consciously sought to combat the perception of apartheid South Africa as a reactionary white backlash against the process of decolonisation.

The republican campaign was spearheaded by Verwoerd himself and the NP leadership, positioning the party as the political arm of Afrikaner republicanism. Very few English-speakers openly supported the republican campaign, the main message of which was a call for white unity and a demand for further entrenchment of white domination; in other words, the republic was presented as a necessary step to safeguard white supremacy in the context of African decolonisation. Moreover, the NP portrayed the coming of the republic as an act of conciliation between the Afrikaans-speaking and English-speaking white populations. A republic would unite the two white groups, and 'bind the people into one nation with one flag, one national anthem and one loyalty'.[21] At the NP republican congress, the *Cape Times* correspondent noted the remarkable change in Afrikaner nationalist rhetoric, with speakers following strict instructions to 'be nice to English-speakers'.[22] Gone were the usual appeals to Afrikaner nationalism, references to the atrocities of the South African War and denunciation of British imperialism. The referendum was perceived by republicans as a moment of national self-realisation marking the break-up of Greater Britain in a South African context.

Throughout the referendum campaign Verwoerd appealed to the English-speaking electorate and used the political crises in other parts of Africa, particularly the turmoil and chaos in newly independent Congo, to underline the imperative of unity in defending white domination. The republican slogan, 'To Unite and Keep South Africa White', amply deployed the fear of the 'black peril' and other scare tactics to ease long-standing ethnic rivalries.[23] Verwoerd's controversial 'Dear Friend' letter, sent to all voting South African whites, made a personal appeal for white unity. Verwoerd outlined how the dynamics of the Cold War had upended international racial solidarity. In this new global configuration, Britain was forced to betray white communities all over the world and thus, if the white South African population was not prepared to take the necessary step and become a republican nation they would 'experience all the suffering of the whites who are being attacked in, and driven out of, one African territory after the other'.[24]

The republicans projected the Crown as foreign and remote, and a dividing factor in the political life of the country. In order to gain 'full' nationhood, South Africa needed a home-grown national symbol as the head of state.[25] Yet, the republican vote was construed as far more than the rejection of the British monarch as head of state; it was also meant to signal adherence to key principles of the postcolonial age. An advertisement proclaimed that a 'Yes' vote would strike a blow for the principle of the right to self-determination of all peoples.[26] Another stated that a 'Yes' to the republic was a vote for the 'DECOLONISATION OF AFRICA'.[27] In sum, the republican movement sold the referendum as an act of mental and constitutional decolonisation, co-opting the prevailing international support for emancipation from the grip of imperial powers, and applying it to themselves.

English-speaking South Africans played a leading role in the anti-republican movement. During the referendum, the ideological and regional fissures that characterised South Africa's English-speaking community were momentarily concealed. The United Party, the main opposition party, was particularly well placed to mobilise across ethnic boundaries. Verwoerd had announced that the republican issue would be decided on the basis of a simple majority of one, which greatly affected the dynamics of the entire campaign.[28] It meant that white anglophones, as a minority community, could only succeed by winning over a portion of Afrikaner votes and hence were obliged to focus less on the language of global Britishness and more on the interests of white South Africans as a whole. Anti-republican campaigners were therefore expressly instructed to suppress, often unsuccessfully, extreme loyalist expressions of shared Britishness and thereby prevent an 'opening for Nats [Afrikaner nationalists] to depict us draped in Union Jacks, etc'.[29]

The first goal of the anti-republican campaign was to expose the insincerity of republican appeals across communitarian divides for white unity. The key message was that the republic would not bring about national unity; rather, anti-republicans saw it as sectional and divisive, jeopardising white unity at a moment when violent unrest in the country and elsewhere made it imperative. Generally, the republican cause was depicted as a campaign for the Afrikanerisation of South Africa and the entrenchment of the political domination of the white majority group.[30] In Durban, a traditional hotbed of 'British' loyalism, the *Natal Mercury* described the referendum as a constitutional power-grab, with the ultimate aim of subordinating and punishing the English-speaking community for 'the unforgiveable sin of being British!'[31]

The monarchy itself occupied a somewhat ambiguous role in the anti-republican campaign, often invoked in very general terms as a symbolic link to the white nations of the Commonwealth. Republicanism, on the other hand, was associated with African authoritarianism and the worldwide spread of communism. As the 'anglicised' Afrikaner and leader of the United Party, Sir De Villiers Graaff asserted, 'there had been good and bad republics and monarchies, but there had never been a communist state under a monarchy nor a communist state that was not a republic', thereby implying that the monarchy formed an anti-communist bulwark.[32] It was claimed, furthermore, that a constitutional monarchy was not antithetic to 'true', post-imperial independence. The monarchy had already been transformed into a national institution, whereas republicanism was portrayed as 'a tremendous disruptive force'.[33] Those who felt the monarchy was 'too' British were impelled to think more about the 'values, the freedoms, the securities which the British political tradition' had successfully produced. These included parliamentary methods of government, the rule of law, a deeply ingrained respect for civil liberties, all values and ideals that the Verwoerd government allegedly regarded as 'a deplorable legacy of British colonialism'.[34] In speeches across the country, white English-speakers and loyal Afrikaners warned that the referendum jeopardised 150 years of historic ties and traditions that South Africans shared with other peoples of the British world.[35]

But the anti-republican campaign did in fact reveal a pronounced hesitancy in relation to the monarchy. On the one hand, the Crown was envisioned as a democratic safety valve and the symbol of distinctly 'British' values. Moreover, a supra-national monarchy was above and beyond sectional interests while a national presidency would almost inevitably cause greater dissension in a multi-ethnic polity such as South Africa.[36] On the other hand, the monarchy was also seen as a constitutional guarantee against the possibility of a black head of state. Republicanism was linked with black nationalism whose real 'creed' was communism.[37] The monarch, then, was both a globally recognised national figurehead for loyal, freedom-loving subjects across the British world and a bulwark against black incursions into racial privilege; in short, a symbol of the inviolable whiteness of South Africa. The anti-republican slogan, 'A Verwoerd Republic Means a Black Future for South Africa', neatly captured this sense that constitutional continuity provided a guarantee against white fears of civil rights abuse and the pervasive 'black peril', because it was simply not possible for apartheid republicanism, cut adrift from its wider racial affinities, to keep South Africa properly white.[38] Thus the republic was 'destructive' and ultimately presaged 'the end of white civilisation in the Union'.[39]

The Commonwealth bond was the key argument. It was the risk of relinquishing Commonwealth membership that allowed the anti-republican campaign to forge a united front, due to the requirement that South Africa would be forced to make a formal application for readmission to the Commonwealth if it became a republic. Thus, it would be left to South Africa's international critics to decide the country's membership and thereby determine its place in the wider world.[40] C. B. Downes, Mayor of Pietermaritzburg, thought that republican status and the possible loss of Commonwealth membership jettisoned 'the one anchorage we have in this storm-tossed world'.[41] Anti-republicans were wedded to a highly specific concept of the Commonwealth, one which emphasised kinship ties to the cohort of white members and paid very little heed to the new membership in Asia and Africa.[42] As a campaign advertisement stated: 'I shall vote anti-republican because I value our close association with the White nations of the Commonwealth'.[43] Republican status meant that South Africa would move from 'the inner circle of the original White Dominions' to 'the outer circle of the newer non-White member states', a common allusion to the loss of racial and kinship ties.[44] Thus, the anti-republican campaign was informed by the idea of British nations bound by a common whiteness. In addition, campaigners emphasised a broad range of potential negative consequences of the loss of Commonwealth membership. Economically, South Africa would lose the benefits of preferential trade with severe consequences for the export sector and a loss of income for ordinary whites.[45] Strategically, South Africa would find itself isolated internationally and become 'a fifth rate state'.[46] Politically, the referendum was sold as a choice between democracy or a ruthless authoritarian regime cut off from the rest of the world. On the final day of the referendum campaign a leader column in the *Natal Witness* predicted that republican status would simply 'cut us loose from our moorings, and set us adrift in a treacherous and uncharted sea, at the very time that the winds of change are blowing up to hurricane force'.[47]

The narrow victory for the republicans was a crushing experience for the white English-speaking community and the whole anti-republican movement. At a republican victory celebration at the Voortrekker Monument, Verwoerd announced that English- and Afrikaans-speaking South Africans had finally 'risen above pettiness and selfishness ...[and] become like the bride and the bridegroom who enter upon the new life in love to create together and to live together as life-mates'.[48] Here, the old ethnic interpretation of the history of the Afrikaner people became a selectively inclusive racist one – of two peoples merging into one. A leader column in the *Natal Witness* published a rebuttal, telling Verwoerd that English-speaking South Africa was not the willing bride of his desire. It was more like 'an ancient tribal marriage by capture, or like a sort of shotgun wedding in reverse'.[49] In the immediate aftermath, Natal and the Eastern Cape became prominent centres of heightened public attention, symbolising the refusal to consummate the new national marriage, embracing the role of the unfaithful wife. In the aftermath of the referendum, English-speaking whites in these provinces openly discussed the option of loyal secession against the imposition of an Afrikaner republic, thus retaining their stake in the 'British' world. Plans for a breakaway Dominion loyal to the monarchy flourished in the press and were given special prominence at spontaneous political rallies that attracted protesters in their thousands.[50]

Yet, the public agonising over the best way to adjust to the new republic also exacerbated internal tensions within English-speaking South Africa. Liberal and progressive opinion demanded a rededication to the principles, values and ideas of 'British' liberalism as a form of resistance to the NP government. To liberals, conservative anglophones were too concerned about 'the symbols of the British tradition and not about its substance'.[51] These ideological cleavages were further accentuated by regional differences. In some parts of the country, Natalian and Cape loyalists were attacked by the press, deriding their call for secession as 'senseless escapism' and a 'rush of blood to the head' that amounted to a wholesale desertion of fellow English-speakers in the rest of the country.[52]

The Natalian secession eventually failed to gain any form of support from Britain or Rhodesia but talk about a possible moral pathway out of the republic continued over the next decades.⁵³ South Africa's withdrawal from the Commonwealth in March 1961 added further to the tensions and dilemmas within the English-speaking community. Increasingly, the British press and British politicians dismissed Anglophone South Africans as aberrant Britons, complicit in sustaining racial discrimination in their country for their own selfish ends.⁵⁴ In the late 1960s, one British journalist described Anglophone South Africa as 'emotionally stateless' in the aftermath of the events in 1960/1. To him, English-speaking South Africans were no longer thoroughly British, but not quite South African either; they had become an 'orphaned people'.⁵⁵ Another writer noted how the English-speaking community had once been 'the inheritor of a vast Imperial world', but after 1961 they had become 'a restricted outcast'.⁵⁶ Unlike other white Dominions undergoing similar processes of disengagement from the British world, English-speaking South Africa was unable to formulate a new white nationalism for a postcolonial age. Some English-speakers, disillusioned by Britain's African policy and developments in the Commonwealth, defected in substantial numbers to the NP.⁵⁷ Yet, as we shall see, the demise of the neighbouring Central African Federation and white Rhodesia's failed struggle for independence from Britain did more to alienate groups of loyal English-speaking South Africans from any residual Greater British feeling.

'Vote Yes, Rhodesia First': the republican referendum in 1969

In November 1965, the Rhodesian Front (RF) issued a unilateral declaration of independence (UDI) in defiance of the London government's insistence on introducing majority rule in Rhodesia. Remarkably, Prime Minister Ian Smith's independence speech was steeped in the language of British loyalism. The open revolt was by no means a rebellion against the Queen of Rhodesia; it was described solely as an act of defiance against the authority of the British government. Having shown a deep sense of loyalty to the British Crown in two world wars, 'the people of Rhodesia' were determined to 'continue exercising our undoubted right to demonstrate the same loyalty and devotion' in the future. Nor did Rhodesians have any quarrel with the British people with whom they had 'the closest affinity'.⁵⁸ With moral standards crumbling across the decolonising world, Smith refused to hand over his country to the 'irresponsible rule' of African nationalists. Successive British governments had time and time again yielded to anti-colonial pressure, which had led to a familiar pattern across Asia and Africa: the ceremonial hauling down of the Union Jack by some 'unfortunate member of the Royal Family' followed by 'the installation of a totalitarian regime'.⁵⁹ Smith described the British policy of decolonisation as a 'philosophy of appeasement and surrender', which his government had resolved to resist by going it alone, thereby striking 'a blow for the preservation of justice, civilisation and Christianity'.[60] In the ensuing years, this myth of the RF's special loyalty to the Crown became increasingly difficult to maintain, and would eventually burst completely during the 1969 republican referendum.

Meanwhile, to the south of the Limpopo, South African whites overwhelmingly sympathised with rebel Rhodesia and backed Smith's independence bid.[61] In general, English-speaking South Africa played a prominent role in providing support for fellow whites in neighbouring Rhodesia. Across the country, Friends of Rhodesia associations proliferated, pledging assistance to 'beleaguered kinsmen' who constituted 'a gallant people in their struggle for freedom'.[62] At a meeting of the Transvaal branch, the Mayor of Pretoria, B. M. van Tonder, fashioned Smith as a modern reincarnation of republican Boer war heroes such as Paul Kruger and General Hertzog.[63] 'Buy Rhodesian' and 'Boycott Britain' campaigns were launched nationwide, in deliberate retaliation against the recent surge in anti-apartheid consumer boycotts and the imposition of economic sanctions against Rhodesia.

In Rhodesia, debates about monarchism and republicanism inevitably became a proxy for gauging popular feeling about UDI. The fact that the Queen was the head of state in both Britain and Rhodesia caused a great deal of confusion and ill-feeling. While the RF continued to profess its loyalty to the monarchy, both national and international press commentary frequently remarked upon how strained the ties really were. The pressures of UDI had a profound impact on the outlook of whites and their ethnic and cultural affiliations. Though Rhodesians had been singled out as among the most 'intensely loyal of British subjects' for years, sooner or later, the *Bulawayo Chronicle* lamented, ordinary Rhodesians would lose this urge to identify themselves with a mother country that had grown so hostile to them.[64] By January 1966, the *Sunday Telegraph* reported that white Rhodesians, who had initially couched their rebellion in the language of loyalism, were veering towards a 'healthier republicanism of the South African type'. While Rhodesians used to speak of their country as 'a nobler Britain in the bush', the British sanctions policy against the illegal regime was effecting a change of heart.[65] The constitutional anomalies of the rebellion itself were also starting to show. Having originally adopted the Queen as the moral crux of their cause (pitting the monarch against herself), the RF was increasingly finding her more of a liability than an asset. To preserve white domination, more and more white Rhodesians grudgingly acceded to shed the cloak of monarchism for a new republican garb. The *New York Times* concurred, arguing that there were 'unmistakeable signs' of a trend in Rhodesia towards a republic and an alignment not with Britain and the Commonwealth but with 'the camp of white-dominated southern Africa'. With each day the protracted struggle with Britain dragged on, 'a bit more sentimentality about "the home country"' was washed away.[66]

The letters pages of the major dailies confirmed press coverage of the new republican trends. With no resolution to the conflict in sight, the time had surely come to 'go the whole hog', in the words of one correspondent, and declare Rhodesia an independent republic.[67] The Queen was portrayed by letter writers invariably as 'the figurehead', 'the mouthpiece', and 'the puppet' of the British left-wing government against whom they had rebelled, making it quite impossible to be loyal to the Queen and consider oneself 'an independent Rhodesian' at the same time.[68] UDI was clearly transforming popular perceptions of the monarchy, from an object of loyalty to a foreign symbol of neo-colonialism and incomplete independence.

These new trends were largely fuelled by the British sanctions policy. Some writers argued that the Rhodesians had discovered a new sense of national purpose by defying British economic warfare. A local journalist described how many Rhodesians now believed that the British sanctions policy was designed to cripple loyal kinsfolk, which was widely perceived as a clear sign of the moral disintegration of 1960s Britain. By defying Britain's left-wing government, the white colonials of Rhodesia had finally 'found themselves'.[69] Desmond Lardner-Burke also stressed the role of sanctions as a unifying element in white Rhodesian nation-building. As Minister of Justice and Law and Order he was responsible for the detention without trial of African nationalists and other political opponents. He saw Rhodesia's struggle for independence as a continuation of the Second World War, only this time the United Kingdom was Germany and Rhodesia had adopted the mantle of plucky Britain, standing alone against foreign tyranny. Once again, a small nation of 'Churchillians' defied a great enemy, fired by the Dunkirk spirit. Lardner-Burke was certain that Rhodesians would suffer as a result of the British sanctions, but it was through suffering that the people would emerge as 'a great Rhodesian nation'.[70]

Yet the republican currents never managed to fully supplant loyalty to the monarchy and support for the Queen. The Queen's official representative in the Rhodesian capital of Salisbury, Sir Humphrey Gibbs, quickly became a focal point for those white loyalists who opposed UDI and for those who genuinely cherished their sense of Britishness and belonging to Greater Britain.[71] Governor Gibbs received a steady stream of letters from private citizens who felt disillusioned and marginalised after UDI, lamenting that true loyalists were 'now voiceless, over-ruled and out-numbered'.[72] These bewildered British subjects urged Gibbs to 'defend our great British heritage and ideals', especially the symbolic ties to the monarchy, and to continue his work for lawful negotiations between Britain and Rhodesia.[73] In the letters pages of the local press, loyal whites could evade RF censorship by describing how the Queen was still the visible symbol of the British connection and embodied global white solidarities.[74] The former Prime Minister Lord Malvern claimed that Rhodesia would gain nothing from 'going the same way as the African states' because the country was virtually a republic already.[75] Echoing the arguments of South African loyalists only a few years earlier, republican status would mark a definitive departure from Britain and the white Commonwealth, leaving Rhodesia at the mercy of Black Africa as 'an even greater outcast'.[76]

Though the RF had continued to profess its loyalty to the Queen after UDI, this state of affairs slowly began to change. The first cabinet minister to signal a change of heart was the Minister of Internal Affairs, William Harper, who, in 1966, suggested that a complete break with Britain and the monarchy would confirm Rhodesia's unwavering determination to stand up for its right to independence on their own terms.[77] In that year, the Queen gave a speech at the opening of the Jamaican parliament which expressed a desire to see majority rule in Rhodesia, triggering a torrent of abuse from disaffected whites.[78] In a broadcast to the nation, Smith blamed the British government for trying to provoke his country into breaking the links to the monarchy.[79] If loyalty to the Queen was 'as natural to the people of this country as it is natural to breathe', the 1966 Queen's speech seemed to confirm suspicion that she was being used as 'a political weapon' against them. Consequently 'the whispers of republic' grew louder.[80] From 1967 the RF dropped the oath of loyalty to the Queen from its party constitution, which marked the party's transition from self-styled champions of empire loyalism to pioneers of a new nationalism.[81]

The so-called Hangings Case in March 1968 was the decisive tipping point. Acting on advice, the Queen had commuted the death sentences of several Africans convicted of murder. The royal reprieve was designed to embarrass the regime and place the RF government in an invidious position; if the Smith regime went ahead with the hangings, it would be an illegal act, and the RF government could no longer uphold the pretence of governing in the Queen's name.[82] However, the Queen's attempt to prevent the executions was overruled by the Rhodesian courts and the executions of three Africans, Victor Mlambo, James Dhlamini and Duly Shadrack, went ahead. An international outcry broke out; in London, Harold Wilson proclaimed that Smith and his rebel regime was 'essentially evil'.[83] In a national broadcast, Smith denounced the British government's 'cynicism' in dragging the Queen into the dispute. Any doubts in his mind about the republican issue had been 'wiped out completely by the antics of Harold Wilson and his Socialist Government'.[84] From that point onwards, he began to argue openly for the idea of Rhodesia as a republican nation, abandoning the language of loyalism as a legitimating prism. Concurrently, British officials hoped that Rhodesians would abandon their aspiration of remaining part of the Queen's Dominions after a possible independence settlement. When Smith announced his intention to hold a referendum on the issue of a republic in 1969, British officials were privately relieved, though this was kept secret to avoid further embarrassment to the Queen.[85]

While the RF had crossed the Rubicon, it is more difficult to gauge the development of popular opinion. The Whaley Constitutional Commission, which had been set up to produce a new constitution for Rhodesia, reported in 1968 that many of its witnesses actually favoured a republican constitution, though many held opposing views. As the report concluded, the Queen provided 'a focal point for loyalty which transcends party political loyalties and a link between English-speaking people throughout the world'.[86] A 1968 poll from the popular weekly newspaper, *Sunday Mail*, based on more than two thousand samples, provides another glimpse of popular opinion on the issue of a republic, indicating a majority in favour. Fuelled by emotions of unrequited loyalty, the proponents of a republic felt disowned by Britain and the British Crown, obliged to watch passively as their image of the monarchy was transformed from an object of reverence to a symbol of 'sentimental rubbish' and a tool of 'discredited, devalued and dishonest Britain'.[87] The real issue, of course, was white minority rule which prevented Rhodesia from receiving the royal acknowledgement that it so desperately craved. Loyalist and moderate opinion, on the other hand, saw support for the republic as a dreadful sign that Rhodesians adhered to the 'undesirable ideas of South Africa'. The support for the monarchy thus also entailed a defence of British-derived constitutional ideals and traditions in the face of South Africa's growing regional and ideological influence. 'We have always been a very "English" colony', one remarked, 'I should hate to break the tie'. Loyalty and affection to the Queen was still visible among those for whom the tie to the monarchy symbolised a thousand years of 'unbroken continuity' and the fundamental principle on which the nature of global British identities was based.[88]

In April 1969, on a visit to Durban, Smith announced his intention to hold a referendum on the republican question in a press interview. Since UDI, he remarked, Rhodesia had de facto been a republic, and the situation now was broadly similar to South Africa's in 1960. Rhodesians claim to loyalty had been 'repudiated'; the Queen no longer acknowledged Rhodesians as her loyal subjects.[89] On 20 May, Smith finally tabled the specific terms of the referendum. He claimed that Britain was obsessed with the idea of black majority rule, but his government would never 'surrender independence'. The Crown had been abused by the left-wing government in London, denying his country's claim to loyalty in the process. Under these circumstances, there was no other option than to accept a republican form of government and a future outside the Commonwealth, like South Africa. The choice had effectively been taken out of his hands, he concluded. In this context, the republic was an assertion of postcolonial sovereignty – only here, sovereignty remained in the hands of the white minority. The republic, Smith promised, would be the last of 'our growing pains on our journey towards full nationhood'.[90]

The RF campaign was remarkably devoid of direct references to monarchy and republicanism. The official slogan, 'Vote Yes! Rhodesia First!', ramped up the significance of the white Rhodesian nation as the prime object of loyalty. Like Verwoerd, Smith made a personal appeal to the electorate in his 'letter to the Rhodesian voter', arguing that whites faced an existential threat as an endangered minority. But the republic would ensure 'the continued presence of the White man and his civilisation in Rhodesia in perpetuity'.[91] 'The whole crux of the issue', Smith emphasised, was whether whites were prepared to hand over power to the black population.[92] The English-born Minister of Internal Affairs, Lance Smith, warned Rhodesians not to look to 'the great White Queen over the water' for future protection, amid constant reminders that black majority rule meant 'irresponsible government' and 'chaos and anarchy'.[93] As one republican advertisement put it: 'Need we remind you of events in the Congo, Nigeria, Ghana, Zanzibar – of the proposed land-grab in Zambia?'[94] The RF campaign dwelt at length on the suffering whites had allegedly experienced in postcolonial Africa, taking voters back to 'the horrors of the Congo' and striking fear into whites with 'grisly reminders of how women, including nuns, were raped, not once but several times'. What had occurred in the 'countries to the north' could so easily happen in Rhodesia. This was the defining template of the entire republican campaign: 'Vote Yes for Rhodesia or perish'.[95]

The opponents of the republic consisted of small political parties, the black parliamentary opposition, university students, church leaders, and business leaders anxious to re-establish legitimate trade relations with the outside world.[96] Throughout the campaign, the old political establishment came out in full support of the monarchy, including three former prime ministers, two of whom issued a joint statement which denounced the republic as 'a complete break with our past'.[97] The proposed constitution would cast the country adrift in unchartered constitutional seas and open the door for apartheid and totalitarianism. The Governor, Sir Humphry Gibbs, released a statement announcing that a republican constitution closed the door to further negotiation with Britain and pushed the country into 'even greater isolation'.[98]

Leaders of the avowedly royalist, relatively liberal Centre Party mounted what resistance they could. Cut off from the monarchy and their 'British heritage', they cautioned, Rhodesia would sink into oblivion as an 'unwanted vassal province of South Africa'. Anyone who thought they could build a republican state on racial segregation, suggested Pat Bashford, was 'as mad as Hitler'.[99] Those kinds of regimes, he underlined, always came to a violent and tragic end. The self-defeating push for a republic would not bring about international recognition of the rebel state, but only succeed in galvanising anti-colonial opposition. A 'Yes' vote to the republic would also bring Rhodesia one step closer to becoming a sixth province of South Africa, while 'the British character' of the country would be 'completely and utterly destroyed'.[100] Other anti-republicans stressed the damaging impact a republic would have on domestic race relations. The former chief justice, Robert Tredgold, predicted the constitutional changes would ultimately bring widespread suffering and set the country on a dangerous path towards violent forms of confrontation which would destroy 'the foundations of civilisation', possibly culminating in a white 'holocaust'.[101] Meanwhile, moderate Africans such as Percy M'kudu and Charles Mzingeli saw the republic as a move towards apartheid which would reduce Africans to outcasts.[102]

The referendum on 20 June 1969 was a resounding success for the RF, with 81.4 per cent endorsing a republic and electing to scrap the monarchy. A 'Yes' majority was returned in all constituencies, but the lowest majorities were to be found in areas with non-white residents and affluent white urban areas.[103] On 2 March 1970, Rhodesia duly became a republican state. In his first presidential address, English-born Clifford Dupont said that the final break with the Crown had not been sought by Rhodesia, and he encouraged Rhodesians to remember that many of their traditions were based on those 'of the old Britain that we had known'. Strikingly, Dupont's speech sounded more like a self-pitying lament for a vanished age than a clarion call for new republican nationalism.[104]

Among defeated and disgruntled loyalists, the new republic seemed a pathetic cause. There were no signs of any genuine popular sentiment behind Smith's new white nationalism, only a pervasive sense of loss and despair. Loyalist reactions were characterised by a mix of disorientation and disbelief. With their sense of attachment to the monarchy thwarted by the majority, a new symbolic void had opened up by the 'severing of the last links with Great Britain' and 'our proud heritage', in the words of one despairing letter to the outgoing Governor Gibbs.[105] Rhodesia had 'reached the end of an era', wrote another, the work of his generation 'ridiculed' by republican rebels. The referendum, some argued, had revealed a generational gap between the old empire loyalists and the new nationalists.[106] With ties to 'the Old Country' broken for good, they would be forced into a closer association with South Africa as a client-state, a fate that appealed to no one.[107] Cut loose from the monarchy, the only 'mother-civilisation' of the future would be South Africa, a country that had already trekked far from its British heritage since the 1960 referendum.[108]

In parliament, debating the result of the referendum, former RF minister Angus Graham (a hereditary peer in the House of Lords) summed up the dynamics that had fuelled a new republican nationalism. In the age of empire, the Crown and the Union Jack had 'stood for something in the world'. With the advent of decolonisation, however, the world had changed profoundly. In this new post-imperial age, Graham argued, 'the old loyalties' had to be put aside in the national interests of Rhodesia. W. M. Irvine, MP for the RF, added that Rhodesia had never actually meant to be 'disloyal' to the Queen. 'We are not leaving her', he remarked, 'She is leaving us'.[109] Such rhetoric merely echoed the widespread myth that Rhodesians had been abandoned by their own, their sense of loyalty, identity and history no longer reciprocated. While the RF adopted the posture and language of a robust 'new' nationalism for a post-imperial future, it could barely conceal a sense of disorientation and a feeling of being cut adrift in an unfamiliar world.

Conclusion

In the 1960s multiple communities of British descendants began to rethink their relationship with Britain and the British Crown. The two republican referendums in South Africa and Rhodesia were part of this deeply unsettling process, marking critical moments in the global history of the break-up of Greater Britain. During the 1960 referendum campaign the majority of white English-speaking South Africans supported the monarchy. In focusing on the importance of the British connection, anti-republican parties emphasised their history, their spiritual and their emotional bonds with the mother country as much as the economic importance of trade preferences and the geostrategic relevance of the link. The protective wings of the British Crown shielded not only against Afrikaner republicanism, but equally against black domination and the spread of communism. The removal of the link to the monarchy thus erased a powerful symbol of community, continuity and common purpose that could not easily be replaced.

In 1969, by contrast, many English-speaking Rhodesian whites had become persuaded to support the idea of a republic. The overwhelming opposition to the retention of the monarchy revealed how much white Rhodesians' understandings had changed since UDI. The RF had gone from thinking squarely in terms of imperial loyalism to embarking on a new nation-building effort under a republican form of government. Yet the transition from a community of rebel loyalists to a nation of republicans was half-hearted. The search for new symbols was not the expression of any resolute sense of post-imperial selfhood. Rather, the scramble for new symbols was embarked upon 'to fill a void in our national life'.[110] The RF mimicked the rhetoric of decolonisation and national self-determination that circulated widely throughout the post-war world. But they also left the structures of settler colonialism and racial hierarchies firmly in place.

By 1970, South Africa and Rhodesia had forged 'white' republics based on a racialised form of nationalism. For both Verwoerd and Smith, these new departures set their countries on a path to complete postcolonial independence, the change of constitution furnishing an emotionally cleansing liberation from British colonial strictures, even as the oppressive structures of racialised colonialism remained deeply entrenched. For the Queen, the scrapping of the monarchy meant that she largely avoided becoming further tarnished by the politics of race, discrimination and state violence in white-ruled southern Africa. The discriminatory laws of apartheid and segregation had been passed in her name. The Queen had been head of state in territories governed by white nationalist oligarchies run rampant. Here too, Greater Britain had become a moral burden, one that was ultimately relinquished with only a minimum of moral compunction.

Notes

1 L. Colley, *Britons: Forging the Nation, 1707–1837* (New Haven: Yale University Press, 1992), pp. 6–7, 193; J. MacKenzie, *Propaganda and Empire: The Manipulation of Public Opinion, 1880–1960* (Manchester: Manchester University Press, 1984), pp. 2, 7, 11. See also A. Olechnowicz, 'Historians and the British Monarchy', in A. Olechnowicz (ed.), *The Monarchy and the British Nation, 1870 to the Present* (New York: Cambridge University Press, 2007).
2 D. Bell, *Reordering the World: Essays on Liberalism and Empire* (Princeton: Princeton University Press, 2016), p. 151.
3 M. McKenna, 'Monarchy: From Reverence to Indifference', in D. Schreuder and S. Ward (eds), *Australia's Empire* (Oxford: Oxford University Press, 2008), p. 262.
4 Exceptions include D. Kenrick, *Decolonisation, Identity and Nation in Rhodesia, 1964–1979* (Basingstoke: Palgrave, 2019); D. Kenrick, 'Settler Soul-Searching and Sovereign Independence: The Monarchy in Rhodesia, 1965–1970', *Journal of Southern African Studies*, 44:6 (2018), pp. 1077–1093; H. Kumarasingham, 'A New Monarchy for a New Commonwealth? Monarchy and the Consequences of Republican India', in R. Aldrich and C. McCreery (eds), *Crowns and Colonies: European Monarchies and Overseas Empires* (Manchester: Manchester University Press, 2016), pp. 283–308; and P. Murphy, *Monarchy and the End of Empire: The House of Windsor, the British Government, and the Postwar Commonwealth* (Oxford: Oxford University Press, 2013). For works on republicanism see D. Lowry, '"These Colonies are Practically Democratic Republics": Republicanism and the British Colonies of Settlement in the

Long Nineteenth Century', in D. Nash and A. Taylor (eds), *Republicanism in Victorian Society* (Stroud, Gloucestershire: Sutton, 2000), pp. 125–139; H. Sapire and A. Grundlingh, 'Rebuffing Royals? Afrikaners and the Royal Visit to South Africa in 1947', *Journal of Imperial and Commonwealth History*, 46:3 (2018), pp. 524–551; M. McKenna, *The Captive Republic: A History of Republicanism in Australia 1788–1996* (Cambridge: Cambridge University Press, 1996); and D. E. Smith, *The Republican Option in Canada, Past and Present* (Toronto: University of Toronto Press, 1999).

5 J. Lambert, '"Welcome Home": White English-Speaking South Africans and the Royal Visit of 1947', *South African Historical Journal*, 69:1 (2017), pp. 101–120, at p. 120; S. Dubow, 'How British was the British World? The Case of South Africa', *Journal of Imperial and Commonwealth History*, 37:1 (2009), pp. 1–27, at p. 16; Kenrick, *Decolonisation*, p. 142; D. Lowry, 'The Queen of Rhodesia Versus the Queen of the United Kingdom: Conflicts of Allegiance in Rhodesia's Unilateral Declaration of Independence', in H. Kumarasingham (ed.), *Viceregalism: The Crown as Head of State in Political Crises in the Postwar Commonwealth* (Basingstoke: Palgrave, 2020).

6 P. Buckner, 'The Long Goodbye: English Canadians and the British World', in P. Buckner and R. Douglas Francis (eds), *Rediscovering the British World* (Calgary: University of Calgary Press, 2005), p. 202; L. Silver, 'A Long Goodbye: Pearson and Britain', in A. McKercher and G. R. Perras (eds), *Mike's World: Lester B. Pearson and Canadian External Affairs* (Vancouver and Toronto: UBC Press, 2017), pp. 217, 223.

7 McKenna, 'Monarchy', pp. 279–281 and *Captive Republic*, pp. 219–226.

8 Cited in S. Ward, *Australia and the British Embrace* (Melbourne: Melbourne University Press, 2001), pp. 142–143.

9 Quote from C. MacInnes, 'Our Own Kings', in J. Murray-Brown (ed.), *The Monarchy and its Future* (London: Allen and Unwin, 1969), p. 143. See also A. Taylor, *'Down with the Crown': British Anti-Monarchism in Debates about Royalty since 1790* (London: Reaktion Books, 1999), p. 231; B. Pimlott, *The Queen: A Biography of Elizabeth II* (London: HarperCollins, 1996), pp. 369–370. From the point of view of British officialdom, see Murphy, *Monarchy and the End of Empire*.

10 'The Queen in Ulster!', *British Movietone*, 7 July 1966, via AP Archive, www.aparchive.com/metadata/youtube/d4db0bd3bed4497dba2ac15803f68398 (accessed 15 September 2020). J. Loughlin, *The British Monarchy and Ireland: 1800 to the Present* (Cambridge: Cambridge University Press, 2007), pp. 356–385. See also Chapter 7, in this volume, by Donal Lowry for more on the perceptions of the Crown in Ulster.

11 Murphy, *Monarchy and the End of Empire*, p. 89.

12 T. Jones, *Ghana's First Republic 1960–1966* (London: Methuen & Co, 1976), p. 26; D. Rooney, *Kwame Nkrumah: The Political Kingdom in the Third World* (London: I.B. Tauris, 1988), pp. 142, 171. In the Gambia the first referendum to make the country a republic failed to get the required two-thirds support of the electorate due to the low turnout in 1965. The second Gambian referendum in 1970 eventually resulted in an overwhelming 70 per cent majority in favour of

becoming a republic. See A. Hughes and D. Perfect, *A Political History of the Gambia, 1816–1994* (Rochester: University of Rochester Press, 2006), p. 346.
13 Murphy, *Monarchy and the End of Empire*, p. 89.
14 A. G. Hopkins, 'Rethinking Decolonization', *Past and Present*, 200:1 (2008), pp. 211–247, at p. 236; J. Lambert, '"An Unknown People": Reconstructing British South African Identity', *Journal of Imperial and Commonwealth History*, 37:4 (2009), pp. 599–617, at p. 609; S. Ward, 'The "New" Nationalism in Australia, Canada and New Zealand: Civic Culture in the Wake of the British World', in K. Darian-Smith, P. Grimshaw and S. Macintyre (eds), *Britishness Abroad: Transnational Movements and Imperial Culture* (Melbourne: Melbourne University Press, 2007), pp. 236–237.
15 The republicans won with a majority of 76,580 votes. While the Orange Free State had been overwhelmingly in favour of the republic (76 per cent for), the majority against a republic was greatest in Natal (76 per cent against). All the big cities (Cape Town, Johannesburg, Durban, Port Elizabeth) except Pretoria were against a republic. See K. Heard, *General Elections in South Africa 1943–1970* (London: Oxford University Press, 1974), Table 50, p. 113.
16 Lambert, 'Welcome Home', p. 118.
17 E. S. Munger, *Afrikaner and African Nationalism* (London: Oxford University Press, 1967), p. 4.
18 S. Dubow, *Apartheid 1948–1994* (Oxford: Oxford University Press, 2014), p. 29.
19 'Message to the People of South Africa, 3 Sept. 1958', in A. N. Pelzer (ed.), *Verwoerd Speaks: Speeches 1948–1966* (Johannesburg: APB, 1966), p. 162. For Verwoerd's transformation, see H. Giliomee, *The Last Afrikaner Leaders: A Supreme Test of Power* (Cape Town: Tafelberg, 2012), p. 75.
20 'Speech of Thanks Addressed to Mr Harold Macmillan, Prime Minister of the United Kingdom, 3 Feb. 1960', in Pelzer (ed.), *Verwoerd Speaks*, pp. 336–339. For more on Verwoerd's speech, see S. Dubow, 'Macmillan, Verwoerd, and the 1960 "Wind of Change" Speech', *Historical Journal*, 54:4 (2011), pp. 1087–1114, at p. 1101.
21 'Speech at Meyerton, 26 Mar. 1960', in Pelzer (ed.), *Verwoerd Speaks*, pp. 374–387; *Natal Mercury*, 28 March 1960; *Cape Times*, 9 September 1960.
22 *Cape Times*, 1 September 1960.
23 For nationalist posters see *Cape Times*, 9 September 1960; and Dubow, *Apartheid*, p. 85.
24 Verwoerd's 'Dear Friend' letter can be found in Archives for Contemporary Affairs (ACA), University of the Free State, Bloemfontein, The Papers of Hendrik Verwoerd, PV93, 1/45/3/4, September 1960.
25 *Cape Times*, 10 September 1960.
26 University of South Africa Library (UNISA), Pretoria, United Party Archive (UP) 133/2: see especially, *Sunday Times*, 29 September 1960, *Cape Argus*, 21 September 1960, and *Cape Times*, 28 September 1960.
27 UNISA, UP 133/2: *Sunday Times* (Johannesburg), 29 September 1960.
28 Heard, *General Elections*, p. 101.
29 UNISA, UP 133/1, memorandum on referendum campaign, undated.

30 UNISA, UP 136: *Eastern Province Herald*, 27 September 1960; and UP, Natal File 68/1: Pamphlet, August 1960. *Rand Daily Mail*, 1 October 1960.
31 *Natal Mercury*, 7 March 1960, editorial.
32 *Cape Times*, 23 September 1960.
33 J. P. Duminy, open letter to Verwoerd, *Cape Times*, 30 September 1960.
34 Quote from *Natal Witness*, 5 August 1960. See also *Cape Times*, 6 September 1960.
35 UNISA, The Papers of Sir De Villiers Graaff (Graaff Papers) 111.3: East London speech, 1 September 1960.
36 *Natal Witness*, 13 February 1960.
37 United Party, *The Case against Republicanism* (Johannesburg: UP Division of Information, 1960), p. 14.
38 UNISA, UP, Natal file 68/1: United Party referendum poster, undated; *Natal Witness*, 4 and 6 October 1960.
39 United Party, *The Case against Republicanism*, p. 13.
40 *Natal Witness*, 8 July 1960; R. Hyam and P. Henshaw, *The Lion and the Springbok: Britain and South Africa since the Boer War* (Cambridge: Cambridge University Press, 2003), p. 264.
41 *Natal Mercury*, 1 October 1960.
42 UNISA, Graaff Papers 111.3: Durban speech 18 August 1960; *Cape Times*, 23 September 1960.
43 Anti-republican advertisements in *Rand Daily Mail*, 4 October 1960; *Cape Times*, 3 October 1960 and *Natal Mercury*, 5 October 1960.
44 *Rand Daily Mail*, 3 October 1960; ACA, Leo Boyd Papers, PV601: Leo Boyd, 'There is no justification for a South African republic in 1961', 7 April 1960.
45 UNISA, Graaff Papers 111.3: Durban speech 16 August 1960; UP 133/1: *Sunday Times*, 11 September 1960; UP 133/2: *Rand Daily Mail*, 21 September 1960 and *Sunday Times*, 18 September 1960; UP 136: *Eastern Province Herald*, 27 September 1960; UP, Natal File 68/1: 'Propaganda Committee', September 1960.
46 UNISA, Graaff Papers 111.3: Klerksdorp speech, 1 October 1960.
47 Front page editorial, *Natal Witness*, 5 October 1960.
48 'Address on the Occasion of the Republican Thanksgiving Festival', in Pelzer (ed.), *Verwoerd Speaks*, p. 427.
49 *Natal Witness*, 19 October 1960.
50 *Natal Mercury* and *Cape Times*, 10 October 1960; *Natal Witness*, 11 October 1960; P. S. Thompson, *Natalians First: Separatism in South Africa, 1909–1961* (Johannesburg: Southern Book Publishers, 1990), pp. 163–166; J. Lambert, '"The Last Outpost": The Natalians, South Africa, and the British Empire', in R. Bickers (ed.), *Settlers and Expatriates* (Oxford: Oxford University Press, 2010), pp. 173–176.
51 *Natal Witness*, 2 November 1960.
52 *Rand Daily Mail*, 10 October 1960; *Cape Times*, 2 February 1961.
53 UK National Archives (UKNA), Kew, DO 161/107: Sir J. Maud, Pretoria, to Sir A. Clutterbuck, CRO, 14 October 1960. See also T. Wilks, *Douglas Mitchell* (Durban: Kings & Wilks, 1980), p. 136.

54 *Cape Times*, 8 June 1961; *Guardian*, 30 June 1961; Hyam and Henshaw, *The Lion and the Springbok*, p. 320.
55 D. Brown, *Against the World: Attitudes of White South Africa* (London: Collins, 1966), pp. 97, 113.
56 F. G. Butler, 'The Nature and Purpose of the Conference', in A. De Villiers (ed.), *English-Speaking South Africa Today* (Cape Town: Oxford University Press, 1976), pp. 12, 14.
57 Heard, *General Elections*, pp. 142–143.
58 *Rhodesia's Finest Hour: The Prime Minister of Rhodesia Addresses the Nation* (Salisbury: Government Printer, 1965). For more on UDI, see B. Schwarz, *The White Man's World* (Oxford: Oxford University Press, 2011), Ch. 7; L. White, *Unpopular Sovereignty: Rhodesian Independence and African Decolonization* (Chicago: University of Chicago Press, 2015), Ch. 4; Kenrick, *Decolonisation*, Ch. 3; Lowry, 'Queen of Rhodesia'.
59 *Bulawayo Chronicle*, 25 January 1966, originally in *Punch*.
60 'Proclamation' in *Rhodesia's Finest Hour*.
61 UKNA, FO 371/187966: H. Stephenson, Pretoria, to Foreign Office, telegram no. 3, 6 January 1966; *Cape Times*, 11 October 1965; *Sunday Times*, 6 February 1966.
62 Quotes from *Rhodesia Herald*, 23 November 1965 and 2 December 1965.
63 *Cape Argus*, 3 February 1966.
64 *Bulawayo Chronicle*, 17 November 1965, editorial.
65 *Sunday Telegraph*, 23 January 1966.
66 *New York Times*, 25 September 1966.
67 Letter to the editor, *Rhodesia Herald*, 25 November 1965.
68 Letters to the editor, *Rhodesia Herald*, 25 November 1965, 17 March 1966 and 26 April 1966, *Bulawayo Chronicle*, 10 February 1966.
69 P. Berlyn, *Rhodesia: Beleaguered Country* (London: Mitre Press, 1967), pp. 74, 97.
70 D. Lardner-Burke, *Rhodesia: The Story of a Crisis* (London: Oldbourne, 1966), pp. 65–66.
71 A. Megahey, *Humphrey Gibbs, Beleaguered Governor: Southern Rhodesia, 1929–69* (Basingstoke: Macmillan, 1998), p. 154.
72 Peterhouse School Archive (PSA), Marondera, Zimbabwe, The Papers of Sir Humphrey Gibbs (Gibbs Papers), Mrs S. Hill to Gibbs, 13 November 1965.
73 PSA, Gibbs Papers, J. de Marie to Gibbs, 14 November 1965.
74 Letters to the editor, *Bulawayo Chronicle*, 21 February 1966.
75 *Sunday Tribune* (Durban), 6 February 1966.
76 Ahrn Palley, cited in *Daily Mail*, 7 February 1966.
77 *Cape Times*, 22 February 1966; *Rhodesia Herald*, 1 March 1966.
78 *The Times*, 5 March 1966. Letters to the editor, *Sunday Mail* (Salisbury), 17 March 1966, *Rhodesia Herald*, 17 March and 26 April 1966.
79 Cory Library, Grahamstown, South Africa, Ian Smith Papers, 2/006(A), 'Speech by the Prime Minister, the Hon I. D. Smith', 27 March 1966.
80 Berlyn, *Rhodesia*, pp. 71, 74.
81 Kenrick, *Decolonisation*, p. 140.

82 *Evening News*, 6 March 1968; M. Facchini, 'The "Evil Genius": Sir Hugh Beadle and the Rhodesian Crisis, 1965–1972', *Journal of Southern African Studies*, 33:3 (2007), pp. 673–689, at pp. 684–685.
83 *Sunday Times*, 8 March 1968.
84 *Rhodesia Herald*, 25 March 1968.
85 Murphy, *Monarchy and the End of Empire*, p. 104.
86 *Report of the Constitutional Commission 1968* (Salisbury: Government Printer, 1968), p. 119.
87 See sample of letters submitted to the *Sunday Mail*, 10 March 1968.
88 Ibid.
89 *Rhodesia Herald*, 4 April 1969.
90 Ibid., 21 May 1969.
91 Ibid., 18 June 1969.
92 Ibid., 20 June 1969.
93 Ibid., 3 June 1969. *Daily Mail*, 31 May 1969.
94 RF advertisement, 'Think!', in *Rhodesia Herald*, 4 June 1969.
95 Quotes from Jack Howman's final broadcast, *Rhodesia Herald*, 17 June 1969.
96 P. Joyce, *Anatomy of a Rebel. Smith of Rhodesia* (Salisbury: Graham Publishing, 1974), pp. 412–420. J. R. T. Wood, *A Matter of Weeks rather than Months. The Impasse between Harold Wilson and Ian Smith: Sanctions, Aborted Settlements and War 1965–1969* (Bloomington: Trafford, 2012), pp. 661–669.
97 Lord Malvern and Sir Roy Welensky, quoted in *Rhodesia Herald*, 13 June 1969.
98 *Rhodesia Herald*, 12 June 1969; Megahey, *Humphrey Gibbs*, p. 167.
99 *Rhodesia Herald*, 30 May and 7 June 1969.
100 Letter to the editor, *Rhodesia Herald*, 12 June 1969.
101 Letter to the editor, *Rhodesia Herald*, 18 June 1969.
102 *Rhodesia Herald*, 19 May 1969.
103 *Rhodesia Herald*, 21 June 1969. Rhodesians voted for the adoption of a republican form of government as follows: 61,130 *for*, 14,372 *against*. The electorate (registered on separate A and B rolls) was made up of 81,572 Europeans (whites), 6,645 Africans, 1,317 Coloureds, and 1,170 Asians. Some 84.5 per cent of those registered cast their votes.
104 C. Dupont, *The Reluctant President* (Bulawayo: Books of Rhodesia, 1978), p. 214.
105 PSA, Gibbs Papers, Mrs Robertson to Gibbs, 25 June 1969.
106 *Rhodesia Herald*, 26 June 1969.
107 PSA, Gibbs Papers, 'Eric' to Gibbs, 22 June 1969.
108 *Rhodesia Herald*, 26 June 1969, editorial.
109 *Rhodesia Herald*, 28 June 1969.
110 *Rhodesia Herald*, 24 August 1974, quoted in P. Godwin and I. Hancock, *Rhodesians Never Die: The Impact of War on White Rhodesia, c. 1970–1980* (Northlands: Pan Macmillan SA, 1993), p. 145.

7

'King's men', 'Queen's rebels' and 'last outposts': Ulster and Rhodesia in an age of imperial retreat

Donal Lowry

In August 1966, against a background of growing civil unrest in Northern Ireland, Captain Terence O'Neill, its Prime Minister, joined his British counterpart, Harold Wilson, and the Home Secretary, Roy Jenkins, for a convivial lunch in Downing Street, after which they settled down for a discussion. 'I suppose', said Wilson, 'Northern Ireland is rather like Rhodesia'. 'Maybe it is', O'Neill replied, with a reference to a recently ousted reformist prime minister, 'but I do not intend to be the Garfield Todd of Northern Ireland'. O'Neill was personally familiar with Rhodesia, having visited it as a member of the Commonwealth Parliamentary Association, and he was a close friend of both the Rhodesian Governor, Sir Humphrey Gibbs, and his wife, Molly, who were then embroiled in a crisis over his government's Unilateral Declaration of Independence (UDI) from Britain on 11 November 1965.[1]

On the face of it, there seems to be little in common between Northern Ireland, an integral part of the United Kingdom itself and situated within the Crown's realms for centuries, and Rhodesia, a colony more than 6,000 miles distant, which had only become a British territory just over sixty years earlier. Yet, as we shall see, Wilson and O'Neill were by no means alone in drawing parallels between these two possessions, both of which were vociferously proud of their loyalty to the Crown and of their historic roles in imperial expansion. Both entities were granted internal self-government at almost the same time in the early 1920s. Indeed, on various occasions over the past century, 'mainstream' Rhodesian, British and Ulster observers, including politicians and academics, would refer to this analogy with comparative ease.[2]

These analogies have been too readily dismissed as emerging merely 'from more extreme Loyalist currents' and from marginal politicians. They have also been attributed to polemically minded writers who have presented such parallels as objective analyses, which could be easily challenged and falsified by scholarly scrutiny.[3] It should be made clear, however, that this essay is *not* concerned with asserting that these comparisons *prove* that Northern Ireland has *objectively* been a 'colonial' territory like Rhodesia. Rather, it is an attempt to explain *why*, and in what circumstances, such diverse observers have drawn such analogies. The experience of the two territories being so different, almost inevitably, many of these observations were superficial. Nevertheless, it would be surely difficult to categorise as marginal or 'extreme' the opinions of such sundry figures as King George V, Winston Churchill, Harold Wilson, three Ulster prime ministers (Sir James Craig, Captain Terence O'Neill and Brian Faulkner); three Rhodesian prime ministers (Sir Charles Coghlan, Sir Roy Welensky and Sir Edgar Whitehead); the first female parliamentarian in the British Empire overseas (Mrs Ethel Tawse Jollie); an American ambassador (Robert C. Good); the Kenyan writer, Elspeth Huxley, and the editors of the *New Statesman* and *Irish Times*, as well as numerous other politicians and observers. These impressions were clearly *subjective* and are not to be confused with, or considered as being on a par with, scholarly critiques but, equally, they are not insignificant comments. Moreover, these perspectives were more widely shared than has often been acknowledged and, as such, deserve examination as a substantial strand of contemporary political sentiment in the context of decolonisation. Historians should surely deal with the opinions of historical figures and not simply elide these dismissively with the assertions of polemicists. As Richard Toye has wisely argued, 'rhetorical analysis is a valuable but neglected tool for Irish and imperial historians'.[4] The subjective opinions of participants should not, therefore, be readily discounted, since such sentiments informed their views and, sometimes, actions as well. Thus, these form part of the *objective* body of historical material to be considered. There is surely something significant – particularly in analyses of the Right – in Enoch Powell's assertion that 'the life of nations, no less than that of men, is lived largely in the imagination'.[5]

Moreover, it has also been asserted that among British settler communities in North America, Australasia and southern Africa, the white settlers did not display the kind of linkage between 'constitutionalism' and national identity manifested in Ulster unionism.[6] On the contrary, issues of constitutional rights, rooted not least in the application of the Durham Formula for self-government, as well as the importance of the Crown, have been at the heart of debates about nationhood in those countries, including, it will be argued, Rhodesia.[7]

'King's men': the emergence of the Ulster–Rhodesia analogy

In June 1921, George V travelled to Belfast to open the first Parliament of Northern Ireland, where he delivered a speech that had been substantially influenced by General Jan Christiaan Smuts, the Prime Minister of South Africa, which called for reconciliation. Widely regarded as momentous, it highlighted the wider imperial focus of Irish affairs:

> [E]verything which touches Ireland finds an echo in the remotest parts of the Empire. Few things are more earnestly desired throughout the English-speaking world than a satisfactory solution of the age-long Irish problems, which for generations embarrassed our forefathers, as they now weigh heavily upon us ... The eyes of the whole Empire are on Ireland today, that Empire in which so many nations and races have come together in spite of ancient feuds, and in which new nations have come to birth within the lifetime of the youngest in this Hall.[8]

One such embryonic nation was Southern Rhodesia. In October of that year, Sir Charles Coghlan, the leader of the Responsible Government Association (RGA) and future premier, arrived in London for discussions with the Secretary of State for the Colonies, Winston Churchill, whose government was then much preoccupied with simultaneous crises in Ireland, Egypt and India. For several weeks, Coghlan and his colleagues had to weave their way through throngs of green ties, rosettes and banners of Irish supporters of Sinn Fein, whose delegation was also visiting London for historic negotiations leading to the establishment of an autonomous Irish state. The crowd also cheered the return of the King from Scotland. This puzzled Coghlan, who must have been unaware of the monarch's recent appeal for peace, which had been composed on the advice of Smuts. Although staunchly proud of his Irish roots, Coghlan regarded the crowd as 'a funny lot, and what between assassinations and good nature one does not know what to make of them'. Disdaining the 'disloyalty' of Sinn Fein, he wondered what they would have made of him, 'a Catholic of Irish name and extraction', and whether they would have regarded him as a 'traitor', with 'a title from the hated foreign government of bloody England'. When he and his delegation met George V, the King remarked that – in its resistance to unification with South Africa, which both the Imperial and South African governments greatly favoured – Rhodesia appeared to be 'the Ulster of South Africa'. Coghlan replied, ominously, perhaps, in light of events of half a century later, by predicting that Rhodesia would prove to be 'just as loyal'.[9]

Such comparisons resonated further during the Anglo–Irish Treaty negotiations. During discussions between the Prime Minister, David Lloyd George, and the Sinn Fein delegates, led by Arthur Griffith, regarding incentives for Ulster to join in a united Ireland, Churchill interjected to remind them that 'Smuts is at this moment offering to Rhodesia inducements to come into the Union [of South Africa] customs, etc.'[10] In Ireland at the same time, Sir James Craig, later Lord Craigavon, the first Prime Minister of Northern Ireland, drew a similar comparison, calling on Irish nationalists to accord the same respect to Unionist wishes for autonomy as Smuts was then allowing the Rhodesians, for 'It was for [the Rhodesians] to say whether and when they are prepared to become part of that larger South Africa …'[11]

As both the King and Smuts observed, the Irish crisis had been followed across the empire, where its effects were keenly felt, not only in colonies and Dominions with substantial Irish-derived populations, but especially in territories where numerically inferior British settler communities sensed a lack of solidarity from the metropolitan state. Before the war, interest had focused on the Ulster loyalist resistance to the Liberal Government's plans for their threat to use any means to prevent the measure, implicitly including force. The paradox of loyalists couching their cause in imperial terms, yet threatening rebellion against a metropolitan government which they regarded as disloyal and prepared to abandon kith and kin to their hereditary enemies, resonated with loyalists throughout the empire; not least because the Ulster resistance involved such prominent imperial figures as Lord Milner, Sir Leander Starr Jameson of the Raid, Rudyard Kipling and Andrew Bonar Law, who stated that the loyalists were 'holding the pass', not only for Ulster, but for the empire.[12]

In Rhodesia in 1911, the Colonial Office feared an Ulster-style revolt by angry white farmers citing the seventeenth-century parliamentarian John Hampden against the ruling British South Africa Company's monopoly control of African labour recruitment. In 1914, the Company's solicitor warned, referring to a scheme to include Southern Rhodesia in an Afrikaner-dominated South Africa: 'God forbid … that we should have to say "Rhodesia will fight and Rhodesia will be right" [a paraphrase of a contemporary Ulster slogan], but if there is any attempt made to put this country under the heel of the Union of South Africa you will know what to do'.[13] In 1919, the Sons of England Patriotic and Benevolent Society of Rhodesia warned that 'The Imperial Government, as indicated in the case of Ulster, seems rather to enjoy putting pressure on a small loyal English [sic] community to surrender its inheritance and liberties to the majority disposal of a much bigger [community] that is – well – not so English and not so loyal'.[14] This feeling was widely shared throughout the Rhodesias, as well as in Kenya, where the settlers threatened, over the issue of Indian immigration – as Elspeth Huxley recalled – 'an original kind of rebellion … paralleled only by the situation in Ulster in 1914'.[15] The settler leaders modelled their declarations on the Ulster Covenant and wondered whether, in the event of a revolt, they would 'have a second Curragh incident' – a reference to the refusal of British officers stationed near Dublin in 1914 to disarm the Ulster loyalists.

Coghlan was greatly emboldened by these manifestations of settler assertiveness, warning: 'We will not part from the British flag [and be compelled to join South Africa] without fighting. If 10,000 [Kenyan settlers] can give all that trouble to the imperial government, what can we do with 35,000 if need be'.[16] Such sentiments were expressed verbally and in print throughout the heated Rhodesian referendum campaign in 1922 that decided whether the territory should unify with South Africa, or seek responsible government, and these frequently referred to parallels with Ireland and Ulster.[17] Advocates of unification made much of General Smuts's imperial credentials during the Great War, but his recent discussions with Eamon de Valera, the Irish leader, suggested to their opponents that the empire was evolving into a decentralised Commonwealth, or even about to disintegrate. These factors were highlighted by Coghlan's expert propagandist, Mrs Ethel Tawse Jollie, later the first female parliamentarian in the British Empire overseas. She noted Smuts's studied avoidance of the terms 'empire' and 'imperial' in his Irish negotiations, words which were still 'spoken with solemnity and reverence' in Rhodesia.[18] She stated to loud applause from a Salisbury crowd that 'as far as loyalty to the throne is concerned we are in no way different to Ulster'.[19]

These opinions reflected an awareness that this was a time of acute crisis for the British Empire, in which the first portents of imperial retreat were discerned.[20] As Jack Gallagher, a leading historian of empire, has noted: '[t]he Irish troubles ... form a kind of intersection between the problems of empire and the problems of domestic British politics'.[21] Certainly, the Irish Unionist leader, Sir Edward Carson, was prominent among those statesmen who were acutely aware of the ominous implications of an Irish withdrawal for decolonisation elsewhere, as well as for Ulster itself:

> If you tell your Empire in India, in Egypt and all over the world that you have not got the men, the money, the pluck, the inclination and the backing to restore order in a country within twenty miles of your own shore, you may as well begin to abandon the attempt to make British rule prevail throughout the Empire at all ... Do not do something which, throughout the length and breadth of our Empire, will turn Ulster against the British connection ... Loyalty is a strange thing ... It is something born and bred in you ... But do not try us too high ... and do not, when we want to stay with you, do anything to turn us out.[22]

Carson could also count on a substantial seam of metropolitan opinion. The Tory *Morning Post* reasserted that Ulster's pre-war armed resistance was justifiable, the product of an 'excess of devotion, which [the British] took to be no sin. For it was England who placed in Ulster this little garrison of her own sons to uphold her throne and maintain her flag'.[23]

It is true, of course, that rhetorical references to empire were conventional and widespread elsewhere throughout the United Kingdom at that time. Moreover, 'nativist' Protestant anti-Catholicism was still endemic in the cultures of Scotland, England and Wales, beyond the Irish and Ulster ethnic diasporas, well into the twentieth century but, following Partition in 1920, the political context in Northern Ireland provided a profoundly different environment from any other region.[24] Not only was the Province divided from the rest of the United Kingdom by sea, but, as the *Morning Post* and many Ulster politicians commonly recalled, a substantial part of its population originated in a formal programme of British colonisation. Migration flows between the neighbouring islands, as well as from Europe, had occurred extensively since time immemorial, but the Ulster Plantation of the early-seventeenth century, in sharp contrast, provided a readily identifiable and frequently recalled point of origin. Since then, despite the obstacle of confessional differences, considerable miscegenation had indeed occurred, although often tellingly disguised by alterations to surnames. Notions of a supposedly immutable distinction between native and settler had endured, enabling an attribution of innate 'racial' characteristics to sectarian differences. In the age of late-Victorian imperialism, this also made an alignment with theories of race and colonisation seem more directly relevant than in other parts of the United Kingdom, whose populations did not derive from such a commemorated moment of conquest and ethnic displacement.[25]

There was also, of course, a manipulative and politicised aspect to theories of race and essentialised racial characteristics which ebbed and flowed according to the needs of unionism from the late-nineteenth century, and such notions of ethnicity were far from fixed or stable. Some emphasised the Scottish aspect of Ulster ancestry, others its English origin.[26] What united them was a sense, unique within the United Kingdom, of Ulster's separateness, having originated in a chronologically identifiable and systematic process of colonisation. This was inescapable, and profoundly marked out the Province from any other part of the United Kingdom. Lord Craigavon referred to 'this outpost of the Empire ... across the Channel – that narrow strait which lies between us, but does not separate us'.[27] 'We are King's Men', he boasted after the outbreak of war in 1940; '*We* shall be with *you* till the end.'[28] This went beyond mere convention. His distinction between 'we' and 'you' are telling. No mainstream political leader of another region of the United Kingdom, however unionist, could frequently refer unselfconsciously and unproblematically to 'England' in speeches and newsreels as 'the mother country'.[29] Moreover, such terms would not have been used had they not resonated with significant sections of the population.

The creation of Northern Ireland as a self-governing region heightened still further the Province's distinctiveness, which further facilitated colonial analogies. Despite its earlier opposition to home rule, Ulster now possessed an elaborate administration of its own, accommodated, after 1932, at Stormont, in a building constructed on a scale more appropriate to one of the great self-governing Dominions. As the Anglican Dean of Belfast, Reverend Brett, declared:

> [This] building ... was regarded as a symbol of a deeply cherished possession; of an attitude of mind as well as a trait of blood. And Ulster identified with the ideal it represented. But the Imperial idea was, after all, but the idea of Ulster.[30]

Stormont housed, in essence, a miniature of Westminster, with a red-benched Senate, a green-benched House of Commons, a Gentleman-Usher of the Black Rod and Serjeant-at-Arms, a Prime Minister and Cabinet, as well as a Privy Council of Northern Ireland. Overseeing this administration, also uniquely within the United Kingdom, was a Governor who, invariably and fatefully, acted on the advice of his Northern Ireland Cabinet, rather than that of the imperial government, largely following the conventions of governors-general in the self-governing Dominions.[31] At State Openings of Parliament, Black Rod would summon senators and members of the House of Commons to the foot of the 'Imperial Staircase' to hear the Governor – in braided court dress, sword and swan-feather-plumed cocked hat – set out in a King's Speech the legislative programme for the forthcoming session, which had been drafted by the Ulster Cabinet. Successive Governors were essential to 'the most important architectural symbol of the North's political identity'.[32] The Province thus possessed – in the words of Lord Carson – 'a new Parliament, with all the paraphernalia and splendour of a new-born Parliament in the Empire', even while remaining within the United Kingdom.[33] Although there was still Ulster parliamentary representation at Westminster, the exclusion of the Province's internal affairs from discussions there emphasised its character as 'a place apart'. The sea-divided distance from the metropolitan island could even seem to lend a measure of enchantment. On the day of the first opening of Parliament, an editorial in the *Belfast Newsletter* attributed Ulster's intense loyalty to its 'frontier mentality':

> [W]e labour under a sense of detachment from the centre of national life and government, and ... this feeling engenders in us a fonder and keener appreciation of what the Sovereign stands for as the binding link in the nation and Empire.[34]

A year later, the Minister of Finance, Hugh Pollock, responded to the Duke of Abercorn's King's Speech as Governor from the Throne thus:

> [We] regard Ulster today as a key-stone of the arch of the British Empire ... Ulster has been selected as the cock-pit of strife by those whose object is the Destruction of the Empire, rather than the mere acquisition of Ulster. Here in this province, the whole principle of Empire is at stake: we the people of Ulster are the children of the Empire.[35]

Unsurprisingly, as Nicholas Mansergh notes, Craigavon himself rarely missed an opportunity, no matter how remote or inappropriate, to refer to the 'loyalty of Ulster'.[36]

A further feature of the Province's distinctiveness within the United Kingdom was the Governor's viceregal residence at Hillsborough Castle, or Government House, in County Down, several miles from Belfast, situated in a town that was admired for its 'very English' character. This was an archetypal urban settlement of the Ulster Plantation, with well-planned streets, a market square and a handsome Anglican parish church, all overlaying an ancient, pre-colonial past. It was noted that William of Orange stayed at the Castle on his way to the Battle of the Boyne in 1690 and the older fort that still stood nearby provided a haunting reminder of this colonial history.[37] 'It makes for a convenient location … as the place of residence of His Excellency the Governor', one Ulster writer recalled, 'and it has come to figure in the minds of Ulster people as a place visited by royalty and many eminent people'.[38] There was also a strong imperial and, incidentally, Rhodesian connection, prominent when the third Duke of Abercorn (1869–1953), the Ulster-born son of the founding president of Cecil Rhodes's BSA Company, was chosen to be the first Governor of Northern Ireland, an office he occupied from 1921 to 1945. He took a continuing interest in Rhodesian affairs and named his daughter 'Mary Cecilia *Rhodesia* Hamilton' in honour of his family's historic connection with that country.[39] Moreover, use of the epithet 'Imperial' appeared to linger longer and more prominently in Northern Ireland discourse than elsewhere in the United Kingdom. Terms such as the 'Imperial Parliament [at Westminster]', the 'Imperial Grand Master [of the Orange Order]' and the 'Imperial Staircase [of the Stormont Parliament]' possessed very different connotations in the context of Northern Ireland than the various Orders of the British Empire, or such educational or commercial institutions as, say, 'Imperial College London' or 'Imperial Chemicals' did on the other side of the Irish Sea.

As late as the 1970s, newspaper letter writers could refer to Northern Ireland being 'an outpost of the Commonwealth', and a 'British outpost in Ireland', while residents of Belfast's Sandy Row commonly referred to their district as 'the heart of the Empire'.[40] These assertions should not, of course, be taken to be on a par with sophisticated academic analyses of colonialism but, rather, as inchoate but nonetheless telling assumptions, underscoring a widespread sense that Ulster was 'a place apart'. Arguments that imperialist sentiment in Ulster was an irrelevant factor, on the grounds that the Province did not produce any great analytical thinkers and that its concerns were overwhelmingly provincial, do not seem entirely satisfactory, for many other communities across the empire were equally dominated by local concerns, where there was little detailed knowledge of its territories or its extent, but where few would readily disregard the importance of such wider attachments. As in all autonomous territories under the Crown, there was no inevitable contradiction between emphases on local or provincial priorities, a popular indifference towards and ignorance of the details of the British Empire, and a general pride in its vaunted 'greatness'. Indeed, such differing elements typically formed composite identities in most colonies of settlement.[41]

An example of the extent to which imperialism informed Unionist identity is provided by Cyril Falls (1888–1971). He had not grown up in the deprived and narrow streets of Sandy Row and can scarcely be categorised as emerging from more 'extreme loyalist currents'. Rather, he was a Dublin-born biographer of Kipling and *The Times* correspondent during the Second World War, who later had the distinction of holding the Chichele Professorship of Military History at All Souls College. In 1936, he published *The Birth of Ulster*, a scholarly account of the Elizabethan conquest and Jacobean settlement of Ulster. Although the volume focused on the early modern history of these events, he was also concerned with the longer-term impact. The 'colonization of the northern province … with English and Scots, from which has sprung a clearly-defined race', he prefaced, 'differed markedly from its parents' stocks and to a far greater extent from its neighbours'. He was brought up to admire 'the Ulster colonists'.[42] Especially significant is the final chapter, titled 'The Fruits', which is concerned with the twentieth century. Here, he celebrates the fact that 'modern Ulster … unlike every other settlement in Ireland … was never swamped or assimilated by its surroundings'. He asserts that the Ulster Protestants had mutated into a local type, distinct from the 'motherland', and he goes on to make an ethnic claim common to many settler societies:

> [The Colony] evolved into something rather different from its parent stock, partly because, though not assimilated, it was in some degree gradually affected by its new environment, partly because all colonies, even in virgin lands, undergo this evolution … One may say that in Belfast [the 'predominant type' of Ulster Scot] approaches the Scot most closely and that in the country districts he has gone farthest towards a new national type. In neither does he resemble the native Irish of Ulster, with whom he dwells side by side. Racial differences have been preserved through over three centuries in an astonishing fashion. An experienced observer walking among the crowds of small farmers on Fair Day in Omagh or Enniskillen could pick out settler from native with ease. He would not, of course, have used those terms. He would say, 'Protestant face'! 'Catholic face'! And he would be right nine times out of ten. If, instead, he were handed a roll of surnames, he could find his way equally well … Moreover, the gap between races and religions – almost synonymous terms – has in recent years grown wider rather than diminished … There are two nations in Northern Ireland, the larger looking across the sea to its motherland of Great Britain, the smaller with its eyes on Dublin.[43]

Royal visits both reinforced and highlighted Ulster's exceptionalism. As in more distant possessions, the monarchy provided a symbol of allegiance which was able to transcend their loyalty to transitory British governments whose reciprocal sense of commitment they may occasionally have found lacking. One such occasion, the coronation visit of Queen Elizabeth II and the Duke of Edinburgh to Ulster in 1953, proved to be a great success, highlighting both the Province's regional exceptionalism and pride in their membership of the wider empire. The couple were guests of the Governor and were greeted throughout Ulster, particularly, if not quite exclusively, in Protestant neighbourhoods. In a special feature, the *Belfast Telegraph* reporter enthused about the visit in terms which highlighted the gubernatorial town's origins in colonial conquest and dispossession:

> All roads lead to Hillsborough, that ancient town in the heart of the country where once stood the stronghold of the Magennises. On this site the first-born of Sir Moyses Hill, that gallant soldier who served the first Elizabeth, built a castle. Now, here is the home of the Governor ... representative in Ulster of Queen Elizabeth the Second. How strangely interwoven are the strands which bind us to our past.[44]

Interwoven indeed; royal tours took place frequently throughout other regions of the United Kingdom, of course, but only in Northern Ireland was there that remembered moment of history, the Plantation and colonisation of Ulster, which gave such occasions a separate poignancy. Noteworthy too at that time, was the extensive personal movie collection compiled for television by the Governor of Northern Ireland, Lord Wakehurst. It indicates that he subscribed, if somewhat naively, to common ethnographical stereotypes of 'industrious' descendants of Scottish and English settlers and 'small dark folk, descendants of the oldest Irish stock' encountered in the highland regions of the Province.[45]

Thus, it cannot convincingly be argued that colonial analogies were either confined to 'extreme Loyalist elements', or to nationalists wishing to undermine the legitimacy of the Union with Britain. Rather, in the decades preceding the Troubles, these were rooted in a common knowledge that the majority of the citizens of Northern Ireland originated in and identified with a colonial settlement, however remote in time, and that its distinctiveness within the United Kingdom was further marked out by its elaborate system of provincial government, more appropriate to an overseas possession than an integral region of the metropolitan state.

The other newly created self-governing state of the 1920s, Southern Rhodesia, was also regarded as a staunch bastion of British imperial loyalty. In 1923, it secured the widest degree of autonomy short of dominion status, with its own Prime Minister, answerable to its own Parliament and a Governor who was advised by his Rhodesian Cabinet, not Whitehall, largely following the convention of the Dominions; in other words, effectively, a Governor who reigned rather than ruled. Its government paid for, appointed and controlled its own armed forces. Significantly, from its early years, it came under the remit of the Dominions Office, later the Commonwealth Relations Office, not the Colonial Office. It had its own High Commissioner in London. In 1948, in common with the Dominions, it passed its own citizenship law and was not treated by British governments for practical purposes as a colony but as an honorary Dominion. It developed a small diplomatic service and could even legally deport British citizens if it so wished, without fear of metropolitan interference.[46] 'The average British-born Rhodesian feels that this is essentially a British country, pioneered, bought and developed by British people, and he wants to keep it so', Ethel Tawse Jollie, argued: 'Rhodesians, as a rule, are intensely imperialistic'.[47] However, she did not claim, it should be noted, neither would she have claimed, that Rhodesians, apart from herself, possessed detailed knowledge of the extent or governance of the empire, nor did Rhodesia produce any important imperial thinkers. Nevertheless, in common with many other citizens of the empire, including Ulster Protestants, what was evident was that they believed in its 'greatness', even if they too, believing themselves to be on the front line of the empire, were compelled to remain constantly vigilant regarding its defence. The colony's 'local Kipling', Henry Cullen Gouldsbury, had warned 'from the Outposts' that they, as frontiersmen, whom Rudyard Kipling had described as 'the Wards of the Outer Marches', would guard 'Greater England' against both external enemies and 'Little England[er]' abdication.[48] By the end of the 1920s, there was already an evident sense of Rhodesia's increasing alienation from Britain. '[Cecil Rhodes's] philosophy … was becoming out-of-date before the Great War shattered our self-complacency and made a kaleidoscope of our moral values', Tawse Jollie lamented. 'His ideas are superseded; only in his country of Southern Rhodesia there still lingers a little of the old faith; the old religious sentiment about the Flag, the Empire and the Traditions of our Race'.[49] Indeed, in many ways, Southern Rhodesia's origins were ideologically fundamentally rooted not in imperial hubris but in reaction to early manifestations of imperial decline.

Sharing much of this critique of metropolitan Britain was Charles Olley (1890–1965), a Belfast-born member of the Orange Order, who caught the populist and imperialist mood of Rhodesia, when its rejection of union with South Africa was frequently likened to Ulster's rejection of a united Ireland. White Rhodesia was also a predominantly Protestant society, but much less sectarian-minded than Ulster, so he tailored his secular political concerns accordingly. He made his mark at the municipal rather than national level of politics, being elected to the Salisbury City Council in 1929, serving as a member for thirty-two years, as well as Deputy Mayor and Mayor. He held very strong views on race, even by contemporary standards, and he typically echoed the fears of the white working class, as a founding president of the

White Rhodesia Council, which advocated mass white immigration. During the 1930s he became closely associated with Henry Hamilton Beamish (1873–1948), the son of a Victorian rear admiral with long roots in Cork, founder of 'The Britons', a notoriously anti-Semitic movement, and an associate of leading international fascists. Beamish was elected to the Southern Rhodesian parliament in 1938, calling on both Ulster and Rhodesia as bastions of Britishness not to obey the 'be-Jewed' British Parliament, from where an alleged international 'Kosher war' to undermine the empire was being waged. In 1939, he was interned for his avowedly pro-Nazi views. Olley joined leading public figures in a petition asking the government for an assurance that Beamish was not being held for his anti-Semitic views, sentiments with which 'forty per cent' of Salisbury agreed. The petition added: 'People think that Beamish has been framed by "Yids"'.[50] Olley also opposed the immigration of Polish Catholics who were religiously and culturally alien, as well as susceptible to communism, who might weaken Rhodesia's character as 'a land of British stock'.[51] He believed that European supremacy should be best secured through the continued entrenchment of the Land Apportionment Act of 1930, the 'Magna Carta' of White Rhodesia, and the early attainment of dominion status. He attacked capitalist interests as being behind the fashionable ideal of 'racial partnership', believing that federation was a conspiracy by big mining interests to line their pockets while depriving white working men of their livelihoods. In 1944 he became a prime mover in the foundation of the inappropriately named Liberal Party, which he hoped would promote his ideals, but broke with it when it flirted with support from local Afrikaners, whom he, as a British nationalist, regarded as republican-minded aliens.

During the Second World War, the Southern Rhodesian parliament debated the implications of the promises of the Atlantic Charter of 1941 for African expectations, as well as the implications of a resurgent Afrikaner nationalism towards the south. Tawse Jollie had been an early advocate of some kind of amalgamation, or federation, with Northern Rhodesia, or at least its strategically important Copperbelt. The outcome of the Second World War heightened her fears for the empire's changing fortunes:

> As Britain moves out of Africa to the north, and as other possessions are lost to her, the African continent becomes of increased importance to the Empire, and with the [republican] political tendencies of the Union [of South Africa] ... making the future of that country as a Dominion within the Commonwealth uncertain, Central Africa is the only part of that continent which offers the possibility of building up a strong new British Dominion closely allied with the Empire and Commonwealth.[52]

As Britain's imperial power faltered, Olley's political philosophy entered the mainstream of settler politics. The populist Dominion Party and, later, the

Rhodesian Front, owed much to his profound influence, with their appeal to the insecurities of white farmers and lower-middle and white working classes. He may indeed be regarded as the prophet and anticipator of the Rhodesian Front, which came to power in 1962. In 1965 his political influence was ending just when the Prime Minister, Ian Smith, was planning a UDI from Britain for November of that year in order to forestall black majority rule. For Olley, UDI was a bold example of direct action against the tide of decolonisation that was well in keeping with his outlook and Ulster loyalist heritage. Before his death, in 1965, Salisbury honoured him with the freedom of the city and made him a Life Alderman.[53]

'Queen's rebels': the British frontiersmen's revolts against decolonisation

As decolonisation advanced from the north, Ulster analogies returned. In 1961, the Irish diplomat, Dr Conor Cruise O'Brien, was appointed United Nations Representative in the former Belgian Congo, where he soon became a bête noire of the Federal Prime Minister, Sir Roy Welensky, who supported Katangese secession, and who exhibited an unusually acute sense of Irish history:

> [O'Brien] was a handsome, witty Irish intellectual and a relentless and deeply suspicious critic of British imperialism ... Suddenly in a position of great power at a crucial juncture in ... what remained of the British Empire he detested so much, with an international force ... He was hostile to the idea of Katanga's secession because he hated the secession of Northern Ireland from Eire; and in me, perhaps, he saw a reincarnation of [the Irish Unionist leader, Sir Edward] Carson. Ireland's woes were to be avenged in Central Africa.[54]

At almost the same time, Sir Edgar Whitehead, the Southern Rhodesian Prime Minister, who was a nephew of the Earl of Middleton, the leader of the southern Irish unionists who had dealt with the British retreat from Ireland in 1921, advocated a subordinate relationship of Northern to Southern Rhodesia, which he called his 'Northern Ireland solution'. In 1963, he also called for Rhodesia's entry into the United Kingdom on the same terms as Northern Ireland, so that the rights of black Rhodesians could be addressed by an overwhelmingly white electorate within the United Kingdom. Such a scheme may now seem bizarre, but just such a proposal seemed recently to have very nearly succeeded in Malta.[55]

The rapidity of British decline so soon after the victory of 1945 had taken white Rhodesians generally by surprise. Initially, it seemed, despite the independence of India and Pakistan in 1947, the British were more actively engaged than ever with their African colonies and the defence of outposts such as Cyprus and Aden, and white Rhodesians rejoiced in British technological achievements, despite wartime exhaustion, manifested in the acquisition of a nuclear deterrent, the winning of air speed records and the possession of such weapons as the Vulcan bomber. This futuristic looking delta-winged strategic jet equipped, among other units, it was noted symbolically, the Royal Air Force's famous 44 (Rhodesia) Squadron, which recalled the colony's own wartime service. Such connections sustained an illusion of sophisticated metropolitan global power. Within a few short years, however, Britain seemed to be in headlong retreat. Reinforced by arrivals of disillusioned settlers from British India and Kenya, white Rhodesians began to distinguish more sharply the Queen from the Queen's government in the United Kingdom. Sir Roy Welensky, who was sworn in as prime minister of the Federation just as the Suez Crisis was erupting, offered his immediate support for the British operation and his undiluted commitment to the monarchy and the Commonwealth.[56] 'I, of course, have no loyalty to your Government whatsoever', he reminded Malcolm Muggeridge. 'But I have a loyalty to the Crown. We look upon the Queen as the Queen of the Federation'.[57] Colin Leys, as astute an observer of Rhodesian politics as any, writing in the late 1950s, thought the attachment to the monarchy exceptional: 'It is not only independent of parties and as much the Crown of Rhodesia as of Britain herself, it is independent of time, and symbolizes vanished epochs as well as (or better than) the present one'.[58] As one opposition MP put it:

> Our loyalty must remain direct to the Crown. The Colonial Office is merely the instrument of whatever government holds power in Britain. By turning our backs on a British Government, we are not turning away from the Crown and the British Commonwealth of Nations.[59]

Increasingly, many Rhodesians seemed bewildered by the pace of these changes and the speed with which perceptions of them in Britain appeared to have changed, from rugged and faithful kith-and-kin warriors to embarrassing relatives they would rather forget. Support for dominion status, seized unilaterally if necessary, now increased greatly. The monarchy, once so central to the Rhodesian sense of themselves, along with their allegiance to the older, 'white' and 'British', Commonwealth, was changing in meaning.[60] Whatever the legal position, there was a widespread political awareness in both Rhodesia and the United Kingdom that the Crown had become somewhat fragmented and that, in the minds of many Rhodesians, as in those of Canadians, Australians and New Zealanders, it was their various national mutations of the monarchy to which they were loyal. Many Rhodesians clearly distinguished the Queen as Queen of Rhodesia, to whom they felt profoundly loyal, from Harold Wilson's legislative instrument, to which they felt little allegiance.⁶¹ Albert Kiralfy, Professor of Law at the University of London, opined in a BBC interview with Anthony King a month before Rhodesia's UDI:

> [Of course, the Rhodesian military's] oath is to the Queen, as Queen of the United Kingdom, but it is now generally recognised that there is no common allegiance of all parts of the Commonwealth to the Crown in quite the same sense. The Queen of Canada, for instance, could be different from the Queen of Australia, so I think this is not a very strong argument on this point.⁶²

Such considerations of loyalty facilitated the revival of another Ulster analogy: the Curragh 'incident' of 1914. Since it would involve action against 'kith and kin', a military intervention against Rhodesian UDI was privately regarded by British service chiefs as 'distasteful', if not unthinkable.⁶³ Robert Good, the American ambassador to Zambia, recalled that 'on everyone's lips' was the precedent of the Curragh 'Mutiny' of 1914 and the question of whether the British Army would remain loyal if ordered to intervene. This analogy was also noted at the time by the *Round Table*'s Rhodesian correspondent and by the Australian Rhodes Scholar and academic, Roger Scott.⁶⁴

Rhodesian apologists for UDI generally attributed evident British abdication and decolonisation to wilful moral decadence and permissiveness, combined with communist conspiracies and infiltrations, even, absurdly, implicating such plainly conservative figures as the Governor, Sir Humphrey Gibbs.⁶⁵ A distinguished jurist and liberal-minded politician, Sir Robert Tredgold, lamented the effectiveness of the Rhodesian Front's propaganda in resonating with the white electorate:

> The white people are told, and many of them seem to believe, incredible things ... They are told and believe that the people of England, in a short generation from 'their finest hour', have lost the qualities that made them great ... They are told and believe that this little pool of white people in the heart of Africa has become the repository of these qualities, as if a small branch of a great tree can live on when the roots have been destroyed.⁶⁶

For sceptical Ulster Unionists, there was far less sense of surprise regarding unrequited allegiance and an evident metropolitan lack of resolve and decline, and this sentiment had as much to do with loyalty to the Crown as with race. Sir Basil Brooke, Viscount Brookeborough, who was a long-standing Prime Minister of Northern Ireland (1943–63), was known for his strongly right-wing opinions and clipped heavily anglicised accent. Ironically, given the Province's sectarian reputation, he was an avowed agnostic, but a cultural Anglican. As an aristocratic kinsman of an Elizabethan adventurer from Cheshire who had settled centuries before in the marches of Donegal and Fermanagh, he subscribed to a common definition of Ulstermen as a 'tough' breed: descendants of Scottish and English Borderers 'who were not exactly made to feel welcome' in the Province. His uncle was Field Marshal Lord Alanbrooke, Chief of the Imperial General Staff, one of several famous Ulster generals. His own life experience extended far beyond the terraced lanes and low horizons of Ulster, having grown up in the British community of Pau in southern France and, after education at Winchester and Sandhurst, soldiered in various parts of the empire.[67] His sense of loyalty is well illustrated by an episode in 1960, when the Northern Ireland government appeared reluctant to accept that the South African High Commissioner to London should open an exhibition in Belfast celebrating the Commonwealth. This was on the grounds that 'mischievous' comparisons might be drawn between the supremacist philosophy of the two states, as Brian Faulkner, Minister of Home Affairs, had warned. The British Home Secretary, R. A. Butler, however, made it clear that he wished the visit to go ahead, despite South Africa's increasingly notorious apartheid policies, because of 'the very great damage' a refusal might do to Commonwealth relations.

Much though Brookeborough identified with the overseas settler empire, it was the growing republicanism of the South African government and their intention to hold a referendum on becoming a republic which most concerned him, rather than apartheid. For leading Ulster families, not least those, such as several of the founders of Northern Ireland, led by Craigavon, who were veterans of the South African War, loyalty to the empire was integral to their identity. Brookeborough himself had served as a British officer in Johannesburg in 1913–1914, where he was impressed by the robust handling of white syndicalists by Generals Botha and Smuts.[68] To him, in contrast, Afrikaner Nationalists were not primarily fellow Protestants, but republican *dis*loyalists and erstwhile allies of Irish republican supporters of the Boers.[69] This connection, thus, had little to do with 'strong affinities and links between Loyalism and South African racial supremacism', analogies of which have been frequently cited and misinterpreted, but, rather, between Ulster loyalism and a sense of Britishness that was seemingly ever more threatened and beleaguered in an age of decolonisation.[70]

'Last outposts': 'Before an Empire's eyes, the traitor claims his price'

In August 1975, six years before his assassination by the Provisional IRA, the Reverend Robert Bradford, MP for Belfast South, warned that 'The time may come when Ulstermen would have to become Queen's rebels in order to remain citizens of any kind'.[71] His alert came after almost a decade of growing violence, in which the very endurance of the state of Northern

Ireland itself had been cast into doubt. There had been significant admiration for Rhodesia's UDI as an assertion of Britishness. Dr Ian Paisley's *Protestant Telegraph* regarded Wilson's opposition to Ian Smith's government as part of a worldwide conspiracy, implicating such culprits as the Common Market, the World Council of Churches, international communism and the United Nations. The Catholic Church, of course, was allegedly at the heart of these machinations and the paper detected evidence of the same 'treacherous' decolonising trends in Ulster as could previously be seen in Gibraltar, Cyprus and Rhodesia. It drew parallels between African 'superstitious throwing of bones' and Romanist sprinkling of holy water. It noted, with reason, the prominence of Irish missionary clergy among leading subversive elements in Rhodesia, for Irish republican-minded missionaries had indeed often rooted their sense of solidarity in parallels they had drawn with Northern Ireland.[72] William Craig, a former Ulster cabinet minister, the founder of the Vanguard Movement and admirer of Rhodesia, advocated a similar UDI to preserve 'British Ulster'. It is also noteworthy that a minority, but nonetheless influential, strand of thinking found in more strident elements in Rhodesia and Ulster was informed by the British Israelite cult, which asserted that the British peoples were the descendants of the Lost Tribe of Israel, even if they did not realise this. Its influence was not inconsiderable within the Orange Order and included at least one cabinet minister, Lord Graham, in the Rhodesian Government. Its providential analyses combined with a widespread notion that the metropolitan British might recover their sense of Britishness by Ulster's and the Rhodesians' patriotic example.[73] There were also, somewhat eccentric, attempts to provide Ulster Protestants with an ethnic connection to the Province which pre-dated colonisation, which paralleled far more outlandish British Israelite efforts to provide white Rhodesians with a pre-colonial aboriginal legitimacy as distant kinsmen of Phoenicians, or other allegedly non-African builders of Great Zimbabwe, which met with considerably less success.[74]

By the late 1960s, Harold Wilson's Labour Government felt assailed by adjacent and distant unrequited loyalists, whose states had enjoyed considerable measures of autonomy, and this had led to fears of United Nations intervention in Ulster, as well as Rhodesia. The Australian United Nations diplomat, George Ivan Smith, who had been an aide to the Secretary General, Dag Hammarskjold, and had been a roving UN ambassador during the Rhodesian UDI crisis, thought that such a prospect put the Northern Ireland Prime Minister, Captain Terence O'Neill, 'off his lunch altogether'.[75] At the time of UDI, an editorial in the *Irish Times* highlighted some historical parallels:

> [The Rhodesian] claim of unswerving allegiance to the British Crown, genuine or not, cannot in context be considered as other than an attempt to salvage sympathy in Britain. [Tory leader] Bonar Law and his friends presented the

Ulster crisis to their followers in the same light that Mr Smith sees the prospect of Rhodesia with a negro majority.[76]

Subsequently, the editor of the left-wing *New Statesman* also seemed struck by some apparent similarities between the two crises:

> When Whitehall fusses, Belfast and Salisbury speak the same language in reply: their ties of blood, their loyalty in war, their more intimate knowledge of the desperate ferocity of their opponents. If that fails, they speak the same coarser dialect: Standing on the constitutional rights acquired in the Twenties, they tell the intrusive British to shove off: 'Whether it be [Harold] Wilson or anyone else who interferes with the just prerogative of the government ... he does so at his peril.' Was it Lord Graham, the [former Rhodesian] Minister of External Affairs, or Captain Orr, the Imperial Grand Master of the Orange Order, who threw down the glove? ... [T]he Unionists are a perfect example of a minority mentality ... Minorities are not scared for nothing; nor merely for their own sins ...[77]

Such comparisons appeared to be borne out by events. In a crucial BBC television broadcast in December 1968, 'Ulster at the Crossroads', the Prime Minister, Captain Terence O'Neill, pointedly warned against ambitions for a Rhodesian-style UDI by elements of his Unionist Party who were opposed to his reforms:

> There are, I know, today some so-called loyalists who talk of independence from Britain ... Rhodesia, in defying Britain from thousands of miles away, at least has an air force and army of her own. Where are the Ulster armoured divisions and the Ulster jet planes? ... These people ... are not loyalists, but disloyalists: disloyal to Britain, disloyal to the Commonwealth, disloyal to the Crown, disloyal – if they are in public life – to the solemn oath they have sworn to Her Majesty the Queen.[78]

O'Neill soon fell from office, due to a widespread party revolt, as did his successor, Major James Chichester-Clark. On the eve of the suspension and eventual abolition of the Northern Ireland Parliament, his successor, in turn, Brian Faulkner, felt he had to warn the Ulster House of Commons that a UDI would be financially disastrous for the Province.[79] His colleague, Captain Robert Mitchell, MP for North Armagh, stated that he had been in contact with people from 'all over the Commonwealth, including Australia, New Zealand and Canada. They were appalled and as dumbfounded as we are at the suspension of this Parliament, because the Government at Westminster are proposing to do away with one of the Parliaments of the Commonwealth'. 'This was totally unacceptable to the other members of the Commonwealth', he concluded.[80] There was indeed consternation when the post of Governor, which many unionists regarded as emblematic of their autonomy and provincial distinctiveness, was abolished; 130,000 signed a petition for the retention of the governorship. Faulkner was not entirely unhappy with that particular change, however. Unlike his aristocratic and landed predecessors, he was a middle-class industrialist with little romantic attachment to tradition. 'I must say that, almost alone among my colleagues, I regarded the office … as rather archaic and colonial', he reflected, regarding the position as an obstacle to Northern Ireland's full integration in the United Kingdom.[81]

Reflecting on these events was Patrick Riddell, a Unionist who had served in both the Northern Ireland and British civil service. He contributed to the Ulster celebration of the Festival of Britain and was a prolific BBC playwright and Belfast *Sunday News* columnist.[82] He readily acknowledged with regret the gerrymandering of local government elections and more generally the scandal of sectarian discrimination. Nevertheless, his analysis reveals familiar colonial tropes. 'Those who regard the native Irish as an inferior race have found much in history to support their argument', he opined, highlighting 'the mist-ridden world of Irish ignorance and dislike of England' and lamented the fact that the British Empire was 'derided' and was now being 'condemned as a thing of wickedness, an evil and repressive power, something to be ashamed of'.[83]

At the other end of the political spectrum was John Hewitt (1907–1987), a leading Ulster Quaker poet who, far from reflecting 'extreme Loyalist currents', identified strongly as a radical dissenter and 'a man of the left', but he too was conscious of the settler origins of his ancestors, as evident in his poem, 'Once alien here'. In his 'Colonial consequence' he writes that 'The colony's so old it's out of touch/with much that's bruited in the Capitol'.[84] In 'A little people', he describes the demographic vulnerability of Ulster Protestants and their unreliable relationship to Great Britain in an era of decolonisation, as well as threats of a UDI:

> But now that empire-Commonwealth runs down,
> new flags, new faces fill the halls of state
> and in embattled company alone
> we misbelieve these vagaries of fate …
> Some would pray our shrunken empire hold
> us closer to her flank beside the throne
> and others, rasher, summon us to fold
> our thin cloak round us close and stand alone.[85]

It is noteworthy, too, that the last words delivered from the dispatch box of the Northern Ireland House of Commons before its suspension by Westminster came from Captain Basil Brooke MP, who was the only surviving son of the first Viscount Brookeborough, his namesake. Not insignificantly, his two brothers were killed in action in the Second World War. Moved by what he and many fellow Unionists regarded as a unilateral metropolitan action lacking moral legitimacy, he recited some oft-quoted lines from Rudyard Kipling's chilling 'Ulster 1912', which expressed sentiments that many white Rhodesians would equally have shared:

> Before an Empire's eyes, the traitor claims his price.
> What need of further lies? We are the sacrifice.[86]

Thus, the reaction of Ulster to the end of empire was inevitably not the same as that of Scotland, for there had been a greater consensual commitment to the empire in Scotland, even among nationalists.[87] While equally riven by sectarianism, there was not in Scotland, as there was in Northern Ireland, as highlighted in the royal tour of 1953, an awareness, or collective 'memory', of ancestral conquest, settlement and dispossession, which so profoundly conditioned reactions to imperial causes. As John MacKenzie has noted: 'the decolonization process ... arguably began with the Irish Treaty of 1922'.[88] There, as Carson had foreseen, the withdrawal from empire began. Striking, if ostensibly superficial, similarities between these two avowedly loyal communities enabled analogies to be drawn that would not have seemed as persuasive in any other part of the United Kingdom. This is not to suggest that colonialism is the only lens through which to view Northern Ireland. Still less is it suggested that such attitudes were constant or unchanging. Nevertheless, these analogies are surely essential to any understanding of prevailing mindsets in Britain, Ulster and Rhodesia, at the end of empire.

Notes

1. T. O'Neill, *The Autobiography of Terence O'Neill* (London: Rupert Hart-Davis, 1972), pp. 86–87.
2. R. Weitzer, *Transforming Settler States: Communal Conflict and Internal Security in Northern Ireland and Zimbabwe* (Berkley: University of California, 1991); D. Lowry, 'A Mirror to Ireland's Face: Colonial Analogies and Ethnic Echoes in Rhodesia/Zimbabwe, c.1910–2019', in J. Woods (ed.), *The Mashonaland Irish Association* (Harare: Weaver Press, 2019).
3. S. Howe, *Ireland and Empire: Colonial Legacies in Irish History and Culture* (Oxford: Oxford University Press, 2000), p. 202; A. Jackson, 'Ireland, the Union, and the Empire', p. 147; and S. Howe, 'Historiography', p. 240, both in K. Kenny (ed.), *Ireland and the British Empire* (Oxford: Oxford University Press, 2004).
4. R. Toye, '"Phrases Make History Here": Churchill, Ireland and the Rhetoric of Empire', *Journal of Imperial and Commonwealth History*, 38:4 (2010), pp. 549–570, at p. 549.
5. Quoted in M. Weiner, *English Culture and the Decline of the Industrial Spirit* (Cambridge: Cambridge University Press, 1981), p. v. See also D. McNeil, '"The

rivers of Zimbabwe will run red with blood": Enoch Powell and the Post-Imperial Nostalgia of the Monday Club', *Journal of Southern African Studies*, 37:4 (2011), pp. 731–745; B. Schwarz, *Memories of Empire, Volume I: The White Man's World* (Oxford: Oxford University Press, 2011), pp. 105–106.
6   Howe, *Ireland and Empire*, pp. 204–205.
7   A. Thompson, 'The Languages of Loyalism in Southern Africa, c. 1870–1939', *English Historical Review*, 118 (2003), pp. 617–650; D. Lowry, 'The Queen of Rhodesia Versus the Queen of the United Kingdom: Conflicts of Allegiance in Rhodesia's Unilateral Declaration of Independence', in H. Kumarasingham (ed.), *Viceregalism: The Crown as Head of State in Political Crises in the Postwar Commonwealth* (London: Palgrave, 2020); G. Martin, *The Durham Report and British Policy: A Critical Essay* (Cambridge: Cambridge University Press, 1972), Chs 1, 4–5; D. E. Smith, 'The Crown and the Constitution: Sustaining Democracy?', in J. Smith and D. M. Jackson (eds), *The Evolving Canadian Crown* (Montreal and Kingston: McGill-Queen's University Press, 2010), pp. 57–72; S. Joyal, 'La Couronne au Quebec', in D. M. Jackson and P. Legasse (eds), *Canada and the Crown: Essays on Constitutional Monarchy* (Kingston: Institute of Intergovernmental Relations, 2012); D. M. Jackson, *The Crown and Canadian Federalism* (Toronto: Dundurn, 2013), Ch.1; P. Boyce, *The Queen's Other Realms: The Crown and its Legacy in Australia, Canada and New Zealand* (Sydney: Federation Press, 2008); J. Curran and S. Ward, *The Unknown Nation: Australia after Empire* (Melbourne: Melbourne University Publishing, 2010).
8   St-J. Ervine, *Craigavon: Ulsterman* (London: George Allen & Unwin, 1949), pp. 421–422.
9   J. P. R. Wallis, *One Man's Hand: The Story of Sir Charles Coghlan and the Liberation of Southern Rhodesia* (London: Longmans, Green and Co., London, 1950), pp. 196–197.
10 T. Jones, *Whitehall Diary, III: Ireland 1918–1925* (London: Oxford University Press, ed. Keith Middlemas, 1971), p. 131.
11 Ervine, *Craigavon*, p. 439.
12 D. Lowry, 'Ulster Resistance and Loyalist Rebellion in the Empire', in K. Jeffery (ed.), *'An Irish Empire'?: Aspects of Ireland and the British Empire* (Manchester: Manchester University Press, 1997), pp. 193–195.
13 J. MacKenzie, 'Responsible Government', *Rhodesian History*, IX (1978), pp. 23–40, at p. 34. See also I. Henderson, 'White Populism in Southern Rhodesia', *Comparative Studies in Society and History*, 14: 4 (1972), pp. 387–399, at p. 393.
14 'The Question for Rhodesia', *Independent* (Rhodesia), 10 February 1921.
15 C. P. Youé, 'The Threat of Settler Rebellion and the Imperial Predicament: The Demise of Indian Rights in Kenya', *Canadian Journal of History*, XII (1978), pp. 347–360; C. J. D. Duder, 'The Settler Response to the Indian Crisis of 1923 in Kenya: Brigadier General Philip Wheatley and "Direct Action"', *Journal of Imperial and Commonwealth History*, XVII (1989), pp. 349–371.
16 E. T. Jollie, *The Real Rhodesia* (Hutchinson: London, 1924), p. 85.
17 Lowry, 'Ulster Resistance', pp. 195–196.

18 E. T. Jollie, 'The Passing of Empire', *National Review*, LXXVII (1922), pp. 810–817, at pp. 810–812.
19 E. T. Jollie, 'The Irish Free State', *Independent* (Rhodesia), 23 December 1922; Jollie, 'Trust General Smuts', *National Review*, LXXVIII (1922), pp. 304–311; Jollie, *The Real Rhodesia*, pp. 91–96; D. Lowry, '"White Woman's Country": Ethel Tawse Jollie and the Making of White Rhodesia', *Journal of Southern African Studies*, 23:2 (1997), pp. 259–282.
20 K. Jeffery, *The British Army and the Crisis of Empire, 1918–22* (Manchester: Manchester University Press, 1986).
21 J. Gallagher, *The Decline, Revival and Fall of the British Empire* (Cambridge: Cambridge University Press, 1982), p. 98.
22 E. Carson, 'I Was in Earnest (1921)', in S. Deane (ed.), *Field Day Anthology of Irish Writing* (Derry: Field Day, 1991), pp. 356, 362; D. G. Boyce, 'Edward Carson', in C. Brady (ed.), *Worsted in the Game: Losers in Irish History* (Dublin: Lilliput Press, 1989), p. 155.
23 Editorial, *Morning Post*, 27 January 1921.
24 D. Jackson, *Popular Opposition to Irish Home Rule in Edwardian Britain* (Liverpool: Liverpool University Press, 2009).
25 E. Hamilton, *The Soul of Ulster* (London: Hurst and Blackett, 1917); G. Walker, 'Empire, Religion and Nationality in Scotland and Ulster before the First World War', in I. S. Wood (ed.), *Scotland and Ulster* (Edinburgh: Mercat Press, 1994), pp. 97–115.
26 J. Loughlin, *Ulster Unionism and British National Identity since 1885* (London: Pinter, 1995), p. 88.
27 J. Craig, 'We are King's Men' (1940), in Deane, *Field Day Anthology*, p. 363.
28 Ibid. – author's italics.
29 Craig, 'We are King's Men' (1940), in Deane, *Field Day Anthology*; Loughlin, *Ulster Unionism*, pp. 25–28; *Craigavon Times*, 7 July 1976, quoted in P. Clayton, *Enemies and Passing Friends: Settler Ideologies in Twentieth-Century Ulster* (London: Pluto, 1996), p. 47.
30 D. Officer, 'In Search of Order, Permanence and Stability: Building Stormont, 1921–32', in R. English and G. Walker (eds), *Unionism in Modern Ireland: New Perspectives on Politics and Culture* (London: Palgrave-Macmillan, 1996), p. 140.
31 D. Lowry, 'A "Supreme and Permanent Symbol of Executive Authority": The Crown and the Governorship of Northern Ireland in an Age of "Troubles"', in Kumarasingham (ed.), *Viceregalism*, pp. 93–127.
32 Officer, 'In Search of Order, Permanence and Stability', pp. 130–147; J. Loughlin, 'Consolidating "Ulster"; Regime Propaganda and Architecture in the Inter-War Period', *National Identities*, 1:2 (1999), pp. 161–177, at p. 173.
33 Carson, 'I Was in Earnest (1921)', p. 360.
34 Loughlin, *Ulster Unionism*, p. 88.
35 D. H. Hume, 'Empire Day in Ireland 1896–1962', in Jeffery (ed.), '*An Irish Empire?*', p. 159.
36 N. Mansergh, *The Government of Northern Ireland: A Study in Devolution* (London: George Allen & Unwin, 1936), p. 233.

37 H. Shearman, *Ulster* (London: Robert Hale Ltd, 1947), p. 144. More generally, see Loughlin, *Ulster Unionism*, esp. Ch. 5.
38 T. Reeves-Smyth, 'Hillsborough Castle Demesne', *Northern Ireland Heritage Gardens Trust Occasional Paper*, 1 (Belfast: 2015); Shearman, *Ulster*, pp. 144–145, 332–338.
39 'Duke of Abercorn', *The Times*, 14 September 1953 – author's italics.
40 *Portadown News*, 10 November 1972 and *Orange Standard*, September 1973, quoted in Clayton, *Enemies and Passing Friends*, p. 44.
41 K. Jeffery, 'Distance and Proximity in Service to the Empire: Ulster and New Zealand between the Wars', *Journal of Imperial and Commonwealth History*, 36:3 (2008), pp. 453–472.
42 C. Falls, *The Birth of Ulster* (London: Constable, 1936), pp. vii, xii.
43 Falls, *The Birth of Ulster*, pp. 230–231. See also J. Cleary, 'Postcolonial Ireland', in Kenny (ed.), *Ireland and the British Empire*, pp. 282–286.
44 G. McIntosh, 'A Performance of Consensus? The Coronation Visit of Elizabeth II to Northern Ireland, 1953', *Irish Studies Review*, 10:3 (2002), pp. 315–329, at p. 322.
45 'The Governor's Notebook' (1955), https://digitalfilmarchive.net/media/a-governors-notebook-179 (accessed 20 February 2020).
46 See D. Lowry, 'Rhodesia, 1890–1980: "The Lost Dominion"', in R. Bickers (ed.), *Settlers and Expatriates* (Oxford: Oxford University Press, 2010), pp. 112–149.
47 E. T. Jollie, 'Southern Rhodesia', *South African Quarterly*, 3 (1921), pp. 10–12.
48 H. Cullen Gouldsbury, 'To England: From the Outposts', *Rhodesian Rhymes* (Bulawayo: Bulawayo Printing and Publishing, 1923), pp. 244–251.
49 E. T. Jollie, '"The Rhodes Idea": Portrait of a Great Imperialist', *Review of Reviews*, 90 (1930), pp. 717–723, at p. 722.
50 B. A. Kosmin, 'Colonial Careers for Marginal Fascists: The Case of Henry Hamilton Beamish', *Wiener Library Bulletin*, XXVII (1973–77), pp. 16–23.
51 C. Olley, 'Another View of Poles', *The New Rhodesia*, 13 December 1946; C. Olley, 'The Case of the White Rhodesia Council', *Rhodesia Monthly Review*, November 1951; A. Mlambo, '"Some are More White than Others": Racial Chauvinism as a Factor in Rhodesian Immigration Policy, 1890 to 1963', *Zambesia*, XXVII:II (2000), pp. 139–160; A. Mlambo, *White Immigration into Rhodesia: From Occupation to Federation* (Harare: University of Zimbabwe Publications, 2002), Ch. 5; B. Tavuyanago, T. Maguti and J. Hlongwana, 'Victims of the Rhodesian Immigration Policy: Polish Refugees from the Second World War', *Journal of Southern African Studies*, 38:4 (2012), pp. 951–965.
52 E. T. Jollie, 'A Rhodesian Dominion', *National Review*, 128 (1947), pp. 279–288, at p. 287.
53 D. Lowry, 'Charles Olley', *Dictionary of Irish Biography* (Cambridge: Cambridge University Press, 2009), https://dib.cambridge.org/viewReadPage.do?articleId=a7113&searchClicked=clicked&quickadvsearch=yes (accessed 15 July 2020).
54 Sir R. Welensky, *Welensky's 4000 Days* (London: Collins, 1964), p. 221.
55 J. R. T. Wood, *The Welensky Papers* (Durban: Bellew Publishing Company, 1983), pp. 1017–1019.
56 M. Muggeridge, *Appointment with Sir Roy Welensky* (London: BBC, 1961), p. 3.

57 C. Leys, *European Politics in Southern Rhodesia* (Oxford: Clarendon Press, 1959), p. 247.
58 Leys, *European Politics*, p. 250.
59 Ibid., p. 247.
60 See Chapter 6, in this volume, by Christian D. Pedersen for more. Also, P. Berlyn, *Rhodesia: Beleaguered Country* (London: Mitre Press, 1967), p. 71; R. Hodder-Williams, 'Rhodesia's Search for a Constitution', *African Affairs*, 69: 276 (1970), pp. 217–235; L. J. MacFarlane, 'Justifying Rebellion: Black and White Nationalism in Rhodesia', *Journal of Commonwealth and Comparative Politics*, 6:1 (1968), pp. 54–79; B. Schwarz, *The White Man's World* (Oxford: Oxford University Press, 2011), Chs 6–7.
61 For these sentiments, see Lowry, 'The Queen of Rhodesia'.
62 B. Goldin, *The Judge, the Prince and the Usurper – From UDI to Zimbabwe* (New York: Vantage, 1990), p. 24.
63 C. Watts, 'Killing Kith and Kin: The Viability of British Military Intervention in Rhodesia, 1964–5', *Twentieth Century British History*, 16:4 (2005), pp. 382–415; P. Murphy, '"An Intricate and Distasteful Subject": British Planning for the Use of Force Against the European Population of Central Africa, 1952–65', *English Historical Review*, 121:492 (2006), pp. 746–777.
64 R. C. Good, *UDI: The International Politics of the Rhodesian Rebellion* (London: Faber & Faber, 1973), p. 60; Rhodesian Correspondent, 'Mr Smith's Rhodesia: Damaged but Determined', *Round Table*, 56: 222 (1965), pp. 114–122, at p. 116; R. D. Scott, 'Northern Ireland: The Politics of Disintegration', *Australian Outlook*, 27: 1 (1973), pp. 40–49, at p. 42.
65 D. Reed, *The Battle for Rhodesia* (Cape Town: Haum, 1966); P. Godwin and I. Hancock, *'Rhodesians Never Die': The Impact of War and Political Change on White Rhodesia, c.1970–1980* (Harare: Baobab Books, 1993), pp. 42–45; D. Lowry, 'The Impact of Anti-Communism on White Rhodesian Culture', *Cold War History*, 7: 2 (2007), pp. 169–194.
66 Sir R. Tredgold, *The Rhodesia That Was My Life* (London: George Allen & Unwin, 1968), p. 255; J. Frederickse, *None But Ourselves: Masses vs Media in the Making of Zimbabwe* (London: Heinemann, 1983).
67 'The Brookeborough Memoirs', *Sunday News* (Belfast), 14 January 1968.
68 B. Barton, *Brookeborough: The Making of a Prime Minister* (Belfast: Institute of Irish Studies, 1988), p. 21.
69 B. Follis, 'Friend or Foe? Ulster Unionists and Afrikaner Nationalists', in D. McCracken (ed.), *Ireland and South Africa in Modern Times* (Durban: University of Durban-Westville, 1996), pp. 172–173; P. Ollerenshaw, 'Northern Ireland and the British Empire-Commonwealth, 1923–61', *Irish Historical Studies*, 36: 142 (2008), pp. 227–242.
70 Howe, *Ireland and Empire*, p. 202.
71 D. W. Miller (with an introduction by J. Bew), *Queen's Rebels: Ulster Loyalism in Historical Perspective* (Dublin: University College Dublin Press, 2007 edn), p. xvii.

72 Lowry, 'A Mirror to Ireland's Face', pp. 172–178; T. Ranger, 'Holy Men and the Zimbabwe War', in W. J. Sheils (ed.), *The Church and War* (Oxford: Oxford University Press, 1983), pp. 449–450, 456.
73 A. Buckley, '"We're Trying to Find Our Identity": Uses of History among Ulster Protestants', in E. Tonkin, M. McDonald and M. K. Chapman (eds), *History and Ethnicity* (London: Routledge, 1989), pp. 183–197; A. D. Buckley, 'The Chosen Few: Biblical Texts in the Regalia of an Ulster Secret Society', *Folk Lie: A Journal of Ethnological Studies*, 24 (1985–86), pp. 5–24; M. Ignatieff, *Mirror, Mirror: Blood and Belonging* (Princeton, NJ: Films for the Humanities and Sciences, 1994); B. J. Graham, 'No Place of the Mind: Contested Protestant Representations of Ulster', *Ecumene*, 1: 3 (1994), pp. 257–281.
74 I. Adamson, *The Identity of Ulster: The Land, the Land and People* (Belfast: Pretani Press, 1982); A. Chennels, 'Settler Myths and the Southern Rhodesian Novel' (Unpublished D.Phil. thesis, University of Zimbabwe, 1982).
75 G. I. Smith, 'Lord O'Neill of the Maine', *Independent*, 25 June 1990.
76 *Irish Times*, 12 November 1965.
77 'Ulster will be Wrong', *New Statesman*, 11 October 1968.
78 T. O'Neill, *Ulster at the Crossroads* (London: Faber & Faber, 1969).
79 *House of Commons (Northern Ireland) Debates*, 28 March 1972, cols.1548–1549.
80 Ibid., cols.1551–1552.
81 B. Faulkner, *Memoirs of a Statesman* (London: Littlehampton, 1978), p. 79.
82 P. Riddell, 'Ulster Farm and Factory', in *The Festival of Britain 1951 in Northern Ireland: Official Souvenir Handbook* (Belfast: Government Printer, 1951), pp. 13–47.
83 P. Riddell, *Fire Over Ulster* (London: Hamish Hamilton, 1970), pp. 13, 61, 68.
84 F. Ormsby (ed.), *The Collected Poems of John Hewitt* (Belfast: Blackstaff Press, 1991), p. 388.
85 Ibid., p. 540.
86 Barton, *Brookeborough*, p. 234.
87 T. M. Devine, 'The Break-up of Britain? Scotland and the End of Empire', *Transactions of the Royal Historical Society*, 16 (2006), pp. 163–180; B. Glass, *The Scottish Nation at Empire's End* (London: Palgrave-Macmillan, 2014), Ch.6; J. Ø. Nielsen and S. Ward, '"Cramped and Restricted at Home"?: Scottish Separatism at Empire's End', *Transactions of the Royal Historical Society*, 25 (2015), pp. 159–185.
88 J. MacKenzie, 'Irish, Scottish, Welsh and English Worlds? The historiography of a Four-Nations Approach to the History of the British Empire', in C. Hall and K. McClelland (eds), *Race, Nation and Empire: Making Histories, 1750 to the Present* (Manchester: Manchester University Press, 2010), p. 13.

8

The tale of two Commonwealths? The (British) Commonwealth of Nations, decolonisation and the break-up of Greater Britain

Andrew Dilley[1]

In 1971 the septuagenarian former Australian Prime Minister Robert Menzies contributed a mournful foreword to his compatriot and octogenarian H. Duncan Hall's monumental study of the *Commonwealth of Nations* (in which Hall returned to a subject he first broached in his 1920 Fabian pamphlet: *The British Commonwealth of Nations*).[2] Menzies took the opportunity to bemoan the post-war transformation of the Commonwealth. He explained that he had become 'acutely and unhappily conscious of a new conception of the Commonwealth' as 'a sort of special agency of the United Nations'. This for Menzies was erroneous as the UN was 'an artificial creation, with a written Constitution and a great paraphernalia of forms and procedures' while 'the Commonwealth is a growth from a recognizable past ... with a minimum of forms and, as many of us grew up to believe, a maximum number of common faiths and instincts'.[3] The changes originated with India's admission as a republic, starting 'a process ... under which more and more Commonwealth countries would be Republics', which meant that 'the evolving Commonwealth would have a less definable structure and would more and more become a loose association ... lacking either common policies or common principles'.[4] However, Britain's likely accession to the European Economic Community (EEC) seemed set to deliver the *coup de grâce* as 'the Treaty of Rome limits the authority of Great Britain in relation to a variety of matters which are purely domestic in character' and hence 'the old Commonwealth idea of an association between fully self-governing nations would be drastically altered; the Commonwealth would cease to be based upon independent sovereignties and would therefore sustain a revolutionary change'.[5] It had, in short, ceased to be the simultaneously tight-knit and decentralised unit Hall described in 1920. Menzies' comments are significant, for few public figures exemplified late 'greater Britishness' more; few mourned its demise more clearly. Menzies reveals how a certain conception of global Britishness had been, but ceased to be, lodged in the interwar Commonwealth of Nations. This chapter argues that any account of the break-up of Greater Britain must pay close attention to the changing nature of the Commonwealth.

Until recently, the Commonwealth tended to attract relatively little attention from imperial and global historians. The 'old' imperial history of Gallagher and Robinson, and Cain and Hopkins, interested in power and denying the significance of institutional forms, bypassed the Commonwealth.[6] The more recent wave of 'British world' publications devoted considerable attention to relations between Britain and the core of the old Dominions.[7] But the British world – generally conceived from the bottom up – tended to keep political forms and states at one remove. Often the concept stretched to encompass a rather broader area occasionally including the United States or pockets of 'Britishness' across the globe.[8] The Commonwealth as an entity and idea became occluded, notwithstanding its significance to contemporaries and the frequent but often unexamined usage of the term in much British world writing.[9] The cultural turn and 'new imperial history' has recently turned more fully to settler colonialism. Bill Schwarz has charted the connections between ideas of whiteness and liberty in the world yet pays little attention to the connection between these and Commonwealth ideas despite their confluence in a figure such as Jan Smuts.[10]

There are some signs that a corner is being turned. The history of the political ideas surrounding Greater Britain and underpinning the interwar Commonwealth, not least those articulated by historians, have been re-examined by Duncan Bell, Tomohito Baji, W. D. McIntyre and Amanda Behm.[11] There has also been renewed interest in the post-war Commonwealth, including Philip Murphy's caustic reassessment, Harshan Kumarasingham's revival of constitutional history, Chris Prior's dissection of fluctuating ideas of Commonwealth in the late 1940s and early 1950s, and Michael Kenny and Nick Pearce's passing discussion within their account of British political discourse on the anglosphere.[12] However less sustained interest has focused on the crucial transition from the interwar to post-1945 Commonwealths, excepting Lorna Lloyd's excellent work on interstate cooperation and diplomacy and Francine McKenzie's important study of the 1947 General Agreement on Tariffs and Trade (GATT) on the crucial symbolic policy of trade preferences, although the shift also serves as an explicit backdrop to David Thackeray's study of British trade networks.[13] The two commonwealths are too rarely placed in the same analytical frame, nor connected sufficiently to broader currents in imperial and global history, not least the history of global Britishness.

This chapter argues that the changing nature of the Commonwealth after 1945 ought to be a crucial element in the story of the break-up of 'Greater

Britain' – taken here to mean a distinct relationship between Britain and the so-called old Dominions – as well as in the history of decolonisation more broadly. To re-examine the Commonwealth's changing nature requires attention to practices of intergovernmental relations and the associated body of political thought, and for these to be set in a global context. Neither set-piece constitutional moments nor a whiggish approach which emphasises continuity over change will get us far, casting the Commonwealth, to use the words of Keith Hancock, as the British Empire defined 'in Aristotelian fashion by its ends'.[14] Rather we must trace the interrelations of states under the Commonwealth umbrella and the way in which these interrelations interacted with the evolving Commonwealth idea and perceptions of global British identity. From this perspective, the period from 1945 to 1970 saw a profound if ragged disjuncture. The new Commonwealth that emerged after 1945, and after Asian and African decolonisation, could no longer be imagined to be a repository of global Britishness or a discrete unit in world affairs. A changed global order superseded and rendered redundant interwar patterns of cooperation simultaneously transformed by expansions. In this context, one Commonwealth ended, another emerged. To elaborate on this case, the next section outlines the development of the interwar British Commonwealth of Nations – Commonwealth 1.0 – and to its close entanglement with ideas of Greater Britain. We then turn to its transformation after 1945 when, under pressure from a growing membership and profoundly altered and US-dominated global order, a new Commonwealth 2.0 emerged which was to be a less intensive forum for interstate cooperation, more focused on North–South dialogue and reimagined in ways that divorced it from notions of global Britishness.

Commonwealth 1.0: the British Commonwealth of Nations, 1880s to 1940s

The late-nineteenth-century flourishing of thought around Greater Britain soon raised a basic question as to how the (supposed) desire for closer cooperation between the United Kingdom and the white settler empire might best translate into institutional practices. Two basic answers emerged: some form of formal federation, or various 'autonomist' variations on 'organic' union. Generally, the autonomist solution, which was based on the notion of voluntary non-binding cooperation within a loose framework of consultation, had more traction than the federalist solution, which promoted the idea of building durable binding pan-imperial institutions. The tensions between the two propositions led the Imperial Federation League to split in the early 1890s.[15] By the First World War the idea of organic union had taken root, not necessarily as the more administratively effective approach to the problem of supranational association, but as the response to what Edwardian commentator Richard Jebb called colonial nationalism and, it ought to be added, to British nationalism.[16] The concern for autonomy was not only characteristic of Dominion leaders like Canadian Prime Minister Wilfrid Laurier who described the British Empire as a 'Galaxy of free nations'.[17] As Herbert Asquith, Britain's Liberal Prime Minister, told the Imperial Conference in 1911: 'we each of us are, and we each of us intend to remain, master in our own household. This is, here at home and throughout the Dominions, the life-blood of our polity'. This was essential in order to 'maintain [...] to the full, in the case of all of us, the principle of Ministerial responsibility to Parliament'.[18] The king-in-parliament, the keystone of British conceptions of sovereignty, 'English liberty' and governance thus turned the original idea of Greater Britain as a consolidated unity into a cluster of Britains.[19]

The terminology of Greater Britain lost traction during the Edwardian period. It failed to capture and include significant white minorities such as the Quebecois and Afrikaners. The term 'empire' continued to be preferred, often used while forgetting the dependent empire, or conceiving that empire as radically different.[20] Notwithstanding some antecedents, the term Commonwealth gained currency during the First World War. It drew from the writings of the classicist Alfred Zimmern and was deployed by the federalist and leading light of the exclusive Round Table Movement, Lionel Curtis, in his *Problems of the Commonwealth*.[21] The 1917 Imperial War Conference postponed discussion until after the war but promised, in Resolution IX, a full discussion of the constitution of the 'Imperial Commonwealth' which encompassed Britain, the Dominions, and also India 'as important portion of the same' – the result of a timely intervention by Sir Satyendra Singha.[22] This lodged India as a member of the interwar Commonwealth, and seemingly ungirding the concept from self-government. The resultant incoherence troubled few and was generally ignored or swiftly glossed down to 1939.[23]

H. Duncan Hall coined the term 'British Commonwealth of Nations' in his 1920 Fabian pamphlet, conceived as an autonomist rejoinder to Curtis. Hall, who exerted a major influence on Jan Smuts, another key architect of the Commonwealth concept, sought to distil the existing relations between Britain and the self-governing Dominions into a model that could carry into the post-1918 world.[24] The phrase was first officially used in the 1921 Anglo–Irish treaty as a substitute for empire – at this stage it acquired a status never achieved by 'Greater Britain'.[25] Southern Ireland's status was henceforth to be identical to Canada's, excepting the additional restrictions within the Treaty. The nature of dominion status remained unclear and the leaders of Canada, South Africa and Ireland continued to push for clarity.[26] This led, in the end, to the 1926 Balfour Declaration following the Imperial

Conference, which explained the Dominions to be 'autonomous communities within the British Empire, equal in status, in no way subordinate one to another in any aspect of their domestic or external affairs'. The 1931 Statute of Westminster gave legal embodiment to this.[27] The legal meaning of dominion status continued to be tested by the Irish, including the right to secede entirely.[28] On the surface, the tale of the 1920s and 1930s was one of change, of the increasing assertion of constitutional autonomy. However, the changes of the period could equally be understood merely as clarifying principles which in practice had always operated, in other words as characterised by continuity. In fact, Hall had coined the term 'British Commonwealth of Nations' as a retrospective description of practice, not a prospective agenda for change.[29] In 1926, Arthur Balfour wrote to Canadian Conservative George Foster that there was 'nothing new' in the declaration or his report for the conference.[30]

The constitutional debates mattered for they clarified and precipitated a political language and concept of the British Commonwealth. Hall sat in a line of interwar writers who sought to decode, with varying degrees of success and satisfaction, the basis and meaning of Commonwealth cooperation. Historians and legal scholars played a crucial role.[31] What they produced though was a body of thought grounded in political practice, all grappling with the reconciliation of association and autonomy. This idea that national autonomy, indeed sovereignty, and close cooperation could coexist became a crucial element in thought on the British Commonwealth of Nations after 1945, integral to the concept of global Britishness as it entered the second half of the twentieth century.

Since theory originated in practice, it is necessary therefore to chart the means of consultation and areas of governance that the British Commonwealth of Nations affected. The monarch as head of state in each part of the Commonwealth acted as a symbol of unity and generated a common British subjecthood. However, as each territory was notionally distinct, the practical implications of this monarchical connection depended on modes of intergovernmental communication and coordination. These evolved from 1880 to 1939 but took place increasingly through several means: a network of High Commissioners (Dominion representatives in London and later British representatives in the Dominions), through intercommunication between the governors-general and the colonial office (a channel reflecting the continued role of the monarch), through dense political and professional networks, through the Committee for Imperial Defence and, crucially, through the colonial and imperial conferences.[32] The periodic consultative conferences performed – before it was fully codified – the essential concept of non-binding cooperation. Hall thought of them as the essence of the Commonwealth concept. Full representation at the conferences was the only reliable indicator of dominion status.³³ They were also supplemented by more specialist conferences, for instance the Imperial Press Conference of 1909 or the Imperial Customs Conference of 1921. These practices were embedded within a dense associational life arranged by groups as diverse as universities, chambers of commerce, journalists and parliamentarians, now richly charted by the British world literature. These networks and groups – this civil society – evolved in dialogue with the budding interstate collaboration embedded in the Commonwealth.³⁴

The evolution of the British Commonwealth of Nations must be set in the global context. Prior to 1918 its sphere of operation was largely unencumbered. British imperial power existed within an international order with few overarching institutions, although there was a growing body of international law. The precise location of sovereignty between Britain and the emerging Dominions was, in practice, defined by the degree to which various Dominions sought to assert themselves, for example Canada with commercial foreign policy.³⁵ In 1895 the abrogation by Britain of commercial treaties with Germany and Belgium created legal space for the policy, then largely anathema in British politics, of preferential trade.³⁶

The new post-1918 international settlement forced greater definition of the nature of the nascent Commonwealth. External relations at the Paris Peace Conferences and in the League of Nations could not easily simultaneously be characterised by the 'one and many' logic at the heart of the concept. Separate representation for the Dominions seemed, to many, to amass votes behind the United Kingdom. The British Empire delegation at Versailles and its successors emerged as a compromise, and there was still a tussle over who should sign.³⁷ Separate representation for the Dominions in the League of Nations followed, again with the same uneasiness in the US Congress that the British were stacking up votes.³⁸ The relationships between the British Commonwealth of Nations and the League of Nations as entities also exercised some political thought including a large part of Hall's study and a section of the Balfour Declaration longer than that dealing with India.³⁹

The League of Nations was a logical international expression of Wilsonian self-determination. It deepened the supranational concept of the British Commonwealth of Nations, which became a cluster of notionally independent states. The British government's short-lived attempt to ensure that this intermediation was to some extent closed – through the maintenance of the doctrine of *inter se* by which appeals for arbitration ought not to be heard beyond the Commonwealth, having been heard within it – proved impossible to maintain when the newly independent Irish government lodged the Anglo–Irish Treaty directly with the League of Nations.⁴⁰ Nonetheless, the League of Nations imposed few practical constraints on the older forms of cooperation inherited from before 1914. While it required the British

Commonwealth of Nations to adopt more clarity of external definition in order to become more obviously sovereign, it did not invade or constrain areas of possible cooperation, nor supersede them.[41]

The interwar global order left considerable scope for cooperation through the existing and evolving practices associated with the British Commonwealth of Nations. Practices such as rare collective agreements (the War Graves Commission cited at one point as the principal example), dense webs of bilateral cooperation, unilateral adoption of policies favouring other members (whether pre-1932 imperial preferences or, say, the United Kingdom's Empire Settlement Act and Marketing Boards), the diffusion of legislation, and considerable legal alignment remained (underpinned by the Judicial Committee of the Privy Council). The significance of the resultant cooperation can be questioned. Exceptions usually have to be outlined. Such doubts and qualifications were the product of an approach to governance which sought to preserve autonomy of action for members.

The areas of governance covered ranged from foreign policy and defence through to trade (and with a lot of caveats currency) to migration, communications and transport. The interwar Commonwealth also functioned as a strategic alliance. There was no obligation on members to support British foreign policy, as became clear in the Chanak Crisis of 1922, hence the United Kingdom subsequently sought to nurture Dominion support, and particularly to ensure – successfully, excepting Eire – full backing in the growing confrontation with the Axis powers.[42] Migration and citizenship allowed relatively unconstrained movement underpinned by a common British subjecthood based on the Crown. Migration within the white settler Empire/British Commonwealth continued to be promoted between the wars, though the flow of people was confined by the 'Natal Education Tests' and the discretion of immigration officials constraining the movement of non-white imperial subjects.[43] The British state especially subsidised a communications infrastructure based on shipping, telegraphs, air transportation and postage which intensified and shaped information flows.[44] Economics, or the sphere of 'men, money, and markets' as Australian Prime Minister Stanley Bruce put it, was a further significant field of cooperation.[45] Attempts to align on various aspects of commercial law can be found. In the 1920s a web of agreements was negotiated between Britain and the Dominions ameliorating double income taxation, moves subsequently translated to international agreements; or, on a more mundane regulatory level, the 1921 Imperial Customs Conference proposed uniform paperwork to demonstrate the origin and content of imports, and hence ease the bureaucracy attendant on preference.[46] After the gold standard was abandoned, the sterling bloc emerged, including non-empire members and excluding Canada.

Preferential trade, as McKenzie rightly argued, became the symbol of British Commonwealth cooperation and, for supporters, of its effectiveness.

Originating in late-nineteenth-century drives to revive enhanced access to British markets for empire-members, preference was a major element in Joseph Chamberlain's tariff reform campaign, launched in 1903. It carried through into the 1920s reaching apotheosis at the Ottawa Economic Conference of 1932 where a web of bilateral preferential agreements was negotiated. Preferential trade involved the concession of better than Most Favoured Nation terms to empire members. Its attractiveness to successive generations of thinkers on the political economy of the Commonwealth was not just that it preserved protection and tariff autonomy but that it used economics to express a certain global moral economy.[47] As Leo Amery wrote in the *Observer* in 1932: 'Mutual preference is the practical expression of a desire to cooperate without that surrender of economic and political autonomy which is involved in any formal customs union with internal free trade'.[48]

British Commonwealth cooperation had sceptics as well as believers. The constitutional expert Sir Ivor Jennings thought its achievements could 'easily be matched with examples of collaboration drawn from Europe, and especially through the technical activities of the League of Nations'.[49] But the key word was 'matched', not superseded. The interwar period offered few more effective examples of international collaboration than the British Commonwealth of Nations. Whatever its practical shortcomings, the experience of cooperation founded on political principles easily deemed 'British' – especially the final sovereignty of parliaments – made the British Commonwealth of Nations a key element in the expression of global Britishness. It was not simply a vague variation on the idea of the English-speaking world, but a more tightly defined practice of interstate cooperation grounded in shared constitutional values.[50]

Commonwealth 2.0: the Commonwealth of Nations and decolonisation

The Second World War seemed to vindicate the Commonwealth method of supranational cooperation. All Dominions except Ireland joined Britain's struggle against the Axis Powers. As well as military cooperation, the formation of the tightly knit sterling area, a lattice of economic controls, and a concerted propaganda effort (as described in Wendy Webster's chapter in this volume) all made the Commonwealth more tangible to contemporaries.[51] When Ivor Jennings published a book studying the British Commonwealth of Nations in 1948, his tone was far less ponderous than in the 1930s.[52] Yet in the two decades or so after 1945 virtually every attribute that characterised the interwar Commonwealth changed.[53] Its membership transformed, its functioning altered to become a broad network of postcolonial states.[54] Non-binding voluntary cooperation remained but now focused on development, on the promotion of broad statements of human rights, and on causes célèbres especially opposing settler hegemony in southern Africa.[55] The changes, however, came not only in response to altered internal composition but also a changed global framework.[56]

One moment became, retrospectively, remembered as a key date in the transition to what might be called a postcolonial Commonwealth: the Declaration of London in 1949 which admitted India as a republic and casually dropped the term British within its text.[57] As we have seen, Menzies retrospectively thought the admission of republics paved the way to a Commonwealth which failed to share all the 'values' of its predecessor. Similarly, Enoch Powell derided the lack of meaning in the Crown's changed status.[58] However, contemporaries were equally likely to see continuity in the Declaration of London, not least in its spirit of compromise. Leo Amery wrote in *The Times*: 'May one who was once concerned in the drafting of the earlier definition of our Commonwealth relationship in 1926 sincerely congratulate the members of the recent conference on a solution which has so closely preserved the essential spirit and even the wording of that definition and of its legal sequel, the Statute of Westminster?' He continued, 'It has changed, in respect of India alone, the historic concept of allegiance as an element in our unity'. However, Amery still felt that India's connection was underpinned by the rule of law and the 'essentially British' type of constitution.[59]

Initially the change in the Commonwealth's composition was minor. Three new members joined the Commonwealth in the late 1940s – Pakistan, India and Sri Lanka – while Ireland left. Practices to promote non-binding voluntary cooperation persisted, even seemingly accelerated in the 1950s. Imperial Conferences were replaced by meetings of Heads of Government and associated meetings of other clusters of ministers, not least finance ministers drawn together by the management of the Sterling Area. These may have had a little less of the grandeur of old but, on the other hand, were more frequent. Voluntary cooperation seemed for a time in the 1950s to have a new lease of life. It survived the far more dramatic expansion of numbers in the late 1950s and 1960s which saw the membership rise to over thirty.[60] The core concept was retained, indeed enhanced, by the founding of the Commonwealth Secretariat in 1965, intended to separate the association more clearly from the British state.[61]

The language of Commonwealth rapidly evolved in ways that reflected changing conceptions. Through the 1950s the words 'empire' and 'British' both became increasingly constrained in meaning. In the interwar period most of the keenest supporters of the British Commonwealth of Nations used the term empire as, if not more, frequently. Officially, as per the 1926 declaration, the British Commonwealth of Nations remained within the empire. During the Second World War, promoted not least by Winston

Churchill and others, it became more common to speak of the British Commonwealth and Empire, the implication increasingly being that the two were distinct and that the term 'empire' applied exclusively to the dependent empire.[62] This tendency for the lexicon to shift can also be seen in the quiet demise of the term 'Dominion' in the 1950s. A term once deemed to distinguish senior Commonwealth members from mere colonies came to be seen as insufficient to meet that end.[63] Similarly, as the Commonwealth expanded to encompass increasing numbers for whom independence meant departure from colonial status within the British Empire, the term British was quietly dropped. While Attlee fudged the issue of correct terminology in 1948, and it was hardly settled in 1949, official usages shifted decisively away from British Commonwealth in the 1950s. Civil society organisations followed suit in tortuous fashion and with at times considerable time lags. Sport provided the most vivid illustration: the British Empire Games were founded in 1930, became the British Empire and Commonwealth Games from 1954 to 1966, then the British Commonwealth Games from 1970 to 1974, only in 1978 catching up to become the Commonwealth Games.[64]

The linguistic gymnastics reflected alterations in composition that were in turn heavily shaped by changes on the world stage. The world after 1945 rapidly took on fundamentally new features, a change profound enough for A. G. Hopkins to argue that collectively a threshold in the history of globalisation had been crossed.[65] The rise of the United States and USSR as global superpowers and the advent of the Cold War altered global realpolitik.[66] The end of the Second World War saw a reconfiguration of international governance under US tutelage more profound than that seen in 1918, and particularly the founding of new more binding international institutions both globally: the UN, which became a more robust successor to the League of Nations, the International Monetary Fund (IMF), the GATT; and regionally, with the North Atlantic Treaty Organisation (NATO) and even the EEC.[67] All tended to have more capacity to bind adherents and required a greater sacrifice of sovereignty than their interwar predecessors. Such new institutions either curtailed or eliminated the space in which voluntary cooperation could operate, or else lessened the relative significance of such cooperation. These changes took time to bed down and work themselves out, meaning that the interwar Commonwealth was superseded piecemeal, almost imperceptibly, which accounts largely for why it is so often overlooked in the eclipse of global Britishness.

The idea of the Commonwealth as a defensive alliance faded after 1945. As Francine McKenzie has shown, it persisted for a time in the thinking of leading Dominions as a counterbalance to the United States.[68] However, in the end, the new US-led alliance that came together during the Cold War sidelined the Commonwealth. The United States itself was not part of the

Commonwealth, nor would become so, and since it would, by virtue of military and strategic might, inevitably assume leadership of the Western powers, the Commonwealth could not become the centre of the anti-Communist struggle. The chief theatres of the early stages of the Cold War, the Far East and Eastern Europe, were not close to the centres of the Commonwealth. The US-led alliance needed to integrate other powers than Commonwealth members and evolved new forms: ANZUS, SEATO and most obviously NATO. NATO's central tenet that an attack on one member was an attack on all constituted an assertion of pooled sovereignty far beyond – indeed in some ways antithetical to – anything in the interwar Commonwealth.[69] Simultaneously, the expanding Commonwealth rapidly came to include members who, led by Jawaharlal Nehru, would also be members of the non-aligned movement, or else would potentially make overtures to the Soviets or Chinese.[70] The hostility between India and Pakistan, and the wars of 1947, 1965 and 1971, further reduced any idea of the Commonwealth as a defensive alliance.[71] To be sure, military cooperation persisted between Britain and the old Commonwealth members, but such cooperation was bilateral or conceived within a broader framework of a Western alliance, or English-speaking world, rather than as a Commonwealth venture.

The demise of preferential trade was even more stark, illustrating precisely how the new forms of international institutions curtailed interwar Commonwealth practices. The general liberalisation of trade in the 1950s was the product of a reversal of US protectionism and a concerted American attack on preferences. The interwar preferential system had grated on American exporters. The United States, as McKenzie has shown, launched a comprehensive assault on preferential trade, which reached its climax at the negotiation of the GATT in Geneva. The 'old' Commonwealth fought a rearguard action that resulted in the retention of existing preferences but prevented any revision or renegotiation of the Ottawa system other than the reduction of preferences. Preferences were ossified and doomed ultimately to erosion by inflation (for preferential margins measured quantitatively) and shifting trade patterns.[72]

The defence of preference led to assertions of the essential unity of the Commonwealth. Thus, in October 1945, a report from a conference hosted by the Federation of Chambers of Commerce of the British Empire London Conference stated that although the 'British Commonwealth of Nations' was 'divided by the sea' and composed of 'States which are themselves each and severally sovereign', this did 'not deprive them of the right to lower the inter-State tariff walls which divide them' since 'the right to this is claimed by every political entity'.[73] Frequently the comparison was made to US states. Such assertions, however, could not be sustained, for each member of the Commonwealth claimed economic sovereignty. The GATT reasserted the sanctity of Most Favoured Nation Status in trade relations between such sovereign entities. Concessions granted to one must be granted to all, except in the context of a Free Trade Area or Customs Union. For a time, GATT seemed impermanent. A backbench Conservative cluster of MPs in the Empire Industries Association argued for greater 'flexibility', a campaign defeated at the 1954 Conservative conference.[74]

The issue of preference again combusted in the 1960s around Britain's application to the EEC. Those defending preferences and opposing entry knew they were defending a fossilised system.[75] At a Commonwealth Industries Association meeting, essentially a backbench lobby group, Conservative MP Maurice Petherick said: 'We ought to have secured the elimination of the restrictive clauses of GATT. We must not be "swallowed up" by the Common Market. There was no doubt the USA was behind this'.[76] EEC membership not only promised the termination of preferences but also the cessation, as Labour leader Hugh Gaitskell pointed out, of the concept of a Commonwealth of autonomous independent states. How, he asked, could the United Kingdom lead such an association while relegated to the status of a 'province' of what he assumed would become a federal Europe.[77] In response, supporters of EEC membership articulated a concept of the Commonwealth compatible with membership of other blocs.[78] This approach was adopted too by Arnold Smith, the first Commonwealth Secretary-General.[79] It was, in many ways, a pragmatic response to changing global governance precipitated by Britain's pursuit of EEC membership. But by limiting important aspects of cooperation by the United Kingdom, the altered conception of an open Commonwealth limited the field within which economic cooperation in the Commonwealth would operate. While predictions that the Commonwealth would break up as a result proved misplaced, the price of survival was a retreat to the margins.[80]

Citizenship rights and migration also evolved, and eroded, from 1945. The 1946 Canadian Nationality Act introduced the concept that each Commonwealth country had separate citizenship. Others followed suit, especially the British with the 1948 British Nationality Act. By the end of the 1940s, only Britain, India and Pakistan allowed free entry to British subjects.[81] In Britain immigration legislation tightened in the following decades under the prospect of waves of migration from the West Indies, South Asia, Africa (not least South Asians fleeing Kenya and Uganda) and finally the prospect of a large wave of newcomers from Hong Kong. The 1962 Commonwealth Immigrants Act made no overt distinction between those from the 'old' largely white and ethnically British Commonwealth and the 'new' Commonwealth, although there was an assumption that the distinction between skilled, semi-skilled, and unskilled migrants with associated quotas would favour migrants from the old Commonwealth. Commonwealth citizens finally lost distinctive rights as the distinction between 'Patrials' (those with UK ancestry) and 'non-Patrials' became the basis of UK Citizenship under the 1971 Immigration Act and for the United Kingdom's accession to the EEC where the principle of free movement introduced a de facto favouring of European over old or new Commonwealth migrants.[82] The distinction was tightened further with the 1981 British Nationality Act.[83] Britishness thus came to be legally defined as an archipelagic concept. Cultural shifts in former Dominions on the Pacific rim, combined with labour shortages, and reduced emigration from the United Kingdom, similarly eroded policies favouring British and indeed white immigration, substituting policies which made little distinction between Commonwealth and non-Commonwealth migrants.[84] The Commonwealth became a less and less meaningful sphere to think about migration and citizenship, simultaneously undermining Greater Britishness and 1950s dreams of a distinctive post-imperial 'multiracial' Commonwealth.

The declining role of the Commonwealth in the spheres of strategy, economics, and migration and citizenship were all related to its expanding membership, and hence divergence from the old 'Greater British' core. As the Commonwealth became larger, the concept of tight-knit voluntary cooperation became less plausible. Expansion, and especially the admission of small states, was a conscious decision which must be understood in a global context.[85] The Cold War created a rationale for Britain to reach out to newly independent colonies to counter the spread of communism. Buttressing Asia against the spread of communism provided an underlying rationale for a new and powerful development agenda, which emerged in the Colombo Plan. The dominant modes of imagining the Commonwealth reconfigured through the 1950s to place its role in fostering north–south dialogue and in promoting development front and centre. The same rationale continued into the 1960s with an ongoing development agenda focused especially on Africa.[86] There was, conversely, little by way of Cold War rationale to maintain the interwar Commonwealth's inner core of settler members who were already embedded in the broader Western alliance led by the United States.

Thus conceptions and practices of Commonwealth cooperation evolved to be compatible with the often contradictory entanglements of members – to be an 'open Commonwealth' as Margaret Ball put it.[87] The reconfigured Commonwealth had its enthusiastic champions in the older members: Patrick Gordon Walker, Lester Pearson and Arnold Smith; and sceptics and critics, such as Menzies and Enoch Powell.[88] It was almost certainly Powell who wrote a scathing letter to *The Times* criticising the Commonwealth as a 'gigantic farce', dominated by nationalists looking for 'any advantage going' while 'resentment against the former ruling power or mother country makes some of them less well disposed to Britain than to Germany, China, or Israel'. The 'old dominions', Powell asserted, had 'no present real ties with Britain other than such as history might have left between any two foreign nations'.[89]

What critics and supporters of the 1960s Commonwealth almost entirely agreed upon was that it had ceased to be exclusively or primarily the repository of relations between Britain and the old Dominions. Yet legacies of Commonwealth 1.0 could be found in surprising places. Julian Amery (son of Leo) argued that the EEC was a worthy inheritor of Chamberlain's federal vision.[90] While J. R. Seeley's 'great Schism' came to be forgotten, Greater Britain reintegrated into the once competing English-speaking world or, more recently, the anglosphere.[91] Very occasionally the idea fostered in the old British Commonwealth of Nations that significant voluntary supranational action could be undertaken, especially on economics, was reapplied to Commonwealth 2.0.[92] These legacies have yet to be fully charted.

Conclusion

The break-up of Greater Britain cannot be thought about without taking account of the changing nature of the Commonwealth of Nations, especially the radical reconfiguration of the Commonwealth from the 1940s and the fact that, unlike the British Empire, the Commonwealth has not in fact ceased to exist. However, after 1945 it gradually ceased to be a repository for a sense of greater British identity, a role formerly served by the interwar British Commonwealth of Nations. Crucially the British Commonwealth of Nations was not just a repository for the 'Britannic Vision', it was an arena in which the component polities encompassed in that vision could collaborate and hence translate that vision into a practical reality of cooperation. The key symbolic institutions of the British Commonwealth of Nations were the monarchy and the Imperial Conferences, but cooperation could find expression across areas including law, strategy, political economy, migration and citizenship. The effectiveness or otherwise of this cooperation was debated by contemporaries, and remains debatable, but its existence pushed Anglo–Dominion relationships beyond political imagination and beyond bilateralism.

The mode of cooperation which evolved, in turn depended upon an international order which, while occasionally forcing unwelcome definition, did not prevent or supersede this mode of cooperation. Thoughts on voluntary cooperation emerged from practice and described an approach to international collaboration generally privileging sovereignty: a form of unity in division. The relevance and importance of these practices faded after 1945. More powerful and binding global institutions superseded or even barred the interwar practices of cooperation in the British Commonwealth of Nations; the growth of the Commonwealth made spontaneous agreement less likely,[1] and its changed composition in the context of the Cold War shifted focus to the new membership and to issues of development and human rights. The Commonwealth was no longer the heir of Greater Britain, but a fundamentally new association built on the majority of the territories of the former British Empire, joined by others from the 1990s, adopting the older practice of non-binding cooperation, and articulating essentially universal values and focusing on their promotion in the developing world. The Commonwealth was no longer a synonym for the British connection.

Greater Britishness evolved as part of broader debates about global association and how to reconcile continued connection with ideas of representative democracy and national sovereignty. The British Commonwealth of Nations served as a practical governmental response to the problem, a practice of interstate relations which was politically viable, at least intermittently effective, and whose existence shaped political theorisation. Understanding greater Britishness, and its demise, cannot be separated from the history of its most practical political expression. Thus, the state needs to be brought back in alongside nation, allowing notions of governance and identity to be considered in conjunction with each other. While this of course cannot be the entire picture, the changing Commonwealth must be treated as more than simply a bit player in either the tale of British decolonisation or the ending of Greater Britain. We must tell the tale of two Commonwealths if Greater Britain's strange death, and its stranger afterlife, are to be fully comprehended.

Notes

1 I would like to thank the participants at the 'Break-up of Greater Britain' conference at Holckenhavn Castle, Nyborg, in 2018 and especially the editors for very helpful feedback on early drafts of this chapter. I would also like to acknowledge the support of the AHRC Early Career Fellowship (AH/M00662X/1) for supporting the research project which fed into this chapter.
2 H. D. Hall, *The British Commonwealth of Nations* (London: Methuen, 1920).
3 R. Menzies, 'Introduction', in H. D. Hall (ed.), *Commonwealth: A History of the British Commonwealth of Nations* (London: Van Nostrand Reinhold, 1971), p. xxii.
4 Ibid., pp. xix–xx.
5 Ibid., p. xxiv.
6 J. Gallagher and R. Robinson, 'The Imperialism of Free Trade', *Economic History Review*, 6:1 (1953), pp.1–15; P. J. Cain and A. G. Hopkins, *British Imperialism, 1688–2000* (Harlow: Longman, 2001).

7 For critical overviews, see R. K. Bright and A. R. Dilley, 'After the British World', *The Historical Journal*, 60:2 (2017), pp. 547–568; S. Howe, 'British Worlds, Settler Worlds, World Systems, and Killing Fields', *Journal of Imperial and Commonwealth History*, 40:4 (2012), pp. 691–725.

8 For such an expansive approach, see G. Magee and A. Thompson, *Empire and Globalisation: Networks of People, Goods and Capital in the British World, c. 1850–1914* (Cambridge: Cambridge University Press, 2010).

9 For instance, the word Commonwealth peppers the chapter by C. Bridge and K. Fedorowich, 'Mapping the British World', in C. Bridge and K. Fedorowich (eds), *The British World: Diaspora, Culture, and Identity* (London: F. Cass, 2003).

10 B. Schwarz, *Memories of Empire: Vol 1: The White Man's World* (Oxford: Oxford University Press, 2011).

11 D. Bell, *The Idea of Greater Britain: Empire and the Future of World Order, 1860–1900* (Princeton, NJ: Princeton University Press, 2007); T. Baji, 'Zionist Internationalism? Alfred Zimmern's Post-Racial Commonwealth', *Modern Intellectual History*, 13:3 (2015), pp. 623–651; T. Baji, 'The British Commonwealth as Liberal International Avatar: With the Spines of Burke', *History of European Ideas*, 46 (2020), pp. 649–665; W. D. McIntyre, *The Britannic Vision: Historians and the Making of the British Commonwealth of Nations, 1907–48* (Basingstoke: Palgrave Macmillan, 2009); A. Behm, *Imperial History and the Global Politics of Exclusion: Britain, 1880–1940* (Basingstoke: Palgrave Macmillan, 2017).

12 P. Murphy, *The Empire's New Clothes: The Myth of the Commonwealth* (London: Hurst, 2018); C. Prior, '"This Community Which Nobody Can Define": Meanings of Commonwealth in the Late 1940s and 1950s', *Journal of Imperial and Commonwealth History*, 47:3 (2019), pp. 568–590; H. Kumarasingham, 'Written Differently: A Survey of Commonwealth Constitutional History in the Age of Decolonisation', *Journal of Imperial and Commonwealth History*, 46:5 (2018), pp. 874–908; M. Kenny and N. Pearce, *Shadows of Empire: The Anglosphere in British Politics* (Cambridge: Polity, 2018).

13 L. Lloyd, '"Us and Them": The Changing Nature of Commonwealth Diplomacy, 1880–1973', *Commonwealth & Comparative Politics*, 39:3 (2001), pp. 9–30; L. Lloyd, 'Britain and the Transformation from Empire to Commonwealth', *The Round Table*, 86: 343 (1997), pp. 333–360; F. McKenzie, *Redefining the Bonds of Commonwealth, 1939–1948: The Politics of Preference* (Basingstoke: Palgrave Macmillan, 2002); D. Thackeray, *Forging a British World of Trade: Culture, Ethnicity, and Market in the Empire-Commonwealth, 1880–1975* (Oxford: Oxford University Press, 2019), pp. 111–141. Saul Dubow's recent re-narration of South Africa's relations with the Commonwealth spans this period but does not pay sharp attention to the transition. See S. Dubow, 'The Commonwealth and South Africa: From Smuts to Mandela', *Journal of Imperial and Commonwealth History*, 45:2 (2017), pp. 284–314.

14 W. K. Hancock, *Survey of British Commonwealth Affairs, Volume One: Problems of Nationality, 1918–1936* (London: Oxford University Press, 1937). 'Whiggism' culminated in N. Mansergh, *The Commonwealth Experience* (London: Weidenfeld & Nicolson, 1969).

15 G. Martin, 'The Idea of Imperial Federation', in R. Hyam and G. Martin (eds), *Reappraisals in British Imperial History* (Cambridge: Cambridge University Press, 1975), pp. 130–131.
16 R. Jebb, *Studies in Colonial Nationalism* (London: Arnold, 1905). On British nationalism, see D. Edgerton, *The Rise and Fall of the British Nation: A Twentieth-Century History* (London: Allen Lane, 2019), pp. 10–25.
17 Quoted and contextualised in G. A. Thompson, 'Ontario's Empire: Liberalism and "Britannic" Nationalism in Laurier's Canada, 1887–1919' (Phd Thesis, University of Oxford, 2016), p. 75.
18 CD5745, *Minutes of the Imperial Conference*, 1911, pp. 22–23.
19 J. P. Greene (ed.), *Exclusionary Empire: English Liberty Overseas, 1600–1900* (Cambridge: Cambridge University Press, 2010).
20 For example, see A. M. V. Milner, *The Nation and the Empire: Being a Collection of Speeches and Addresses* (London: Constable, 1913).
21 McIntyre, *Britannic Vision*, pp. 119–120.
22 CD 8566, *Imperial War Conference*, 1917, pp. 5, 49–50.
23 The 1926 Balfour Declaration devoted six elusive lines to India's 'special position', E. 129, Imperial Conference, 1926, Inter-Imperial Relations Committee, p. 2.
24 Hall (ed.), *Commonwealth*, pp. 190–197.
25 Hall, *British Commonwealth of Nations*; McIntyre, *Britannic Vision*, pp. 35–36, 107.
26 P. G. Wigley, *Canada and the Transition to Commonwealth: British—Canadian Relations 1917–1926* (Cambridge: Cambridge University Press, 1977); G. Martin, 'The Irish Free State and the Evolution of the Commonwealth, 1921–1949', in R. Hyam and G. Martin (eds), *Reappraisals in British Imperial History* (Cambridge: Cambridge University Press, 1975), pp. 201–223.
27 E. 129, Imperial Conference, 1926, Inter-Imperial Relations Committee, p. 1; P. Marshall, 'The Balfour Formula and the Evolution of the Commonwealth', *The Round Table*, 90:361 (2001), pp. 541–553.
28 D. K. Coffey, '"The Right to Shoot Himself": Secession in the British Commonwealth of Nations', *The Journal of Legal History*, 39:2 (2018), pp. 117–139; McIntyre, *Britannic Vision*, pp. 222–235.
29 Hall, *British Commonwealth of Nations*.
30 Archives Canada, MG II.D.7.12 (George Foster Papers), File 1919–1932, Arthur Balfour to Foster, 5 May 1927.
31 McIntyre, *Britannic Vision*.
32 K. C. Wheare, *The Constitutional Structure of the Commonwealth* (Oxford: Oxford University Press, 1960), pp. 128–149; J. E. Kendle, *The Colonial and Imperial Conferences, 1887–1911: A Study in Imperial Organization* (London: Longmans, 1967); Lloyd, 'Us and Them'. The term imperial replaced colonial in 1911.
33 McIntyre, *Britannic Vision*, pp. 79–81; Hall, *Commonwealth*.
34 Hall, *British Commonwealth of Nations*, pp. 372–378.
35 Wigley, *Canada and the Transition to Commonwealth*, pp. 6–26; B. Fergusson, *Rt Hon W. S. Fielding*, two vols. (Windsor, NS: Lancelot Press, 1971), pp. II, 39–66.
36 L. Trainor, 'The British Government and Imperial Economic Unity, 1890–1895', *The Historical Journal*, 13:1 (1970), pp. 68–84.

37 R. F. Holland, *Britain and the Commonwealth Alliance, 1918–1939* (London: Macmillan, 1981), pp. 4–6; Wigley, *Canada and the Transition to Commonwealth*, pp. 67–95.
38 Wigley, *Canada and the Transition to Commonwealth*, pp. 111–117.
39 Hall, *British Commonwealth of Nations*, pp. 329–370; E. 129, Inter-Imperial Relations Committee, pp. 4–6.
40 Martin, 'Irish Free State', p. 209; R. B. Stewart, *Treaty Relations of the British Commonwealth of Nations* (New York: Macmillan, 1939), pp. 358–362.
41 S. Pedersen, 'Back to the League of Nations', *The American Historical Review*, 112:4 (2007), pp. 1091–1117; S. Pedersen, *The Guardians: The League of Nations and the Crisis of Empire* (Oxford: Oxford University Press, 2016).
42 Holland, *Britain and the Commonwealth Alliance*.
43 S. Constantine, *Emigrants and Empire: British Settlement in the Dominions between the Wars* (Manchester: Manchester University Press, 1990). R. Bright, 'Asian Migration and the British World, 1850–1914', in K. Fedorowich and A. Thompson (eds), *Empire, Identity and Migration in the British World* (Manchester: Manchester University Press, 2013).
44 S. J. Potter, *News and the British World* (Oxford: Oxford University Press, 2003); S. J. Potter, *Broadcasting Empire: The BBC and the British World, 1922–1970* (Oxford: Oxford University Press, 2012); D. Cryle, '"Cornerstone of the Commonwealth": The Press Union and the Preservation of the Penny Cable Rate, 1941–67', *Journal of Imperial and Commonwealth History*, 42:1 (2014), pp. 153–170.
45 W. K. Hancock, *Survey of British Commonwealth Affairs, Volume Two: Problems of Economic Policy, 1918–1939* (London: Oxford University Press, 1942).
46 National Archives, London, DO 35/218/10: Double Income Tax Relief, 1930; Cmd. 1231: Imperial Customs Conference, 1921.
47 I. M. Drummond, *Imperial Economic Policy, 1917–1939* (London: Allen and Unwin, 1974); McKenzie, *Redefining the Bonds of Commonwealth*.
48 *Observer*, 10 April 1932.
49 I. Jennings, 'The Constitution of the British Commonwealth', *Political Quarterly*, 9:4 (1938), pp. 465–479.
50 On the distinct concept of the English-Speaking World, see P. Clarke, 'The English-Speaking Peoples before Churchill', *Britain and the World*, 4:2 (2011), pp. 199–231.
51 N. Mansergh, *Survey of British Commonwealth Affairs: Problems of Wartime Co-operation and Post-War Change 1939–1952* (London: Oxford University Press, 1958).
52 I. Jennings, *The British Commonwealth of Nations* (London: Hutchinson, 1948).
53 Lloyd, 'Britain and the Transformation'.
54 W. D. McIntyre, 'Commonwealth Legacy', in J. M. Brown and W. R. Louis (eds), *Oxford History of the British Empire, Vol. 5: The Twentieth Century* (Oxford: Oxford University Press, 1999).
55 Murphy, *Empire's New Clothes*.
56 Dubow, 'Commonwealth and South Africa', pp. 8–9.

57 R. J. Moore, *Making the New Commonwealth* (Oxford: Clarendon, 1987).
58 McIntyre, *Britannic Vision*, pp. 49–50.
59 *The Times*, 28 April 1949. See also H. Kumarasingham, *A Political Legacy of the British Empire: Power and the Parliamentary System in Post-Colonial India and Sri Lanka* (London: I.B. Tauris, 2012).
60 K. Srinivasan, 'Nobody's Commonwealth? The Commonwealth in Britain's Post-Imperial Adjustment', *Commonwealth and Comparative Politics*, 44: 2 (2006), pp. 257–269.
61 W. D. McIntyre, 'Britain and the Creation of the Commonwealth Secretariat', *Journal of Imperial and Commonwealth History*, 28: 1 (2000), pp. 135–158.
62 Wheare, *Constitutional Structure*, pp. 4–6.
63 W. D. McIntyre, 'The Strange Death of Dominion Status', *Journal of Imperial and Commonwealth History*, 27: 2 (1999), pp. 193–212.
64 https://web.archive.org/web/20170416125811/http://thecgf.com/games/story.asp (accessed 15 August 2019).
65 A. G. Hopkins, 'Introduction: Globalization, an Agenda for Historians', in A. G. Hopkins (ed.), *Globalization in World History* (London: Pimlico, 2002), pp. 7–9.
66 O. A. Westad, *The Cold War: A World History* (London: Penguin, 2018).
67 E. Borgwardt, *A New Deal for the World: America's Vision for Human Rights* (Cambridge, MA: Belknap, 2005); M. Mazower, *No Enchanted Palace: The End of Empire and the Ideological Origins of the United Nations* (Princeton, NJ: Princeton University Press, 2009).
68 F. McKenzie, 'In the National Interest: Dominions' Support for Britain and the Commonwealth after the Second World War', *Journal of Imperial and Commonwealth History*, 34:4 (2006), pp. 553–576.
69 Article 5, The North Atlantic Treaty, 4 April 1949.
70 Mansergh, *Survey of British Commonwealth Affairs*, pp. 363–365.
71 J. D. B. Miller, *Survey of Commonwealth Affairs: Problems of Expansion and Attrition, 1953–1969* (London: Oxford University Press, 1974), pp. 45–62.
72 McKenzie, *Redefining the Bonds of Commonwealth*.
73 London Metropolitan Archives CLC/B/082/MS18287/8: Federation of Chambers of Commerce of the British Empire, Congress Report, 1945, p. 9.
74 University of Warwick, Modern Records Centre, MSS 221 [Empire/Commonwealth Industries Association] 2/1/2/3: Executive Committee, 1947–1956, 17 November 1954.
75 S. Ward, *Australia and the British Embrace: The Demise of the Imperial Ideal* (Carlton South, Vic.: Melbourne University Press, 2001); J. D. B. Miller, 'The Commonwealth after De Gaulle', *International Journal*, 19:1 (1963), pp. 30–39.
76 University of Warwick, Modern Records Centre, MSS 221 [Empire/Commonwealth Industries Association] 1/1/2: General Meetings and Council, 1935–1967, AGM of Commonwealth Industries Association, 25 July 1961.
77 Speech by Hugh Gaitskell against UK membership of the Common Market (3 October 1962), p. 7, www.cvce.eu/content/publication/1999/1/1/05f2996b-000b-4576-8b42-8069033a16f9/publishable_en.pdf (accessed 27 March 2020).

78 R. Toye, 'Words of Change: The Rhetoric of Commonwealth, Common Market and Cold War, 1961–3' in L. J. Butler and S. E. Stockwell (eds), *Winds of Change: Harold Macmillan and British Decolonisation* (Basingstoke: Palgrave Macmillan, 2013).
79 A. Smith, *Stitches in Time: The Commonwealth in World Politics* (London: Andre Deutsch, 1981), pp. 182–183.
80 G. Arnold, *Economic Co-operation in the Commonwealth* (Oxford: Pergamon Press, 1967).
81 Lloyd, 'Britain and the Transformation', p. 340.
82 I. Spencer, *British Immigration Policy since 1939* (London: Routledge, 1997), pp. 116–117, 143–144 and *passim*.
83 A. Dummett, 'The New British Nationality Act', *British Journal of Law and Society*, 8:2 (1981), pp. 233–241.
84 This was not smooth. See E. Richards, 'Migrations: The Career of British White Australia', in D. Schreuder and S. Ward (eds), *Australia's Empire* (Oxford: Oxford University Press, 2008), pp. 174–185.
85 W. D. McIntyre, 'The Admission of Small States to the Commonwealth', *Journal of Imperial and Commonwealth History*, 24:2 (1996), pp. 244–277.
86 A. Adeleke, 'Playing Fairy Godfather to the Commonwealth: The United States and the Colombo Plan', *Commonwealth & Comparative Politics*, 42:3 (2004), pp. 393–411; Y. Bangura, *Britain and Commonwealth Africa: The Politics of Economic Relations 1951–75* (Manchester: Manchester University Press, 1983).
87 M. M. Ball, *The 'Open' Commonwealth* (Durham, NC: Duke University Press, 1971).
88 Smith, *Stitches in Time*, pp. 487–513; P. G. Walker, *The Commonwealth* (London: Secker and Warburg, 1962); Miller, *Survey of Commonwealth Affairs*, pp. 487–516.
89 Ibid., pp. 356–357.
90 J. Amery, *Joseph Chamberlain and the Tariff Reform Campaign* (London: Macmillan, 1969), pp. 1050–1054.
91 Kenny and Pearce, *Shadows of Empire*.
92 Murphy, *Empire's New Clothes*, pp. 225–232.

9

Greater Britain and its decline: the view from Lambeth

Sarah Stockwell[1]

On 17 October 1950 the Archbishop of Canterbury, Geoffrey Fisher, and his wife, Rosamund, disembarked from the *Dominion Monarch* in Fremantle at the start of an Australian tour. Mrs Fisher disliked flying so the pair travelled by ship, docking briefly in South Africa where Fisher's brother was bishop of Natal. Five weeks later Australian bishops waved them off from Sydney with a rousing rendition of 'For they are jolly good fellows'. The couple proceeded to spend a month in New Zealand. In all, over sixty-five days, Fisher travelled 1,400 miles by sea, 1,734 miles by air, 1,560 by train and 3,700 by car and gave 138 addresses and sermons.[2] He was entertained by politicians as well as Church leaders, dining with the New Zealand Cabinet and lunching at Parliament House in Canberra. In Adelaide he gave an open-air service for some 5,000 children and broadcast an address as part of a national service; the first time Fisher had been heard throughout Australia.[3] Meanwhile Mrs Fisher had her own engagements with 'the wives' and members of the worldwide Anglican Mothers' Union.[4] The tour (which originated in an invitation to attend centennial celebrations of the foundation of a Church of England settlement in Canterbury, New Zealand)[5] was the Fishers' first visit down under and the first by any archbishop of Canterbury. As he preached and partied his way across Australia, visiting sixteen of the country's twenty-five Anglican dioceses, Fisher was enthusiastically received. As the couple entered Sydney in a cavalcade of horses, crowds flocked to their open-top car. It was, Mrs Fisher later wrote, 'one of the proudest moments of my life. The streets were thickly lined with people. We had to wave back to them and I tried to be like the Queen.'[6]

The reception the Fishers received places their visit squarely within the political, social and cultural worlds of Greater Britain. It illustrates how cultures of Britishness survived into the post-war era, with the result that something resembling a Greater Britain as imagined by Charles Dilke and John Seeley in the nineteenth century could be said still to exist in the 1940s and 1950s, before declining thereafter.[7] In Australia, with its significant Scottish, Welsh, Irish Protestant and Catholic communities, 'Britishness' was hardly monochrome and was inflected by differences of class as well as region and religion. Nevertheless, as a key proponent of the 'Englishness' synonymous with a particular form of 'Britishness', the Church of England and its clergy had played a significant part in the evolution of this British world.[8] During the First World War, Anglican clerics were influential proponents of imperial loyalty. After the war, burgeoning Australian nationalism co-existed alongside imperial attachment within the Church of England in Australia, but the Church remained manifestly middle class and English in character, a bastion of the British race patriotism which in the late nineteenth century had become central to the Greater Britain concept.[9] As late as 1959 most bishops in New Zealand were still English while nearly half of all Australian diocesans were English-educated.[10]

In turn, the transformation of the domestic Church of England into the global Anglican Communion was profoundly shaped by both the idea and existence of Greater Britain. The Communion (a term that had begun to be used in the 1840s with reference to the Protestant episcopal churches of Britain and America) began to assume more concrete form in the 1850s. Since 1867 bishops from around the Communion had met at Lambeth in conference every ten years; an innovation which owed much to Bishop Selwyn of New Zealand. Thereafter understandings of the Anglican Communion as a sort of confederacy of local and national churches had been influenced by Seeley's concept of Greater Britain.[11] The Communion as it had evolved by the mid-twentieth century did not map precisely onto Greater Britain: missionary activity had resulted in the creation of dioceses in locations beyond the empire or where there was no settled British community; conversely, other Christian denominations were significant within Greater Britain. But the two were nevertheless intimately intertwined. Acts of special worship, including national days of prayer, observed throughout the empire, saw the Church of England exercise spiritual and moral guidance not just to the British nation but to Greater Britain too.[12] Deep into the 1950s Fisher continued to conceive the community to which he ministered as incorporating a wider British world.[13]

Nowhere was the connection between the Communion and Greater Britain stronger than in Australia and New Zealand, the geographical focus of this chapter. More Anglicans in the Communion resided in Australia than anywhere else outside Britain. In both Australia and New Zealand, Anglicans were the largest single denominational groups, even though the Church had not succeeded in achieving establishment status.[14] The Antipodean churches also played an important regional role as a centre of Anglican mission in Polynesia and East Asia. In short, Greater Britain had provided a context in which the Church flourished overseas and was part of the geographical and spiritual imaginary of English Anglicans.

This chapter explores English Anglican ideas of this Greater British world after the Second World War through analysis of views of Australia and New Zealand. There is a rich historiography of the Anglican church in its different national settings, including the Australian.[15] There is also a burgeoning scholarship on post-war Greater Britain, and the chronology and dynamics behind its decline, with historians principally pointing to political and economic changes occurring from the 1950s and 1960s, especially Britain's turn to Europe.[16] Growing secularisation and shifting church membership are also acknowledged as among the factors contributing to a withering of transnational cultures of Britishness.[17] But, in contrast to the attention paid to it in accounts of the nineteenth and early twentieth centuries, religion is rarely foregrounded in analyses of Greater Britain in this period, and there has been little investigation of English Anglican perspectives. This chapter considers the 'view from Lambeth', the London home of the Church of England's most senior figure and symbolic head of the worldwide Communion.

A first section charts how, after the war, senior English Anglicans visiting Australia, including Fisher, were beguiled by its Britishness and returned convinced of the central role Australia (and New Zealand) should play in a Communion in which there were disintegrative forces at work. Yet even as they were heartened by their experiences, anxieties about the erosion of the 'Anglican-ness' of the old Dominions, especially Australia, increased. As shown in the second section, English Anglicans feared that the Church was losing ground to Catholics, Australia's second largest Christian denomination: a latter-day expression of an anti-Catholicism that had been fundamental to ideas of Britishness in earlier periods and which had been articulated by 'ultra-Protestant' elements within Britain and the Dominions between the wars.[18] The Church of England responded by trying to restock Greater Britain not just with white people but with Anglicans. This chapter hence argues that it was the implications of the decline of Greater Britain for their own Church that chiefly animated English Anglicans. But this focus did not preclude imperial sentiment and, although they acted principally to defend their Church, they did so in ways which entailed consciously reinvigorating the British connection.[19]

Allies in the battle against the 'forces of materialism and unbelief': Australia, New Zealand and the Anglican Communion

In the post-war world, Fisher travelled more extensively than any archbishop before him. Despite their pageantry, his overseas tours were anything but simply ornamental. They were designed to reinforce the Communion in the face of perceived challenges to its vitality and to a Western Christian order more generally. From the late 1930s Soviet communism, world war and the dawn of the atomic age had engendered among many English Anglicans what has been described as a 'grand narrative of world crisis' in response to which some form of spiritual renewal was required.[20] After the war, the onset of the Cold War era raised new concerns about an expansionist atheist communism that intersected with others about growing materialism.

There were other potentially disintegrative forces at work within the Communion as national and cultural differences became more problematic.[21] The most recent Lambeth Conference had taken place in 1930. But it had proven an alienating experience for bishops from the Anglican Church of Canada and Protestant Episcopal Church of the United States of America, who had reportedly found themselves observers rather than participants at proceedings dominated by a clique of English bishops associated with All Souls and Balliol, Oxford. The war had since prevented a further meeting, and, on becoming archbishop, Fisher toured Canada and the United States, seeking to re-engage the North Americans in advance of the next conference scheduled for 1948 amid concerns that, should he fail, this might prove the last such meeting.[22] Attended by 369 bishops from all parts of the Communion including Japan, the 1948 Conference laid the groundwork for new initiatives, including the establishment of a new Anglican Congress, which met for the first time at Minneapolis in 1954. Under Fisher's leadership, the Communion, Colin Podmore notes, became 'less English-dominated'.[23] The immediate dangers of fragmentation had been averted, but a shift in the economic power base within the Communion was occurring that saw it increasingly underwritten by American money. This corresponded to a growth more generally of American influence, material and spiritual, including in Australia, as evidenced by the response to Billy Graham's 1959 crusade.[24] Concurrently, issues of race increasingly intruded on the established order of Anglicanism in Africa. Forward-thinking English Anglicans advocated changes to churches still very 'colonial' in complexion, and, in the context of post-war African political change, Fisher began grouping old colonial dioceses into independent provinces to take their place within the Communion. But steps towards dismantling racial hierarchies in Africa were tentative at best, and between Anglicans there were significant differences of view as to the appropriate response to apartheid in South Africa and towards the Federation of Rhodesia and Nyasaland.[25]

The Church of England in Australia (as it was still officially known) was not immune from difficulties either. Financial precarity exacerbated problems of ministry in remote and sparsely populated dioceses and was made worse by the Depression. The Church's role was less significant in the Second World War than it had been in the First, and in post-war Australia it was more marginal to public life than earlier. The Church was also divided both geographically and theologically. Differences of church party between Anglo-Catholics and evangelicals that troubled the Church in England had been exported overseas. They had acquired a distinct character in small Australian dioceses that 'assumed the ecclesiastical colour of their bishop', recreated for subsequent generations in local theological colleges.[26] In South Africa such differences had led to the formation of a schismatic 'Church of England in South Africa' after some evangelical Anglicans refused to join the new Church of the Province of South Africa created in 1870. In Australia the principal fissure was between Anglo-Catholics based in the dioceses of Brisbane, Adelaide and Rockingham, and evangelicals in that of Sydney. While the Sydney evangelicals had not followed the South Africans in breaking away from the Church of England, they supported them. The differences with their fellow Australian Anglicans had also bedevilled past attempts to agree a constitution for an independent Australian Church even though there were those within it who wished to increase its autonomy.[27] As a result, the Anglican Church in Australia was still legally part of the Church of England, and unable to depart theologically or liturgically from it; should it do so, it would be deemed in the eyes of the Australian law to have formed a new church and be liable to forfeit all property held as the Church of England in Australia. In contrast the Anglican church in New Zealand had attained its independence from Canterbury in 1858.[28]

The lack of constitutional independence was uncomfortable for both the Australians and for the Church of England. Sydney evangelicals who cleaved to particular Reformation practices had objected to a reform of Canon Law currently underway in England which they feared might prove binding in Australia as well as England.[29] Fisher's first reaction on learning of the evangelicals' objections had been to tell them 'To mind your own business', but he realised that the complex legal relationship made this impossible, underlining for Fisher a conviction that the 'right course is for the Church in Australia to acquire a self-governing' constitution.[30]

The continuing appointment of English-born bishops to key positions could also be a source of tension. The practice reflected in part an ongoing cultural cringe, with English candidates sometimes perceived as better than home-grown. As Edward Woods, the Bishop of Lichfield, whom Fisher had sent on a 'great mission' to Australia and New Zealand, reported from New Zealand in early 1948, 'most thoughtful people out here agree that it is desirable that from time to time there should be an infiltration from the Homeland into the ranks of both Bishops and Clergy'. It was he said 'quite natural, that a first-rate education in England at one of the best public schools and then Oxford or Cambridge, coupled with all the sense of history and culture which a man unconsciously absorbs in our country represents qualifications which in the nature of the case are unobtainable in a new country'.[31] With so many of the senior Australasian bishops themselves English-educated, a preference for imported personnel constituted a form of self-legitimation, undoubtedly contributing to an English bias deep into the 1950s. As the Anglophile and Oxbridge-educated, Australian Bishop of Geelong, John McKie, explained in 1957 concerning the selection of the next archbishop of Melbourne, there was a strong current of opinion that the Church 'should not depend on England to fill our chief positions of leadership', but the 'Australian field' was not strong and the Australians would accept an English appointment if he was 'head and shoulders in ability above the locals'.[32] Fisher proposed the English Bishop of Middleton, Frank Woods: 'in Oxford terms ... more an alpha-beta or beta ++' and 'a bit liable to be over exuberant and enthusiastic and passionate when he gets worked up in a speech', characteristics that might 'go down very well in Australia'– comments that did not address McKie's concerns about intellectual quality but revealed a different cultural prejudice.[33]

Yet while there were tensions and difficulties both within the Church and in its relations to the Church of England, the strength of the British connection impressed senior visiting English Anglicans. The 'ardent loyalty of people in these two Dominions to our institutions at Home and especially to the Throne has to be seen to be believed', wrote the Bishop of Lichfield, commenting on the intense interest shown in the recent royal wedding.[34] This event probably reinforced in the minds of the public an association between Church and Crown, and, since he had officiated at the wedding, Fisher's own prominence. The influential Bishop of Chichester, George Bell, who spent two months in Australia in 1949 followed by three weeks in New Zealand, was similarly struck.[35] Admittedly, as this volume's editors remark in their introduction, encountering Greater Britain first-hand could prompt feelings of difference rather than familiarity. 'I found', Fisher observed in a broadcast following his Australasian tour, 'in different physical setting, men and women very like ourselves; very close to us in a thousand ways, while still conspicuously different'.[36] For Fisher this 'difference' lay not just in the 'physical setting' (a landscape 'so vast as to be monotonous'), or, as we have seen, in his view of the Australians' character, but in the youthfulness of the two Dominions.[37] The 'pressure of materialism', he commented, was as heavy as in Britain and 'perhaps heavier for these countries are without many of the witnesses to a spiritual world which speak among us here: ancient churches, cathedrals, and the heritage of their musical tradition'.[38] But, like his colleagues, Fisher was struck by the Britishness, and more specifically Englishness, of those he met: he found Australians 'more English than the Canadians in feel and temper'.[39] This perception should not surprise us. These visitors' experience of Australia and New Zealand was filtered through the lens of churches still English in character, dished up for their delectation in carefully managed occasions. For example, Fisher's triumphant entry into Sydney in 1950 was orchestrated by the city's English and evangelical Archbishop, Howard Mowll.[40] 'I cannot exaggerate', Fisher said on his return, 'the strength of the British tradition, as it exists in Australia and New Zealand. It really is good for an Englishman to go there and be refortified in his own faith in the British tradition.'[41]

Other English Anglicans, hoping that the British laity could be similarly fortified, aimed to capitalise on the 'remarkable impact' of Fisher's Australian tour to promote the Church and Communion at home. A public reception to welcome Fisher back was arranged at Central Hall Westminster. Perhaps because of the efforts of Cyril Garbett, the Archbishop of York (who warned it would 'be a disaster if the hall were only half-filled'), Fisher was greeted by a 'huge audience' and received not only by Garbett but also by the Prime Minister, Clement Attlee.[42] The Society for Promoting Christian Knowledge, convinced that movie footage of Fisher's tour offered 'a unique opportunity for impressing the importance of the worldwide Anglican Church with the rank and file of the Church of England', acquired the rights to the newsreel. This was broadcast to 'church people' in parish halls and churches.[43] In the film's concluding message, Fisher duly reminded the British (in words reflecting the iconography and language of the recent war) that while they thought of themselves as 'standing alone', they had 'allies' in the fight against the 'forces of materialism and unbelief'.[44] Perhaps with the recent expulsion of Western missionaries from China weighing heavily, Fisher had already set out in an address given in Australia a vision of the Commonwealth and Christian faith working in partnership. Together they could combat the dangers of 'Imperialist Communism, aggressive and atheist' as well as 'the profounder menace of materialism'.[45]

Above all, in an uncertain and changing world order, these Anglicans returned convinced of the importance of Britain's most 'British' and Anglican Dominions within the Communion. On his return Bell declared the 'necessity of a far fuller realisation of the interdependence' of the Church of England and the Anglican churches in Australia and New Zealand. It was 'a matter of the highest importance for the Anglican Communion as a whole', Bell judged, while also suggesting the 'same applies to Canada and the other Churches of the Anglican Communion'.[46] In this context, it seems fitting that during Fisher's tour three Australian opals were set within the processional Primatial Cross of Canterbury, which had been taken out of England for the first time since its manufacture in 1883.[47]

In Australia, as in Britain, it was not until the 1960s that significant secularisation occurred.[48] Yet British ambitions to see Australia and New Zealand play a greater role within the Communion seem to have reflected an appreciation of the Australasians' Britishness as much as their Christian witness. This may simply be because the bishops associated an adherence to Christian faith with Britishness (and, for Fisher, 'British tradition' undoubtedly encompassed Protestantism). But it may also reflect the pattern of developments occurring in the wider Communion. As noted earlier, Fisher had set out to strengthen the Communion, working with forces that otherwise threatened to weaken it. He had sought to hold the Americans to the Communion, building a strong relationship with the Presiding Bishop of the Episcopal Church of the United States. However, as he set out to breathe new life into an idea of the Communion as a confederation of independent churches, it seems plausible that – with the American church increasingly influential in the Communion – the perceived value of Anglicanism in the Antipodes lay at least in part in its Britishness.

To achieve closer association between the Australasian and English churches, Bell proposed the introduction of a newsletter to be sent to all diocesan bishops in the Communion, and greater Church of England hospitality and support for Australian and New Zealand candidates for ordination studying in Britain. He also wanted more extensive exchange of personnel, including the occasional appointment of an Australasian-born bishop to an English see.[49] Both he and Fisher appreciated, however, that the most urgent task was rationalising the Australian church's legal status to enable it to exercise leadership within Australia *and* the Communion. As Bell reflected, Australia badly needed 'someone who, by virtue of his office, will have the prestige and authority of the Archbishop of Canterbury', thereby enabling the Church to provide 'effective corporate witness and raise an effective voice of moral leadership in the affairs of the Dominion'.[50] In Sydney, Fisher, addressing the House of Bishops and General Synod, similarly argued that a new archbishop of Australia 'would represent the whole Church in the continent' and 'would have freedom to travel representing the Church of Australia'.[51]

On the long voyage home from New Zealand, Fisher busied himself adapting a draft constitution previously prepared by Francis de Witt Batty, the Bishop of Newcastle in the Province of New South Wales.[52] He also proposed the Australians adopt the rather long-winded title 'the Church of Australia in communion with the Church of England', to be known more succinctly as the 'Church of Australia', a shorthand title that, had it been adopted, would not have played well with Australia's other churches.[53] In the event, it took Fisher's entire archiepiscopate – and extended negotiation and constitutional revision led by Batty – before the new independent province was finally created. Even then, at the insistence of the Diocese of Sydney, the new province was still known until 1981 as the 'Church of England in Australia'.[54] The constitutional negotiations became mired in contention over whether the English Reformation doctrine of the prayer book and the 39 Articles should be included as one of several fundamental declarations establishing the church and its relationship to the Church of England and Communion, in effect a struggle between parties each deploying different constructions of Englishness. The vexed question of the balance of power between individual diocesan synods and the General Synod was equally problematic. At one stage Fisher and Batty even contemplated proceeding with the creation of a Church of Australia without the Sydney diocese.[55]

Managing the transition to independence of the Australian Anglican Church might look like a decolonising act by an English archbishop impatient with the Australians' inability to get their own house in order, but, as Stuart Piggin argues, it was principally designed to ensure Anglicanism retained a 'position of influence world-wide' relative to other churches.[56] Through the new constitution Fisher also aimed to maintain his own authority. He inserted a declaration requiring the Australian church to secure the consent of the Archbishop of Canterbury, as president of the Lambeth Conference, before any alterations could be made to the first part of the constitution (comprising the 'fundamental declarations'), and a further stipulation that any revision must also be subject to the approval by the diocesan synods and the General Synod. This would act as 'a brake on any hasty or unwise alteration' and serve as a declaration of the Australian's 'solidarity with the Anglican Communion' and 'desire to preserve it'.[57]

Laying 'religious and spiritual foundations' in a 'new period of Commonwealth building'

Yet even as English Anglican elites were impressed by Australian and New Zealand's Britishness, and sought to bolster the position of the Australian church within the Communion, they became increasingly concerned about potential threats to this Britishness and, more specifically, to its Anglican variant. They worried Anglicanism was losing ground in Britain's most Anglican Dominions. With hindsight we can see that secularisation, the product of social, cultural and generational change, was one of several forces that would eventually weaken the Anglican church.[58] However, although there were concerns about materialism, and an awareness that not all those who self-identified as Anglican were 'full' churchgoers, it was the risks from changing patterns of immigration that were seen as most threatening to the Anglican hegemony. These were not the result of decolonisation. But factors associated with imperial decline – British economic weakness and changing priorities – are nevertheless part of the wider context here since it was the withdrawal of British governmental funding for

Anglican overseas settlement that initiated some of the discussion around the issue. As the rest of this chapter shows, English Anglican efforts to shore up the Anglican element of the Australian population, as well as elsewhere in the old Commonwealth, led to new efforts to facilitate Anglican overseas migration.

The Church had a long tradition of encouraging emigration. From the 1840s the Church, like other religious institutions, ministered to migrants both during their journeys and upon arrival.[59] In 1925, following the introduction of government subsidies for approved organisations sponsoring migration under the Empire Settlement Act of 1922, the Church had also formed an Advisory Council for Empire Settlement.[60] Like other voluntary bodies funded under the Act, the Council was responsible for the selection of emigrants, while a network of 'daughter organisations' helped them procure work and accommodation on arrival.[61] Government funding was cancelled in the mid-1930s amid economic difficulties and the Council's activities were suspended in the war, but the Council resumed work in 1947. By then the government subsidy met 75 per cent of the Council's administrative expenses with private subscriptions contributing some of the remaining costs. Within a few years the Council had overseen the emigration of 2,000 adults and 235 children.[62]

Historians have commented on the significant denominational rivalries evident in discussions of post-war emigration to Australia. But they focus on child-migration and principally on other denominations. They also place most explanatory weight on how Australian demand fed the rivalries.[63] Analysis of the domestic Church of England shows that concerns at the British end were as significant – albeit that they were partly shaped by information received from overseas colleagues. Each migrant ship bound for Australia left British shores carrying between one and two thousand people, of whom approximately three quarters were – at least nominally – Anglican. Even so Anglicans were alert to what Fisher referred to in 1947 as the Roman Catholic 'menace',[64] evidence of the 'inbred opposition' to Roman Catholicism with which he admitted he had grown up.[65] Such was the level of concern at this stage that non-Catholic British churches agreed to cooperate under the guidance of the Church of England to discuss Roman Catholic activity.[66] The following year Fisher objected when the Australian government agreed to provide quarters on-board ships only for chaplains planning to settle in Australia. He feared that this favoured Catholic interests since it was easier for unmarried chaplains to relocate. At his request, the Archbishop of Sydney intervened with the Australian prime minister who agreed to drop the stipulation.[67]

A few years later, anxiety about Roman Catholicism was also the primary factor behind changes to the Council for Empire Settlement. By 1952 the

Council's position had become precarious. In Britain's straitened post-war financial situation, the government reduced its financial commitment to migration and withdrew its subsidy to the Council.[68] In these circumstances the Church Assembly established a commission to make recommendations about the future role of the Church with regard to migration and to review the Council's constitution and functions.[69] The commission included the Council's existing chair, Lord Bessborough, as well as Bell, William Wand, the Anglo-Catholic Bishop of London, and the Conservative MP Enoch Powell. When the commission reported in 1954, it emphasised the importance of laying 'religious and spiritual foundations' in a 'new period of Commonwealth building' and, particularly, the need to maintain a flow of Anglican migrants. The Council, with the active support of the Australian, New Zealand and Canadian churches, was subsequently reconstituted as the 'Church of England Council for Commonwealth and Empire Settlement'. The change meant that for the first time the Council became an official body of the Church Assembly, which also now undertook to provide financially for it.[70]

This development had Fisher's full support, his recent Australian tour having underscored for him the value of emigration. 'How good it would be', he had said in his home broadcast, 'if a million or two of our people could go and see these lovely countries for themselves! Yes, and the best of them would want to stay there'.[71] He advised Bessborough that the commission 'must contain people of real standing' so that their report would impress the Church Assembly. 'I want', he said, 'to make a real success of this most important task'.[72] But the Assembly's new commitment to emigration owed most to the bishops of Chichester and London, Bell and Wand. Bell, like Fisher, had not only returned from Australia convinced of the importance of strengthening Australia's position within the Communion, but was also one of the Church's most senior figures and closely engaged with foreign affairs. Wand, a former army chaplain to Australian forces at Gallipoli, had served as Archbishop of Brisbane from 1934 to 1943. While in Australia he was a controversial figure, disliked for his style and reforming zeal and resented by local Anglicans who had hoped for a home-grown archbishop. But he was also a passionate advocate of Britishness, as revealed by his pamphlet published after the fall of Singapore in 1942, *Has Britain Let Us Down?* His robust defence won approval within the British government and may have influenced Churchill's decision to select him first for the see of Bath and Wells and then as Fisher's successor as Bishop of London following Fisher's own appointment to Canterbury.[73]

During discussions in the Assembly, both Wand and Bell were staunch in their support of the Council's work. With other denominations 'active among emigrants and overseas communities', Wand feared that if the

Council was unable to continue its activities the Church would lose ground. For his part, Bell emphasised the importance of the 'redistribution of our citizens over the whole of the British Commonwealth'. Most attention focused on Australia, to which most emigrants were destined. In line with its attempt to maintain a national identity in which whiteness, and more specifically, Britishness played a key part, the Australian and New Zealand governments had introduced assisted passages schemes to help certain categories of migrant. As already noted, Anglicans constituted a higher proportion of the population in Australia than in any other Commonwealth country. Even so, with its significant Irish-emigrant population, and growing numbers of new arrivals from continental Europe, there was, in Wand's words, 'intense competition'. The Vatican, realising 'the difficulties in Europe', as Wand put it rather opaquely, was doing its utmost to build a strong church in the Pacific region. The Anglican Church, he advised, needed to work to maintain its existing numerical superiority. Richard Howard, the Provost of Coventry, who in 1954 had just returned from a fundraising tour of Canada, provided useful supporting evidence from North America. The 'British', he warned, were now less than 40 per cent of the population of Canada, while 47 per cent was Roman Catholic. 'On the minds of everybody', he remarked, 'there lay the burden of the need for British emigration to Canada, particularly Protestant emigration', and, more specifically 'Church of England emigration'.[74]

Its future secured at least for the time being, the Council oversaw the emigration of nearly 1,200 in the next two years.[75] However, concerns that Anglicanism was losing ground continued. Claims about the onwards march of Catholicism were buttressed by reference to worrying statistical evidence; whether these figures came from Australian Anglicans or were collected independently by the Council is unclear. Either way they were used to paint an alarming scenario of the steep decline of the Britishness, and by extension, Anglican-ness of the Australian population. In 1956 the Council's secretary, Miss Jones, reported that the Catholic population of Australia had grown 10 per cent in the last five years, while the number of 'foreign' migrants now exceeded British.[76] By 'foreign' Jones presumably meant European and, probably more specifically, Southern European. While the 'White Australia' policy remained in force until the 1970s, in 1951 Australia had opened its doors to more non-British white migrants by broadening the assisted passages scheme to include migrants from Europe.[77] 'People', the Bishop of Coventry, the vice-chair of the Council, declared upon his return from Australia in 1959, 'were pouring in from Europe and elsewhere and British numbers were steadily going down'. Local Anglicans, he noted, were extremely worried. Indeed, in October the official journal of the Perth diocese published a letter from its archbishop under a title that paraphrased the

Australian government's recent 'Bring out a Briton' venture as 'Bring out an Anglican'.[78] A year later, in view of data showing that only 38 per cent of all emigrants to Australia were now Anglican, a fall of 7 per cent in ten years, the importance of maintaining Anglicanism within the Dominions was argued once again.[79]

One way to do this was by encouraging child migration. Children drawn from the Church of England's own Children's Society,[80] as well as from local authority and 'broken homes',[81] were sent to residential institutions mostly in Western Australia.[82] In New Zealand (where there were no Church of England homes) they were placed with foster parents.[83] Despite the importance some within the Council attached to it, child migration was increasingly out of step with the climate of opinion at home. Under the Children Act of 1948 children had ceased to be cared for under the Poor Law and became the responsibility of local authorities, and, as ideas of child welfare developed, local authorities prioritised keeping children with their families in preference to their removal to foster families or via emigration.[84] The year after the introduction of the Children Act, Jones complained to Australia House about the difficulties the Council was experiencing in getting local authorities in Britain to identify children for emigration.[85]

By the mid-1950s there were some within the Church who were more critical of child migration, but Bell and Wand both continued to emphasise its importance and their obligation to assist Australian Anglican residential homes by sending children to them.[86] There were apparently no formal arrangements in place to monitor the welfare of these child migrants. However, Jones visited every Australian Anglican children's home during a visit in 1955. She concluded that she 'was very satisfied with all she saw'.[87] A Commonwealth Relations Office fact-finding mission on child-migration to Australia was more sceptical.[88] By the 1960s the Council had ceased to sponsor child migrants. Yet, as Gordon Lynch, Janet Fink and Geoffrey Sherrington argue, for a time different denominational societies not only became a key source of ongoing support for child migration as they responded to demand from overseas residential homes for British children, but also became crucial in sustaining an older pattern of placing child migrants in residential care.[89]

As well as trying to maintain Anglican migration, the Council sought to ensure that migrants were Anglican in more than just name, and to improve the quality of its provision for migrants, amid worries that the Catholics managed a more efficient operation.[90] It focused particularly on improving the reception of Anglicans on their arrival overseas. To this end, Jones encouraged every Australian diocese during her Australian tour to establish a committee to welcome arrivals, and the Archbishop of Sydney agreed to assist with the creation of a single organisation to handle Anglican migration in Australia.[91]

While it was the importance of maintaining Anglican migration to Australia that was most prominent in the minds of Council members, the Council's remit encompassed the Commonwealth generally. For example, Jones and the Council's assistant secretary visited South Africa and Rhodesia, where the Council worked in close cooperation with the Southern Africa and Rhodesia Settlement Association.[92] At the request of the Anglican Church of Canada, Jones and an Anglican minister also became involved in tending to Britons leaving under the Canadian government's 1950s 'Air Bridge to Canada', part of a broader scheme of loans to selected migrants. The pair were to be found 'almost every day' at the air terminal at Waterloo, and in a little over five months they had waved goodbye to over 17,000 individuals, commending them to the Anglican Church at the other end.[93] The Bishop of New Westminster in Vancouver reported that this work helped 'hold many to this Church'.[94]

The anti-Catholicism coursing through these discussions illustrates that those involved principally understood their mission to support migration as one of faith, and partisan at that, rather than of Commonwealth. Nevertheless, the two were impossible to disentangle, and reinforcing Anglican communities in the Dominions inevitably also meant promoting Britishness. Some – notably lay Anglican Council members – explicitly invoked a broader Commonwealth imperative. For example, Sir Colin Jardine, a retired English army officer, worried that, 'unless there is sufficient migration to preserve the British character of the family group of Nations of which Great Britain is the centre, it is going to be extremely bad for this country'.[95] Conversely, there were some Church Assembly members who deplored what they (with justification) saw as the Council's 'anti-Roman Catholic' bias and blatant 'touting for migrants'.[96]

These complaints corresponded to objections from some quarters that it was inappropriate for the Assembly to be financially supporting the Council. Such was the undercurrent of resistance, that Fisher appointed a new enquiry into the Council's work barely four years after the initial commission.[97] This reported positively, but doubts continued.[98] Some Assembly members considered that the Church had more important priorities, including the provision of assistance to migrants arriving in, rather than departing from, Britain. They pointed out the anomalies of the current situation in which the Church was doing more to enable the integration of Britons settling in the Commonwealth into an Anglican community than it did for migrant arrivals at home.[99] In 1964, after protracted discussion with various Church organisations, the Council's vice-chair suggested that the Council, like Anglican missionary societies that similarly became involved in working with Commonwealth arrivals,[100] assume responsibility for dealing with immigrants as well as emigrants; an example of how expertise associated with an imperial endeavour was repurposed at the end of empire. But as Jean Smith shows in this volume, an older pattern of Commonwealth migration continued deep into an era of decolonisation in the form of ongoing British settlement in Australia and the other former Dominions. Renamed in 1958, the Council for Commonwealth Settlement (and later Overseas Settlement, and then Committee for Overseas Settlement) was only finally wound up in 1981.

Conclusion

With hindsight we can see that the fifteen-year period after 1945, on which this chapter has focused, was the Indian summer of both Greater Britain and Anglicanism in its old heartlands. In the aftermath of world war, visiting English Anglicans had been encouraged by what they perceived as the Britishness of Australia and New Zealand; at the same time, Fisher's tour may in some small way have contributed to maintaining this British orientation. Anglican leaders returned convinced of the important role the Australasian churches had to play in a Communion in which there were wider changes afoot. They focused on trying to strengthen the position of the Church within Australia by assisting it, finally, to become legally independent of the Church of England. They also aimed through emigration to maintain the numerical strength of Anglicanism down under amid fears that it was losing ground to Roman Catholicism. Denominational rivalries would later recede as ecumenical cooperation rose, but this chapter illustrates how they were as operative at the end of empire as they had been in an earlier phase of empire-building.[101] It has also shown that post-war Anglican elites, described elsewhere as the last generation to equate Britain's status as a Christian nation with Britain's 'greatness',[102] remained significantly invested in the political, social and cultural worlds of Greater Britain.

Yet forces of change would soon weaken both Greater Britain and Anglicanism in its established centres. Despite efforts to 'send out' Anglicans, and ongoing British Commonwealth migration, the changing profile of immigrants to Australia, coupled with social change, realised the Church of England's worries: Anglicanism was overtaken by Roman Catholicism in the Dominion in which it had most flourished. Together with secularisation in Britain and the other old Dominions, this saw the centres of global Anglicanism shift from the old Commonwealth, not (as many in the 1950s expected) towards America,[103] but to the new, especially in Africa. And, by permitting Australian Anglican dioceses legally to depart from Church of England conventions, the independence in 1962 of the Australian Anglican church eventually played into the development of a more nationally focused church. This had attendant implications for the extent to which the Australian Anglican church continued to serve as a reservoir of a white Englishness within the country.[104] The changing climate was evident when Fisher's successor as archbishop, Michael Ramsey, spent a few weeks in Australia and New Zealand in 1965. For all that some wished his visit had been longer, it is clear that it lacked the impact that had characterised Fisher's fifteen years earlier. Since the late nineteenth century the Communion and Greater Britain had been mutually constitutive of each other; so too was the relative decline of Anglicanism in Australia and the break-up of Greater Britain.

Notes

1 I am very grateful to Alana Harris and Arthur Burns for their comments on this chapter, as well as to staff at Lambeth Palace Library and the Church of England Record Centre.
2 'Welcome Home to the Archbishop of Canterbury', *Church Times*, 2 February 1951, p. 1.
3 Lambeth Palace Library [hereafter LPL], Fisher 68, ff. 42–43, Bishop of Adelaide to Fisher, 1 June 1950.
4 LPL, Fisher 272, ff. 253–268, 'Travels', pp. 9, 12.
5 LPL, Fisher 68, f. 1, Archbishop of New Zealand to Fisher, 14 March 1949.
6 LPL, Fisher 327, ff. 213–232, Mrs Fisher's account of Australian visit, p. 18; E. Carpenter, *Archbishop Fisher: His Life and Times* (Norwich: The Canterbury Press, 1991), pp. 479–485.
7 S. Ward, *Australia and the British Embrace: The Demise of the Imperial Ideal* (Victoria: Melbourne University Press, 2001), esp. pp. 24–30, 236–255; A. G. Hopkins, 'Rethinking Decolonization', *Past and Present*, 200 (2008), pp. 211–247.
8 M. Gladwin, *Anglican Clergy in Australia 1788–1850: Building a British World* (Woodbridge: Royal Historical Society, 2015); G. A. Bremner, *Imperial Gothic: Religious Architecture and High Anglican Culture in the British Empire, c. 1840–1970* (New Haven, CT: Yale University Press, 2013); H. M. Carey, *God's Empire: Religion and Colonialism in the British World, c. 1801–1908* (Cambridge: Cambridge University Press, 2011).
9 B. H. Fletcher, 'Anglicanism and Nationalism in Australia 1901–1962', *Journal of Religious History*, 23:2 (1999), pp. 215–233; R. Frappell, 'Imperial Fervour and Anglican Loyalty, 1901–1929', in B. Kaye (ed.), *Anglicanism in Australia: A History* (Victoria: Melbourne University Press, 2002), pp. 76–99, esp. 93–94.
10 W. M. Jacob, *The Making of the Anglican Church Worldwide* (London: Society for Promoting Christian Knowledge, 1997), pp. 292–293.
11 E. Radner, 'The Anglican Communion and Anglicanism', in J. Morris (ed.), *The Oxford History of Anglicanism. Volume IV: Global Western Anglicanism, c. 1910–present* (Oxford: Oxford University Press, 2017), pp. 303–328, esp.

p. 311; S. Piggin, 'Australian Anglicanism in a World-Wide Context', in Kaye, *Anglicanism in Australia*, pp. 200–222.

12 J. Hardwick and P. Williamson, 'Special worship in the British Empire: from the seventeenth to the twentieth centuries', *Studies in Church History*, 54 (2018), pp. 260–280.

13 S. Stockwell, '"A Sort of Official Duty to Reconcile": Archbishop Fisher, the Church of England and the politics of British decolonisation in East and Central Africa', in T. Rodger, P. Williamson and M. Grimley (eds), *The Church of England and British Politics since 1900* (Woodbridge: Boydell and Brewer, 2020), pp. 240–261.

14 I. Breward, 'Anglicanism in Australia and New Zealand', in Morris (ed.), *Oxford History of Anglicanism*, pp. 331–361, esp. p. 331.

15 For example, S. Piggin, B. Kaye, I. Breward and B. Fletcher cited above.

16 For Australia see, Ward, *Australia and the British Embrace*, pp. 236–255; J. Curran and S. Ward, *The Unknown Nation: Australia after Empire* (Victoria: Melbourne University Press, 2010), pp. 26–44. See introduction for more references.

17 P. Buckner, 'The Long Goodbye. English Canadians and the British World', in P. Buckner and R. Douglas Francis (eds), *Rediscovering the British World* (Calgary: University of Calgary Press, 2005), pp. 181–207, esp. p. 202.

18 L. Colley, *Britons: Forging the Nation 1707–1832* (New Haven, CT: Yale University Press, 1992); G. Vaughan, '"Britishers and Protestants": Protestantism and Imperial British Identities in Britain, Canada and Australia, from the 1880s to the 1920s', *Studies in Church History*, 54 (2018), pp. 359–373.

19 Rowan Strong's study of an earlier period leads him to argue similarly that Anglicans acted from grounds of faith rather than ideological attachment to empire: *Anglicanism and the British Empire, c. 1700–1850* (Oxford: Oxford University Press, 2007), pp. 283, 294.

20 S. Brewitt-Taylor, *Christian Radicalism in the Church of England and the Invention of the British Sixties, 1957–1970* (Oxford: Oxford University Press, 2018), Ch. 1.

21 Radner, 'Anglican Communion', p. 316.

22 Carpenter, *Archbishop Fisher*, pp. 452–462.

23 C. Podmore, 'The Development of the Instruments of Communion', in Morris (ed.), *Oxford History of Anglicanism*, pp. 271–302, esp. pp. 483–484.

24 D. Hilliard, 'Australia: Towards Secularization and One Step Back', in C. Brown and M. Snape (eds), *Secularisation in the Christian World* (Abingdon: Routledge, 2016), pp. 75–92.

25 J. Stuart, *British Missionaries and the End of Empire: East, Central and Southern Africa, 1939–1964* (Grand Rapids, Michigan, and Cambridge: Eerdmans, 2011), esp. Chs 1–3; S. Stockwell, 'Anglicanism in an Era of Decolonization', in Morris (ed.), *Oxford History of Anglicanism*, pp. 160–185.

26 Frappell, 'Imperial Fervour', pp. 83–92, quote p. 87; T. Frame, 'Local Differences. Social and National Identity 1930–66', in Kaye (ed.), *Anglicanism in Australia*, pp. 100–123.

27 Piggin, 'Australian Anglicanism', pp. 214–215.

28 Jacob, *Making of the Anglican Church*, pp. 142–143, 274.

29 LPL, Fisher 39, f. 314, Fisher to F. de Witt Batty, Bishop of Newcastle, 13 January 1948.
30 Ibid., f. 317, Fisher to H. S. Begbie, Archdeacon of Sydney, 19 January 1948; Carpenter, *Archbishop Fisher*, p. 487.
31 LPL, Fisher 47, ff. 115–118, Woods to Fisher, 30 January 1948.
32 LPL, Fisher 190, ff. 135–137, McKie to Fisher, 3 February 1957; 'The Right Revd. John McKie', obituary, *Independent*, 14 April 1994.
33 Ibid., ff. 141–142, Fisher to Bishop [of Geelong], 15 March 1957.
34 LPL, Fisher 23, ff. 260–267, Woods to Fisher, 31 December 1947.
35 LPL, Bell 94, ff. 34–39, Bell to Fisher, 1 February 1950.
36 LPL, Fisher 68, ff. 209–210, text of Fisher's broadcast World Today, 6 February 1951.
37 LPL, Fisher 290, Tour Diaries, ff. 64–65, referenced in R. Frappell, L. Frappell, R. Nobbs and R. Withycombe (eds), *Anglicans in the Antipodes: An indexed catalogue of the papers and correspondence of the Archbishops of Canterbury, 1788–1961, relating to Australia, New Zealand and the Pacific* (Westport, CT: Greenwood Press, 1999).
38 'Forward in Fellowship', *Movietone News* (1950), www.youtube.com/watch?v=bygTN_ntQ7U (accessed 14 December 2018).
39 LPL, Fisher 290, Tour Diaries, ff. 23–24.
40 LPL, Fisher 68, ff. 49–50, Mowll to Fisher, 16 June 1950.
41 'Welcome Home to the Archbishop of Canterbury', *Church Times*, 2 February 1951, p. 1.
42 LPL, Fisher 68, ff. 172–173, Bishop of Dover to Garbett, 19 December 1950; f. 174, Garbett to '[Rev. J] Long', 1 January 1951.
43 Ibid., f. 238, F. N. Davey, SPCK, to Fisher, 7 May 1951.
44 'Forward in Fellowship', *Movietone News* (1950).
45 LPL, Fisher 74, ff. 412–416, text, Fisher's Perth broadcast.
46 LPL, Bell 94, ff. 34–39, Bell to Fisher 1 February 1950.
47 'Forward in Fellowship', *Movietone News* (1950).
48 S. Piggin, *Evangelical Christianity in Australia: Spirit, Word and World* (Oxford: Oxford University Press, 1996), pp. 125–127, 172; Hilliard, 'Australia: Towards Secularization'. On Britain, C. Brown, *The Death of Christian Britain: Understanding Secularization, 1800–2000* (London: Routledge, 2009).
49 LPL, Bell 94, ff. 34–39, Bell to Fisher, 1 February 1950.
50 Ibid.
51 LPL, Fisher 79, ff. 199–202, 'Meeting of the Australian House of Bishops', 22 November 1950.
52 LPL, Fisher 79, f. 207, copy Fisher to Batty, 15 February 1951; Carpenter, *Archbishop Fisher*, pp. 485–491; Frame, 'Local Differences', pp. 119–120.
53 LPL, Fisher 79, ff. 208–223, 'Suggestions relating to a Constitution of the Church of Australia. Submitted to the Bishop of Newcastle (N.S.W.) by the Archbishop of Canterbury' (February 1951), p. 1.
54 Jacob, *Making of the Anglican Church*, pp. 273–277; Breward, 'Anglicanism in Australia', p. 349.

55 LPL, Fisher 165, ff. 106, 111, Batty to Fisher, 5 March 1956; Fisher's reply, 6 April 1956. The negotiations are best followed in J. Davis, *Australian Anglicans and their Constitution* (Canberra: Acorn Press, 1993).
56 Piggin, 'Australian Anglicanism', pp. 213–216.
57 LPL, Fisher 79, ff. 208–223, 'Suggestions relating to a Constitution of the Church of Australia', pp. 4–5; ff. 224–234, 'Suggested re-draft of "revised draft"', p. 3.
58 Hilliard, 'Australia: Towards Secularization'.
59 H. M. Carey, 'Religious nationalism and clerical emigrants to Australia', in K. Fedorowich and A. S. Thompson (eds), *Empire, Migration and Identity in the British World* (Manchester: Manchester University Press, 2013), pp. 82–106.
60 M. Harper and S. Constantine, *Migration and Empire* (Oxford: Oxford University Press, 2010), p. 18.
61 *Church Assembly. Report of Proceedings*, XXXII, no 2, 12 November 1952, Bishop of London, pp. 260–265.
62 Ibid., XXXIV, no 1, 18 February 1954, pp. 89–90.
63 See G. Lynch, *Remembering Child Migration: Faith, Nation-Building and the Wounds of Charity* (London: Bloomsbury, 2016), pp. 58–59; G. Sherrington, '"Suffer Little Children": British Child Migration as a Study of Journeyings between Centre and Periphery', *History of Education*, 32:5 (2003), pp. 461–476; J. Fink, 'Children of Empire', *Cultural Studies*, 21:6 (2007), pp. 847–865; and briefly Fletcher, 'Anglicanism and Nationalism in Australia', pp. 225–226.
64 LPL, Fisher 27, f. 325, Fisher to Rev. R. E. Burlingham, 22 March 1947; Fisher 44, f. 271, Fisher to Mowll, 30 October 1948.
65 A. Chandler and D. Hein, *Archbishop Fisher, 1945–1961. Church, State and World* (Farnham: Ashgate, 2012), pp. 106–109.
66 LPL, Fisher 27, f. 329, Bessborough to Fisher, 25 June 1947; f. 336, Fisher to Bessborough, 4 July 1947.
67 LPL, Fisher 44, f. 271, Fisher to Mowll, 30 October 1948; f. 275, Mowll to Fisher, 12 November 1948.
68 The Church seems still to have received some funding in relation to child migrants and in 1960 the Commonwealth Relations Office agreed to provide ad hoc help with the Council's costs: PP. 1955–6, Cmnd. 9832, *Child Migration to Australia. Report of a Fact-Finding Mission* (London: HMSO, 1956), para. 3; LPL, Fisher 239, f. 261, Duncan Sandys to Fisher, 17 October 1960.
69 *Church Assembly*. XXXIV, no 1, 18 February 1954, p. 87.
70 *Church Assembly*, XXXVI, no. 2, 20 June 1956, p. 234. The Council comprised ten Assembly members; six chosen by the archbishops of Canterbury and York; and up to three co-opted members. The Assembly voted it annual subventions of £3,500–£5,000: Archdeacon of Halifax, *Church Assembly*, XXXX, no. 1, 16 February 1960, pp. 21–23.
71 LPL, Fisher 68, ff. 209–210, copy of text.
72 LPL, Bell 183, f. 16, copy, Fisher to Bessborough, 13 May 1953.
73 W. Wand, *Changeful Page: The Autobiography of William Wand Formerly Bishop of London* (London: Hodder & Stoughton, 1965), pp. 148–152; H. Riley (revised,

R. Brown). 'Wand, John William Charles', *Oxford Dictionary of National Biography*, https://doi.org/10.1093/ref:odnb/31798 (accessed 7 June 2018); F. R. Arnott, 'Wand, John William Charles (1885–1977)', *Australian Dictionary of Biography*, National Centre of Biography, Australian National University, http://adb.anu.edu.au/biography/wand-john-william-charles-8976/text15795 (accessed 7 June 2018).
74 *Church Assembly*, XXXIV, no 1, 18 February 1954, pp. 94–96.
75 Bell, *Church Assembly*, XXXVI, no. 2, 21 June 1956, p. 291.
76 Church of England Record Centre, Bermondsey, London [hereafter CERC], CECES/1A/1, minutes, fourth Council meeting, 9 February 1956, draft annual report to Church Assembly.
77 For this, and Australian immigration policy generally, see Chapter 12, in this volume, by Jean P. Smith.
78 CERC, CECES/1A/1, agenda and minutes, nineteenth Council meeting, 11 November 1959; appendix, 'Some results of the Bishop of Coventry's Visit to Australia'; also Fletcher, 'Anglicanism and Nationalism in Australia', pp. 225–226.
79 Archdeacon of Halifax, *Church Assembly*, XXXX, no. 1, 1960, 16 February 1956, pp. 21–23.
80 Formerly Waifs and Strays Society.
81 Those 'where parents had divorced' or whose home was 'unhappy'.
82 *Church Assembly*, XXXIV, no 1, 18 February 1954, p. 90.
83 LPL, Bell 183, f. 39, minutes, fourth commission meeting, appendix 2.
84 K. Paul, 'Changing Childhoods. Child Emigration since 1945', in J. Lawrence and P. Starkey (eds), *Child Welfare and Social Action in the Nineteenth and Twentieth Centuries: International Perspectives* (Liverpool: Liverpool University Press, 2001), pp. 121–143, esp. p. 125; S. Constantine, 'The British Government, Child Welfare, and Child Migration to Australia after 1945', *Journal of Imperial and Commonwealth History*, 30:1 (2002), pp. 99–132, at p. 100–105.
85 National Archives of Australia, Research Guides, note to file A436, 1949/5/6347, http://guides.naa.gov.au/good-british-stock/chapter3/church-of-england.aspx (accessed 24 July 2019).
86 *Church Assembly*, XXXVI, no. 2, 20 June 1956, p. 227–229.
87 CERC, CECES/1A/1, minutes, fourth meeting, 9 February 1956, draft annual report. In 2018 the Church apologised for its part in child migration: Anglican Communion News Service, www.anglicannews.org/news/2018/03/child-abuse-inquiry-begins-public-hearing-into-church-of-england-safeguarding-failures.aspx (accessed 11 June 2018).
88 *Child Migration*, paras. 23, 36–40.
89 Lynch, *Remembering Child Migration*, pp. 58–59; Sherrington, 'Suffer Little Children', pp. 461–476, esp. p. 470; Fink, 'Children of Empire', pp. 847–865, esp. pp. 852–853.
90 Archdeacon of Maidstone, *Church Assembly*, XXXVIII, 1958, no. 2, 18 June 1958, pp. 291–293; Rev. G. V. Gerrard, *Church Assembly*, XXXVI, no. 2, 20 June 1956, p. 232–233.
91 CERC, CECES/1A/1, minutes, fourth Council meeting, 9 February 1956, draft annual report; Bell, *Church Assembly*, XXXVI, no. 2, 20 June 1956, p. 235.

92 CERC, CECES/1A/2, Report by Brown on visit to South Africa, tabled with agenda for Council meeting, 17 February 1960.
93 CERC, CECES/1B, minutes, General Purposes Committee, 11 September 1957.
94 Bell, *Church Assembly*, XXXVII, no. 2, 20 June 1957, p. 323.
95 CERC, CECES/1A/1, minutes, eleventh Council meeting, 24 May 1957.
96 CERC, CECES/1A/1, minutes, fourth Council meeting, 9 February 1956.
97 LPL, Fisher 217, ff. 271–272, Fisher to Sir Griffith Williams, 7 January 1959.
98 LPL, Fisher 239, ff. 242–244, 'Church Assembly. Report of the Standing Committee of the Church of England Council for Commonwealth Settlement' (1960).
99 For example, Mr A. C. Cropper: *Church Assembly*, XXXVI, no. 2, 20 June 1956, p. 233.
100 J. Clark, 'CMS and Mission in Britain: The Evolution of a Policy', in K. Ward and B. Stanley (eds), *The Church Missionary Society and World Christianity 1799–1999* (Grand Rapids, Michigan and Cambridge: Eerdmans, 2000), pp. 319–343.
101 For a different example of Anglican anxieties about Catholicism at the end of empire, see Stockwell, 'A Sort of Official Duty to Reconcile'.
102 A. Chapman, 'The International Context of Secularization in England: The End of Empire, Immigration and the Decline of Christian National Identity, 1945–1970', *Journal of British Studies*, 54 (2015), pp. 163–189.
103 Radner, 'Anglican Communion', p. 319.
104 B. H. Fletcher, 'Anglicanism and National Identity in Australia since 1962', *Journal of Religious History*, 25:3 (2001), pp. 324–345, esp. pp. 326–327.

10

From *Pax Britannica* to *Pax Americana*? The end of empire and the collapse of Australia's Cold War policy

James Curran

Speaking in October 1968, Australian Prime Minister John Gorton attempted to come to grips with the new circumstances facing the nation's strategic culture and outlook. 'We have come to a watershed in Australian affairs', he said. 'No longer can we, as we have done for two centuries say "We are Australian. We are protected by the British Navy. We do not need to protect ourselves ..."'. Gorton's statement formed part of an ongoing effort by Australian leaders to come to terms with the British government's decision, announced in January that year, to speed up its planned withdrawal from South East Asia. Coming after Britain's abortive attempt at the beginning of the decade to join the European Economic Community, the Wilson government's decision to bring the curtain down on a British military presence in the region dealt another significant blow to the imperial ideal in Australian politics and culture. Australia was facing up to a world without Britain.

Gorton did feel able, however, to add a touch of reassurance to this solemn pronouncement. Despite such a 'basic change in the history of this nation', he went on to say, Australia was not entirely alone. 'We are, for our own security, dependent more on the United States Government providing the protection understood to be provided under the ANZUS pact', a treaty signed by Australia, New Zealand and the United States in September 1951.[1] The Prime Minister had some grounds for confidence in believing there to be a genuine community of interest between Australia and the United States. After all, at the time of his speech there were nearly 8,000 Australian troops fighting alongside the American military in South Vietnam.

But Gorton's optimism concerning the US alliance demands closer scrutiny. Only five months earlier, Australian confidence in its great power ally had been badly shaken, not only by the Tet Offensive, but also by a speech in which President Lyndon Johnson declared a unilateral halt to the bombing campaign against North Vietnam – a decision taken without any prior consultation with the Australian government. In the same speech, Johnson had also revealed that he would not seek the Democratic nomination for President at the elections due later that year. In Canberra, the combination of yet more setbacks on the ground in Vietnam combined with doubts over America's long-term policy in Asia. Fears of American retreat and isolationism resurfaced, and Australia now seemed to be staring down the barrel of a region without both of its 'great and powerful friends'. Amid this kind of uncertainty, it is little wonder that Gorton's stress on the 'protection *understood* to be provided' (emphasis added) by ANZUS seemed a touch equivocal. Indeed, the phrase reflected long-standing concerns among Australian politicians and policymakers about the nature of the American guarantee afforded to the country under the terms of ANZUS. In short, the troubling currents emanating from Australia's reaction to the end of empire looked most unlikely to be calmed by stronger voices of reassurance from American leaders and policymakers in Washington.

Yet it has been a dominant theme in the historiography of Australia's relations with the world that the United States has been an ever-present saviour at moments of Anglo-Australian crisis. Historians have tended to see in this evidence for Australia's persistent mentality – and policy – of great power dependence. When Britain's chips are down, so the story habitually runs, 'Uncle Sam' is there to soothe frayed Australian geopolitical and cultural nerves. The three most dramatic international circumstances the Commonwealth faced last century have tended to be viewed in this light. Thus in 1907 when Prime Minister Alfred Deakin became indignant at British indifference to Australian security concerns in the Pacific, he defied the Colonial Office in London and issued to the American President Theodore Roosevelt a direct invitation for his Great White Fleet to visit Australia. Its presence in Australian waters was to warn a rising Japan, which only two years before had trounced Russia at the Battle of Tsushima straits.[2] Deakin's actions have long been interpreted as a moment of heroic Australian defiance of Britain, a circumventing of British authority and a dramatic episode heralding a nascent Australian–American military brotherhood in the Pacific. The same interpretations have often coursed through treatment of the most infamous of all Australian 'turns' away from London towards Washington in 1941, when Labor's wartime leader John Curtin 'looked' to America 'free of any pangs' as to the country's traditional kinship with the United Kingdom. Curtin was doing so as Japan was sweeping down through South East Asia, thus proving hollow a decade of British assurances about the impregnability of its naval base in Singapore.[3] Finally this mentality is again seen to have been pervasive in the 1960s as Britain made its European intentions clear and began to withdraw from East of Suez. Australia, by committing forces to Vietnam, was thereby guaranteeing that even with the British departure from South East

Asia, its remaining great power ally would continue to help keep the Asian communist threat at bay and thus safeguard Australian security.

What is so little noted in these episodes, however, is the transience of the American life raft at these moments of national peril. Following the Great White Fleet's visit, the Americans explicitly rejected Deakin's call for them to extend their Monroe Doctrine to the South Pacific; in the Second World War, there was nothing to suggest that Curtin's remarks at the end of 1941 represented a major departure in Australian foreign policy, or that he envisaged a long-term security relationship with the United States continuing into the peace. Indeed, in the mid to late 1940s the United States rejected time and again Prime Minister Ben Chifley and External Affairs Minister H. V. Evatt's entreaties for some kind of security arrangement with the Americans in the Pacific, even on one occasion refusing to issue a basic presidential statement of support for Australia.

What these episodes do provide, however, is a window onto a more persistent problem in thinking about the history of Australian national security, namely that the United States had for some time hovered somewhat tentatively on the edges of the strategic and sentimental assumptions about Greater Britain in the Australian context. Recent scholarship contends that a broader context of Anglo-Saxonism, not British race patriotism, determined Australia's global racial orientation from the late nineteenth century.[4] And it is true that the father of Australian Federation himself, Sir Henry Parkes, had on occasion incorporated the United States into his vision of the destiny of the British race – in 1888 he had in somewhat grandiloquent fashion set out his hope that the Australian colonies might 'hold out their hands to the states of America' to form 'one great empire' with the mother country.[5] Nevertheless the Australian example tends to confirm Srdjan Vucetic's broader observation that the 'status of the United States in the discourses of Britishness was liminal'. If 'folk theories' of history drew on metaphors of the family to nominate Australia and New Zealand as Britain's daughters in the Southern seas, America was 'their somewhat estranged sister or distant cousin'.[6] That is not to say, though, as Duncan Bell points out, that America did not play a crucial role in imperial discourse in the late nineteenth century, and not only in its status as a potential rival to British power. Anglo–American tensions since the war of independence taught imperial unionists a stiff lesson: that 'the demands of colonial subjects had to be treated seriously'. In addition, the United States was exhibiting the success of a federal model – 'proving that individual liberty was compatible with vast geographical extent'.[7]

Even so, for all the attempts to cast Britishness in its Australian context as a virtual subcategory that included white Americans, clear reservations remained in the national consciousness about whether the United States should be considered a true constituent part of the Greater Britain concept. Thus, for example, Australian leaders resented the belated entry of the United States into the First World War. They decried the failure of their fellow Anglo-Saxons to come immediately to the rescue of the British Empire. Australia's Prime Minister Billy Hughes blamed the Americans for the failure of the British Empire to achieve the peace it was entitled to at the end of the war – it was 'not a good peace' for the British Empire as it did not restore Britain's dominant world position. Speaking of the United States, Hughes thundered that 'she who did not come into the war to make anything has made thousands of millions out of it … she has a good chance of beating us for world mercantile supremacy'.[8] This Australian resentment of the Americans lingered on into the interwar period. Robert Menzies confided to his diary after his first visit to the United States as Attorney General in 1935 that 'one thing which impresses the mind is that we err if we regard the Americans as our blood cousins. The majority of them are not Anglo-Saxons … they have … no sense of Imperial Destiny except so far as it sounds in terms of collaring the world's trade'.[9] Here America was being contrasted with the British peoples and the British Empire of which Australia was a proud member.

Even after the signing of the ANZUS treaty in September 1951, Australia and New Zealand strove to ensure, for much of the 1950s, that the agreement was not seen as incompatible with loyalty and devotion to Britain. Indeed, as Vucetic shows, they claimed that their new alliance with Washington along with the more traditional Commonwealth defence arrangements were 'now two parts of a single and indivisible project'. Australians would have readily agreed with their New Zealand counterparts that they were not 'selling out to the Americans'.[10] Significant Anglo–Australian defence cooperation in the 1950s gave more than a little substance to these lofty claims, but by the 1960s, the currents of decolonisation, a receding Britain and an uncertain American posture in Asia combined to erode what one senior Australian political journalist, Alan Reid, had called an era of 'glorious certainty'.[11]

This period oversaw nothing short of the collapse of Australia's Cold War policy – namely the desire to keep the Americans and the British engaged in South East Asia. Britain's withdrawal from the region, as has been shown in several works, elicited the expected last ditch, and ultimately unsuccessful, Australian appeals to Britain's global role. Doubts over America's long-term regional posture meant that Australia was almost back at the point it had been in the early 1950s, namely profoundly uncertain about what protection it was afforded under the treaty arrangements with the United States. But the crunch came when Canberra was leant on by both Britain and America to take up more of the security slack in the region, particularly over the defence of Malaysia and Singapore following the dissolution of its short-lived federation. Fearful once more that such a commitment might bring it into conflict with Indonesia or China, Australia could not be sure that its American ally would come to its aid. Thus once more did intense geopolitical anxieties animate the Australian strategic imagination.

The argument presented here has three dimensions. Drawing on official records from archives in Washington, London and Canberra, the chapter first explores how the British government's announcement concerning its withdrawal from the region introduced new and difficult problems for policymakers in Canberra. Australia found itself under significant pressure from both of its great power protectors. Britain was asking for Australian military support to assist in the ongoing defence of Malaysia and Singapore, an arrangement that was intended as a warning to Jakarta that it should not again seek to threaten regional stability after the adoption of its 'Confrontation' policy towards the creation of the new Malaysian Federation. In Washington, the administrations of Lyndon Johnson and then Richard Nixon joined Britain in pressuring Australia to increase its defence commitments in South East Asia. Alarmed at the potential security vacuum in the region with Britain's forthcoming withdrawal, US officials feared a symbolic retreat of Western power at a time when despair about the situation on the ground in Vietnam was reaching new levels.

Second, the chapter details how the Australian government, fearful of its forces in the region coming under attack by either China or Indonesia, renewed their efforts to extract a firmer guarantee from successive US administrations regarding America's obligations under the terms of the ANZUS treaty. These efforts were the primary focus of Prime Minister Gorton's official visits to Washington in 1968 and 1969. Those visits provoked another round of exhaustive deliberations in the innermost councils of the American national security community as to precisely what ANZUS obliged America to do. Finally, the article shows that, as a result of the profound differences between Australian expectations for the treaty and American realities, officials and politicians in Canberra had at last to resign themselves to accepting the limitations inherent in the treaty.

In the historiography of Australia's relations with the world, the British military withdrawal from South East Asia in the late 1960s has elicited two broad responses. The first is related to the impact of the decision on Australia's strategic circumstances, the second to the consequences of this period for Australian cultural identity and orientation. The first view stresses the Wilson government's decision as a critical step in forcing Australian leaders and policymakers to face up to the reality of a region no longer sheltered by great power protection. Following on from Britain's first attempt to join the European Economic Community (EEC) from 1961–63, the decision announced by the British government of Harold Wilson in July 1967 to bring home all British military forces from 'East of Suez' is widely regarded as one of the 'shocks' that initiated not only a fundamental reassessment of Australia's defence posture but ultimately its relationship with the countries and cultures of Asia. Scholars such as Andrea Benvenuti, John Darwin, David Goldsworthy and Stuart Ward have mapped the sense of profound discomfort that attended Australia's reaction to this British decision.[12] While the Australian government's reaction to the Wilson announcement did not prompt quite the same emotional, outraged cries of abandonment that had coloured the official response to Harold Macmillan's attempts at British EEC entry earlier in the decade, nevertheless the Australian government of Harold Holt vehemently objected to the British move for two reasons. In the first instance, it raised the prospect of massive additional costs in maintaining Australia's 'forward defence' posture in the region in Britain's absence, requiring the 'recasting of Australian external policy in fundamental terms'. Second, the British presence was an important counterweight to the ongoing and far more crucial presence of the United States in the region. In early 1966, the Foreign Affairs and Defence Committee in Canberra had stressed that the 'vital thing for Australia was to have the United States remain in the area and everything must be measured against this. Any prospect that the British would abandon their presence in South East Asia must tend to embarrass and undermine present United States policy'. Australian concerns were related not so much to anxiety about the British relationship in itself as to the impact of Britain's withdrawal on the wider strategic situation.[13]

A second interpretation of these events has nurtured the powerful view, expressed both at the time and since, that the decline of British imperial power in South East Asia and the readiness of governments in Canberra to support the United States in South Vietnam showed that Australia had simply switched one dependency on a great power for another, that it had leapt from the British imperial embrace into the American orbit. Historian Geoffrey Serle even believed that the country's 'transition from a British colony to an American province' had occurred so swiftly that Australia was about to become a hybrid nation: 'Austerica', with his fellow citizens destined 'to become just slightly different sorts of Americans'. What Serle saw as the irresistible 'logic of satellitism' – inherited from long experience with Britain – would likely prevail in Australian habit and thought. The more Australians pronounced their independence, the 'more and more Americanised and dependent' they would become.[14] Just over a decade later Humphrey McQueen could still assert that Australia almost overnight had morphed from 'British sycophant' to 'American lickspittle'.[15] It is the purpose of this chapter to test the assumption that the collapse of Britishness and decolonisation automatically resulted in strategic dependence on Washington and cultural Americanisation.

The dilemmas of ANZUS and Australian security in the era of Vietnam

The confidence of Australian leaders in the ANZUS treaty was somewhat offset by the state of chronic unease they felt concerning the nature and level of America's commitment to Australian security.[16] This anxiety derived primarily from the wording in Article IV of the pact, which held that in the event of 'an armed attack in the Pacific Area on any of the Parties' each 'would act to meet the common danger in accordance with its constitutional processes'. Australian officials were all too aware that the wording was not as emphatic a declaration as that contained in the equivalent provision in the NATO treaty, which stipulates that an 'attack on one constitutes an attack on all'. As a consequence, they were reluctantly forced to accept that their American ally was never going to invest ANZUS with the same kind of strategic weight as the Atlantic pact.

Australian disappointment over the American interpretation of its treaty obligations under ANZUS was manifest most visibly in the early 1960s when the United States and Australian governments disagreed over Indonesian President Sukarno's desire to annex the Dutch-held territory of West New Guinea and over his policy of 'Confrontation' towards the creation of the new Malaysian Federation. It is the latter case that is most relevant here, for the government in Canberra met bluntly Washington's reluctance to promise military assistance in the event of Australia becoming involved in armed conflict with Indonesian forces. Throughout 1962 and 1963, Australian diplomats and political leaders embarked on a sustained campaign to elicit some kind of stronger guarantee from the White House. Indeed, they were relentless in their pursuit of a form of words that they hoped would provide the sort of security they clearly struggled to find within the language of the ANZUS treaty itself. President John F. Kennedy, however, delivered a blunt message to his junior alliance partner. Contrary to Australian expectations, it was not the US view that American forces would be automatically engaged if Australian troops in North Borneo came under fire from Indonesia guerrilla units. During a crucial meeting with the Australian External Affairs Minister, Sir Garfield Barwick, in October 1963, Kennedy put the situation in the starkest possible terms: the American people had 'forgotten ANZUS and are not at the moment prepared for a situation which would involve the United States'.[17]

Although the Americans did agree to come to Australia's aid under the terms of ANZUS if Indonesians attacked Australian armed forces, they placed so many conditions on their consent which, in the given circumstances, almost emptied the agreement of any meaning. In a formal memorandum handed to Barwick, the United States laid down the law as they saw it. They required, first, that Australia should consult with them before sending troops to Borneo. Furthermore, the promise of aid would apply only to a conventional military attack on Australian forces and not to a guerrilla or subversive war. And lastly, in the event of the Australians invoking the agreement, US assistance would be limited to air, naval and logistical support. As the Defence Committee in Canberra subsequently noted, the 'agreed note is cautiously worded as regards the obligations of the United States'.[18] The government in Canberra had little choice but to accept that this was how it had to be. But the episode raised doubts about the meaning of the ANZUS alliance, and therefore about the nation's ability to rely on America for support or even consultation about issues which touched its vital interests in the region. In 1964, the best that Australian Prime Minister Robert Menzies could tell the parliament about the treaty was that it was a 'contract based on the utmost goodwill, the utmost good faith and unqualified friendship. Each of us will stand by it'.[19]

'Goodwill' may have been a remarkably shallow commodity on which to base Australia's faith in the Alliance, but it showed too that the habits of relations with Britain were being carried over into its attitudes towards the US alliance. More specifically, as the Australian External Affairs Minister Paul Hasluck subsequently explained, Menzies' statement was also 'an implicit rejection of the procedure of trying to define more exactly in writing what Articles IV and V mean and of attempts to describe in advance what would happen under ANZUS in various hypothetical situations'. As such, Menzies' words were to assume an almost canon-like status in the language of Alliance diplomacy. But this was intended to be the most silent of diplomatic canons. Hasluck was firmly of the view that the best policy for Australian officials to follow was to simply keep quiet, for the 'more we try to spell out the meaning of Article IV and V the narrower that meaning will become'. In the wake of the disappointment over President Kennedy's interpretation of America's ANZUS obligations in the Confrontation dispute, the head of Australia's external affairs department, Arthur Tange, stated that Australia had been 'put on notice by a former President that the American understanding of its obligations was such as to exclude help from them to Australia in certain circumstances'.[20] The so-called lifeline of American support – so crucial in an age of British imperial retreat – appeared to be on life support. Thus the assumption that Australia moved seamlessly from a fading *Pax Britannica* to the supposed iron-clad guarantees of a *Pax Americana* is highly problematic.

All of this raises again the problem of studying the dissolution of the British Empire in the era of Vietnam. In his 2002 presidential address to the American Historical Association, Wm. Roger Louis explained that events in Vietnam, Malaysia and Singapore were not merely interconnected but can be 'studied in such a way as to illuminate the spirit of the age – a deeply anti-imperial age, but then as now not without its champions of the British imperial mission or the American cause in Vietnam'.[21] But Louis' focus was primarily on the view from Washington and London, thus leaving aside the dilemma for those in the region who were not only being asked to fill the strategic vacuum left by British departure, but who were doing so at a time of great uncertainty for the United States in Vietnam and the region more broadly. A. G. Hopkins, on the other hand, does concede a place for the Dominions in terms of a Cold War global strategy formulated by the United States and Britain. But his attention is focused neither on South East Asia, nor is it on how the Dominions responded to the unravelling of this strategy. Indeed, when he does identify the moment that Canada, Australia and New Zealand 'freed themselves from reliance on Britain' it was merely, he says, to 'become dependent on the US for military supplies and protection'. But this new dependence, he notes, 'was no greater than that of much of the rest of the world'.[22]

But with the announcement of Britain's intended military withdrawal from South East Asia, Australian anxiety about the nature of the American guarantee under ANZUS only intensified. New demands made the question of America's obligations a vital question in Australian strategic thinking and planning. American policymakers were now looking to their alliance partners in Canberra not only for ongoing support in the war in Vietnam, but for an assurance that Australian forces would step up to fill the strategic void left by British departure from the region.

In particular the American and British pressure on Canberra to increase its defence commitment to Malaysia and Singapore presented the Australian governments of Harold Holt (1966–1967) and John Gorton (1968–1971) with an acute dilemma. Eager to satisfy the requests from its great power ally in Washington, they decided once again to seek a set of assurances from US presidents and officials about Washington's commitment to assisting Australia under ANZUS. Caught in a geopolitical whirlwind not of its own making, the Australian government looked to ANZUS as an anchor in a post-imperial world. But just as in previous eras when Australian leaders had continually sought assurances from Britain to protect the Australian continent from an attack by a hostile Asian power, so they would now likewise struggle to convince Washington that it would need to come to Australia's aid at a time of military crisis. It is perhaps not surprising, then, that even as Canberra moved with a more purposeful tread into the American orbit, its practice of managing a great power relationship appeared to be haunted by the ghosts of its own strategic past: most especially in the continued seeking of a common, concerted policy.

The defence of Malaysia/Singapore: Australia as the new 'Sheriff'?

The question over whether the Australian government would increase its commitment to the defence of Malaysia and Singapore arose out of a proposal by the Malaysian leader Tunku Abdul Rahman in mid-1967 for 'Five Power' talks – involving Australia, Britain, Malaysia, New Zealand and Singapore – to discuss defence arrangements in the region following Britain's withdrawal.[23] Singaporean Prime Minister, Lee Kuan Yew, had put the matter in characteristically blunt terms: would Australia, which had been content to play the role of 'Deputy Sheriff' to Britain or America in the region, now step up to play the role of Sheriff as the two major powers retreated?[24] Initially, Prime Minister John Gorton had sounded enthusiastic at the prospect of 'falling in' with the 'strong desire' of Singapore and Malaysia for an Australian defence presence. At the opening of the Australian parliament on 12 March 1968, the government signalled its intention to 'discuss the size and role of an Australian contribution to continued defence arrangements which embrace a joint Singapore/Malaysia defence effort'.[25] Australia already maintained an infantry battalion and supporting units at the Commonwealth Brigade Headquarters in Malacca, Malaysia, along with two air force squadrons at Butterworth in northern Malaysia and four ships based in Singapore.

But that early Australian support seemed to be overtaken by chronic vacillation following the Tet Offensive and Johnson's withdrawal from the American presidential race for 1968. It was at this point that Australian concerns over British and possible American withdrawal from the region merged. Wanting on the one hand to devise a policy acceptable to Britain, the Australian Cabinet were also mindful of the ongoing uncertainty over future American policy in the region given the worsening situation in Vietnam.[26] The result was a determination to maintain flexibility and freedom of manoeuvre in Australia's strategic posture, but 'flexibility' was fast becoming a euphemism for a government increasingly prone to what one newspaper came to describe as 'Defence Dither'.[27] It was also around this time that the Philippines pressed once more its claim to the Malaysian state of Sabah.

While some ministers in the Australian government were keen to see an ongoing Australian commitment to Malaysia and Singapore as emblematic of Australia's policy of 'forward defence' in the region – that is, keeping the threat from Asia as far away from Australia's shores as possible – the Prime Minister continued to waiver. Gorton's equivocation had only one cause: whether the Americans would 'back him up' should Australian forces get into trouble. As Dean Rusk put it, Gorton 'reportedly would like a firm guarantee of US protection before committing Australian troops'.[28] As Peter Edwards has suggested, this was 'one of the major questions ... hanging over that commitment'.[29] New archival evidence can now reveal just how painful a process this was for Australian and American policymakers. Based on previous experience, the Australians surely knew they faced an uphill task. As one American policy brief put it, 'there is nothing in the legislative history to show that the Congress (or the executive for that matter) understood that the United States, through the ANZUS treaty, was authorising Australia and New Zealand to create defence commitments for us to other states'.[30] As a result, American advisers in the Department of State deemed it 'prudent to continue to avoid flat statements that ANZUS applies to Australian forces in third countries'.[31]

The Australian government had not, however, left all the diplomatic heavy lifting until President Johnson's speech of March 1968. The effort to discern American thinking on ANZUS and its application to the Malaysia/Singapore question started well before. In October 1967, Paul Hasluck had left with Dean Rusk and Robert McNamara a memorandum containing a number of questions about the applicability of the treaty should Australia decide to keep its forces in Malaysia and Singapore. He was, in essence, asking not only for further consultations with Washington over its position on ANZUS, but also for the right for the then Australian Prime Minister, Harold Holt, to be able to make a statement to the Australian people concerning American military support in the event of hostilities involving Australian troops.[32] In a formula that betrayed both desperation and assumption in equal measure, Hasluck conveyed to Rusk his view that 'ANZUS must be kept alive, but the fact that the Treaty did apply should not be hammered in public'.[33]

For the Americans the Hasluck memorandum had a familiar ring. But in Washington there was an eagerness to underline the changed circumstances. Not only had Singapore now withdrawn from the Malaysian Federation but Indonesia, under the leadership of new president Suharto, had put down a Communist insurrection in October 1965, and shifted its foreign policy from 'confrontation' against Malaysia to cooperation with its southeast Asian neighbours.[34] The American reply was therefore decidedly guarded, and came in the form of a letter from Samuel Berger, Deputy Assistant Secretary of State for East Asian and Pacific Affairs, to Australia's Ambassador in Washington, Keith Waller. Berger had already told Waller privately that the circumstances of 1963, when President Kennedy and Garfield Barwick had negotiated a secret memorandum over the application of the ANZUS treaty to Australian forces in Malaysia, had 'disappeared', and that 'any public statement would be likely to cause difficulties for the US and, in the nature of things, it would have to fuzz the US commitment under ANZUS. From the US point of view, the less that had to be said by anybody the better ... '. As Waller put it soberly in his report back to Canberra, this was 'as much as we can expect from the US at this time'.[35] The formal correspondence from the Department of State put it even more forcefully, spelling out that 'we would not favour Australia justifying or explaining its position in terms of the ANZUS commitment'. For the Americans, it was almost as if this were a treaty that dare not speak its name. In Canberra, Australian officials could only note that 'current US policy offers no grounds that the United States Government would be more prepared now than in the past to define more closely its commitment under the ANZUS treaty'.[36]

Dealing with John Gorton

John Gorton was a very different kind of leader to his predecessor, Harold Holt, with whom President Johnson had established a close working relationship. Not only had Johnson been the first US president to visit Australia – at the height of cooperation over Vietnam in October 1966 – but he had also returned to Australia in late 1967 to attend Holt's funeral, following the latter's disappearance at sea. Initial US assessments were hopeful that Gorton could be 'even more valuable than Holt because of his self-confidence and forcefulness and his insistence on putting Australia's interests first'. The American Ambassador in Canberra did however see that the new leader was a work in progress, and 'until Gorton has succeeded in establishing the image he would like, involving both an idea of Australia first and rough-hewn independence, it will be necessary to take the thorns with the roses'.[37]

It did not take long for the thorns to show. Gorton's attempt at assertive nationalism had already aggravated a White House increasingly desperate to maintain a united allied front at a time when the situation in Vietnam continued to spiral out of control. Almost upon coming to office in January 1968, Gorton had stated bluntly that Australia could not increase its commitment of manpower to the conflict, which then numbered around 8,000. American distrust of the new Australian prime minister was also sparked by Gorton's alarmed reaction to Johnson's critical speech at the end of March 1968. In the wake of the Tet Offensive, in which the Vietcong had been able to strike seemingly at will at US and allied targets in south of the country, the somewhat rosy American ideas of progress in Vietnam took a fatal blow. This move towards de-escalation caught the Australian government by complete surprise. Only days before, Hasluck had strongly defended the US bombing policy in the parliament. Furious at the lack of consultation about the policy change, Gorton had privately remarked that this was 'no way to treat an ally'.[38] In the press, journalist Alan Ramsey likened the American decision to 'little short of stabbing in the back'.[39] The Prime Minister confided to one reporter his fear that the United States was on the cusp of returning to pre-Second World War isolationism. Yet Gorton saw even more portents of doom ahead; one assessment by the State Department argued that the Australian leader viewed Johnson's retirement from politics as 'possibly foreshadowing a US retreat from Southeast Asia, which would leave Australia in an agonising position'.[40] It was not far from the mark. As

Australian Minister for the Air, Peter Howson confided to his diary in the days following Johnson's broadcast: 'To my mind it's the first step of the Americans moving out of South East Asia and ... within a few years, there'll be no white faces on the Asian mainland ... from now on, and to a much greater extent, we shall be isolated and on our own'.[41] The generation of leaders, policymakers and strategic thinkers in the 1960s were having to prepare for an eventuality that their predecessors would have struggled to imagine. As John Gorton himself put it on one occasion, his incredulity unmistakable: 'who would have thought that suddenly at this point in the nation's history, all the old conceptions would have to be taken out, have to be re-examined, to be reassessed because the world had changed ...'[42]

In the wake of Johnson's speech, Gorton referred publicly to the anxiety among his colleagues about a possible change in US Asia policy. But he went even further, suggesting that it may become necessary for Australia to abandon its policy of 'forward defence' and adopt what he called an 'Israeli-type' defence posture. Secretary of State Dean Rusk advised President Johnson to try to influence Gorton's thinking in a 'more helpful direction'. He pressed the president to make it clear that the types of comments the Prime Minister was making about America's future in Asia 'can only contribute to producing the very result Gorton fears: a US public mood of isolationism'.[43]

On the cusp of Gorton's visit to the United States, American attitudes had hardened. The president's closest advisers struggled to take Gorton seriously, labelling him 'not a profound thinker ... a conclusion jumper' and a leader who 'lacks experience in foreign affairs'.[44] While they respected his refusal to 'have either himself or Australia taken for granted', they underlined the inherent limits to this brash style. Amid so many regional uncertainties, not only in Vietnam but also in the projected British military pull-out from South East Asia, US officials pointed to a 'growing realisation that, whatever its will, Australia cannot realistically adopt a meaningful independent stance'.[45]

For the White House, the most crucial issue was the question of Australian commitment to maintain its presence in Malaysia and Singapore after the British withdrawal from 1971. Dean Rusk advised Johnson that while Gorton had announced a tentative decision in favour of remaining militarily engaged in the region, he was now 'backing away from this' and 'reportedly would like a firm guarantee of US protection before committing Australian troops'. But still the Americans were as immovable on this point as they had been over the Indonesia–Malaysia Confrontation episode in 1963, and the Secretary of State merely told the President that there was no need to alter the 'special understanding' that had been reached between John F. Kennedy and Garfield Barwick. On that occasion, while strongly encouraging the Australians to remain in the region, there was no need to 'give them a blanket guarantee of protection under ANZUS'.[46]

It was clear after his meeting with the President that the Americans had been true to their word. In answer to questions on this subject from the Australian press, Gorton's mixture of contorted speech and confused reasoning was laid bare:

Journalist: From what (Assistant Secretary of State for East Asia and Pacific Affairs) Mr (William) Bundy told us in the White House conference, he defined the ANZUS treaty as applying to forces of all the signatories in the Pacific Area. But he left ambiguous whether this would apply to Australian forces in Malaysia, Singapore ... Have they in fact expressed any opinion on whether ANZUS does apply in that?

Gorton: I wouldn't say any definite ... I don't know I can give you any definite answer to that either. ANZUS is a treaty – I think it does apply in the three defined areas.

Journalist: It does or does not?

Gorton: I think it applies in certain defined areas. But I would want to check this with the External Affairs people before I was sure that that was correct. But by and large, I think it has been, what shall I say – I cannot think of the exact words – a matter – never spelled out whether it applied in Malaysia and Singapore area or not.

Journalist: But that is exactly the point. It has never been spelled out. The point is have you made a judgment in your mind now as to whether it would apply to these two countries?

Gorton: Well, you are asking really the sort of questions which one can pursue it to the point where it is the whole sort of subject of discussions. And I do not think I am free to do that.[47]

Following this press conference, the chronic uncertainty over the US interpretation of ANZUS – which had only been expressed in strict privacy – now tumbled into Australian domestic politics and created new difficulties for Gorton. The leader of the Labor Opposition, Gough Whitlam, was only too ready to highlight the government's discomfort, emphasising 'the extraordinary admission that the Prime Minister of Australia cannot tell his people or his Parliament what Australia's rights and obligations are under ANZUS'. Reading out aloud what one newspaper report called 'an embarrassing series of quotations from Gorton's news conferences in the United States', Whitlam attacked their 'vagueness' about the ANZUS treaty.[48]

The Australian Prime Minister had badly miscalculated. On his return to Canberra, Gorton's senior foreign affairs adviser, Alan Griffith, gave a devastating appraisal of the Washington visit to an American diplomat: the whole exercise had been 'a bit of a disaster', not least because Gorton had 'overplayed his mission of sounding out US intentions in Asia'. It was apparent to the Australian press, Griffith noted, 'that the President and others had turned the tables on him by pointing up that it was for Australia and other Asian powers to set the course in Asia; the US performance in that area would depend upon Australia and others carrying at least a fair share of the burden'.[49]

By 1969 it was the new Nixon administration's turn to deal with a less obliging Australian ally. In the figure of John Gorton – who had said publicly that he had no wish to 'follow America blindly' – they continued to bristle at a style unseen in previous Australian leaders.[50] William Crook, American Ambassador in Canberra, believed that Gorton had a 'bone and marrow suspicion that we are trying to push him around'. He was, quite simply, a 'very difficult man' who needed to be 'told the facts of life'.[51] Even the British sensed that the president–prime minister relationship had to be 'rebuilt anew'.[52] Though he 'wound up rather jaundiced' by his experiences with Johnson, Gorton was being told by senior Australian officials that Nixon was a 'man with whom he can have a proper relationship without fear that he is being dominated or annexed'. Those same officials, however, were not entirely well-informed about Nixon. Keith Waller told Governor General Lord Casey that he had 'simply no idea of the line the new president will take' towards Australia.[53]

Gorton did, however, win some early kudos with the new administration on account of his announcement in February 1969, barely a month after Nixon's inauguration, that Australia would maintain its forces, including ground troops, in Malaysia and Singapore after the British pull-out in 1971. Moreover, Gorton set no 'specific terminal date' for the Australian commitment. Nevertheless, he did make it clear that contingencies were conceivable with which Australian forces might not be able to cope, and that 'if such a situation should arise we would have to look to the support of allies outside the region'. He could only have had America in mind.[54] Regardless of this qualification, one US policy analyst remarked that in so doing Gorton had decided Australia would go 'all the way with ... forward defence', thus equating this decision firmly with former Prime Minister Harold Holt's declaration on the south lawn of the White House in 1966 that Australia was 'all the way with LBJ' in Vietnam. It was, the brief added in a patronising Churchillian touch, Gorton's 'finest hour'.[55]

But such interpretations aptly captured the Washington mood. Nixon's Secretary of State, William Rogers, noted that the decision 'put an end to a year-long, meandering public foreign policy debate on "forward defence" versus "fortress Australia"'.[56] The former had won. The *Bulletin* magazine reported that there were 'shouts of joy' in Washington at the news, and Rogers was especially relieved, since Gorton now seemed no longer likely 'to seek a specific US guarantee of the safety of his ground forces before committing them'.[57] And extracting that guarantee had reportedly been the 'only one thing on his mind' before coming to Washington to see Nixon.[58] But as Gorton confided to Rogers, he was repeatedly questioned whether ANZUS applies to 'this and that' but now recognised that he 'could not be always trying to spell out the meaning of the treaty in the absence of concrete situations. To do so ... might well result in narrowing the application of the treaty unnecessarily rather than clarifying it'. The 'best he could look for was something general in nature'.[59] It was a somewhat crestfallen resignation to the realities. But it meant the Americans could retreat to the safety of their tried and tested 1963 formula: that in the event of any military contingency in Malaysia or Singapore requiring their support, the United States 'would of course stand ready to consult fully and promptly on what support we might give'.[60] It was the very conditionality in statements such as this that so troubled Australian policymakers.

Kissinger knew, though, that Gorton was still likely to 'test the firmness of US Asian commitments' and while he didn't seek 'legal precision', he was after a 'real and personal feeling that we intend to stick by Australia'.[61] And those warming words were always much easier to put in the presidential speeches and meeting briefs. Some American officials even surmised that Gorton was so 'blunt', so 'down to earth', so desirous of a 'man-to-man approach', so 'impatient of formalities and diplomatic nuances' that literally any kind of assurance from the United States on ANZUS might hit the spot. 'He is the sort of man who, if he hits it off with the President, might even be content with an oral exchange and a handshake over a scotch and soda'.[62] Never before – and probably not since – have the critical articles of the ANZUS treaty been reduced to the protocols of the saloon bar. Gorton too had made it clear that 'it would be very embarrassing to the government of Australia to be taken unaware by changes in US policy in areas of common concern, such as Vietnam and China'.[63]

The Americans had done their homework, knowing instinctively what kind of approach would appeal to Australian instincts. Over the preceding decade US diplomatic reporting from Canberra had gone to great lengths in charting the eroding 'capital' of feeling in Anglo-Australian relations, and there is every reason to suggest that the proposed application of a 'real and personal' touch as a means of assuaging Gorton's anxieties derived from that close study of the dwindling basis for sentiment in Canberra's ties with London. Likewise, it shows a sensitivity to the kind of rhetorical and emotional currency that coloured Australian defence policy for nearly a century, namely that specific, legally binding defence guarantees were unnecessary if the requisite reservoir of mutual goodwill and understanding were assured. This strategy certainly suited the Nixon White House, which, like its predecessors, remained steadfast in refusing to be drawn openly on what the ANZUS 'guarantee' involved. The same ironically goes for Australian prime ministers like Gorton. As the awkward and rambling syntax of his press conference outside Blair House showed, he was simply not used to thinking in contractual or legal terms when it came to the politics of the US alliance. It was surely enough that Australia was not only contributing forces to Vietnam but that it was seen to be responding to wider, 'Western' defence obligations in the region brought on by the British military withdrawal. The sober reality, of course, was that Australians were witnessing once more the thwarting of a deep assumption at the core of their strategic policy: the belief that their interests with a great power protector would ultimately coincide. Long-cherished beliefs in the viability of imperial defence took a long time to die in Canberra, even outliving the Fall of Singapore in 1942. By 1969, the ANZUS treaty was not even two decades old, but Australian policymakers were facing up once more to the reality that their major ally would not utter the magic words of an iron-clad commitment to the defence of Australia.

Conclusion

To return, then, to the original proposition: the conventional wisdom in much Australian historiography that the shock of empire's end was buffeted by the American connection. If that was the case in strategic terms, it was a most uncertain one. By mid 1969 following Nixon's enunciation of his Guam doctrine – effectively saying the United States would never again get involved in a land war in Asia – Australian ministers were wailing about having no more white faces on the Asian mainland. But they also had to give up on going to Washington asking for clarification on Article IV of the ANZUS treaty. Writing in *The Age* around this time, Australian journalist Sam Lipski concluded that the idea of some special bond between the two countries had been found wanting. Americans, he said, 'do not quite understand the Australian expectation that mates who have worked together, played together, or fought together will always put their loyalty to one another ahead of other relationships'.[64] Lipski argued that the logical consequence of this was that American policy, was 'not oriented towards special relationships with other nations, even when they share our language and ancestral descent ... However much individual Americans may come to prefer Aussies to their other friends and relatives, Washington policies are conducted with a certain cosmic impartiality'.[65] While the American alliance remained the central principle around which the nation's defence was based, both sides of Australian politics left behind the era of 'great and powerful friends' and instead embraced the imperative of comprehensive engagement with the countries and cultures of Asia.

Notes

1. John Gorton, Speech to the Flinders Electorate Liberal Party Luncheon, Mornington, 14 October 1968, www.pmtranscripts.gov.au (accessed 10 July 2015).
2. N. Meaney, *The Search for Security in the Pacific* (Sydney: Sydney University Press, 1976).
3. See J. Curran, *Curtin's Empire* (New York: Cambridge University Press, 2011).
4. See, for example, M. Lake, *Progressive New World: How Settler Colonialism and Transpacific Exchange Shaped American Reform* (Cambridge: Harvard University Press, 2019).
5. Parkes, speaking at the dedication of Centennial Park, cited in N. Meaney, 'Australia and the World', in N. Meaney (ed.), *Under New Heavens: Cultural Transmission and the Making of Australia* (Sydney: Heinemann, 1989), p. 395.
6. S. Vucetic, *The Anglosphere: A Genealogy of a Racialised Identity in International Relations* (Stanford: Stanford University Press, 2011), p. 58.
7. D. Bell, *Reordering the World: Essays on Liberalism and Empire* (Princeton: Princeton University Press, 2016), p. 185; see also Bell, *The Idea of Greater Britain: Empire and the Future of World Order, 1860–1900* (Princeton: Princeton University Press, 2007), pp. 231–260.
8. Hughes, letter to Munro Ferguson, 17 May 1919, quoted in N. Meaney, *Australia and World Crisis, 1914–1923* (Sydney: Sydney University Press, 2010), pp. 396–397.
9. Menzies, diary entry, 15 August 1935, quoted in A. W. Martin, *Robert Menzies: A Life, Volume 1: 1894–1943* (Carlton: Melbourne University Press, 1993), p. 166. For a fuller treatment of Menzies' views of the US, see F. Yuan, 'Heir to the Empire: Robert Menzies and the United States of America' (BA Hons thesis, University of Sydney, 2017).
10. Vucetic, *Anglosphere*, p. 66.
11. Alan Reid, *The Bulletin*, 24 August 1968.
12. A. Benvenuti, 'A Parting of the Ways: The British Military Withdrawal from Southeast Asia and its Critical Impact on Anglo-Australian Relations, 1965–68', *Contemporary British History*, 20:4 (2006), pp. 575–605; A. Benvenuti, 'The British Military Withdrawal from Southeast Asia and its impact on Australia's Cold War Strategic Interests', *Cold War History*, 5:2 (2005), pp. 189–210; S. Ward, *Australia and the British Embrace: The Demise of the Imperial Ideal* (Carlton: Melbourne University Press, 2001); J. Darwin, *The Empire Project: The Rise and Fall of the British World-System 1830–1970* (Cambridge: Cambridge University Press, 2009); D. Goldsworthy, *Losing the Blanket: Australia and the End of Britain's Empire* (Carlton: Melbourne University Press, 2002).
13. J. Curran and S. Ward, *The Unknown Nation: Australia after Empire* (Carlton: Melbourne University Press, 2010), pp. 45–46.
14. G. Serle, 'Austerica Unlimited', *Meanjin Quarterly*, 26:3 (1967), pp. 237–250, at p. 249.
15. H. McQueen, *Gallipoli to Petrov: Arguing with Australian History* (Sydney: Angus & Robertson, 1980), p. 174.

16 D. McLean, 'Australia in the Cold War: A Historiographical Review', *International History Review*, 23:2 (2001), pp. 299–321; see by the same author, McLean, 'From British Colony to American Satellite? Australia and the USA during the Cold War', *Australian Journal of Politics and History*, 52:1 (2006), pp. 64–79.
17 Memorandum of Conversation, President Kennedy and Garfield Barwick, 17 October 1963, in E. C. Keefer (ed.), *Foreign Relations of the United States* (FRUS), 1961–63, Vol XXXII, Southeast Asia (Washington: US Department of State, 2004), pp. 750–753.
18 National Archives of Australia (NAA), Canberra, Defence Committee, 7 November 1963, A1838 TS686/1/1, Part 1.
19 Menzies, *Commonwealth Parliamentary Debates (CPD)*, House of Representatives, 21 April 1964, p. 1280.
20 NAA, Minute, Tange to Hasluck, 10 February 1965, A1838, TS686/1/1, Part 1.
21 Wm. R. Louis, 'The Dissolution of the British Empire in the Era of Vietnam', in Wm. R. Louis (ed.), *Ends of British Imperialism: The Scramble for Empire, Suez and Decolonisation* (London: IB Tauris, 2006), p. 557.
22 A. G. Hopkins, 'Rethinking Decolonisation', *Past and Present*, 200 (2008), pp. 211–247, at p. 240.
23 P. G. Edwards with G. Pemberton, *Crises and Commitments: The Politics and Diplomacy of Australia's Involvement in SouthEast Asian Conflicts, 1948–1965* (Sydney: Allen & Unwin, 1992), p. 199.
24 Lee Kuan Yew, cited in C. Bell, *Dependent Ally: A Study in Australian Foreign Policy* (Melbourne: Oxford University Press, 1984), p. 87.
25 Cited by J. L. Richardson, 'Australian Strategic and Defence Policies', in G. Greenwood and N. Harper (eds), *Australia in World Affairs 1966–70* (Melbourne: F. W. Cheshire, 1974), p. 244.
26 Edwards with Pemberton, *Crises and Commitments*, p. 194.
27 *Sydney Morning Herald*, 11 December 1968, cited in S. Ward, 'Security: Defending Australia's Empire', in S. Ward and D. Schreuder (eds), *Australia's Empire* (Oxford: Oxford University Press, 2008), p. 254.
28 National Archives and Records Administration (NARA), Washington DC, Memorandum, Rusk to President, 24 May 1968, SNF, 1967–69, Box 1860, RG 59.
29 Edwards with Pemberton, *Crises and Commitments*, p. 203.
30 NARA, Visit of John Gorton, 'Background Paper: Scope of US Commitment under ANZUS treaty in the event of armed attack upon Australian and New Zealand Forces in Malaysia or Singapore', Department of State, 1 May 1969, Bureau of East Asian and Pacific Affairs, Subject Files, Box 34, RG 59.
31 NARA, Visit of John Gorton, Background-Position Paper, 29 April 1969, Department of State, Bureau of East Asian and Pacific Affairs, Subject Files, Box, 34, RG 59.
32 NAA, Memorandum, Hasluck to Rusk, 9 October 1967, quoted in 'The ANZUS treaty', Prime Minister's Brief for Visit to the US, April 1969, A1838, TS 686/1/1, Part 2.

33 Memorandum of Conversation, Secretary Rusk and Minister Hasluck, Washington, 9 October 1967, in *FRUS 1964–68*, Vol XXVII (Washington: US Government Printing Office, 2000) p. 70.
34 NARA, Correspondence, Donald E Neuchterlain, Office of the Assistant Secretary of Defense, to Robert S Lindquist, Director, Australia, NZ and Pacific Affairs, Department of State, 21 November 1967, in Subject Numeric Files, 1967–69, Box 1516, RG 59.
35 NAA, Inward Cablegram, Australian Embassy Washington to Canberra, 9 January 1968, in A1839, TS 686/1/1, Part 1.
36 NAA, Correspondence, Samuel Berger to Keith Waller, 17 January 1968; and comments by Australian officials both quoted in 'The ANZUS treaty', Prime Minister's Brief for Visit to the US, April 1969, A1838, TS 686/1/1, Part 2.
37 NARA, Cable, 'Gorton's General Attitude towards US', American Embassy Canberra to Department of State, 27 March 1968, SNF, Box 1863, RG59.
38 NARA, Memorandum, Rusk to Rostow, 2 May 1968, SNF, 1967–69, Box 1860, RG 59.
39 Cited in J. M. Van Der Kroef, 'Australia Looks to Nixon', *National Review*, 11 February 1969.
40 NARA, Memorandum, Rusk to Rostow, 2 May 1968, SNF, 1967–69, Box 1860, RG 59.
41 P. Howson, *The Life of Politics* (Melbourne: Viking Press, 1984), p. 415.
42 John Gorton, Speech to the Henty Electorate Dinner, 14 September 1968, transcript, www.pmtranscripts.gov.au (accessed 22 July 2019).
43 NARA, Memorandum, Rusk to President, 24 May 1968, SNF, 1967–69, Box 1860, RG 59.
44 NARA, Memorandum, Rusk to President, 24 May 1968, SNF, 1967–69, Box 1860, RG 59.
45 NARA, Telegram 5576, Cronk to Secretary of State, Assessment of Gorton Government, 13 May 1968, SNF, 1967–69, Box 1861, RG 59.
46 NARA, Memorandum, Rusk to President, 24 May 1968, SNF, 1967–69, Box 1860, RG 59.
47 NAA, Inward Cablegram, Press Briefing by Prime Minister at Blair House, 28 May 1968, A 1838, TS 686/1/1, Part 1.
48 *Canberra Times*, 5 June 1968.
49 NARA, Memorandum of Conversation, Alan Griffiths and John Dorrance (US Embassy, Canberra), 21 June 1968, in Telegram A-615, Prime Minister Gorton's Performance to Date, 5 July 1968, SNF, 1967–69, Box 1861, RG 59.
50 Gorton, quoted in *Age*, 3 February 1969.
51 NARA, Telegram 758, Ambassador to Bundy, 6 February 1969, SNF, 1967–69, Box 1859, RG 59.
52 The National Archives (TNA), London, Correspondence, John Freeman (British Embassy, Washington DC) to Sir Charles Johnston (British High Commissioner, Canberra), 30 April 1969, FCO 33/2256.
53 NAA, Correspondence, Keith Waller to Lord Casey, 8 November 1968, M4323 2003/9.

54 NAA, Gorton, Ministerial Statement on Defence, 25 February 1969, *Commonwealth Parliamentary Debates*, House of Representatives, in A 1838, TS 686/1/1, Part 1.
55 NARA, Visit of John Gorton, Scope Paper, 12 March 1969, Bureau of East Asian and Pacific Affairs, Subject Files, Box 34, RG 59.
56 Richard Nixon Presidential Library (RNL), Yorba Linda, California, Memorandum, Rogers to the President, 29 April 1969, Nixon VIP Visits, Box 910.
57 *Bulletin*, 12 July 1969, p. 35; RNL, Memorandum, Rogers to the President, 29 April 1969, Nixon VIP Visits, Box 910.
58 NARA, Memorandum, Robert Moore to Ambassador Winthrop G. Brown, 20 February 1969, Bureau of East Asian and Pacific Affairs, Office of Australia, New Zealand and Pacific Island Affairs, Subject Files, Box 34, RG 59.
59 NARA, Memorandum of Conversation, Prime Minister Gorton's Meeting with the Secretary, 6 May 1969, in SNF, 1967–69, Box 1863, RG 59.
60 NARA, Memorandum, Rogers to the President, 29 April 1969, ibid.
61 RNL, Memorandum, Kissinger to the President, undated, National Security Files, VIP Visits, Box 910.
62 NARA, Memorandum, Robert Moore to Ambassador Winthrop G. Brown, 20 February 1969, Bureau of East Asian and Pacific Affairs, Office of Australia, New Zealand and Pacific Island Affairs, Subject Files, Box 34, RG 59.
63 NARA, Memorandum of Conversation, Prime Minister Gorton's Meeting with the Secretary, 6 May 1969, SNF, 1967–69, Box 1863, RG 59.
64 Sam Lipski, 'Americans just can't fathom our "mateship" philosophy', *The Age*, 31 January 1969, in NAA, 250/9/1, A1838, Part 10.
65 Ibid.

11

Boundaries of belonging: differential fees for overseas students in Britain, c. 1967

Jodi Burkett

In the final weeks of 1966, the British government announced that, starting in the 1967–1968 academic year, the annual fees for overseas students would triple from £70 to £250. The fees for 'home' students would remain the same. This was both a cost-saving measure and another step in Britain's global withdrawal from empire and from the notion of Greater Britain. The charging of differential fees required drawing a clear line between who belonged and who did not, who were insiders and who were outsiders, within British higher education and wider society.[1]

The overseas movement of students and other scholars has a long history and is intimately bound up with empire.[2] As Tamson Pietsch has demonstrated, networks of students and scholars created a 'British academic world' that was crucially important in the late nineteenth and early twentieth century. In the early twentieth century this British imperial academic network was imagined as 'expansive, masculine, familial, connected and co-operating'.[3] Oxford, Cambridge and London, argues Hilary Perraton 'saw themselves as at the apex of an imperial University structure'.[4] A. J. Stockwell too has traced the important, if complicated and sometimes ambivalent, imperial connections of students and higher education.[5]

Changes in the British Empire from the early twentieth century had an impact on overseas students and British universities more generally. The networks that Pietsch described were destabilised in the interwar period and 'finally unwound' in the 1960s.[6] During the 1960s, as the 'winds of change' swept through Africa and the majority of the colonies became independent, overseas students became an increasingly complicated 'emblem of Britain's changing role in the world'.[7] Jordanna Bailkin highlights the 'supreme paradox' of the colonial system, which was 'heightened in the postcolonial metropole' and coalesced, at least partly, around education and the image of the overseas student.[8] For Stockwell, one of the most significant things that happened to students from former colonies in Britain at the end of empire was their renaming from 'colonial' to 'overseas' students.⁹ Sarah Stockwell's exploration of public administrative training of overseas students shows a clear continuity between colonial and postcolonial eras.¹⁰ These courses were seen as an important means through which the 'continuance of the British tradition and British ideals in administration in the colonies' could be ensured.¹¹

Students coming to Britain from colonial, or 'developing' countries had to face discrimination that their white counterparts from the 'developed' world did not. Sarah Stockwell has noted that the 'first appearance of non-white and non-Christian students' gave rise to 'tensions' and that some Oxford and Cambridge 'colleges had been reluctant to accept students of colonial origin'.¹² There are a number of examples given by Stockwell and Pietsch of academics and administrators at these universities who voiced reluctance to teach 'non-white' students, particularly those from Africa, although Indian students also faced discrimination.¹³ Hakim Adi argues that for West African students in Britain, it was the discriminatory treatment they received which made them acutely aware of their 'colonial status' and worked to undermine, rather than reinforce, their sense of belonging within the empire and support for the imperial project.¹⁴ Both Perraton and Stockwell highlight the findings of the Franks Commission which explored Oxford practices in 1966 and found that 'Oxford colleges treated overseas students badly'.¹⁵ While not explicitly stated, it was not white students from Canada or Australia who were badly treated, but black and brown students from Britain's former empire who, as Perraton argues, came to dominate the image of what it meant to be 'a commonwealth student' by the end of the 1970s.¹⁶ As Labour MP Frank Judd commented, 'the easily identifiable overseas students are the coloured ones', which he argued, automatically linked the discussion of overseas student fees in 1967 to 'an already undermined public opinion on this issue of racialism'.¹⁷ This chapter explores this racialisation of overseas students. In their campaigns against the increase in overseas student fees even student leaders, including the National Union of Students (NUS) exhibited an amnesia about empire when it came to Australia, Canada and New Zealand, but a heightened sense of imperial responsibility in relation to students from Africa in particular. This amnesia was not, however, one-sided as the student press in both Australia and Canada were entirely silent about the increase in UK fees and its potential impact on students from those countries who wanted to study in Britain. The NUS worked tirelessly to oppose racism and racial discrimination and their policies on overseas students became intimately intertwined with this activity. In their pursuit of a cosmopolitan, multicultural, multi-ethnic and multiracial Britain they continued to perpetuate ideas which normalised whiteness and reinforced narrowing racial understanding of belonging within Britain.

There are many estimates of the number of overseas students in Britain in this period. According to the British Council, in the early 1960s there were around 43,044 overseas students in Britain, of which 13,919 were studying in universities.[18] Perraton has found that 'into the 1960s more than half of all overseas students continued to come from the Commonwealth' although which part of the Commonwealth is unclear.[19] In 1967, the government said there were 32,000 overseas students who 'had nine-tenths of their fees subsidised from British public funds'. Of these, more than a quarter came from countries 'with a national income per head as high as or higher than our own' including 'the United States, the old Dominions, Western Europe [and] Scandinavia'.[20] This, of course, differed depending on the type of institution that overseas students were attending. In 1966–67 the largest single group of overseas students to British universities was from the United States, with India and Pakistan not far behind.[21] The largest single group of overseas students attending polytechnics and technical colleges on advanced courses were from Nigeria, with Norway the only country in the top eight 'sending countries' with no imperial connection.[22] For nurse training it was the West Indies which dominated overseas student numbers with Jamaica in the top spot.[23] One of the significant issues in the debates and discussions about overseas students is the lack of understanding or awareness about these different groups of students and, in general, who overseas students were. There were systematic biases towards those attending universities as they were 'for many years treated as temporary visitors of little interest to the home office' whereas those in technical colleges and polytechnics were more directly affected by changes in immigration policy which were enacted during the 1960s and 1970s.[24]

No matter where overseas students were coming from, they were elites and, in the main, wealthy. Many overseas students who travelled to Britain were not the first in their families to do so. Adi found that West African students in the early twentieth century often came from families who 'maintained a tradition of educating their children in Britain over several generations' and were, in the main, 'male and from wealthy, even royal, families'.[25] Often overseas students had to prove they had sufficient funds, or provide a deposit, before enrolling in British universities.[26] Bailkin has also illustrated the elite nature of overseas students travelling from Africa in the 1930s.[27] For those at polytechnics, Perraton argues that 'most of these students were lower middle class or "artisan class"'.[28] The elite nature of overseas students was reinforced by scholarship schemes such as the Rhodes scholarship which was set up after the Second World War to bring 'the most promising young men' to Britain and reinforce imperial links.[29]

In the late 1960s there was an acknowledgement that many overseas students came from privileged backgrounds. As the government argued in

1967, it was certainly not the case that 'all the students from the Middle East, from India, or from Pakistan came from poor families'.³⁰ Welsh Labour MP Ednyfed Davies too argued that 'some overseas students from Asia and Africa are very wealthy and spend enormously here'.³¹ Sitting alongside this, however, was a view of students coming from certain places as being backward, poor and in need of help. There was a long history of this. For example, Bailkin talks about programmes created by the British Council in the 1950s to prepare overseas students before they came to Britain in which 'elite young men and women ... were shocked to find themselves being instructed on how to eat with a knife and fork or use the toilet'.³² For many people it was not the individual circumstances of students, so much as what country they came from, that indicated their wealth. For example, Scottish Labour MP M. S. Miller argued that he had 'no objection to an increase in the fees paid by students from ... [Australia and New Zealand] or from the United States' as those students 'are rich'. Students from developing countries, he continued, 'need more help from us than ever before', citing that in places such as India and Pakistan '£1 per week is not an uncommon wage for a working man'.³³ There was no acknowledgement that the vast majority of students from these countries, like those from the United Kingdom, were not the children of working men.³⁴

By the early 1960s it was clear to the British government that universities needed reformation to be able to cope with the increased number of students and to be financially sustainable. In 1961 they appointed Lord Robbins to chair the Committee on Higher Education and his report was published two years later in 1963. While Robbins was principally tasked with examining the state of Higher Education in Britain, the committee did not view British higher education in isolation but explored developments in a range of other countries. The Robbins report was positive about the presence of overseas students in Britain seeing their presence as valuable for fostering 'a sense of international community on both sides' and giving Britain 'diplomatic and economic advantages'. Students coming from 'developing' countries also provided 'a helpful contribution to their country's advancement'.³⁵

In terms of finances, Robbins calculated that the British government provided a 'total annual subsidy' of around £9 million towards the education of overseas students.³⁶ Robbins did not suggest that this 'subsidy' should end, but explicitly saw it as 'a form of foreign aid' and problematic because it was being lumped together with education spending.³⁷ One of Robbins' particular concerns about the existing fee structure was that the British government 'receives no credit' for the subsidy as it was invisible, meaning that overseas students and foreign governments were not sufficiently *grateful* for its receipt. Robbins recommended 'that the level of fees be revised so that in future they meet at least 20 per cent of current institutional expenditure'.³⁸

Harris argues that the Robbins report was the 'moment at which overseas students began to be conceived politically and economically as a dimension of UK commercial interests and cultural and foreign policy'.[39]

This chapter aims to address a gap within the existing literature by exploring the attitudes and reactions of students to these changes. The ability to get a good, although far from complete, understanding of the views of students on this, and many other issues has increased in the last decade with the digitisation of student newspapers at several universities. Student newspapers offer a window, although partial and somewhat distorted, into the debates and discussions taking place within local student unions and campuses. This chapter uses the student newspapers of the universities of Leeds, Warwick, Newcastle and Imperial College London. Each newspaper is unique, each has an editorial line that shifts and changes, that is sometimes in sympathy with the NUS Executive and sometimes diametrically opposed. It is often impossible to tell exactly who wrote pieces within the newspaper, as they remain unsigned. Despite these caveats and the many difficulties associated with using these newspapers as a historical source, they also allow us to hear the voices of students themselves on a wide range of issues where, in the past, we would have only heard the views of the NUS, university authorities or government.

This chapter will first provide a quick summary of the key decisions and responses to the decision to raise overseas student fees for the 1967–68 academic year. The rest of the chapter will examine three themes that emerged within the debate about this decision, by students, university officials and within the government. The first theme examines arguments related to Britain's world role, the second explores how education for overseas students was understood and conceptualised as 'overseas aid', and the third addresses how 'overseas students' were being racialised in these debates. The chapter argues that the understanding and conceptualisation of overseas students within these debates excluded overseas students from any sense of belonging within Britain or the Commonwealth. This was done either by ignoring their presence, particularly students from Australia, Canada and New Zealand, or reframing them as 'dependent' charity cases in need of Britain's help and altruism, rather than members of a 'Greater British' family.

The Government decision and reaction

During its first few years of office, the Wilson government focused on trying to limit numbers of overseas students as a way to get control of financing.[40] It was only when the issue of grants and student fees came up for their normal five-year review in 1966 that the decision was taken to increase fees.

Criticism of the decision came quickly from all sides. By the end of January 1967, seventy-four Labour backbenchers had signed a motion asking Anthony Crosland, Secretary of State for Education and Science, to revoke the decision.[41] Vice-Chancellors and Principals of universities and colleges across the country were swift to condemn the decision. The Principal of Ruskin College, H. D. Hughes, objected to the move, calling it a 'false economy' and saying that it created a 'financial apartheid in higher education'.[42] The Senate of Leeds University deplored the 'discriminatory action' of the Government, while Durham University sent a telegram to Crosland asking him to reconsider.[43] The Senate at Warwick also deplored the government action saying that there was 'an element of discrimination involved' in the policy, that it would cut the flow of students from 'underdeveloped countries' and therefore 'stop one of the most effective forms of development aid', and that in cutting the number of students from 'developed overseas countries, we deprive ourselves of some of *our* best talent'.[44] This phrasing is telling, illuminating the understanding of students from 'developed' countries as part of 'us', of belonging here, while those from developing countries are simply in need of 'aid' which will be discussed further later in the chapter.

It was not until 28 February 1967 that Crosland met with Vice-Chancellors to discuss the changes. Despite their rhetorical opposition, many university authorities did quickly agree to adhere to the government's decision. For example, the Vice-Chancellors at Leeds agreed not to oppose the new overseas student fees after receiving the 'firm assurance from the Government that the size of its hardship fund would be such as to enable some assistance to be given to overseas students beginning courses in October 1967'. They also 'pressed for assurance that a pattern of differential fees for home and overseas students should not be a continuing feature of the university fee structure'.[45] On this point, however, they received no government assurances and there was no further discussion. It was this idea, that there should be parity or equality in fees across the board and that differential fees were discriminatory against overseas students that fuelled most protests by students.

The method for imposing the increase – simply cutting grants to universities by £250 for each registered overseas student – allowed for a certain amount of autonomy. Both Bradford and Hull universities refused to charge the new fees and Bradford continued this refusal until 1975.[46] Perhaps the most prominent institution to refuse to increase fees was Oxford. This may, in part, have been the result of their training of overseas students for public administration.[47] In order to offset the cost of not imposing the new fees, Oxford created an independent fundraising group.[48] Oxford continued not to charge overseas students the increased fee into 1970, although they were reporting in 1969 that it was costing more than had been expected.[49] Those who advocated that Oxford should not charge the increased fees argued that it was 'central to the university's claim to be international that it should not discriminate between students on grounds of nationality or residence'.[50] It was felt by some that increasing the fees at Oxford would damage the institution's 'high status and immense reputation in the world', while some countered that this principled stance was unnecessary as only 307 of the 1,244 overseas students at Oxford came from 'poorer countries'.[51]

Reactions among students in the United Kingdom were unanimously negative, although the level of opposition activity varied substantially between institutions. At the national level, the NUS condemned the decision, but their ability to take action was hampered by their existing constitution, and divisions within the student movement. In 1967 the NUS constitution prevented the organisation from taking a stand on political issues that did not affect students *because* they were students. The raising of overseas student fees fit within this proscription but became embroiled within the political debates then taking place within the NUS and the student movement more broadly. In 1967 the Radical Students Alliance (RSA) held their first conference and declared their intention to provide a focus for students with a more politicised vision of the role of the student movement and union. They quickly seized on the issue of overseas student fees as a key issue that students should be mobilised around, and where they saw the NUS leadership failing.[52] National actions around overseas student fees were, therefore, embroiled in this internal debate within the student movement over the role of student organisations, the student movement and the place of students within society more generally.

The student press argued that significantly more overseas students would be affected by the fees increase than the Government suggested. They most often cited that 'two thirds of the overseas students in this country' were supported only by family, although it was not clear where this figure came from.[53] At Imperial College London, the student press argued that a significant number of overseas students suffered financial hardship quoting the statistic that '34% of overseas students in Britain ... live on £40 a month or less'.[54]

A group of left-wing students sent a letter to *The Times* in the third week of January denouncing the suggestion that the fees increase would 'encourage more of these students to obtain places in their own countries' saying that such places were not available. Instead, they argued, the policy would simply mean fewer students 'from the developing world' being 'given opportunities for study in higher education' at all. This letter was signed by the presidents of nineteen students' unions from universities, polytechnics and colleges across England and Wales, as well as Thabo Mbeki of the Coordinating Committee of Overseas Student Organisations and S. K. Boateng, General Secretary of the Ghana Union of Great Britain and Ireland.[55]

The NUS launched a national campaign to protest against the decision at a meeting in Euston on 23 January. The NUS Executive agreed to fight the government's proposal 'in all possible ways' and briefed all 650 institutions of higher education across the United Kingdom asking them to 'hold local protest meetings and write to local MPs'.[56] The first major student protest took place on 1 February, with between 3,500 and 4,000 students 'of all nationalities' queuing up to lobby their MPs.[57] The Leeds student newspaper reported that 'many students hinted at racial discrimination'. They quoted students from Thailand, Malaysia, South Africa, Greece and the United States, most of whom, bar the American, said that the increase would have a serious and detrimental impact on their own studies and deter students from their home country from coming to Britain in the future. The student from the United States, on the other hand, saw that the fees increase would have the opposite effect. The impact of the new policy, the American student said, was that 'there will be a loss of students from under-developed countries and a rise from countries that can afford to educate them, like mine'.[58] This activity did meet with some success as Crosland, as well as the Minister of State and the Under-Secretary of State for Scotland met with NUS and Scottish Union of Students (SUS) representatives on 8 February to discuss the fees increase.[59]

However, this also led to some criticism from within the student movement. Leeds *Union News* editor Dave Williams, criticised the NUS Executive, and the NUS President Geoff Martin in particular, for complaining that 'British students don't give a damn about the increase in fees for foreign students' while focusing on 'negotiation at high level' and not 'organizing propaganda and meetings to bring the situation home to the average student'.[60] Leeds student, Jack Straw, was heavily involved in the activities surrounding opposition to the raising of overseas student fees. Straw was Vice-President of the Leeds Student Union in 1967 and elected President in February to take over the role that summer. He helped to organise the mass boycott of lectures to be held on 22 February, sending letters to all union presidents across the United Kingdom asking them to attend a meeting at Leeds to discuss 'the necessity or otherwise of calling a one-day lecture boycott'.[61]

As early as February there were also reports of overseas students withdrawing from British universities because they could not afford the new fee regime despite the fact that it did not come into effect until the following September and was limited to a £50 increase for students already enrolled in Britain. A second-year student from Ghana was reported to have left Manchester University as he could not afford the new fees.[62] The new fees were also seen as institutionalising racial discrimination. Miss Stella Njoku, the Secretary of the Afro-Asian Society, was quoted in the Leeds *Union News* saying that the new fees made it 'silly' to 'try to make overseas students seem welcome' as it was 'not just a few landladies or students [who] practised racial discrimination, but the British Government would seem to make it their policy'.[63]

Of course, not all students, or even all student activists, supported the campaigns and protests against the government's proposal. The president of the Imperial College student union, Tony Duke, agreed that overseas student fees should not be increased, but feared that any militant action, such as a strike, would 'unnecessarily prejudice staff–student relations'.[64] This division within the Students' Union reflected divisions within the student body itself which was articulated within the letters page of the student newspaper. Dimitris Alatzas, writing on behalf of 'English' students argued that excluding overseas students, by charging them high fees, would lower the standards within UK universities and that 'the 5 million pounds spent on foreign students should be regarded as an investment bringing its due return and not as a charity'. On the other hand, Rob Collinge argued that university places funded by British taxpayers should go to British students first.[65] *Felix*, the Imperial College student newspaper, also reported that some colleges disagreed with the protest against the fees increase. The College of Estate Management voted 101–76 against a motion to deplore the rise in fees against the wishes of its own union president, Mike Slade, and the visiting NUS speaker.[66] The division between different groups of students did not strictly follow party political lines, although in some ways it did mirror positions taken within national politics. For example, just as the Conservative Party was against the move to increase overseas student fees, arguing that they were discriminatory and detrimental to Britain's international leadership position, the Federation of Conservative Students (FCS) who was, in 1967, the largest student political group in the United Kingdom, with approximately 10,000 members, opposed the policy for similar reasons.[67] The size and strength of the FCS highlights one of the particular blind spots of student newspapers as they are virtually absent from student newspapers before the 1980s.

The debate about overseas student fees and notions of belonging

In the remainder of this chapter I will explore the three most significant, and interrelated, aspects of the debates about overseas student fees: what they said about Britain's international role, how they linked to discourses about education as a form of foreign aid, and the racial characterisation of overseas students. Underpinning each of these debates are arguments about where the boundaries of Britain do, or should, lie; about how Britain should go forward no longer a 'great' power; and what that meant for their responsibilities and relationships with other nations and individual students.

Lee argues that the emotional nature of the debates about overseas student fees were 'the result of fundamental difficulties encountered in the attempts to retain Britain's place in the world'. Increasing fees for overseas students, he argues, 'brought to the surface a whole range of doubts and feelings of guilt'.[68] In the main, this came through as concerns about the 'responsibility' that Britain had to former colonies and how Britain could, or should, fulfil their 'duty' to the world. For example, Lord Mitchison in the House of Lords argued against the fees increase saying that 'we have a responsibility towards the emergent countries ... and a general responsibility to the world'.[69] When referencing Britain's work with 'developing' nations there was an acknowledgement of widespread feelings of, and rejection of, shame.[70] Empire was discussed in euphemisms throughout the debate, particularly in reference to the 'language, history and tradition' that made Britain an 'attractive' country to overseas students,[71] although there were fears voiced that this 'natural' connection was being lost in favour of Britain's Cold War competitors.[72]

Criticisms were also voiced that the policy would make Britain too insular. Frank Judd, Labour MP for Portsmouth West, argued that 'Britain was in danger of losing any sense of worldwide perspective and becoming morbidly self-centred'.[73] This was clearly linked to the end of empire and Britain's changing international position. As Richard Hornby, Conservative MP for Tonbridge, argued, it was particularly important for overseas students to continue to come to Britain, as Britain was 'trying to feel our way and to understand what it means to be a medium-sized Power which wishes to exert influence and to play a proper part in the world'.[74] Others, such as Frank Judd and Patrick Wolrige-Gordon, Conservative MP for East Aberdeenshire, were concerned that the raising of overseas student fees would damage Britain's international reputation. Wolrige-Gordon thought the policy made Britain look 'mean, niggardly and niggling'[75] while Judd worried that the policy was evidence of a 'Little Englander attitude ... growing in Britain'.[76] The student press also echoed this concern with growing British insularity and the move away from ideas of Greater Britain. The Imperial College newspaper, *Felix*, published a full-page article titled 'Fees Increase – Symptom of Insularity' in which student journalist and Commonwealth Scholarship holder from South Africa, David Potter, argued the government's proposal was 'callous ... wrong [and] ... immoral'. He outlined a number of reasons for this, but fundamentally the problem was 'the indifference it shows to the world outside'.[77] Throughout the debate, then, there was a sense that maintaining low fees, or subsidies, for overseas students kept elements of Britain's 'greater' past and maintained the imagined borders of Greater Britain.

The introduction of higher fees for overseas students marked a clear transition from Britain as the leader of the empire and Commonwealth, to a provider of 'overseas aid'. As Lee has put it, this decision on fees marked 'the point at which Britain shed the role of being a mother country'.[78] It was in the 1960s, argues Sarah Stockwell, that 'British–Commonwealth relations came chiefly to be defined as developmental'.[79] This, according to Nicholas Tarling, directly impacted on the way that overseas students were viewed, as those from 'developed' countries were seen in terms of an educational 'exchange' while those from 'developing' countries came under the auspices of 'aid'.[80] Throughout the debates on overseas student fees there was widespread agreement that educating students in Britain was one of the best means of providing foreign aid, partly, at least, because it would not be 'squandered'.[81] Students advocated for education as aid calling for 'educational aid, not military aid'.[82] This form of aid was seen as superior to the work of non-governmental organisations such as Oxfam, with some students arguing that 'war on ignorance surely supersedes war on want'.[83]

The raising of overseas student fees was seen by some as a backhanded way of cutting foreign aid and, by extension, removing some of Britain's responsibility to former colonies.[84] Recent cuts to the overseas aid and development programme were cited as evidence of 'the declining priority given by the Government to overseas aid generally'.[85] The government denied this and suggested that raising overseas student fees would benefit newly independent countries as it would encourage bright students to stay at home and study at institutions in their own countries.[86] Students took a dim view of this argument, suggesting that the policy would 'restrict students from coming here from under-developed countries, so they will remain under-developed'.[87] Some Labour backbenchers argued that while they should be 'proud of their tradition in granting independence to countries in the fight against colonialism', the new fees policy meant this was in danger of becoming a 'hollow exercise' as these countries would not have the trained personnel they needed.[88] According to backbenchers, the Labour Party's colonial record and Britain's image as a progressive force and moral leader in the postcolonial world was under threat.

The main criticism that students made of the increase in overseas fees was that it was discriminatory. They argued it would taint universities by introducing 'discrimination into institutions which have attempted to be "without regard to colour, creed or race"'.[89] While the intent of this protest was laudable in many ways, it relied on a misunderstanding of the nature of overseas students and stereotyped assumptions about them which drew on, and reinforced, racialised ideas of 'developing' countries.

The government took great pains to argue that the policy was not discriminatory as it applied universally to anyone who had not been resident in

Britain for three years or more. In making no distinction based on 'nationality, race, birth or origin', the policy was colour-blind, making 'no distinction between black and white, between Asian and European, between African and North American'.[90] The government did concede, however, that it was not enough to be fair, the policy had to *look* fair. To this end, they agreed to set up a hardship fund to help 'students from the underprivileged sections of even developed countries'.[91]

However, for some critics, the policy needed to discriminate in order to be fair. In the House of Lords, Fenner Brockway called for the government to 'differentiate between overseas students from Europe, North America and Australia ... and students from the developing countries' when assessing what fees students should pay.[92] Similar calls to treat students from 'developing' countries as a 'special case', or to discriminate 'in favour of the needy' were made within the House of Commons.[93] Some student activists supported the idea of 'selectively subsidising some students from abroad' while some politicians argued that this idea was itself racist.[94]

Racialised stereotypes of overseas students most often came through in discussions about where overseas students came from and what their family background was. Reginald Maudling argued that the 'most deserving' of overseas students were those who 'came as a result of their own families scraping the money together over a long period'.[95] In the House of Lords, Brockway argued that 'many of those students who come even from developing countries have parents such as oil sheikhs who can well afford to pay the higher fees',[96] whereas students coming from Africa were often characterised as coming from small villages where fellow villagers 'and clans club together to send their best boys over here for education'.[97] Labour MP James Johnson also used the language of 'best boy in the village' in voicing concern for overseas students.[98] The repeated image of rural villages sending 'boys' to be educated in Britain gives an important insight into how overseas students were imagined.

There were also concerns raised that increasing fees would decrease access to higher education for those students who opposed the politics of their home state.[99] During the debate about overseas student fees overseas, students from Libya occupied the Libyan Embassy to protest about the cancelling of their grants by their home state due to political disagreements, so it was evident that this could be an issue.[100] In the main, this issue was discussed in relation to students from South Africa. Conservative MP William Van Straubenzee highlighted what he referred to as 'a strange order of priorities' when overseas students who supported the apartheid regime and were sponsored by the British Council would be cushioned from the fees increase, while those who opposed apartheid and were supported by the United Nations Training Programme would have to pay the full increase.[101] In the late 1960s a number of students' unions were setting up scholarship funds to support black South African students to come and study in the United Kingdom, although the impact of increased fees on these funds was not discussed in 1967.[102]

Throughout the debate within Parliament the focus was most often on students from the 'new' Commonwealth or the 'developing world'. There was some recognition, however, that the 'old' Dominions were being neglected or forgotten. Conservative MP Frank Judd commented that 'some feeling had been expressed by the High Commissions in this country' that there had been 'a lack of consideration on our part for the older ties which we have with the Commonwealth'.[103] The government seemed keen to shift the language within the overseas student fees debates away from using the term 'commonwealth' to distance the government from any sense of obligation towards these students, referring to them instead as simply 'foreign'. Many backbenchers, however, worked hard to try to remind the government of these imperial ties. John McNamara, Labour MP for Hull North, read out a letter from the High Commissioner of Jamaica saying that Britain had 'lost a wonderful opportunity of discriminating in favour of Commonwealth students'.[104] Judd also read out a letter from the Kenya High Commission listing the significant impacts of the new policy on Kenyan students.[105] Dr M. S. Miller, Labour MP for Glasgow Kelvingrove, quoted a letter from South African students highlighting the racially discriminatory nature of higher education within their country and reminding MPs that making special allowances for students from the Commonwealth would leave South African students out in the cold.[106] James Johnson also quoted a cable from Mauritius saying that the new fees would 'deprive poor students higher studies' and that in raising fees Britain was 'sacrificing long-term interests' for the sake of immediate needs.[107] The language used throughout the debates sought to distance Britain from its former empire, to classify overseas students as 'foreign' and in need of aid rather than people who, a few short years before, had been part of the Greater British family and continued, for the most part, to be part of the Commonwealth.

Conclusions

The decision to raise overseas student fees in 1967 was a significant step in restricting the boundaries of belonging within Britain. Decisions about fees for tuition, as well as accommodation during the 1970s, continued this trend towards shrinking the imagined boundaries of Greater Britain. As the 1970s came to a close, the Thatcher government introduced 'full-cost' fees for overseas students, solidifying overseas students as a lucrative market rather than members of imperial education networks.

There was significant and sustained opposition to the increase in overseas students' fees from a range of quarters. However, the precedent that students who had not been resident within the United Kingdom for three years, except for those from the European Economic Community and then the European Union, should pay more appears to have been accepted. The boundaries regarding which students should be subsidised, and which should not, were mapped out in the debates that took place in the 1960s. They did not follow governmental policies about citizenship or nationality and they did not change when new immigration or nationality laws were introduced in the 1970s and 1980s. This reflected the clear and determined policy of Harold Wilson's Labour government to not 'appear' discriminatory by linking fees to residency rather than citizenship or nationality.

The National Union of Students held a much more militant line about fees increases, particularly overseas student fees, during the 1970s than they had in the late 1960s. This was largely a reflection of the changes which took place within the organisation at the end of the 1960s in which the more militant students represented by the Radical Students Alliance were able to gain the upper hand and amend the constitution, allowing the NUS to take a political stance. This resulted in significant national action around the overseas student fees increases in the spring of 1976 and a sustained campaign that carried on into the early 1980s.[108] During the late 1970s, the issue of overseas students' fees was one upon which the NUS hung their banner of opposing racism.[109]

The introduction of differential fees in 1967 was a significant step in undermining the idea of Greater Britain. Overseas students from the Commonwealth and former colonies were being actively transferred from the realm of one of 'us', of students who the British government and academic institutions had a duty to educate and protect, to foreigners like all others. While students from different countries were seen differently, and often treated as representatives of their home country, collectively they were increasingly a market that universities could tap into. While there were no explicit mentions of empire in the debates about overseas student fees, the connections and assumptions made within the debates clearly showed a clash between Britain's political frontiers and the imagined frontiers of Greater Britain. In the late 1960s the pervasiveness of concerns and debates about Britain's global obligations and responsibilities to those in former colonies speaks volumes about how those in government and wider British society were attempting to re-imagine Britain's role in the postcolonial world. In exploring the issue of overseas student fees we can see how the demise of the belief in Greater Britain permeated wider conversations about what it meant to be British and how one could inhabit this collective selfhood in vastly changed global circumstances.

Notes

1. K. Paul, *Whitewashing Britain: Race and Citizenship in the Postwar Era* (London: Cornell University Press, 1997); B. Schwarz, *The White Man's World* (Oxford: Oxford University Press, 2011).
2. J. M. Lee, 'Overseas Students in Britain: How Their Presence Was Politicised in 1966–1967', *Minerva*, 36:4 (1998), pp. 305–321, at p. 313.
3. T. Pietsch, *Empire of Scholars: Universities, Networks and the British Academic World 1850–1939* (Manchester: Manchester University Press, 2013), p. 10.
4. H. Perraton, *A History of Foreign Students in Britain* (Basingstoke: Palgrave Macmillan, 2014), p. 54.
5. A. J. Stockwell, 'Leaders, Dissidents and the Disappointed: Colonial Students in Britain as Empire Ended', *Journal of Imperial and Commonwealth History*, 36:3 (2008), pp. 487–507.
6. Pietsch, *Empire of Scholars*, p. 8.
7. J. Bailkin, *The Afterlife of Empire* (Berkeley: University of California Press, 2012) pp. 97–98.
8. Ibid., pp. 95–96.
9. Stockwell, 'Leaders, Dissidents and the Disappointed'.
10. S. Stockwell, *The British End of the British Empire* (Cambridge: Cambridge University Press, 2018).
11. Stockwell, *The British End*, p. 96.
12. Ibid., p. 102.
13. Stockwell, *The British End*, p. 103 and Pietsch, *Empire of Scholars*, pp. 72, 178–179.
14. H. Adi, *West Africans in Britain 1900–1960: Nationalism, Pan-Africanism and Communism* (London: Lawrence & Wishart, 1998), p. 3.
15. Stockwell, *The British End*, p. 127. See also Perraton, *A History of Foreign Students*, p. 105.
16. Perraton, *A History of Foreign Students*, p. 85.
17. Frank Judd, House of Commons Debates [hereafter HC Deb] 23 February 1967 vol. 741, cols 2030–2031. There is extensive literature on attitudes to race and immigration in this period. See material cited in note 1.
18. Quoted in Perraton, *A History of Foreign Students*, p. 93.
19. Ibid., p. 85.
20. Anthony Crosland, HC Deb 23 February 1967 vol. 741, cols 1990–1991.
21. Perraton, *A History of Foreign Students*, p. 85.
22. Ibid., p. 88.
23. Ibid., p. 89.
24. Ibid., p. 94.
25. Adi, *West Africans in Britain*, p. 3. Bailkin, *Afterlife of Empire*, gives similar examples, p. 95.
26. P. Lancaster, *Education for Commonwealth Students in Britain* (London: Fabian Commonwealth Bureau, 1962), p. 4.
27. Bailkin, *Afterlife of Empire*, p. 102.

28 Perraton, *A History of Foreign Students*, pp. 66–67.
29 Pietsch, *Empire of Scholars*, p. 49.
30 Crosland, HC Deb 23 February 1967 vol. 741, cols 1990–1991.
31 Ednyfed Davies, HC Deb 23 February 1967 vol. 741, cols 2017–2018.
32 Bailkin, *Afterlife of Empire*, p. 108.
33 Dr M. S. Miller, HC Deb 23 February 1967 vol. 741, cols 2012–2013.
34 E. G. Edwards, *Higher Education for Everyone* (Nottingham: Spokesman, 1982), p. 75.
35 L. Robbins, *Higher Education: Report of the Committee Appointed by the Prime Minister under the Chairmanship of Lord Robbins 1961–63* (London: HMSO, 1963), pp. 66–67.
36 Ibid., p. 67.
37 Ibid., p. 67.
38 Ibid., p. 214.
39 R. Harris, 'Overseas Students in the United Kingdom University System', *Higher Education*, 29: 1 (1995), pp. 77–92, at p. 79.
40 Perraton, *A History of Foreign Students*, p. 108.
41 '74 MPs join in student fee protest', *The Times*, 30 January 1967, p. 1.
42 'Financial Apartheid in Colleges: Ruskin principal condemns rise in foreign students' fees', *The Times*, 5 January 1967, p. 7.
43 'Minister agrees', *The Times*, 2 February 1967, p. 11.
44 'Strike?', *Warwick Giblet*, 34, 2 February 1967, p. 1. Emphasis added.
45 'V-Cs not to oppose overseas fees rise', *Union News*, Leeds, 326, 17 March 1967, p. 3.
46 'University revolt on higher fees', *The Times*, 28 January 1967, p. 7; E. G. Edwards, 'Overseas Student fees', letter to the editor, *The Times*, 28 November 1975, p. 17.
47 See Stockwell, *The British End*, pp. 93–141.
48 'Oxford Aim to Cushion Fees', *The Times*, 12 June 1967, p. 3.
49 'Costly stand on fees', *The Times*, 18 June 1969, p. 3.
50 'Dons oppose higher fees', *The Times*, 6 February 1970, p. 15.
51 'Oxford fees defeat', *The Times*, 11 February 1970, p. 2.
52 K. Cavanaugh, 'IC Acts on Fees: Lobby of Parliament Petition. Possibility of a strike', *Felix*, 18 February 1967, p. 1.
53 'Government fees decision shocks overseas students', *Newcastle Courier*, 25 January 1967, p. 1. 'Minister agrees to talks on fees increase', *The Times*, 2 February 1967, p. 11.
54 'Hardship for overseas students?', *Felix*, 241, 18 January 1967, p. 1.
55 'College Fees', Letter to the editor of *The Times*, 21 January 1967, p. 9.
56 'Campaign against higher tuition fees begins', *The Times*, 23 January 1967, p. 13.
57 'Minister agreed to talks on fees increase', *The Times*, 2 February 1967, p. 11.
58 P. Crossley, 'Mass Lobby of Parliament', *Union News*, Leeds, 320, 3 February 1967, p. 1.
59 Crosland, HC Deb 23 February 1967 vol. 741, col. 247.
60 D. Williams, 'Agitation needed', *Union News*, Leeds, 319, 27 January 1967, p. 2.

61 'Lecture Boycott Planned if Lobby Unsuccessful', *Union News*, Leeds, 320, 3 February 1967, p. 1.
62 *Warwick Giblet*, 36, 16 February 1967.
63 'Academic shutdown backed by A.G.M.', *Union News*, Leeds, 321, 10 February 1967.
64 D. Sullivan, 'Duke says No to strike', *Felix*, 18 February 1967, p. 1.
65 Letters to Felix, 'Fees – two opposing views', *Felix*, 244, 1 March 1967, p. 5.
66 J. Mullaly, 'C.E.M. favour fee increases', *Felix*, 244, 1 March 1967, p. 2.
67 'Protecting the status quo', *Warwick Campus*, 27, 11 October 1967, p. 7.
68 Lee, 'Overseas Students in Britain', p. 306.
69 Lord Mitchison, House of Lords Debates [hereafter HL Deb], 14 February 1967 vol. 280, col. 259.
70 J. Johnson, HC Deb 23 February 1967 vol. 741, cols 2021–2024.
71 Crosland, HC Deb 23 February 1967 vol. 741, col. 1989.
72 *The Times*, 2 February 1967; Wolrige-Gordon, HC Deb 23 February 1967 vol. 741, col. 2020.
73 'MPs protest at student fees' *The Times*, 24 January 1967, p. 11.
74 R. Hornby, HC Deb 23 February 1967 vol. 741, cols. 2004–2005.
75 Wolrige-Gordon, HC Deb 23 February 1967 vol. 41, col. 2020.
76 Judd, HC Deb 23 March 1967 vol. 743, col. 1905.
77 D. Potter, 'Fees Increase – Symptom of Insularity', *Felix*, 18 February 1967, p. 11.
78 Lee, 'Overseas Students in Britain', p. 320.
79 Stockwell, *The British End*, p. 133.
80 N. Tarling, 'Making a Difference: Overseas Student Fees in Britain and the Development of a Market in International Education', *Britain and the World*, 5:1 (2012) pp. 259–286; at p. 259.
81 'Strike?', *Warwick Giblet*, 2 February 1967, p. 1; HC Deb 2 February 1967 vol 740, col. 747; Davies, HC Deb 23 February 1967 vol. 741, col. 2018.
82 'MPs protest at student fees', *The Times*, 24 January 1967, p. 11.
83 T. Fisher, 'Opinion', *Newcastle Courier*, 1 February 1967, p. 4.
84 HC Deb 2 February 1967 vol. 740, col. 747.
85 HC Deb 2 February 1967 vol. 740, col. 745. Emphasis added.
86 A. Oram, HC Deb 2 February 1967 vol. 740, col. 745; W. Van Straubenzee, HC Deb 23 February 1967 vol. 741, col. 2035.
87 'Student revolt likely against government's fees proposals', *Newcastle Courier*, 1 February 1967, p. 1.
88 Judd, HC Deb 23 February 1967 vol. 741, col. 2032.
89 T. Hinxman, 'Editorial', *Warwick Giblet*, 34, 2 February 1967, p. 3.
90 Crosland, HC Deb 23 February 1967 vol. 741, col. 1993.
91 Miller, HC Deb 23 February 1967 vol. 741, col. 2014.
92 Fenner Brockway, HL Deb 19 January 1967 vol. 279, col. 215.
93 G. Roberts, HC Deb 23 February 1967 vol. 741, col. 2037; Scott, HC Deb 23 February 1967 vol. 741, col. 2010.
94 A. Thompson, 'Letter to the editor', *Warwick Giblet*, 36, 16 February 1967; 'Union – Concern? Busy meeting adjourned', *Felix*, 242, 1 February 1967, p. 1;

HL Deb 19 January 1967 vol. 279, col. 216; Miller, HC Deb 23 February 1967 vol. 741, col. 2014.
95 Maudling, HC Deb 23 February 1967 vol. 741, col. 1986.
96 HL Deb 19 January 1967 vol. 279, col. 216.
97 Johnson, HC Deb 2 February 1967 vol. 740, col. 747.
98 Johnson, HC Deb 23 February 1967 vol. 741, cols 2022–2023.
99 Scott, HC Deb 23 February 1967 vol. 741, cols 2010–2011.
100 J. Mullaly, 'Hunger strike at Libyan Embassy', *Felix*, 243, 18 February 1967.
101 Van Straubenzee, HC Deb 23 February 1967 vol. 741, col. 2036.
102 'Union – Concern? Busy meeting adjourned', *Felix*, 242, 1 February 1967, p. 1; J. Mullaly, 'ICSASAF underway', *Felix*, 18 February 1967, p. 3.
103 Judd, HC Deb 23 February 1967 vol. 741, col. 2031.
104 HC Deb 21 March 1967 vol. 743.
105 Judd, HC Deb 23 February 1967 vol. 741, col. 2029.
106 Miller, HC Deb 23 February 1967 vol. 741, col. 2012.
107 Johnson, HC Deb 23 February 1967 vol. 741, col. 2021.
108 *Leeds Student*, 133, 5 March 1976; *Warwick Boar*, 71, 16 February 1977; 'Wave of unrest spreads', *Leeds Student*, 154, 18 February 1977, p. 1.
109 'NUS No to Racism', *Darts*, no. 416, 7 May 1977, p. 2; 'Join the Fight Against Racialism', *NUS News*, 2:4, 9 October 1981, p. 7; *NUS News*, 12 June 1981, p. 3; 'Overseas fees conference', *NUS News*, 1:2, 17 April 1981, p. 5; 'LSE students occupy room in fee protest', *The Times*, 4 March 1981, p. 4; 'Court order against sit-in students', *The Times*, 10 March 1981, p. 3.

12

Persistence and privilege: mass migration from Britain to the Commonwealth, 1945–2000

Jean P. Smith

In the summer of 1963 there was a flurry of British newspaper articles highlighting rising rates of migration. Just a year after the 1962 Commonwealth Immigrants Act marked the beginning of restrictions on the entry of Commonwealth migrants to the United Kingdom, these articles spoke to a different kind of postcolonial migration, the large numbers of British migrants leaving the United Kingdom. Headlines such as 'The Rising Flood of Emigrants' in the *Financial Times*, 'Rush to Emigrate' in the *Daily Mail* and 'Record Number Leaving for Australia' in *The Times* speak to a growing interest in rising rates of emigration.[1] Though it had continued at a steady rate since the Second World War, 1963 saw the beginning of a dramatic and sustained increase in British emigration. Until the 1980s, the majority of British emigrants moved to the settler colonial nations of 'Greater Britain': Australia, Canada, New Zealand, South Africa and Rhodesia.[2]

This increase coincided with both the final stages of the long drawn-out process of decolonisation and, as mentioned above, with the passage of legislation that restricted migration from the Commonwealth and eventually redefined British nationality in terms of descent. Though it has received less scholarly and popular attention than immigration to the United Kingdom after the Second World War, emigration from the United Kingdom was significant, outpacing immigration until late in the twentieth century.[3] From 1946 to 2000, more than 8 million Britons emigrated and, of these, more than 5 million moved from the United Kingdom to countries in the empire and former empire.[4] British migration to what had been termed 'Greater Britain' not only continued during and after the era of decolonisation, but actually increased, in large part due to the institution of recruitment programmes and the offer of assisted passages or loans by the receiving countries. In the case of South Africa, it was the end of formal imperial ties that led to increased British migration as the apartheid state only began to offer subsidised passages after its declaration of Republic and exit from the Commonwealth in 1961.

This migration and the state policies that shaped it speak to the persistence of many of the assumptions upon which the idea of Greater Britain was based long after the term itself had lost political or cultural currency. Primary among them was the assumption of racial and cultural affinity, the basis for the belief that white British migrants were the most desirable and would easily assimilate in the receiving countries, which in turn would hold the most appeal for British migrants. This continues to have echoes in the post-Brexit discussions of the 'Anglosphere' and particularly proposals for the creation of a common zone of free movement between the United Kingdom and other (largely white) English-speaking countries of CANZUK (Canada, Australia, New Zealand and the United Kingdom).[5] The lack of scholarly and popular attention given to post-war British emigration, despite its scale, that it is taken for granted or considered unremarkable that so many people would move from the United Kingdom to these settler colonial nations and that these nations would not only welcome them but aid their migration, also speaks to the persistence of these assumptions.

Migration both to and from the United Kingdom in this period was shaped by legislation and policies that cannot, like the migrations themselves, be understood without considering the legacies of the British Empire and in particular, imperial and settler colonial ideologies of race. These ideologies informed restrictions, both implicit and explicit, placed on the entry of migrants of colour as well as the recruitment and subsidy of 'white' or 'European' migrants in all of these nations including the United Kingdom.[6] British migrants were favoured to varying degrees, more so in Australia, New Zealand and Rhodesia than in South Africa and Canada where their recruitment had to be balanced, at least in political rhetoric, with the concerns of Afrikaner and Quebecois nationalism.

Though British migration to these settler colonial nations was the continuation of a long-running trend in migration, a kind of afterlife of the migrations that originally constituted and sustained Greater Britain, the immigration policies and particularly the subsidised schemes that enabled this migration were undertaken at great expense not purely in the service of the empire or Commonwealth, but also of the racialised nation-states of Australia, New Zealand, South Africa, Rhodesia and Canada.[7] Their migration policies, both in terms of restriction and recruitment, had long prioritised their own perceived national self-interest. This is reflected in their late-nineteenth century disputes with the imperial authorities over the restrictions placed on the entry of British subjects of colour. That the British government in challenging these restrictions was more concerned with the appearance of imperial unity than with the protection of the rights of British subjects of colour is illustrated by the various compromises reached, that restrictions be based on implicit rather than explicit racial grounds such as language tests or the continuous passage requirement.[8] Marking a change in priorities in the wake of imperial collapse and when faced with the mass migration of Commonwealth citizens of colour, the British government's approach to migration by the 1960s became more like the long-running approach of the settler colonial nations. Though implicit rather than explicit, the restrictions placed on Commonwealth migration to the United Kingdom from 1962 onward drew on the racial ideologies of empire, while at the same time prioritising the nation at the expense of the imperial or as it was increasingly re-branded the Commonwealth connection.

Though the immigration policies and practices of these countries were not identical, and varied over time based on economic and political circumstances, all had a preference for European and, with the exception of South Africa, especially British migrants that persisted late into the twentieth century. Despite these similarities, scholars have generally considered these migration policies and programmes separately in terms of the histories of individual receiving countries. They are also rarely connected to histories of immigration restriction.[9] This essay contends that these recruitment schemes and the preferential treatment provided to British and other European migrants were just as much part of racialised immigration regimes as policies of restriction. Looking at both aspects of the migration policies of these countries together reveals the longevity and scale of the privilege provided to British and to a lesser, though still significant degree, other European migrants. This chapter begins by outlining British migration to the empire and former empire in the second half of the twentieth century and then shows how this migration was shaped by the immigration policies of the main receiving countries of Australia, Canada, New Zealand, South Africa and Rhodesia. This transnational approach demonstrates both the persistence of the imperial networks of migration of Greater Britain long after the end of formal empire, and the ways in which the racial ideologies of empire were constituent parts in the making of postcolonial nations.

An outline of British emigration, 1945–2000

Statistics on British emigration are, as James Hammerton has noted, 'notoriously unreliable' but even given the caveats below, the available data show a clear trend for large-scale migration from the United Kingdom across the second half of the twentieth century, largely to the settler colonial nations of 'Greater Britain' until the 1980s.[10] The graphs below draw on the statistics collated by the Overseas Migration Board up to 1964 and from *International Migration: Migrants Entering or Leaving the United Kingdom*, the MN series, published by the Office of Population, Censuses and Statistics thereafter.

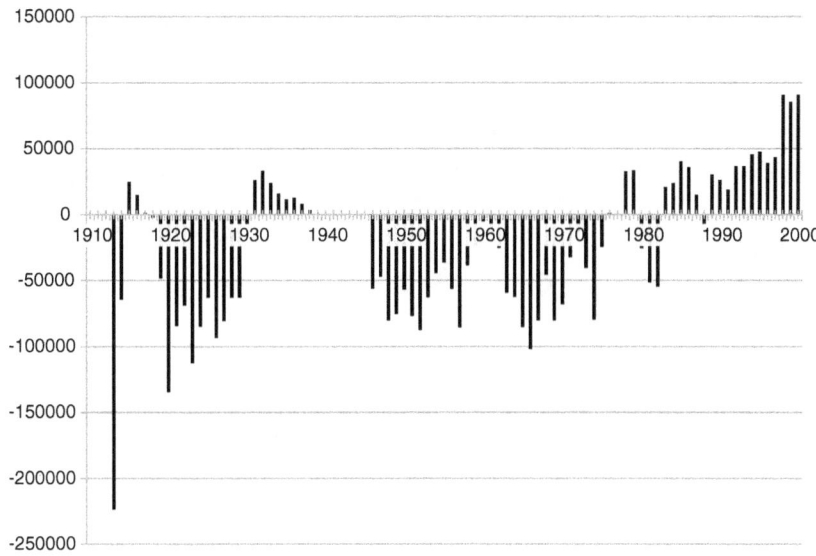

Figure 12.1 Net migration between the United Kingdom and the empire/former empire, 1913–2000

Despite some limitations, explained below, these sources provide the best available overall sense of the picture of migration to and from the United Kingdom, drawing on data from both the United Kingdom and the main receiving countries. Migration to and from the Republic of Ireland and its predecessor, the Irish Free State, are not included after 1923. Before 1963 the data are largely based on shipping records and so do not include those who travelled by air. From 1963 onwards the data are from the International Passenger Survey, a random sample of passengers leaving by both air and sea routes, and from the records of arrivals kept by the receiving countries. Emigrants are defined as those intending to leave the United Kingdom for more than one year, having lived in the United Kingdom for at least one year. Because of this, the figures do not take into account people who left or returned sooner than they anticipated, nor do they account for return migration.[11]

Figure 12.1 shows the net migration balance between the United Kingdom and the empire and former empire from 1913 to 2000, except for the Second World War years, for which statistics are not available.[12] Even given the limitations of the available data, the larger volume of migration to the empire and former empire than from those countries up to 1976 is evident. Figure 12.2 illustrates the total number of British emigrants in the second half of the twentieth century, the proportion that went to the former empire and, from 1964, those who went to Europe and the United States.[13]

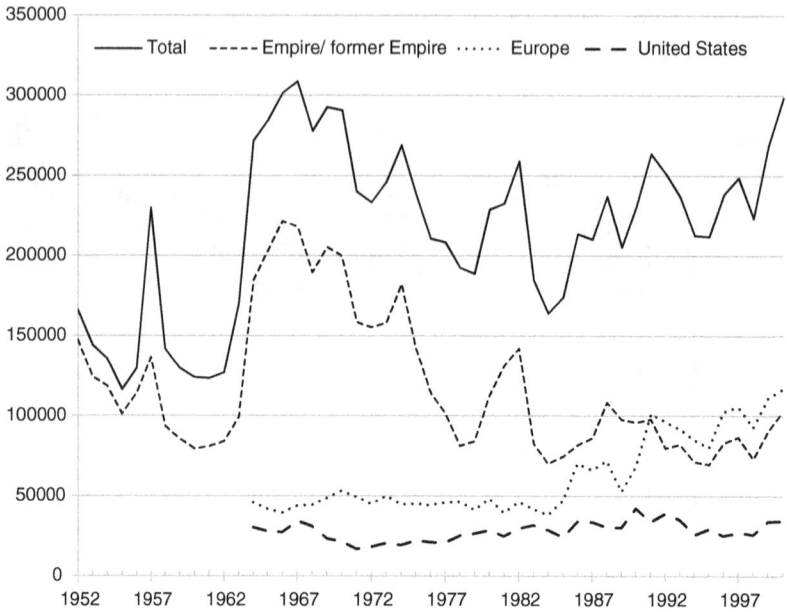

Figure 12.2 Emigration from the United Kingdom, 1952–2000

The graph shows a clear trend towards movement to the empire and former empire in the decades after the Second World War. Only in the 1990s did Europe begin to overtake the former empire as the most popular destination.[14] While steady numbers moved to the United States throughout the period, more Britons overall moved to Commonwealth destinations such as Australia and Canada. These statistics do not indicate which proportion of migrants returned or how long they stayed abroad. Though knowledge of these details could open further avenues of analysis, it is significant that so many people left the United Kingdom, regardless of whether they returned.

Figure 12.3 shows rates of migration from the United Kingdom to the settler colonial nations of Australia, Canada, New Zealand, South Africa and Rhodesia.[15] The large volume of migration in this period indicates ongoing links between the United Kingdom and these nations. It also reflects the relatively easy access British migrants had to these countries and the subsidies and other inducements that facilitated their passage.

Though Australia and Canada received the most migrants, followed by New Zealand, Britons also moved to South Africa and Rhodesia in this period.[16] Most significantly, this migration did not end when these countries left the Commonwealth in the early 1960s. On the contrary, there was a significant increase in British migration to the region in the 1960s and 1970s,

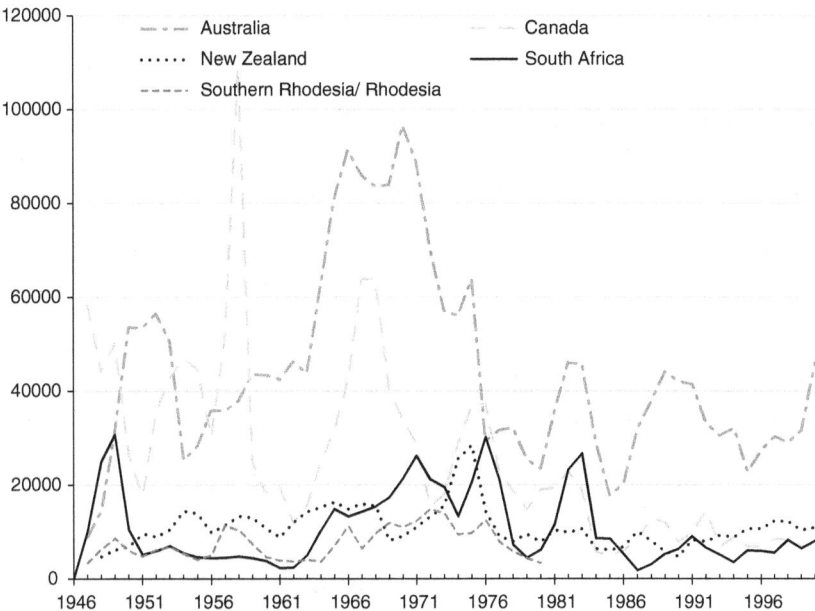

Figure 12.3 Emigration from the United Kingdom to the empire/former empire by destination, 1946–2000

especially to South Africa, even as South Africa and Rhodesia came under increasing international criticism for their segregationist policies. As discussed in more detail below, both countries began actively recruiting 'white' migrants at this time, offering subsidised passages.

Though undoubtedly the availability of subsidised migration schemes and their promotion influenced the decisions of would-be migrants, they do not offer a complete explanation for these migration flows or how their decisions and experiences were understood by migrants themselves. Just as they had for centuries, many left seeking opportunities and a better lifestyle as well as travel and adventure. This was often tied to negative perceptions of a decolonising and increasingly multicultural United Kingdom.[17] This was a new expression of an idea with a long history: that the settler colonial nations of the British Empire were or had the potential to be better Britains, free of the blights of industrialisation and hierarchies of class. Though often framed as egalitarian, the racialised appeal of making a new life in 'white' nations abroad was a crucial element. Remarkably, these motivations seemed to survive the demise of empire and Greater Britain for decades afterwards in the choices of the migrants themselves.

The legacy of the long history of empire settlement is also evident in the way that British people saw migration to the empire and later the Commonwealth as a potential option well beyond the political chronology of decolonisation. From 1948 to 1975, between 30 and 40 per cent of the British public surveyed by Gallup, expressed the wish to emigrate, largely indicating the settler colonies of Australia, Canada, New Zealand and South Africa as their most desired destinations.[18] While this is much larger than the number of people who actually left the United Kingdom, these polls indicate awareness of the possibility of migration, likely influenced by friends and family who had emigrated as well as recruitment campaigns. Eric Richards has argued that such polls are of 'questionable reliability', pointing to a 2002 poll that found that 54 per cent of Britons would emigrate 'if given the chance'.[19] While clearly such polls do not reliably predict rates of emigration whether in 1948 or 2002, they do indicate the persistence of the idea in the British imaginary that emigration was both possible and desirable, even, given the example Richards cites, into the twenty-first century.

It is clear that there are complexities here over time and place; someone moving to Southern Rhodesia in the late 1940s likely had different motivations as well as a different experience than someone moving to Australia in the 1970s, and rates of migration fluctuated over time. There are important continuities, however, both in terms of where British emigrants chose to go, and in terms of the state polices that enabled their migration. Through the 1980s the majority of emigrants from the United Kingdom went to nations that were or had once been part of the empire, and only in the 1990s did they begin to move in larger numbers to European destinations, notably France and Spain. Parts of the former empire remain popular destinations for British migrants into the twenty-first century, especially Australia, as reflected by television shows such as the BBC's *Wanted Down Under*, which has been running since 2007 and Channel 5's *A New Life in Oz* which premiered in 2017.[20]

The scale and longevity of continuing British emigration to the Empire-Commonwealth has been obscured in part by the focus on immigration to the United Kingdom, even though migration from the United Kingdom to the former empire outpaced migration from the former empire from the Second World War up to 1976.[21] In part, the attention granted to mass immigration from the Commonwealth to the United Kingdom stems from its perception as something new and, for many, threatening, especially in relation to the arrival of people of colour. This also explains the greater attention paid to immigrants of colour from the former empire, given that the largest group of immigrants to the United Kingdom in this period (and historically) came from Ireland, with significant numbers from continental Europe, Australia, New Zealand and Canada.[22] While there is a long history of people of colour living in the United Kingdom, the beginning of mass migration marked a change in migration patterns and appeared to many an inversion of the deep-rooted, and often implicit racial hierarchies of empire. Mass migration from the United Kingdom to the former empire, and especially to the settler colonies of Australia, New Zealand, Canada, South Africa and Rhodesia, by contrast, was nothing new.

Immigration restriction and recruitment in Australia, Canada, New Zealand, South Africa and Rhodesia

Though migration from the United Kingdom to the settler colonial nations was long-established, what was different in the post-war period was the extent to which British emigrants received state support. As well as benefitting from what Hammerton has termed the 'colonial dividend' that smoothed the path for their move – existing Commonwealth links, similar institutions, networks of family and friends, and the use of English in the former Dominions and Rhodesia – British migrants were also able to take advantage of subsidised migration schemes.[23] Though there had been previous assisted passages, notably the soldier settlement schemes after the First World War, in the decades after the Second World War British migrants were supported by far more comprehensive and wide-reaching state subsidies largely funded by the receiving countries.[24] These lasted late into the twentieth century. Australia and New Zealand offered subsidised passages until 1982 and 1974 respectively, while Canada provided loans to migrants. Following South Africa's declaration of Republic in 1961 and Rhodesia's Unilateral Declaration of Independence (UDI) in 1965, both nations began to offer subsidised passages, which continued until 1991 and 1980 respectively.

As well as benefiting from free or assisted passages, British migrants were aided by immigration policies that favoured their admission or that of Europeans in general. In Canada, such policies continued into the 1960s. In Australia, the 'White Australia' policy lasted until the 1970s. In New Zealand, it was only the introduction of a points-based system of immigration in 1987 that completely ended preference for migrants from Europe. In South Africa, racial discrimination in immigration law continued until 1991 and in Rhodesia until the end of settler rule in 1980.

The role of migration and its restriction in the formation of imperial and settler colonial cultures in the period up to the Second World War is well established. Works by James Belich, and Gary Magee and Andrew Thompson have shown how mass migration to the settler colonies of the British Empire (and in the case of Belich also the United States), facilitated by the development of modern technologies of communication and transportation, was crucial to the development of these nations.[25] As Marilyn Lake and Henry Reynolds, and Robert Huttenback have shown, equally important to the creation of settler colonial nations, were migration restrictions on racial lines.[26] Such policies continued after the Second World War working in tandem with assisted passage schemes which aimed to recruit European and especially British migrants.

Probably the best known of these was the 'White Australia' policy and the accompanying 'Ten Pound Pom' scheme of subsidised migration, which Hammerton and Alistair Thomson have described as the 'largest planned migration of the twentieth century'.[27] The United Kingdom–Australia Free and Assisted Passage Agreement came into operation in March 1947 and provided assisted passages to more than one million migrants until its conclusion in 1982. In its original form, the scheme was jointly financed by the British and Australian governments under the Empire Settlement Act, however, it was largely funded by the Australian government from the early 1950s and British government funding was withdrawn completely in 1972. Selected migrants received a passage, temporary housing and assistance with finding employment on the condition that they remained in Australia for two years. Civilians paid a contribution of £10, teenagers £5 and children and veterans received free passage. All veterans were eligible for the scheme, but civilians were recruited to fulfil labour needs in Australia, with a preference for single migrants under the age of 45.[28]

The exact parameters of the scheme varied over time depending on economic and political developments and migration flows, although its basic structure remained in place for thirty-five years. Immigration targets were reduced in response to the recessions of 1952/3 and 1961 and then raised again when the economy improved. Though in the immediate post-war years the Australian government prioritised single migrants with specific skills, nominated by Australians who could provide them with accommodation, by the late 1950s the scheme was opened to all who met the health requirements and had no significant criminal record. The assisted passage scheme was widened to include other European countries from 1951, and Australia operated a separate scheme for displaced persons which recruited more than 170,000 migrants from 1947 to 1953. This was the first time that the Australian state subsidised migrants who were not British.[29] As this suggests, these policies were primarily intended to build up the white population of Australia, and while there was a preference for British migrants, other European migrants were also admitted and recruited. The largest number of immigrants consistently came from the United Kingdom until 1996 when they were surpassed by those from New Zealand.[30] This was due to both the long-running networks of migration between Australia and the United Kingdom and the preference of the Australian government for British migrants, who were considered to be more easily assimilated.[31]

This preference was reflected in the range of schemes that targeted British migrants specifically. In 1952, the Commonwealth Nomination Scheme was introduced, whereby Britons without a personal sponsor could be housed in migrant hostels. Other initiatives included the 'Bring Out a Briton' scheme introduced in 1957, which encouraged Australians to sponsor British migrants, and the 'Nest Egg' scheme introduced in 1959 for migrants with at least £500. British migrants were given preferred status when they applied and provided with better ships and conditions. Ninety per cent of British migrants to Australia in the 1960s travelled under the assisted passage scheme, with almost 80,000 coming in the peak year of 1969.[32]

In 1972, with the election of a Labor government under Gough Whitlam, the special privileges accorded to British migrants as well as the 'White Australia' policy came to an end. In 1979, a points system was introduced, although assisted passages, despite being scaled down continued until 1982.[33] They had been, alongside the 'White Australia' policy a form of social engineering, favouring British migrants, followed by those from other European countries. By contrast, there was very little assistance provided to migrants from elsewhere in the world or to people of colour in the United Kingdom, who were unable to access assisted passages.[34]

Immigration restrictions based on race and nationality and subsidised passages were employed in a similar way in New Zealand. New Zealand provided unrestricted access to 'any citizen by birth of the British Commonwealth who was wholly of European ancestry', had no criminal convictions and met health requirements. By the mid-1950s, this has been changed to the subtler, 'readily assimilable to the New Zealand way of life', although this was an entirely subjective measure that left much discretion to immigration officials. This policy changed after a review in 1974 to a system with more emphasis on skills and qualifications, although potential for assimilation was still considered, and priority was given to immigrants from certain 'source' countries, including the United Kingdom, until the passage of the 1987 Immigration Act.[35]

The New Zealand government also ran and solely funded an assisted passage scheme from 1947 until 1975, which brought in 76,673 immigrants, the majority of whom were British. As in Australia, the exact parameters of the scheme changed over time depending on rates of migration and economic circumstances. Originally open only to single British migrants of 'European race and colour', between 20 and 35 years old in specific occupational categories, later older migrants, married migrants and those in a wider range of occupations became eligible. Similarly, the migrant's contribution to the fare changed over time. Initially it was free for veterans, with other migrants paying £10. It was made free for all migrants in 1950. A fare of £25 for single migrants and £50 for families was introduced in 1961, which was reduced to £10 in 1970. Like Australia, New Zealand operated a nomination scheme.[36]

The New Zealand government also recruited migrants from other European countries, although British migrants were preferred. In 1950 the scheme was opened to migrants from the Netherlands, Austria, Denmark, Switzerland and Germany. Following an increase in migration, the assisted passage scheme was scaled back in 1956, and again in 1958, at which time Danish, Swiss, Austrian and German migrants were excluded, reflecting the priority placed on British migrants. In 1960, the recruitment of unskilled single men was restricted to those nominated by family members, and a new scheme was introduced by which employers paid the migrant's passage, receiving a £100 subsidy from the New Zealand government. By 1968, the annual target for migrants was reduced to 500 and the nomination scheme was cancelled. In 1970, the nomination scheme was re-introduced following a labour shortage due to a rise in export prices and the government loosened skill requirements and abolished quotas on the subsidised scheme. Assisted passages came to an end in 1975 and all preference for migrants from 'source countries' ended in 1987.[37] As this suggests, the scheme was intended to serve the perceived national interest, and so varied according to economic or political circumstances.

A focus on the perceived interests of the racialised nation state over the imperial connection was also clear in South Africa and Rhodesia. In both cases it was their departure from the Commonwealth and the end of formal imperial connection that led to the institution of subsidised schemes for white migrants. Yet, even in these cases, the legacies of imperial migration pathways meant that more migrants moved to both South Africa and Rhodesia from the United Kingdom than from any other nation.

In South Africa, except for temporary migrant labour from surrounding countries, only migrants defined as 'white' by the apartheid government were admitted. Given Afrikaner nationalist opposition to mass migration from the United Kingdom, there was no subsidised migration scheme in the 1940s and 1950s. Even the Smuts government, in power from 1939 until 1948, though less vocally opposed to British migration than the Nationalist Party governments thereafter, only implemented a very limited scheme, with an agreement with the Union-Castle steamship line to delay the reconditioning of some of their ships that had been used as troop ships so that they could provide passages for migrants to South Africa, given the post-war shipping shortage.[38] From the mid-1950s, however, the South African government gradually began to pursue a more active immigration policy. In 1955 there was the establishment of a new Directorate of Immigration and in 1956 the government provided £25,000 to the Intergovernmental Committee on European Migration to facilitate the immigration of Hungarian refugees. In 1960, the South African government began providing financial support to the private South African Immigration Organisation (Samorgan), which recruited skilled workers in the United Kingdom and provided loans for their passages to South Africa, and also to Transa, a similar organisation that operated in West Germany, Austria and Switzerland.³⁹

After the 1961 declaration of republic, the South African government embarked on a recruitment drive aimed at reinforcing its white population in the face of rising white emigration. The achievement of the long-held Afrikaner nationalist goal of complete independence from the United Kingdom had eliminated much of the previous concern over mass British migration. Incentives included free passages and temporary housing for eligible immigrants as well as help with permanent housing and employment. Approved immigrants were offered R120 or the cost of a passage, which was comparable to the assisted passage schemes to Australia and New Zealand. It was arguably more generous, because unlike the other schemes, there was no minimum residency requirement. The scheme was very successful, dramatically increasing rates of British and wider European migration to South Africa in the 1960s and 1970s. Though the South African government recruited across Europe, they were most successful in the United Kingdom. For much of the period in question, more migrants came from the United Kingdom than any other country, except for short periods when British migrants were surpassed by those from Rhodesia/Zimbabwe and Mozambique in the run-up to and after independence in those countries. Though active recruitment ended in 1982 and the assisted passage scheme was limited to skilled migrants with offers of employment thereafter, it continued to operate until December 1991, and the same year, as part of the dismantling of apartheid legislation, the Aliens Control Act removed racial discrimination in immigration law.⁴⁰

Though there was more public and official support for European and particularly British immigration in Southern Rhodesia than in South Africa after the Second World War, the government ultimately took a more cautious approach than its southern neighbour in the post-war years, imposing quotas even for British migrants who met the financial and health requirements.⁴¹ A plan to offer free passages to British ex-service personnel after the Second World War was never implemented because of the number of migrants who arrived at their own expense. Concerns about the provision of housing and employment suitable for white people in the racial hierarchy of the minority settler colonial state led the Southern Rhodesian government to impose restrictions on 'European' immigration, beginning with non-British subjects in 1946 and expanding to British subjects by 1948.⁴² In 1952, the Southern Rhodesian government implemented a quota system, which limited immigration to 10,800 'Europeans' annually or 7 per cent of the existing 'European' population. Within this overall quota were further restrictions by country, which demonstrated a preference for British migrants: 4,560 admitted from the United Kingdom, 4,560 from the Union of South Africa, 600 from other British territories in Africa, 360 from other parts of the British Empire and Commonwealth and 720 from 'alien' territories. In part, these restrictions were intended to keep 'European' unemployment low, they were also an attempt to limit the number of white South African migrants, especially Afrikaners, out of concern that the arrival of too many would dilute the Britishness of white Southern Rhodesian culture. In 1953, Southern Rhodesia joined the Federation of Rhodesia and Nyasaland and these limits were increased to 6,000 each for the United Kingdom and South Africa, 800 for the rest of British Africa, and 800 for 'alien' countries.[43] Other than two short-lived and limited schemes for skilled British workers implemented in 1951 and 1955, there was no formal recruitment scheme until after UDI.[44]

The mid-1950s saw some renewed enthusiasm by both the Federal and Southern Rhodesian governments for promoting European immigration, but this was very much contingent on economic circumstances. The quota system was abandoned in 1955, the Federal Government implemented a nomination scheme and the small-scale loan scheme mentioned above. Quotas, albeit at a higher level, were reintroduced after an economic downturn in 1958, however, and though they were loosened again the following year, uncertainty over the looming break-up of the Federation led both the Federal and Southern Rhodesian government to take a cautious approach in the early 1960s.[45]

Following the collapse of the Federation in 1963 and Rhodesia's unilateral declaration of independence in 1965, the Rhodesian government began a campaign to recruit British and other European migrants, offering a £60 grant towards passages, and the reimbursement of some relocation expenses. This assistance was comparable to that offered by South Africa, Australia and New Zealand and was granted on the condition that migrants remained in Rhodesia for three years. The increasingly embattled minority regime also ran promotional schemes including those that enlisted white Rhodesians to personally appeal to their friends and relatives overseas to move to Rhodesia, such as the Settler '74 campaign. These efforts were largely unsuccessful, however, as the war between the Rhodesian government and anti-colonial forces intensified. The United Nations imposed sanctions against migration to Rhodesia and the British government prohibited its promotion. Assisted migration schemes came to an end with Zimbabwean independence in 1980.[46]

Unlike Australia, New Zealand, South Africa and Rhodesia, the Canadian government did not introduce subsidised passages, although it did offer selected immigrants from the United Kingdom and other European countries interest-free loans to cover their passages, lending more than $50,000,000 between 1951 and 1970. Migrants had two years to repay the loan. The Canadian government also provided easier access to migrants from the United Kingdom, the United States and France from 1949 until a points system was introduced in 1967. Out of these, more effort was made to recruit British immigrants. A larger administrative apparatus was set up in the United Kingdom along with a more active campaign of recruitment. More British immigrants went to Canada than any other nationality in the decades after the war, about a third between 1946 and 1965.[47]

The Canadian government also implemented other initiatives to facilitate British and wider European migration. They made arrangements with shipping companies and airlines to transport Britons at discounted rates immediately after the war. Like Australia and New Zealand, Canada implemented a scheme for displaced persons in Europe, admitting more than 166,000 between 1947 and 1952.[48] In 1957, to accommodate both large numbers of Hungarian refugees admitted after the failed Hungarian uprising of the previous year and a spike in British migration following the Suez crisis, the Canadian government worked with the Intergovernmental Committee for European Migration to charter flights at cheap rates to Toronto and further West, the 'air bridge to Canada', intended in part to even out the distribution of immigrants between eastern and western Canada.[49] There were some programmes for would-be migrants to Canada from outside of western Europe, but these were very limited in scale. From 1951, 150 citizens of India, 100 citizens of Pakistan and 50 citizens of Ceylon were allowed annual entry. Though in 1957 the quota for India was raised to 300, this was a tiny fraction of those coming from Europe and the quotas were not always filled. A scheme for domestic workers implemented in 1955 allowed the entry of just 100 immigrants annually from Jamaica and Barbados.[50]

Explicit preference for immigrants from particular national backgrounds remained in Canadian law until 1962, and in 1967 the Canadian government implemented a points system based on age, education, occupational skills, employment prospects and proficiency in English or French.[51] The loan programme was also extended to immigrants from Commonwealth countries in the Caribbean in 1966 and worldwide from 1970, although a 6 per cent interest rate was introduced in 1967, contributing to a dramatic drop in the loans granted.[52] These changes provided greater access to Canada for immigrants from countries beyond western Europe and the United States, although it was often still easier for European and American migrants to gain entry under the points system, which was primarily intended to gain more skilled labour rather than to end racial discrimination.[53] Rates of migration from the United Kingdom and other European countries remained high, and the Canadian government and the provincial governments continued to invest more in promotional campaigns there than in other regions, even after the change in legislation.[54]

Conclusion

The immigration policies of these five countries, in terms of both immigration restriction and incentives such as subsidised passages and loans all gave priority to British and other European immigrants in the decades after the Second World War. Though the form these policies took varied between countries and over time, such preferences based on nationality and race continued as late as the 1980s, as did mass migration from the United Kingdom to the settler colonial nations of Greater Britain. This continuity, taken together with the increasing restrictions on immigration in the United Kingdom beginning in 1962, reveals the lasting legacy of imperial racial ideologies in the immigration policies of all these nations. Yet, as the willingness of the settler colonial nations to admit and even recruit other 'white' or 'European' as well as British migrants demonstrates, these immigration policies, like increasing British restrictions on Commonwealth migration, were deployed primarily in the service of the racialised nation, itself a legacy of the racial logic of empire.

These policies and the continued influx of British and, as time went on, European migrants also served to perpetuate settler colonial structures in these countries, which, as Lorenzo Veracini has argued, did not disappear with independence from the United Kingdom.[55] Even though the end of explicit national and racial restrictions has led to greater access to migrants from around the world, the points systems that replaced them, while ostensibly neutral, continue to discriminate implicitly, given language and education requirements.[56] While British migrants gradually lost their privileged status, and migrants from other parts of Europe and later the world began to come to these countries in larger numbers, this process was gradual and came later than has often been assumed.[57] British migrants retained privileged access both in terms of entrance and subsidised passages until the 1960s in the case of Canada, until the 1970s in the cases of New Zealand, Australia and Rhodesia and until the 1980s in the case of South Africa. Even after the end of subsidised passages, Britons continued and continue to move to these countries, especially to Canada, Australia and New Zealand. While it seems unlikely that a CANZUK free movement zone will come into being in the foreseeable future, the persistence of the idea reflects the ongoing legacy of the migration that created Greater Britain, and its continuing ideological resonance.

Notes

1 *Financial Times*, 16 August 1963; *Daily Mail*, 23 May 1963; *The Times*, 20 May 1963.
2 The colony of Southern Rhodesia (present-day Zimbabwe) became known as Rhodesia following the independence of Zambia, previously the colony of Northern Rhodesia in 1964. The country will be referred to as Rhodesia for the period after 1964 and in general, and Southern Rhodesia for the period prior to 1964.
3 Exceptions include K. Paul, *Whitewashing Britain: Race and Citizenship in the Postwar Era* (Ithaca: Cornell University Press, 1997), pp. 25–63; A. James Hammerton and A. Thomson, *Ten Pound Poms: Australia's Invisible Migrants* (Manchester: Manchester University Press, 2005); A. J. Hammerton, *Migrants of the British Diaspora since the 1960s: Stories From Modern Nomads* (Manchester: Manchester University Press, 2017); J. P. Smith, '"The Women's Branch of the Commonwealth Relations Office": The Society for the Overseas Settlement of British Women and the Long Life of Empire Migration', *Women's History Review*, 25:4 (2016), pp. 520–535. Eric Richards covers the period from 1600 to the 1980s, although his main emphasis is on the nineteenth century. E. Richards, *Britannia's Children: Emigration from England, Scotland, Wales and Ireland since 1600* (London: Hambledon and London, 2004).
4 See Figure 12.2. Here the 'former empire' refers to countries that were part of the empire in the nineteenth century (therefore excluding the United States) but later gained independence, except for the Irish Free State/Republic of Ireland. Looking at emigrants with British nationality the estimate for total departures is 8,334,772 and for departures to destinations in the empire and former empire the estimate is 5,075,962. Including all nationalities, the estimate for total departures is 10,549,772. None of these estimates account for return migration as detailed below. Looking at a slightly different period, 1951–1998, Timothy Hatton estimates a figure of 7.3 million emigrants to all non-European destinations. T. J. Hatton, 'Emigration from the UK, 1870–1913 and 1950–1998', *European Review of Economic History*, 8:2 (2004), pp. 149–171, at p. 153.
5 D. Bell and S. Vucetic, 'Brexit, CANZUK, and the Legacy of Empire', *The British Journal of Politics and International Relations*, 21:2 (2019), pp. 367–382.
6 The United Kingdom also recruited 'white' migrants from Europe, most significantly from displaced persons camps after the Second World War. Kathleen Paul estimates that the Atlee government recruited 345,000 migrants from Europe at a cost of £18.1 million. Paul, *Whitewashing Britain*, p. 78.
7 Bernard Kelly makes a similar argument regarding the migration scheme for British ex-servicemen to Australia after the Second World War. B. Kelly, '"Masters in Their Own House": Britain, the Dominions and the 1946 Ex-Service Free Passage Scheme', *Journal of Imperial and Commonwealth History*, 44:1 (2016), pp. 121–139.
8 R. A. Huttenback, 'The British Empire as a "White Man's Country" – Racial Attitudes and Immigration Legislation in the Colonies of White Settlement', *The Journal of British Studies*, 13:1 (1973), pp. 108–137; M. Lake and H. Reynolds,

Drawing the Global Colour Line: White Men's Countries and the International Challenge of Racial Equality (Cambridge: Cambridge University Press, 2008), p. 5; R. V. Mongia, 'Race, Nationality, Mobility: A History of the Passport', in A. Burton (ed.), *After the Imperial Turn: Thinking With and Through the Nation* (Durham: Duke University Press, 2003), pp. 196–214.

9   For an exception with regard to Australia, see A. C. Palfreeman, *The Administration of the White Australia Policy* (Melbourne: Melbourne University Press, 1967), p. 2.

10 Hammerton, *Migrants of the British Diaspora*, p. 241.

11 According to Eric Richards 16 per cent of British emigrants to Australia returned between 1959 and 1964 and the proportion was higher for New Zealand and Canada. Richards, *Britannia's Children*, p. 267. James Hammerton and Alistair Thomson estimate a 25 per cent return rate for British migrants to Australia across the post-war period. Hammerton and Thomson, *Ten Pound Poms*, p. 264.

12 Data for Figures 12.1 and 12.2 as follows. Data for 1913–1953 from Cmd. 9261. Commonwealth Relations Office, *First Annual Report of the Overseas Migration Board* (London: HMSO, 1954), p. 29. Data for 1954–1963 from Cmnd. 255, Commonwealth Relations Office, *Overseas Migration Board Statistics for 1963* (London: HMSO, 1964), p. 13. Data for 1964–1974 from Office of Population, Censuses and Statistics, *International Migration: Migrants Entering or Leaving the United Kingdom*, Series MN, No. 1 (London: HMSO, 1974), pp. 44–45. Data for 1975–1984 from Office of Population, Censuses and Statistics, *International Migration: Migrants Entering or Leaving the United Kingdom*, Series MN, No. 11 (London: HMSO, 1984), pp. 6–7. Data for 1985–1990 from Office of Population, Censuses and Statistics, *International Migration: Migrants Entering or Leaving the United Kingdom*, Series MN, No. 17 (London: HMSO, 1990), pp. 6–7. Data for 1991–2000 from Office of Population, Censuses and Statistics, *International Migration: Migrants Entering or Leaving the United Kingdom*, Series MN, No. 27 (London: HMSO, 2000), pp. 6–7. As the measure here is the empire and former empire rather than the Commonwealth, statistics for South Africa and Pakistan have been included for the years that they left the Commonwealth: 1961–1994 in the case of South Africa and 1972–1989 in the case of Pakistan.

13 The graph begins in 1952 as, prior to that year, the Overseas Migration Board statistics only included the total number of emigrants to Commonwealth destinations. The figures include all migrants who had established residence in the United Kingdom regardless of nationality.

14 Hammerton, *Migrants of the British Diaspora*, pp. 211–213.

15 Because of the way that migration statistics were collected in Southern Rhodesia/Rhodesia, the graph includes British migration to Southern Rhodesia for 1946–1955, British migration to the Federation of the Rhodesias and Nyasaland for 1956–1964 and 'European' migration to Rhodesia from 1965 to 1979 as statistics by nationality are not available. During the Federal period, the majority of British migrants went to Southern Rhodesia. The 'European' figures include large numbers of white migrants from Africa who left in the run-up to

Persistence and privilege 269

or after independence, particularly Portuguese settlers from neighbouring Mozambique, which gained independence in 1975. Though migration from Britain did continue in this period, it was limited due to sanctions. A survey conducted by the United Kingdom Office of Population Censuses and Surveys found that 1,300 British migrants intended to move to Rhodesia in 1971; 1,200 in 1972; and 700 in 1972, between 7 and 9 per cent of total 'European' migration recorded by the Rhodesian state in those years. This might be lower than the actual number as 'intending' immigrants might not have been truthful, given the sanctions. Even so, it does suggest that rates of migration directly from the United Kingdom were much lower than previously. Cited in *Southern Africa: Immigration from Britain: A Fact Paper by the International Defence and Aid Association* (Geneva: Centre Europe Tiers Monde, 1975), p. 26. Unless indicated, statistics are based on country of last permanent residence. Data for Australia, 1946–1964. Cmnd. 2861. Commonwealth Relations Office, *Overseas Migration Board Statistics for 1964* (London: HMSO, 1954), p. 13. Data for Southern Rhodesia (by birthplace) for 1946–1955 Cmd. 9835. Commonwealth Relations Office, *Second Report of the Overseas Migration Board* (London: HMSO, 1956), p. 32. Data for the Federation of Rhodesia and Nyasaland (by birthplace) for 1956, and Canada (by racial origin), New Zealand (by place of birth and for years ending 31 March) and South Africa for 1946 to 1956. Cmnd. 336. Commonwealth Relations Office, *Third Report of the Overseas Migration Board* (London: HMSO, 1957), pp. 22, 27, 29, 30. Data for South Africa for 1957–1964 from Republic of South Africa Bureau of Statistics, *Report No. 286: Statistics of Immigrants and Emigrants 1924–1964* (Pretoria: The Government Printer, 1964), p. 4. Data for Canada, New Zealand, and the Federation for 1957 and 1958 (data for 1957 from the Federation includes the Republic of Ireland) from Cmnd. 975. Commonwealth Relations Office, *Fifth Report of the Overseas Migration Board* (London: HMSO, 1960), p. 6. For 1959 Cmnd. 1243. Commonwealth Relations Office, *Sixth Report of the Overseas Migration Board* (London: HMSO, 1960), p. 6. For 1960 and 1961 Cmnd. 1905. Commonwealth Relations Office, *Overseas Migration Board Statistics for 1961* (London: HMSO, 1962), p. 7. For 1962 and 1963 Cmnd. 255, Commonwealth Relations Office, *Overseas Migration Board Statistics for 1963* (London: HMSO, 1964), p. 9. Data for Rhodesia for 1964–1979, J. Brownell, *The Collapse of Rhodesia: Population Demographics and the Politics of Race* (London: I.B. Taurus, 2011), p. 125. Data for 1964 to 2000 for all other countries as for Figures 12.1 and 12.2.

16 The sharp rise in migration to Canada in 1956 and 1957 was caused by both the introduction of the 'air bridge' the previous year and shipping difficulties to Australia and New Zealand caused by the Suez Crisis. Cmnd. 336. *Third Report*, pp. 9, 18.

17 Hammerton, *Migrants of the British Diaspora*, pp. 27–53, 57–58; D. Conway and P. Leonard, *Migration, Space and Transnational Identities: The British in South Africa* (Basingstoke: Palgrave Macmillan, 2014), pp. 154, 171–174; Hammerton and Thomson, *Ten Pound Poms*, p. 72.

18 G. H. Gallup (ed.), *The Gallup International Public Opinion Polls: Great Britain 1937–1975* (New York: Random House, 1976), pp. 171, 187, 217, 249, 361, 401, 451, 481, 613, 621, 661, 702, 732, 789, 813, 878, 1036, 1071–1072, 1219, 1298, 1441.
19 See Note 15; Richards, *Britannia's Children*, p. 355.
20 D. Sriskandarajah and C. Drew, *Brits Abroad: Mapping the Scale and Nature of British Emigration* (London: Institute for Public Policy Research, 2006), p. viii.
21 See Figure 12.2.
22 T. Modood and J. Salt, 'Migration, Minorities and the Nation', in T. Modood and J. Salt (eds), *Global Migration, Ethnicity and Britishness* (Basingstoke: Palgrave Macmillan, 2011), p. 3; Paul, *Whitewashing Britain*, pp. 64, 90–110; C. Wills, *Lovers and Strangers: An Immigrant History of Post-War Britain* (London: Allen Lane, 2017), pp. xii, 50, 114.
23 Hammerton, *Migrants of the British Diaspora*, pp. 51–52.
24 M. Harper and S. Constantine, *Migration and Empire* (Oxford: Oxford University Press, 2010), pp. 290–293; K. Fedorowich, *Unfit for Heroes: Reconstruction and Soldier Settlement in the Empire between the Wars* (Manchester: Manchester University Press, 1995).
25 J. Belich, *Replenishing the Earth: The Settler Revolution and the Rise of the Anglo-World, 1783–1939* (Oxford: Oxford University Press, 2009); G. B. Magee and A. S. Thompson, *Empire and Globalisation: Networks of People, Goods and Capital in the British World, c. 1850–1914* (Cambridge: Cambridge University Press, 2010).
26 Lake and Reynolds, *Drawing the Global Colour Line*, pp. 106–137; Huttenback, British Empire as a 'White Man's Country'.
27 Hammerton and Thomson, *Ten Pound Poms*, p. 9.
28 Ibid., pp. 30–31.
29 R. T. Appleyard, *Immigration: Policy and Progress* (Sydney: Australian Institute of Political Sciences, 1971), pp. 8–9, 11, 21.
30 J. Jupp, *From White Australia to Woomera: The Story of Australian Immigration* (Cambridge: Cambridge University Press, 2002), pp. 12–13.
31 S. Ward, *Australia and the British Embrace: The Demise of the Imperial Ideal* (Melbourne: Melbourne University Press, 2001), pp. 26–27.
32 Hammerton and Thomson, *Ten Pound Poms*, pp. 31–34.
33 Ibid., p. 33.
34 Jupp, *From White Australia to Woomera*, p. 18; Hammerton and Thomson, *Ten Pound Poms*, p. 31; Richards, *Britannia's Children*, p. 264; Hammerton, *Migrants of the British Diaspora*, pp. 64–65.
35 M. Hutching, *Long Journey for Sevenpence: An Oral History of Assisted Immigration to New Zealand from the United Kingdom, 1947–1975* (Wellington: Victoria University Press, 1999), pp. 73–74; Paul, *Whitewashing Britain*, p. 43.
36 Hutching, *Long Journey for Sevenpence*, pp. 49–74.
37 Ibid., pp. 49–62, 68–73.
38 S. Peberdy, *Selecting Immigrants: National Identity and South Africa's Immigration Policies, 1910–2008* (Johannesburg: Wits University Press, 2009), pp. 88–92.

39 F. G. Brownell, *British Immigration to South Africa, 1946–1970* (Pretoria: Government Printer, 1985), pp. 43–48.
40 Peberdy, *Selecting Immigrants*, pp. 120–123, 143–144, 268–289; Conway and Leonard, *Migration, Space and Transnational Identities*, pp. 39–40.
41 Paul, *Whitewashing Britain*, pp. 30–31. On the surge in post-war migration to southern Africa and its relationship to travel during the Second World War, see J. P. Smith, '"Transformation to Paradise": Wartime Travel to Southern Africa, Race and the Discourse of Opportunity, 1939–1950', *Twentieth Century British History*, 26:1 (2015), pp. 52–73.
42 *The Statute Law of Southern Rhodesia* (Salisbury: The Government Printer, 1947), pp. 109–125.
43 Ian Smith Papers, Cory Library, Grahamstown, South Africa (hereafter Ian Smith Papers), 1/78/002, Memorandum on Immigration, 23 July 1954.
44 Paul, *Whitewashing Britain*, p. 31. Ian Smith Papers, 1/78/004, Immigration Policy, 24 October 1955, pp. 3–5. The later scheme, which provided interest free loans of between £30 and £120 to skilled workers was very small in scale compared with the contemporary recruitment schemes in Australia, New Zealand and Canada, assisting just over 500 migrants in 1957. The National Archives of the United Kingdom, Kew, CO 1015/1248, Annex A. The Federation of Rhodesia and Nyasaland Assisted Passage Scheme for Immigrants from the United Kingdom.
45 Cmnd. 975. *Fifth Report*, p. 23. Brownell, *The Collapse of Rhodesia*, p. 117.
46 Brownell, *The Collapse of Rhodesia*, pp. 14, 117–130.
47 M. Barber and M. Watson, *Invisible Immigrants: The English in Canada since 1945* (Winnipeg: University of Manitoba Press, 2015), pp. 22–26; A. Richmond, *Post-War Immigrants in Canada* (Toronto: University of Toronto Press, 1967), pp. 3–4, 9, 11, 14–18.
48 Richmond, *Post-War Immigrants in Canada*, pp. 9, 15.
49 V. Knowles, *Strangers at our Gate: Canadian Immigration Policy, 1540–2006* (Toronto: Dundurn Press, 2007), pp. 173–176. See Figure 12.3 for the increase in British migration at this time.
50 Richmond, *Post-War Immigrants in Canada*, pp. 11, 13.
51 P. S. Li, *Destination Canada: Immigration Debates and Issues* (Oxford: Oxford University Press, 2003), p. 23.
52 N. Kelley and M. Trebilcock, *The Making of the Mosaic: A History of Canadian Immigration Policy* (Toronto: University of Toronto Press, 2010), p. 363.
53 Li, *Destination Canada*, pp. 24–25.
54 Knowles, *Strangers at our Gate*, p. 177.
55 L. Veracini, *The Settler Colonial Present* (London: Palgrave Macmillan, 2015).
56 A. K. Boucher, 'How "skill" definition affects the diversity of skilled immigration policies', *Journal of Ethnic and Migration Studies*, 46:2 (2019), pp. 1–18.
57 Stephen Constantine estimated a change in the 1940s, calling for more research into the specifics of each receiving country. S. Constantine, 'British Emigration to the Empire-Commonwealth since 1880: From Overseas Settlement to Diaspora?', *Journal of Imperial and Commonwealth History*, 31:2 (2003), pp. 19–28.

13

'The mouse that roared': the Falklands and Gibraltar in Thatcher's (Greater) Britain

Ezequiel Mercau

At the beginning of April 1982, Spanish president Leopoldo Calvo Sotelo was busy shuttling around Andalusia, campaigning for his party, *Unión de Centro Democrático* (UCD). While touring the south of Spain on 2 April, news of the Argentine invasion of the Falklands/Malvinas Islands reached Europe, threatening to derail the fragile diplomatic progress that Madrid had recently made with London over Gibraltar. Keen to dissociate the two disputes, the president gave an ad hoc press conference while on a bus journey from Algeciras to Tarifa the next day. He did not mince his words and stated clearly that Gibraltar and the Malvinas were 'different and distant', and thus no links should be drawn between them.[1] Spain and Britain, in fact, had agreed to open the so-called 'Garlic Wall' frontier gates separating the Rock and the mainland (which had been closed by Franco in 1969), and to begin the Lisbon negotiations on 20 April 1982. Yet, as a piece in the *Gibraltar Chronicle* put it a few weeks later, while throughout the British–Argentine conflict there was a clear attempt by London and Madrid to officially distinguish the two disputes (given the similarities drawn in the public sphere), 'the fact remains that both Spaniards and Gibraltarians have become more entrenched in their attitudes towards each other because of the Falklands crisis'.[2]

There is no shortage of allusions to the connections between these two post-imperial disputes, both of which loomed large in the 1980s, and which remain live issues to this day – not just in terms of the disagreements themselves, but also in the way in which they are used as reminders of Britain's unfinished imperial business.[3] Too often, however, this coupling of the Falklands and Gibraltar remains superficial. Here are two overseas territories claimed by larger, Spanish-speaking countries who, especially since the era of decolonisation, have both consistently and persistently accused Britain of perpetuating colonialism and of maiming their territorial integrity. Undeniably, there is some logic in regarding these two cases in parallel, but perhaps the obvious superficial links have served to obscure the deeper and more significant dynamics at work.

I argue here that a closer look at the imperial dimensions of these issues can shed some light. Though both disputed territories have (particularly in recent decades) tried to make a case for the defence of their right to self-determination, they have done so in the broader context of their attachment to an idea of Britain. This has not merely been a marriage of convenience, but rather the result of decades – indeed, over a century – of imperial endeavour, which bound Gibraltarians and Falkland Islanders to a global community of British sentiment.

This chapter thus examines the evolution of the Falklands and Gibraltar disputes in the broader context of the unravelling of the transcontinental idea of Greater Britain in the wake of empire, taking as a focal point a number of crises in the early 1980s. This was a time of uncertainty in both British Overseas Territories – a time of transition, of hopeful expectations and of worrying disappointments. At the heart of all this was the evolving nature of these communities' bond with Britain, which had until then been the solid bedrock of their national identification. But the gradual transformation of the British state and of metropolitan Britons' self-perception, coupled with the emergence of increasingly intractable diplomatic tensions with Argentina and Spain respectively, had rapidly eroded the shield of Britishness under which both Gibraltarians and Falkland Islanders took shelter.

Here I focus particularly on the British Nationality Act of 1981 and on the Falklands War and its immediate aftermath, while paying attention to other concurrent events, especially the decision to close the Royal Naval Dockyard in Gibraltar. Because they directly impinged on these communities' self-identification, these events provoked an emotional rollercoaster in both territories, thrusting Gibraltarians and Falkland Islanders in all directions – ranging from an embrace of Britishness, declarations of loyalty and a reaffirmation of a deep spiritual bond, to rising suspicions, doubts and fears, an alarming breakdown of mutual trust, a desire to move away from the 'colonial' stigma, and even talk of seeking independence from Britain. Doubtless, there are many differences between the Falklands and Gibraltar, and this chapter does not gloss over them or attempt to lump the two cases together without regard for the distinctiveness of each one. But only by examining them side by side can we appreciate that some of the key forces driving the local responses to these international events transcend the territories themselves. Moreover, looking at these two cases together through the transnational prism of Greater Britain can help us better understand their disproportionate reverberations in Thatcher's Britain. To paraphrase one of the Rock's political leaders, in the 1980s the Falklands and Gibraltar were like 'the mouse that roared'.[4]

Popular feeling and issues of national identity, though somewhat elusive, can be measured and discerned by focusing on political culture in a broad sense, observing the contours of popular opinion, of dominant attitudes and ways of understanding reality.[5] Indeed, grasping the dynamics of these disputes matters. Discussions about national identity in the Falklands and in Gibraltar were never merely academic or ornamental. In the case of the South Atlantic Islands, they reached a critical point with the outbreak of war in April 1982 – when, more than ever, their livelihood and future was at stake. While Gibraltar was fortunate enough not to experience the same drama, the incessant claims from their neighbour north of the border meant that their British connection was always an issue, with very direct consequences for their future existence.

Imperial origins

These two disagreements originated, in many respects, as a direct result of Britain's imperial expansion – Gibraltar, in the early eighteenth century, and the Falklands in the nineteenth. The more recent iterations of both disputes, however, date from the 1960s – a decade of imperial unravelling. In fact, both Spain and Argentina presented these at the United Nations as cases for decolonisation, in response to the General Assembly's Resolution 1514 (XV) from 1960. Matters began to heat up from that point onwards on the Iberian peninsula, as Madrid gradually introduced restrictions on Gibraltarians, who responded with a referendum in September 1967 in which, under the banner of 'British we are, British we stay!', they overwhelmingly voted in favour of remaining under British rule. Curiously, the inhabitants of the Rock, unlike the Falkland Islanders, had ancestors from a wide variety of ethnic and national backgrounds: Maltese, Portuguese, Genoese, North African Sephardic Jews, Moroccans, Menorcans and Britons.[6] It is commonly argued that their attachment to Britain was amplified over the ensuing years thanks to Franco's decision in 1969 to introduce a total blockade – cutting off all links and communications between the Rock and Spain – in response to Gibraltar's new constitution and to Britain's renewed commitment to back the Gibraltarians.[7] Some also argue that the evacuation of Gibraltar's civilian population to Britain during the Second World War was an important factor in the crystallisation of Gibraltar's Britishness.[8] About a decade later, as a newly democratic Spain sought to join NATO and the European Economic Community (EEC), talks resumed between Spain and the United Kingdom, culminating in the Lisbon Agreement of 1980, whereby Spain reaffirmed its desire to restore its territorial integrity, while respecting the interests of Gibraltarians, and Britain expressed its commitment to the wishes of the inhabitants of the Rock.[9]

Moving seven thousand miles southwest to the Falklands/Malvinas, a key point that reignited this quarrel was the 1965 UN Resolution requesting Britain and Argentina to find a satisfactory solution to the disagreement, bearing in mind Resolution 1514 on decolonisation, and respecting the interests of the Falkland Islanders. After a promising start for Argentina, UN negotiations failed, partly through the efforts of the Falklands lobby, which would develop into a powerful ginger group in the United Kingdom over the ensuing years, making it its business to campaign on behalf of the Islanders under the battle cry of 'Keep the Falklands British'. The population of the archipelago, though miniscule at under 2,000 inhabitants, was largely descended from English, Scottish, Welsh and Irish settlers, and was staunchly loyal to the 'mother country'. The Falklands lobby played an important role in raising awareness in the British Parliament and media about the Islanders' family bonds with Britain – not infrequently stressing that the Kelpers (as they are sometimes called) were white and spoke with the same accents as people in metropolitan Britain. During the 1970s, Buenos Aires focused its efforts on a 'hearts and minds' campaign in the Islands, with occasional attempts at resolving the sovereignty dispute through diplomatic means. While some progress was made, this strategy ultimately proved insufficient, particularly as Argentina fell into a period of economic and political instability, culminating in a military dictatorship that wreaked havoc in the country. Britain continued negotiating with Argentina throughout, while secretly making contingency plans for war. The beginning of the 1980s saw a possible leaseback solution scrapped. The bond of kinship uniting colony and 'mother country' had by now been severely damaged, however, and many Islanders increasingly viewed British diplomats and leaders with suspicion, often accusing them of betrayal.[10] But, faced with the alternative of Argentine sovereignty (and even if more than a few entertained the thought of 'going it alone'), they continued to hope that Britain would 'not let them down'.[11]

Britain, meanwhile, found itself by the early 1980s in a dire economic situation, with spiralling unemployment and growing social unrest, sometimes triggered by racial tensions. Over the previous two decades, Britain had undergone a significant process of adaptation from the world's biggest empire to a small country off the north-western confines of Europe. On taking up office in 1979, Margaret Thatcher, on top of the tough domestic battles facing her premiership, had inherited a number of post-imperial headaches – among them, Gibraltar and the Falkland Islands. It is in this context that we must understand the tensions generated by the British Nationality Act of 1981.

Citizenship, defence and the economy: the rollercoaster of 1981

The year 1981 provoked in Gibraltarians and Falklanders a whirlwind of emotions, as a number of events and revelations threatened their link with

Britain and their livelihoods. These mainly had to do with citizenship, the defence of their territories and their economic survival.

The issue of British citizenship was not a new one. Since the early 1970s, there had been demands in Westminster for a new citizenship law that would realign nationality and immigration. Prior to the bill, three immigration acts (1962, 1967 and 1971) had progressively restricted the number of immigrants from the former empire with right of abode in the United Kingdom, even though under the British Nationality Act of 1948 they were still considered British nationals. The new nationality bill, originally conceived by Labour but ultimately tabled and implemented by the Conservatives, set out to create three distinct types of citizenship: British Citizens (people with UK-born parents or grandparents), who would have right of abode in the United Kingdom; and British Dependent Territories' Citizens (born or naturalised in the dependencies) and Overseas Citizens, neither of whom would enjoy right of abode in Britain. Contrary to what the law had stipulated until then, Britishness would now be granted on the basis of 'the right of blood', rather than 'the right of soil' (acquired by birth in a territory).[12]

Though many point out that these restrictions over the years were not aimed at arresting the intake of overseas British settlers and their descendants, Falkland Islanders and Gibraltarians alike felt threatened by this bill, which would potentially strip many of them of British citizenship. Gibraltar's efforts to amend the nationality bill succeeded, while those of the Falklanders' failed. In both places, however, this event became an occasion to proclaim once again their loyalty to Britain, while prompting complaints and accusations against London. As we shall see, this was not an isolated matter; a number of other key episodes punctuated this period, giving it a more dramatic flavour.

In the case of the South Atlantic archipelago, about a third of its population (600–700 Islanders), some of whom could trace their British ancestry back to the original settlers in the nineteenth century, would only qualify for British Dependent Territories' Citizenship. Given the deteriorating relationship between Britain and the Falklands during the previous decade, this move was perceived by many Kelpers as the death knell of their British connection. In the broader context of renewed attempts, under the Conservatives, to find a solution to the sovereignty dispute with Argentina through a leaseback proposal, all the signs seemed to point in one direction – and it was not good news for the Falklanders.

Despite verbal assurances from British ministers that Islanders would be treated favourably, the latter found it particularly difficult to comprehend London's reluctance to enshrine this special treatment into law. An intervention from a member of the Falklands lobby at a meeting with the junior foreign minister, Nicholas Ridley, sums up this view: why, he asked, could the government 'not distinguish between them (and other people in similar positions in other Dependencies) and those, like the Chinese in Hong Kong, who were not of British origin'? To this, Ridley retorted that 'any attempt to develop the nationality debate on these lines would be bound to attract criticism of racialism'.[13] Hong Kong was, indeed, one key issue behind the nationality debate.

As the discussions progressed, it became clear that metropolitan British and Kelper understandings of Britishness had diverged significantly. The UK government's emphasis on the right of soil over the right of blood collided head-on with the Islanders' understanding and position. Their case, in fact, rested largely on the notion that they had 'no other "mother country"'.[14] Ironically, even though the British Nationality Bill might well have been influenced by a desire to more firmly align Britishness with 'whiteness', it also left out a significant number of 'white overseas Britons', whose families had left Britain generations earlier.

The Islanders, who had repeatedly experienced frustration at London's attitudes towards them, became increasingly apprehensive, and some even began to question the value of their own British connection. One prominent example was Neil Watson, one of the original members of the local branch of the Falkland Islands Committee, who protested that he had a 'nagging feeling that we are preparing our lines of retreat', concluding: 'there is no way that I regard Britain as home' (even if he was, by no means, in favour of Argentine sovereignty over the Islands).[15] He was not alone in this. A report from the United Kingdom Falkland Islands Committee (UKFIC, the most important organ of the Falklands lobby) to the Foreign Office from October 1981, in fact, added that 'some Islanders were now considering seriously the question of independence'.[16] This suggested a loss of faith in the capacity of their Greater British link to serve as a bedrock for the miniscule Kelper community, undermining their internal harmony in the process.

To compound the matter, the bill received Royal Assent on 30 October, prompting the editor of the *Penguin News* to write, amid a mood of 'resigned anger' in the Falklands:

> In a place where people have become well aware that loyalty expressed over many generations is swiftly forgotten, they are not surprised that they have been pushed a little further out into the cold.[17]

This had taken place only a few months after the announcement that the ice patrol HMS *Endurance* would be withdrawn from the South Atlantic after the southern summer of 1981–1982, which had left the Islanders indignant.

For Gibraltar, the battle was fought along similar lines, but with its own peculiar hues. Specifically, given that it was the only British overseas territory *within* the EEC, it could claim special treatment without compromising

Britain's dealings with other territories. This perhaps put some distance between their plight and that of the Falklanders, which might explain the conspicuous lack of solidarity between them.

One of the key arguments put forward from the Rock was that they were not primarily concerned with immigration. As explained in a letter agreed to by the leaders of the three parties in the Gibraltar House of Assembly and signed by the inhabitants of the Rock:

> For us it is a matter of National Identity. The people of Gibraltar cannot achieve independence, it seems, because of the commitments of the British Government under the Treaty of Utrecht. We consider that the historical relationship that exists between the people of Gibraltar and the people of the United Kingdom is unique. The closeness of the people of Gibraltar to Britain is we believe unparalleled in any other territory and we ask that we get our rightful status, that of British Citizens which is what we are.[18]

As with the Falkland Islanders, for the Gibraltarians this was a fight that went far beyond the pragmatism that seemed to be driving the Bill. Citing a unique relationship and closeness was a strategy that had been used by other overseas Britons in the past – which was accompanied here, as it often was the British world over, by a reminder of Gibraltar's wartime contributions. Moreover, through this particular emphasis, the Rock's leaders perhaps sought to assuage any fears that Gibraltarians might decide to move en masse to the United Kingdom. In a letter to Lord Ferrier, one of Gibraltar's supporters in Britain, stressing their Britishness and loyalty, assured the Conservative peer that there was no risk of Gibraltarians flooding into Britain: 'I am sure Gibraltarians are quite happy with life in their Mediterranean peninsula. But they like to be called British and would wish to be welcomed as first-class British citizens when they come to Britain'.[19]

Peter Isola, leader of the Democratic Party of British Gibraltar (DPBG), echoed these sentiments in an interview at the end of January 1981, bewailing this worrying trend – perceived not quite as 'a casting adrift' but certainly as 'a move away' from Britain.[20] The Gibraltar Union of Students, meanwhile, submitted a memorandum to the Foreign Affairs Committee, stressing Gibraltar's Britishness, illustrated in its institutions – a British inheritance, but not an imposition – and its contribution during the Second World War. Similar to messages from Falkland Islanders and their supporters, this note stressed 'racial and religious integration' at a time when 'intolerance and prejudice were rife in the rest of Europe, including England'.[21] Even if Gibraltarians could not use this strategy to portray themselves as more quintessentially British than metropolitan Britain, as the Kelpers had done, they could still point to their British traditions and virtues. In any case, despite their awareness of their mixed ethnic make-up, their supporters still claimed that Gibraltarians were 'more British than the British', as the Conservative MP Albert McQuarrie, chairman of the British Gibraltar Group in Westminster, told the Commons in June 1981.[22] This common refrain was often accompanied by a reminder of their loyalty 'to Crown and Country'. Yet these manifestations of allegiance could not fully paper over the cracks that were beginning to appear on the Rock's Britishness.[23]

A number of events during this period served to simultaneously augment both the tensions and the lingering allure of a Greater British mentality in Gibraltar. The Defence Review of June 1981, which had announced the scrapping of HMS *Endurance* to the chagrin of the Kelpers, brought its share of ominous news to Gibraltar. The Rock's inhabitants learnt that the Royal Navy's Dockyard in Gibraltar, alongside a number of other dockyards in Britain, would be closed down in the ensuing years. London promised to consult Gibraltar's leaders on the matter before making a final announcement, but the latter still expressed grave concern over the possible impact that this would have on the Rock's future livelihood.[24] Indeed, it was predicted that almost one thousand jobs would be lost directly, and up to two thousand would be threatened, putting one in five members of the labour force in a precarious situation, reducing national income drastically and producing great damage to the economy.[25] Gibraltarians, though deeply distressed by this news, were temporarily distracted by the decision of Prince Charles and Diana Spencer to begin their honeymoon in Gibraltar at the start of August, from where they would set out on a cruise trip. Though it was the briefest of visits, barely lasting two hours, the locals made much of this episode, seeing it as an opportunity to exhibit their Britishness with great flair, and thus boost support for their plight in Westminster.[26] The town was draped in red, white and blue for the occasion 'and Union Jacks of every imaginable size, shape and form (hats, swimsuits, dresses, jackets, cars) were out on display'.[27] The fact that the royal visit coincided with the anniversary of the British arrival in Gibraltar in 1704 was seen as particularly symbolic: 'Gibraltar stands today as British as ever and with a determination to remain so which fully justifies its well founded faith in the future', reported *Vox*.[28]

Yet even this joyous occasion was marred by the negative press it got in the United Kingdom, often reproduced in local newspapers. For instance, one piece saw Gibraltar's outpouring of Britishness as an atavistic impulse, warning that 'one day, the British colony in Europe is going to have to find a new status, more in keeping with the last years of the 20th century'.[29] Similarly, a piece in the *Sunday Times* decried the support for Gibraltar in the House of Lords as an 'echo of empire',[30] while another scoffed at the Chief Minister's extolling of 'Gibraltar with a list that is almost a parody of British virtues' – which apparently included 'flower shows, dog shows, the housewives' association, charity fetes, the philatelic club, the clay-pigeon shoot'.[31] Remarks of this kind had also featured in the context of the Falklands dispute, and would become more pronounced during the South Atlantic war. These negative vibes were perhaps compounded by the House of Commons Foreign Affairs Select Committee report published at the end of August 1981, which recognised that regional autonomy in the Spanish constitution would be an important element in the future solution to the dispute, while questioning British jurisdiction over the isthmus (not mentioned in the Treaty of Utrecht), and stating that Gibraltar should be reminded that Her Majesty's Government's primary responsibility was to the British Parliament.[32]

All of this provoked angry reactions in Gibraltar. One astonished reader, for instance, pointed out that the 'provisions of this Bill are certainly not a joke for the people of what remains of the old Empire', adding that the 'Gibraltarians, who are very loyal British subjects and very proud of being so, fiercely resented this discrimination and protested very strongly'. Interestingly, this reader pointedly reminded Britain about its reduced status since decolonisation. 'Great Britain', he declared, 'is no longer an island off the continent of Europe, possessing a huge empire, it is now a European country and Gibraltar is more akin to the Channel Islands than to any of the erstwhile colonies'.[33] This effort to be seen as different from other colonies was becoming increasingly common in Gibraltar – something which would later jar with the fervent expressions of solidarity with the Kelpers during the war.

Taken together, these unsympathetic views from Britain (in conjunction with Spanish accusations of 'colonialism') may well be seen as a key reason why Gibraltarians sought to move away from their 'colonial' status, stressing Gibraltar's geographical proximity to Britain and proposing that it be granted a status similar to the Channel Islands.[34] Michael Mifsud, one of Gibraltar's most popular supporters in Britain, developed this line of thought in an interview broadcast on a popular radio station in London saying that, 'born of naturalised immigrants to a Crown Territory, Gibraltarians cannot be any different, by law, in status to any metropolitan Briton', and explaining that the word 'colonial' was repugnant and insufferable to Gibraltarians, since it went against the truth and 'our national heritage'.[35]

This was clearly a period of mixed feelings for Gibraltarians. While some doubted Britain's willingness and capacity to 'sustain and maintain' Gibraltar, others felt the Rock should not seek to 'go it alone', when Britain had 'always stood by us'.[36] Independence was generally not afforded much consideration in Gibraltar – not least because of the Treaty of Utrecht, which stated that Spain would get first preference should Britain decide to pull out of Gibraltar. In contrast, desires for independence were occasionally voiced in the Falkland Islands (even if they always remained a fringe view), perhaps as a result of almost two decades of frustrating relations with Britain. Where one might have expected Gibraltarians and Falkland Islanders to join forces – namely, the fight for British citizenship – there were hardly any references to one another in their respective discussions. Indeed, given the fact that both communities of besieged 'loyal' Britons had resorted, over the years, to the verities of Greater Britain, it might seem surprising that there was so little solidarity between them on this matter. As we shall see, this trend changed during the Falklands War. But perhaps the point here is that an attachment to Greater Britain was often accompanied by a mentality that was at once global and transnational, on the one hand, and parochial and provincial, on the other. In this particular case, it was clearly not expedient for Gibraltar to seek common cause with the Falklands, since, for very practical purposes, the Rock sought to make the case for British citizenship based on arguments that stemmed primarily from its geographical location, not from its place in the British family. However, they still emphasised their long-standing British connection, manifesting their loyalty and pro-British sentiments in a similar way to the Kelpers.

The citizenship battle came to a happy conclusion for Gibraltarians on 27 October 1981, when an amendment was passed, allowing them to avail of full British citizenship. The British Gibraltar Parliamentary Group – a ginger group not unlike the Falklands lobby – was acknowledged as having played a crucial role by threatening 'a massive Tory rebellion at the House of Commons'.[37] The news of the victory was received with great relief on the Rock. Hot on the heels of the announcement, Gibraltar's House of Assembly passed a motion rejoicing at the decision of Westminster, showing gratitude to the supporters of the Rock and expressing 'to the British Crown its reaffirmation of the loyalty and affection of the people of Gibraltar'.[38] Enthusiastic Gibraltarians called for the establishment of a 'Day of Britishness' on the anniversary of the citizenship victory.

But all was not well. Statements from the leaders of the main political parties reveal that this event did not bring about the restoration of an idyllic state of unadulterated Britishness. Far from it. Beneath the thin veneer of allegiance, could be sensed underlying anxieties about Gibraltar's future and the desire for a more distinctive Gibraltarian identity. In his account of these events, Chief Minister Sir Joshua Hassan, for one, did not omit to mention the 'severe British Government resistance' that had preceded the eventual victory in Westminster. For the leader of the Gibraltar Socialist Labour Party, Joe Bossano, this event had singled out the support for Gibraltar in Westminster as 'unique among the colonies', something that the Rock ought to exploit. Meanwhile, Peter Isola, leader of the right-of-centre DPBG, felt compelled to clarify that British nationality in no way eroded Gibraltarian identity, 'no more than British Nationality erodes the identity of the Welsh, the Scots or the people of the Channel Isles'. 'We have not fought for a place of refuge', he declared, 'we have fought against the erosion of our nationality and finally after 17 years we have regained our rightful status'. And finally, Robert Peliza, head of the Integration with Britain Party, argued, in an intriguing statement, that this had been the decolonisation of Gibraltarians; 'now', he added, 'we have to think very hard about decolonising the territory … Gibraltar is our home town and Britain is our nation'.[39]

This undercurrent of unease can also be gleaned from an interesting conversation that took place in the letters' pages of the *Gibraltar Chronicle* a few weeks after the nationality decision. Tagging this event as a 'Pyrrhic victory', the politician Cecil A. Isola worried that this new development would pave the way for an eventual repatriation of Gibraltarians into Britain. Tellingly, in order to bolster his case, he resorted to the lessons of European decolonisation in Africa:

> If recent history is anything to go by we shall have our 'exit visas' assured in 1983. What happened to the British Rhodesians, Tanganyikans, Kenyans, French colonies of North Africa and a host of other Europeans who preferred their 'home' status. Any exceptions to their enforced return?[40]

Clearly, Isola was expressing the concern – shared by others – that retaining full British citizenship would facilitate a potential negotiated agreement between Britain and Spain, whereby Gibraltarian 'Britons' would be repatriated to the United Kingdom. Isola was a member of the DPBG, and therefore not an opponent of Gibraltar's British link. Yet he was evidently coming at this question from a post-imperial perspective, which led him to question the value of clinging to British citizenship in the climate of the time.

Keen not to allow this perspective to mar one of the finest achievements of his tenure as Chief Minister, Joshua Hassan took it upon himself to make a swift response. His reply (deliberately or not) blatantly missed Isola's main point. Hassan argued that history had shown, particularly since 1969, that, 'obstinately, Gibraltarians … simply will not go away'. Of course, Isola had not argued that the Nationality Act would be an incentive for Gibraltarians to willingly move to Britain, but rather that it may be used against them in future negotiations, forcing them to abandon Gibraltar for their so-called 'home' in the United Kingdom. Hassan's response highlighted instead what he considered the *true* rationale behind the citizenship campaign, namely 'sentiment'. He cited at length a memorandum sent to the British government in October 1980, which stated that the wishes of Gibraltarians did not stem from a desire 'to achieve a practical gain', but rather 'primarily and essentially from the deep roots of our relationship'. The memorandum stressed the very close connections that inhabitants of the Rock had enjoyed with Britain for a very long time, and pointed out that, while depriving them of British citizenship 'would in no way weaken our resolve to remain linked with Britain', this deterioration of the British bond 'would be a matter of the utmost disappointment and regret to us all in Gibraltar'.[41] Here, very clearly, the memorandum – and, by extension, Hassan – was deploying a Greater British logic: this was a matter of respecting a family relationship that went back generations. And, while he accentuated Gibraltarians' undying loyalty, which would not be diminished even if Her Majesty's Government were to strip them of their legal Britishness, he also showed how this act would tarnish their attachment. Whether he was aware or not, this stress on sentiments of affinity echoed the cries of those stranded overseas Britons amid the turmoil of decolonisation, who mourned the distancing of their 'mother country'.

Yet Hassan's honeymoon period was not to last. In the midst of their rejoicing after the citizenship victory, the inhabitants of the Rock had a rude awakening when the United Kingdom formally announced that the Royal Naval Dockyard would close down in 1983. This decision had a clear air of finality about it. No consultation with Gibraltarian leaders had been carried out, apparently breaking the pledge made only a few months earlier.[42] The various political leaders reacted strongly against this decision, expressing grave concern. The Trades Council, moreover, called a walk-out among all unions in support of Bossano's motion against the closure of the dockyard.[43] A general sense of being let down by Britain pervaded the Rock.[44] The weekly *Vox* condemned this latest affair 'as a blow below the belt and a shocking breach of the commitment to us by the British Government'.[45]

This sense of foreboding trickled down to ordinary citizens. Lord Carrington reported to the Prime Minister that 'public concern was running high'.[46] One Briton living in Gibraltar, for instance, felt 'disgust and shame' at the manner in which this had been announced, contrasting the loyalty and brave efforts of the locals to guard their Britishness with this apparent flouting of the British sense of fair play – heretofore a sure marker of Britishness. In lamenting the loss of one of Britain's characteristic virtues, he was unwittingly echoing typical British settler sentiments.[47] That the Governor himself, in his Christmas message, felt the need to give reassurances to those who feared that this was all 'part of a plan to weaken Gibraltar's links with Britain' was perhaps a sign of the pervasiveness of this growing mistrust.[48]

Gibraltarians received the support of their friends in Britain, with the Conservative MP Michael Latham protesting in the Commons that this was 'not an honourable way in which to treat some of Her Majesty's most devoted and loyal subjects',[49] and Labour's John Silkin telling Gibraltarians at a mass rally in Gibraltar that 'problems of the people of Gibraltar, the existence of British Gibraltar, is as much a concern of the British Labour Party as if you lived in the shadows of Big Ben'.[50]

But the wounds inflicted by the dockyard bombshell were deep. At that very rally, Joe Bossano reminded Britain of its 'moral and political obligation' towards Gibraltar, which arose from past imperial policies and dynamics: 'Gibraltar depends on the defence economy because for two-and-half centuries it has suited the United Kingdom to have Gibraltar to assist it in its defence of its world-wide interests'. Whitehall's latest decision had had an unprecedented impact on Gibraltar, which had never had any 'doubt where we stood and who our friends were. For the first time in our history', Bossano protested, 'we are now in a position of being made to doubt the integrity and the meaningfulness of the pledges made by the Conservative Government in the UK'.[51] If the citizenship battle had witnessed meek complaints and assertive expressions of loyalty, this unexpected turn of events brought out more vocal accusations from the Rock, showing an increasingly fraying relationship. A major event on the other side of the planet only a few months later would once again throw this bond into convulsions.

'The days of doubt are over': The Falklands War

On a calm, sunny morning in early April 1982, the peacefulness of another loyal British community thousands of miles away was rudely disturbed by foreign armed forces. Argentina's military junta had ordered the invasion of the Falkland Islands only a few days earlier, and on 2 April, when Galtieri came out onto the balcony of the *Casa Rosada* presidential palace in Buenos Aires to greet the euphoric crowds, it all seemed like a fait accompli. The British response, as is well known, was swift and decisive and, within three weeks, the Task Force reached the South Atlantic and began the 'recovery' of the Islands. In Britain, feelings of dejection in the aftermath of the Argentine takeover were quickly replaced by the hopeful mood of a seemingly resurgent nation. This was accompanied by the growth of Greater British affections for the Kelpers in the United Kingdom. What had been until then a distant and unknown British colony had suddenly been shunted into the limelight by Galtieri.

Arguments to the effect that the Islanders were kith and kin who ought to be defended increasingly filled the public sphere. In Westminster, British politicians were reminded that the Islanders were 'British in stock and tradition', and that Britain had a 'moral duty, a political duty and every other kind of duty' to protect them.[52] Newspaper editorials called for the defence of 'our loyal subjects' as though 'it were the Isle of Wight which had been invaded'.[53] 'Ordinary people do care about their kith and kin', readers were told, because 'blood is thicker than water, even when the water involved is 8,000 miles of ocean'.[54] Members of the public wrote to the Falkland Islands

Office in London (closely linked with the Falklands lobby) in support of 'this small part of Britain'.[55] One notable letter expressed this Greater British sentiment very clearly: 'Britishness is also a state of mind, even over eight thousand miles your Britishness will enhance ours. Your loss will diminish us'.[56] Others vehemently opposed this viewpoint, claiming that this was an anachronistic mentality that did not fit in with Britain's reality in 1982. As the violence escalated in May and June, the Greater British paradigm became increasingly obscured by a more 'dominant imperial' memory of gunboats and conquest, conferring on the conflict an enduring imperial stigma.

In the wake of the Argentine invasion, given the jubilant reaction of the Spanish press, Thatcher feared that the Iberians would follow suit and attempt to recover Gibraltar. Despite assurances in a report stating that 'we have *no reason to believe* that there is an increased military threat to Gibraltar from the Spanish Government', the Prime Minister still felt uneasy. 'This is surprisingly like the Falkland Islands assessment before invasion. 1000 soldiers with a land boundary, no air-cover, etc', she scribbled at the bottom of a memo from the Foreign Office to No. 10.[57] In the end, these fears proved unfounded.

Gibraltar had, until then, not overtly associated its plight with that of the Falklands in any significant way. Now, this perceived act of aggression from Argentina provoked a flood tide of solidarity with the South Atlantic archipelago. Politicians drew parallels with their experience under General Franco's thumb, even if the government itself did not explicitly express its support for the Falklands until almost a month into the conflict.[58] When it did, donations were sent to the Falkland Islands Office, and the Gibraltar Victuallers' Association surpassed its fundraising target for the Falklands Task Force Fund.[59] Though this spirit of solidarity was triggered by a shared experience of hostile neighbours, it sometimes found deeper roots. *Vox*'s reporters waxed lyrical about the deep spiritual communion between the two besieged territories. 'There can hardly be a community in the free world', argued one piece, 'that is more conscious, or feels more deeply, the fate that befell the British Falkland Islanders ... than the Gibraltarian community', in part due to their resolve 'to remain British in a British territory'.[60] Another editorial highlighted the 'enormous similarities' between the two 'in the unwavering defence of all we hold so precious under our British heritage: freedom, life under law, and respect for the individual'. 'Few peoples', concluded the author, 'have as many similarities as the Falkland Islanders have with the Gibraltarians'.[61]

Beneath these proclamations of affinity, however, the connections drawn between the two disputes often showed a more mundane, parochial and self-interested side. Gibraltar – and, specifically, the Royal Naval Dockyard – played an important role in the war. Whitehall was keen, nonetheless, to 'avoid seeking – and, indeed, do what we can to avoid – publicity about Gibraltar's role in support of the task force', in order 'not to inflame Spanish attitudes'.[62] For the Gibraltarians, however, this was a unique opportunity to make a strong case in favour of saving the dockyard from its impending closure. One notable event was the refitting of the school cruise liner SS *Uganda* into a hospital ship in April. *Vox* reported the event with gusto:

> On Monday morning the transformed Uganda was ready and at 9 o'clock she was towed out of the dock to the strains of 'Rule Britannia' and 'Hearts of Oak' played over loud speakers from the ship turning in the harbour made for open sea preceeded [sic] by the Royal Fleet Auxiliary 'Olma'.[63]

This account underscored both the British trappings surrounding the whole event and implied Gibraltar's readiness to help the 'mother country' in need. For Joe Bossano, the Falklands crisis had 'provided practical proof of the British Government's mistaken Defence policy' threatening scores of dockyard workers on the Rock and in Britain.[64] Meanwhile, the Minister for Education, Major Frank Dellipiani, protested that 'in the same way as the Falklanders need military support, Gibraltar needs economic support to maintain its identity'.[65] And the Governor proudly noted that many would be convinced 'more than ever that Gibraltar will always rise to an occasion when called upon, as it has done so many times in the past'.[66]

These sentiments were joined by a growing relief and a renewed confidence in Britain as the war wore on. For the chairman of the Gibraltar branch of the European Movement, this signalled a new beginning:

> The days of doubt are over. Britain is showing that she is a force to be reckoned with, even at a time of temporary material weakness. Once again Gibraltar has been able to prove that we have a part to play in our common cause, as we have throughout her history, and as we shall in the future.[67]

In Gibraltar, Union Jacks were 'appearing on windows and balconies spontaneously'. This renewed embrace of Britishness reached its climax with the eventual British victory on 14 June 1982, when, after seventy-four days of conflict in the Falkland Islands, the Argentine Governor of the Malvinas signed the instrument of surrender. Britain's victory in the South Atlantic was hailed with great rejoicing on the Rock. Hassan immediately sent Mrs Thatcher a telegram of congratulation, and the main opposition party, the Democratic Party of British Gibraltar, commended 'Margaret Thatcher and her Government and indeed … the people of Britain for their staunchness in upholding British sovereign rights and wishes of the Falkland Islanders against unprovoked aggression'.[68]

But if the conflict had witnessed a re-flourishing of Greater British impulses, the aftermath of the war showed that these did not herald the full restoration of a past family bond. Rather, they seemed to be more like twitching nerves capable of shaping contemporary events. In Britain itself, despite Mrs Thatcher's declaration that, as a result of the war, Britain 'had ceased to be a nation in retreat' and had 'instead a newfound confidence', the Falklands had, in fact, polarised the country more than they had united a resurgent nation.[69] Over the ensuing years, the Falklands would continue to reappear in the national conversation, deployed by the Right as a tool to increase patriotic fervour, or by the Left as a device to upbraid their political opponents for perpetuating unfinished imperial business. In the Falklands, where one would have expected the British victory over Argentina to have finally assuaged all fears and healed all internal divisions, tensions continued to simmer beneath the surface. Islanders increasingly favoured accentuating their distinctiveness, given that a return to the colonial past was becoming more and more unthinkable, but they remained uneasy about their future.[70]

In the midst of all this, Gibraltar had not come away from the South Atlantic conflict unscathed. The role of the Foreign Office in the lead-up to the South Atlantic conflict – perceived as duplicitous – had raised suspicions about its intentions for Gibraltar, where faith in Britain's diplomats had suffered a severe blow.[71] In the aftermath of the war, questions about Gibraltar's own relationship with Britain resurfaced once again. It seemed clear that time was running out for Gibraltar's colonial status.

The very likely prospect of the reopening of the frontier gates over the following months (it had already been postponed twice because of the South Atlantic conflict), had aroused fears of an identity loss in Gibraltar, given the inevitable increase in contact with Spain and the 'lessening of the UK British presence in the form of the defence economy'. The solution, according to a *Gibraltar Chronicle* editorial, was to develop Gibraltar's own institutions and encourage more local involvement in political and social life, thus strengthening the 'Gibraltarian culture and society'. 'Gibraltar is different – our challenge is to keep it that way', concluded the piece.[72] This was not all that different to a trend of accentuating the distinctiveness of the local identity, which had begun in the Falklands some years before, and which would continue to grow after the war. This is no coincidence. Both colonies had traversed different but connected paths, and perhaps it was this latest intensification of the bonds of Greater Britain as a result of the South Atlantic conflict – bringing along with it a host of imperial memories of a different kind – which had made their attachment seem all the more obsolescent.

This theme of bringing Gibraltarian identity up to speed with the contemporary geopolitical reality of Europe in the 1980s was explored in different arenas. One prominent example of this was a leader in the *Gibraltar Chronicle* from mid-August 1982. The editor, Jon M. Searle, plumbed the depths of the

Rock's British connection, conscious of the territory's own challenges (not least the looming closure of the dockyard and its potential impact on the economy), plus the added uncertainty caused by the forthcoming Lisbon talks between Britain and Spain. 'Gibraltarians', argued Searle, 'are caught between the stable but dying fortress economy supported by the colonial power, Britain, and the uncertainties of developing new industries with which to support themselves'. This brought Gibraltarians face-to-face with the 'problem of finding an evolution from our colonial status', acceptable both to Britain and Spain. In light of this challenge, the citizenship victory seemed somewhat trivial to those who chose to remain in Gibraltar. In Searle's view, the answer was not independence – which he saw more as 'a cry from the heart' than as 'a reasoned solution' – but a condominium. Regardless of the merits of this proposal, it is very telling that Searle felt the urge, at this time, to sound a warning bell for Gibraltarians: 'We are awaking from our false dreams of security, we have done our share of hooting'.[73]

Another very prominent case was the farewell dinner speech of the outgoing Governor of Gibraltar, Sir William Jackson, on 29 September 1982. Enlightened by four years of tenure, Jackson now counselled going after a 'dominion status' of sorts. Not *full* dominion status, but a situation whereby 'the Rock would be on a par with the Channel Isles and the Isle of Man which are certainly not considered colonies'.[74] The re-emergence of this eagerness to distance Gibraltar from other colonies at this point is not insignificant, coming shortly after the Falklands War, during which such heartfelt fellow feeling with the Kelpers had been invoked by Gibraltarians. In a way, this trend suggests that those expressions of solidarity only a few months earlier were perhaps hollower than they had appeared to be.

Following a similar line of thought, for others, the logical progression for Gibraltar's status was full integration with Britain. One *Gibraltar Chronicle* reader even presented this as 'the decolonisation of Gibraltar'.[75] This unusual understanding of decolonisation might be construed as a clever and calculated strategy to wrongfoot those (particularly in Spain) who claimed that Gibraltar must be decolonised through a British exit from the territory – that was, indeed, how the dispute had been reignited at the United Nations in the 1960s. So, while it proposed a different course of action, this idea followed the same logic as the desire for Gibraltar to be treated more like the Channel Islands and less like other colonies. It was not merely a matter of geographical location. There was a growing realisation in the eyes of Gibraltar's leaders that it was becoming increasingly untenable for the Rock to keep its colonial status – a fact that had been brought to the limelight by the imperial dimensions of the Falklands War.

This growing uneasiness with the colonial relationship would be aggravated by a seemingly insignificant spat between the Gibraltar government and London. After two forced deferrals, 15 December was finally set as the agreed date for the reopening of the 'Garlic Wall' frontier gates. Since 1969, the gates had always remained open on the British side, closing only between 1 a.m. and 6 a.m. The idea was that they would now open on both sides (for pedestrian traffic only) and remain open for the entire day. Just days prior to the agreed date, however, the Gibraltar House of Assembly passed a motion to keep the gates closed during the usual five hours during the night. At this, British Foreign Minister Francis Pym intervened immediately, and Chief Minister Hassan had to relent. This last-minute intervention was perceived as heavy-handed by many in Gibraltar. The Chief Minister bemoaned this decision publicly in a televised statement: 'We are naturally very disappointed', he argued, 'that the British Government have taken a different view and we believe that our disappointment will be felt generally by the people of Gibraltar who expressed great support for the stand we took'.[76] Joe Bossano, meantime, decried it as a 'totally unacceptable exercise of colonial rule', arguing that it highlighted Gibraltar's 'colonial situation', since this was a matter for the people of Gibraltar to decide, not for 'a Government 2000 miles away'.[77] This was not to be the definitive reopening of the gates, however. Two more years would pass before normal links with Spain were restored. Yet the channels of communication between Gibraltar and Britain, while fully open, were increasingly coming under severe strain.

Conclusions: the legacies of Greater Britain

Both the Falklands and Gibraltar have evolved significantly since the 1980s. They have become more self-confident territories, as shown in the 2002 Gibraltar referendum – held unilaterally by the Gibraltar government, without British approval – and in the 2013 Falkland referendum, both of which produced overwhelming majorities in favour of retaining the status quo.[78] Their level of self-government and autonomy has increased, also economically. Both territories are affluent and, in many regards, less dependent on the UK state: the Falklands' economy has grown exponentially since the mid-1980s, with the development of the fisheries' industry, and more recently through oil exploration, while Gibraltar's has diversified thanks to its 'offshore tax status, as well as the development of VAT-free trading, tourism, bunkering, online gaming and acting as a hub for cruise liners'.[79]

The self-identification of Falkland Islanders and Gibraltarians has also evolved into a more complex form, which stresses distinctiveness and self-determination above loyalty and sameness, while still retaining a strong foundation of Britishness. It can be argued that both identities are a legacy of Greater Britain, both in terms of their origins and of their transformation over the decades. As the Gibraltarian Joseph Garcia described it, in the early 1980s, 'you could feel there existed in Gibraltar the embryo of what we could call Gibraltarian nationalism. A resistance to Spain, but also to old colonial Britain'.[80] Discerning the consequences of the events presented here on Gibraltar and the Falklands is a challenging task: to what extent did they signify a moment of reckoning, effecting profound changes? What long-term impact, if any, did they have on their sense of identity and belonging? A far more detailed study would be required to answer these questions in full. Here I will limit myself to making a few exploratory suggestions. No single event can explain these – subtle but real – transformations witnessed in the Falklands and Gibraltar. Viewed through the lens of Greater Britain, nevertheless, they reveal some interesting features.

For the Falklanders, the events in the run-up to the war were confirmation of British disinterest in their windswept colony. The war itself and Britain's victory in the South Atlantic, ushered in a new era in the Falklands – but not quite a return to a Greater British idyll. An emphasis on seeking a more distinct Falkland status, combined with a more independent economy – also one far less dominated by the Falkland Islands Company – and a changing demography, has given the Falklands a different complexion to the one it had pre-1982. In the case of Gibraltar, the nationality victory gave the British Gibraltar Group a massive confidence boost. Gibraltar's prominent role in the Falklands War, however, was not enough to prevent the eventual closure of the dockyard, as some had hoped. But this event, nonetheless, proved to be beneficial in the long term, as it forced Gibraltar to diversify its economy and be less dependent on the Royal Navy. It could be argued that the events of the early 1980s paved the way for the development of a more confident Gibraltarian identity in the decades to come.

The idea of Greater Britain, which had become almost entirely obsolete, still resonated in the context of the Falklands and Gibraltar in the early 1980s. This lingering purchase was limited and partial, and it had different hues in each territory. For decades, the Kelpers had played the 'kith-and-kin' card (often to great effect), while Gibraltarians had resorted to stressing loyalty, wartime contributions and a long-standing partnership with Britain, given their varied ethnic background. In both cases, their arguments had resonated among many in the United Kingdom, in no small part thanks to the relentless efforts of their respective lobby groups.

During the South Atlantic conflict, these revived Greater British impulses in the United Kingdom were eclipsed by an imperial memory of conquest, gunboats and glory. This accentuated political divisions within Britain – which were exacerbated in the aftermath – to the point where it became expedient to make the relationships with Gibraltar and the Falklands ostensibly less 'colonial'.

Both territories, in different ways, punched well above their weight in the 1980s. This would have been virtually unthinkable without the abiding allure of a 'British world' mentality, which had ensured over the years that any attempts to compromise on British sovereignty would be met with public outrage and stiff opposition in Parliament and in the media. The Falklands and Gibraltar indeed proved to be 'the mouse that roared' in Thatcher's Britain. Without due regard for the imperial dimensions of both disputes, their disproportionate impact cannot be fully understood.

Notes

1. Cited in *El País*, 4 April 1982.
2. *Gibraltar Chronicle*, 22 May 1982.
3. For a few recent examples in the British media, see: *Independent*, 2 April 2017; *New Statesman*, 26 January 2016; *The Week*, 27 January 2012.
4. *Gibraltar Chronicle*, 29 October 1981.
5. More developed arguments about the usefulness of studying political culture and rhetoric can be found in E. Mercau, *The Falklands War: An Imperial History* (Cambridge: Cambridge University Press, 2019), pp. 15–17.
6. P. Gold, *Gibraltar: British or Spanish?* (Oxon: Routledge, 2005), p. 1.
7. See, for instance, P. Gold, 'Identity Formation in Gibraltar: Geopolitical, Historical and Cultural Factors', *Geopolitics*, 15:2 (2010), pp. 367–384, at p. 371; S. Constantine, 'Monarchy and Constructing Identity in "British" Gibraltar, c. 1800 to the Present', *Journal of Imperial and Commonwealth History*, 34:1 (2006) pp. 23–44, at p. 37. For a different perspective, see G. Stockey, 'Us and Them: British and Gibraltarian Colonialism in the Campo de Gibraltar c. 1900–1954', in A. Canessa (ed.), *Bordering on Britishness: National Identity in Gibraltar from the Spanish Civil War to Brexit* (Cham: Springer International Publishing, 2019), p. 94; and, more generally, G. Stockey, *Gibraltar: 'A Dagger in the Spine of Spain'?* (Sussex: Sussex Academic Press, 2014).
8. Gold, 'Identity Formation in Gibraltar', p. 369. But, for a different perspective, see D. Lambert, '"As Solid as the Rock"? Place, Belonging and the Local Appropriation of Imperial Discourse in Gibraltar', *Transactions of the Institute of British Geographers*, 30:2 (2005), pp. 206–220, at p. 214.
9. For more on Gibraltar–Spanish relations, see Gold, *Gibraltar: British or Spanish?*, Chs 3–5.
10. For more on the 1960s and 1970s, see also: M. A. González, *The Genesis of the Falklands (Malvinas) Conflict* (Basingstoke: Palgrave Macmillan, 2014); A. Donaghy, *The British Government and the Falkland Islands, 1974–79* (Basingstoke: Palgrave Macmillan, 2014); Mercau, *Falklands War*.
11. Margaret Thatcher Foundation, Cambridge (THCR) ALW 040/325/12, Hunt to Carrington, 4.
12. See Mercau, *Falklands War*, pp. 61–66.

13　The UK National Archives (TNA) FCO 7/3981, Minutes of meeting: Ridley–UKFIC, 11 March 1981.
14　TNA FCO 7/3814, Frow to Sir Nigel Fisher, 28 August 1980, fol. 57.
15　*Falkland Islands Enquirer*, 23 October 1981.
16　TNA FCO 7/3981, Minutes of meeting: FCO–UKFIC, 14 October 1981, fol. 12.
17　*Penguin News*, 29 November 1981.
18　*Gibraltar Chronicle*, 28 January 1981. A few days later, the *Gibraltar Chronicle* reported that more than 8,000 signatures had been collected among the members of the public. *Gibraltar Chronicle*, 3 February 1981.
19　*Gibraltar Chronicle*, 20 June 1981.
20　*Gibraltar Chronicle*, 30 January 1981.
21　*Gibraltar Chronicle*, 11 April 1981. On the Falkland Islanders' references to this topic, see Mercau, *Falklands War*, pp. 26–27, 63–65.
22　House of Commons Debates [hereafter HC Deb] 2 June 1981 vol. 5, cols 879–882.
23　See, for instance, *Vox*, 16 August 1980; *Gibraltar Chronicle*, 10 June 1981.
24　See, for instance, *Gibraltar Chronicle*, 21 June 1981; *Gibraltar Chronicle*, 1 July 1981; *Gibraltar Chronicle*, 10 July 1981.
25　Gold, *Gibraltar: British or Spanish?*, p. 34.
26　*Gibraltar Chronicle*, 27 July 1981.
27　*Gibraltar Chronicle*, 3 August 1981.
28　*Vox*, 1 August 1981.
29　*Gibraltar Chronicle*, 27 July 1981.
30　Cited in *Gibraltar Chronicle*, 12 October 1981.
31　Cited in *Gibraltar Chronicle*, 7 December 1981.
32　Gold, *Gibraltar: British or Spanish?*, p. 32.
33　Originally published in *Sunday Times*, 18 October 1981; cited in *Gibraltar Chronicle*, 19 October 1981.
34　Letter to the editor, *Gibraltar Chronicle*, 15 August 1981.
35　*Gibraltar Chronicle*, 9 September 1981.
36　Letter to the editor, *Gibraltar Chronicle*, 23 September 1981; Letter to the editor, *Gibraltar Chronicle*, 25 September 1981.
37　*Gibraltar Chronicle*, 27 October 1981.
38　*Gibraltar Chronicle*, 28 October 1981.
39　*Gibraltar Chronicle*, 29 October 1981.
40　Letter to the editor, *Gibraltar Chronicle*, 20 November 1981.
41　Letter to the editor, *Gibraltar Chronicle*, 21 November 1981.
42　See TNA PREM 19/769, Armstrong to PM, 11 November 1981, fol. 51.
43　*Vox*, 19 December 1981.
44　See *Gibraltar Chronicle*, 24 November 1981; *Gibraltar Chronicle*, 25 November 1981.
45　*Vox*, 28 November 1981.
46　TNA PREM 19/769, Carrington to PM, 30 November 1981.
47　Letter to the editor, *Gibraltar Chronicle*, 27 November 1981.
48　*Gibraltar Chronicle*, 29 December 1981.
49　HC Deb 8 December 1981 vol. 14, col. 714.

50 *Gibraltar Chronicle*, 11 January 1982.
51 Ibid.
52 HC Deb 3 April 1982 vol. 21, col. 634, 638.
53 *Daily Express*, 3 April 1982.
54 *Sunday Telegraph*, 11 April 1982.
55 Imperial War Museum (IWM) Documents.3011/76/1154, Max Hull to FIO, 7 April 1982.
56 Imperial War Museum (IWM) Documents.3011/76/1154, Elizabeth Stacey to FIO, 14 April 1982.
57 TNA PREM 19/770, Holmes (FCO) to Coles (No. 10), 5 April 1982, fol. 166.
58 *Gibraltar Chronicle*, 30 April 1982; *Vox*, 1 May 1982.
59 *Gibraltar Chronicle*, 10 May 1982; *Gibraltar Chronicle*, 8 June 1982.
60 *Vox*, 17 April 1982.
61 *Vox*, 15 May 1982.
62 TNA PREM 19/770, Richards to Coles, 8 April 1982, fol. 154.
63 *Vox*, 24 April 1982.
64 *Gibraltar Chronicle*, 7 April 1982. The British Gibraltar Group decided to take this line of action also: *Gibraltar Chronicle*, 14 April 1982.
65 *Gibraltar Chronicle*, 4 May 1982.
66 Cited in *Gibraltar Chronicle*, 24 April 1982.
67 *Gibraltar Chronicle*, 18 May 1982.
68 *Gibraltar Chronicle*, 16 June 1982.
69 THCR 1/17/94, MT speech at Conservative rally (Cheltenham), 3 July 1982.
70 See Mercau, *Falklands War*, p. 172.
71 *Vox*, 24 April 1982. See also *Gibraltar Chronicle*, 8 July 1982.
72 *Gibraltar Chronicle*, 29 May 1982.
73 *Gibraltar Chronicle*, 14 August 1982.
74 *Gibraltar Chronicle*, 1 October 1982.
75 Letter to the editor, *Gibraltar Chronicle*, 28 May 1982. Interestingly, in more recent years, in an attempt to distance themselves from the colonial stigma, Gibraltarian leaders have spoken of the 'decolonisation' of Gibraltar as a fait accompli. Stockey, 'Us and Them', p. 94.
76 TNA PREM 19/1038, Williams to FCO, 14 December 1982, fol. 238.
77 *Gibraltar Chronicle*, 15 December 1982.
78 See Gold, 'Identity Formation in Gibraltar', p. 372.
79 Gold, 'Identity Formation in Gibraltar', p. 373. On the Falklands, see Mercau, *Falklands War*, pp. 177–180.
80 J. J. Garcia, *Gibraltar: The Making of a People* (Gibraltar: MedSun, 1994). See also, Lambert, 'As Solid as the Rock'.

14

Falling Rhodes, building bridges, finding paths: decoloniality from Cape Town to Oxford, and back

Stephen Howe

Ideas of intellectual decolonisation are, one might venture, as old and as diverse as are empires and colonialism themselves. Certainly, calls for political transfers of power to be accompanied by intellectual transformations, decolonisation of minds, have been a major part of modern anti-colonial thought everywhere it has manifested itself.

For most of the modern era, such projects of intellectual transformation took place largely outside the institutions of formal, state-sponsored education: schools, colleges, and universities. They were undertaken by independent public intellectuals, whether these were politicians or poets; by discussion groups, journals and publishing houses, research centres, or political formations either not linked to the university system, or occasionally existing uneasily, informally, even semi-secretly within it. Good examples might include *Présence Africaine* in Paris or the New World group in the Caribbean. Where the protagonists were university teachers or students, although they were of course likely to be very critical of existing power structures and regimes of knowledge, and regard the institution as a site for political struggle, this was rarely their main concern; their ambitions were broader and bolder. In the 'golden age' of student protest, generally thought to have been in the late 1960s, transformations in universities themselves were generally, at most, a secondary object; the activists had grander ambitions of total social change. True, in the United States especially, students in many institutions were in that era calling for more localised kinds of change, especially for provision of Black Studies (and in some cases other ethnic minority studies or departments), and for increased recruitment of African-American and other minority students and faculty. It may be noted that these calls were primarily for *additive* kinds of change rather than wholly transformative ones.

In the very recent past, the picture has been quite radically altered. The notion of decolonising the university itself has taken centre stage in several countries, as well as in transnational networks of debate and of activism. In this contribution, I do not of course attempt to sketch a history of these movements, in the United Kingdom itself, in the anglophone world, or more globally. Rather, I seek to indicate some major features of the dominant discourses in these developments, and to suggest both the potential and the problems inherent in these. In particular, I interrogate uses of the word and concept decolonisation itself, and that of decoloniality. An original intention of this chapter was – in line with the focus of the volume as a whole – to discuss relevant debates as 'Anglospheric' phenomena, discussing interlinked debates across multiple territories of what some once called Greater Britain. However, although there have been shared themes and mutual influences among British, South African, North American, Australian and other English-language sites of dispute over imperial legacies and decoloniality, such interconnections have been perhaps just as salient across Europe, all over Africa, to and from Latin America, and more. The divergent paths of 'colonial legacies' debates in different Anglophone spheres, plus the corresponding renaissance of pan-European, pan-African and near-global ones, are themselves further evidence of a 'break-up of Greater Britain'. Thus, for example, Australia's 'history wars', since their initiation by Keith Windschuttle around 2000, developed mostly in isolation from any other, potentially partly parallel, Anglospheric arguments. Therefore, this chapter engages mainly with bilateral British–South African inter-influences plus briefer invocation of those from the United States.

There are, it should immediately be noted, some methodological problems associated with this task. These were well summarised by Saul Dubow:

> African and international echoes of the Fallist campaigns have to be unpicked very carefully. Tracing the circuits of knowledge around Fallism and decoloniality is perilously difficult, but they are becoming clearer as participants reflect on this moment in books and memoirs. These concepts are not necessarily subject to the same kinds of logic that we might apply to other historical ideas, partly because questioning is apt to be couched in the language of identity politics such as positionality, gender, race and power.[1]

The warning is certainly apt in relation to the decolonial idea, which has moved with remarkable speed from referring to a fairly specialist if not esoteric body of mainly Latin American thought, to becoming a globally resonant slogan. The central thrust of much of this thought is to urge the necessity for a decolonisation of knowledge more far-reaching than anything achieved by existing critical projects. This involves, inter alia, dismantling the seemingly inextricable bond forged long ago between modernity and 'coloniality', and uncovering the multiple ways in which a coloniality of being and thinking persists far beyond and long after the apparent ends of colonialism's political forms. It insists that history is not linear and singular but multiple, containing always innumerable simultaneous projects and possibilities, and espousing a 'transmodern' world vision that links together various sites of colonised conditions and consciousness around the globe. For some of those concerned, deconstructionist methods and/or postmodernist claims necessarily implied a profound critique of ethnocentrism and thus of imperialism, in that they undermined the formative intellectual self-images of the West. A bit earlier, related assertions were advanced for existentialism, and for surrealism, and also among the fascinating new maps of recent intellectual history now being developed one might here add ones about existentialism's impact among Arab intellectuals, recently studied by Yoav Di Capua, or surrealism's in the Caribbean.[2]

If the more ambient, and more specifically intellectual, backdrop to current calls for the transformation of universities is the decolonial idea, the more immediate and more directly political impetus is summarised in two catchphrases: Rhodes Must Fall and Black Lives Matter. Again, there is no intention here of summarising the eventful global lives of these two tags. A few 'signposts' must suffice.

South Africa's 'Rhodes Must Fall' battles started in early 2015, with student demands for the removal of a huge bronze statue of Cecil John Rhodes which had adorned the University of Cape Town (UCT) campus. Protest and direct action soon spread to other South African universities – though mainly the historically elite, white, Anglophone ones – with the focus on other aspects of their public symbolism, such as UCT's art collections, and on a broader decolonial agenda. The movement was soon followed by and intertwined with a second protest campaign, #FeesMustFall, from September 2015 onwards, which centred on the prohibitive costs of higher education. The twin struggles involved episodes of serious personal violence and injuries (perpetrated both by some protestors and by police and campus security), the destruction of buildings, and burning or censoring artworks. But it also involved serious and intense debates among students and others not only about issues of 'race', but also ones of gender, social class, language and political philosophy. And it rapidly generated a substantial critical literature, some of it purely agitational but much of it of an indubitably high intellectual level.[3]

British student decolonial initiatives began several months after the South African ones, near the end of 2015, and were in part inspired by them and by some South African students studying in the United Kingdom. There too Cecil Rhodes was an initial focus, with demands for the removal of his statue at Oriel College Oxford. This, though, was argued to be just part of a more general and long overdue decolonisation of Oxford University; on 9 March 2016 students in Oxford held a 'Mass March for Decolonisation' as part of the wider campaign. As in South Africa, the movement rapidly spread to numerous other universities, with varying degrees of intensity. In Britain too, it began to address more specifically academic and intellectual concerns, including ones of university curricula and research. However, these British developments have not apparently thus far (as of September 2020) stimulated intellectual debate of a scale, weight and seriousness parallel to those in South Africa.[4]

Again Oxford – plus interventions from Cambridge – was something of a flashpoint. The focus was especially *Ethics and Empire*, a five-year interdisciplinary project led by theologian Nigel Biggar and (initially) imperial historian John Darwin, and held under the auspices of Biggar's McDonald Centre.[5] Its aims were stated to be, via an investigation of historical debates over the ethics of empire, to develop 'a nuanced and historically intelligent Christian ethic of empire' and thus enable a 'morally sophisticated negotiation of contemporary issues such as military intervention for humanitarian purposes in culturally foreign states, the cohesion of multicultural societies, and settling imperial pasts'.[6] Biggar meanwhile had already begun, and was to continue, to make polemical interventions on a range of related issues including the Rhodes Must Fall campaign, in a variety of mostly conservative media outlets. These included repeated claims that a one-sidedly leftist, morally condemnatory, view of imperial and colonial histories had become the imposed orthodoxy across vast swathes of the academic world, including relevant Oxford seminars and courses, with differing views silenced, excluded, even intimidated.[7]

Reactions from many of Biggar's Oxford colleagues, and from scholars of imperial and colonial studies elsewhere, were very negative. On 19 December 2017 a group of Oxford academics published an open letter, sharply criticising the project on both scholarly and political grounds. They were joined three days later with a letter signed by more than 170 international academics and offering a similar critique. An Oxford anti-racist student group, Common Ground, expressed itself yet more sharply: 'The proud announcement of this project, following on the heels of Biggar's article, reflects a university that has shown itself to be singularly incapable of reckoning with its colonial past'.[8] It should however perhaps be stressed that, contrary to Biggar's claims, none of these collective statements demanded the suppression or censorship of the project or of his views; though one individual contributor to the controversy, Cambridge's Priyamvada Gopal, did appear to make such a call. Meanwhile Oxford's Chancellor Chris Patten claimed that the demand to remove the Rhodes statue was part of a general attack on free speech. He urged campaigners to read Karl Popper's *The Open Society and Its Enemies*, 'the most important book for any undergraduate', and if they still felt unable to embrace British traditions of toleration and fair play, then they should consider being educated elsewhere.[9]

After a period of relative quiescence, the Oxford and other British campaigns were revitalised in 2019–20, now stimulated by developments far from academia, and far from the island shores. A series of clearly unjustifiable police killings of African Americans, plus renewed calls for the removal of Confederate and other monuments linked with the legacies of slavery or racism, prompted the movement Black Lives Matter in the United States. This too spawned sister movements in Britain and several other countries, including campaigns for the removal of statues and other memorials commemorating morally compromised historical figures, not least our old acquaintance Cecil Rhodes. And now, in contrast to the previous round, Oriel College announced that it would accede to the demand for removal of the statue.

Surely far more important than rows over statues or other symbols and *lieux de mémoire*, in the longer term and especially for those concerned with furthering intellectual enquiry, is the overarching or underlying thematic of both decoloniality and Fallism: that universities confront the structural and epistemological legacy of colonialism. Here, questions both sharply pointed and profound are posed about the very nature of knowledge and its pursuit in higher education. But are they well posed, in the current movements and debates, and likely to lead to enlightening answers? What follows here will suggest some grounds for scepticism, albeit from a standpoint of strong sympathy and solidarity with (most of) the declared aims of the insurrectionary movements concerned, and in the conviction that conceptual clarity is as desirable and helpful for activists as for analysts.

My aim is therefore (paraphrasing Jonathan Jansen, to whose recent writings my debt here is very great) to interrogate the 'politics of knowledge' – especially but not only the relationship between knowledge-claims and power relations, or claims to authority – involved in the academic decolonisation movements. It seems, as intimated earlier, apt to begin with the idea of decolonisation itself. The word has all too often been used by recent protestors and others, in South Africa, the United Kingdom, and elsewhere, as if its meaning were both self-evident and all-embracing. Yet it is surely far indeed from being so.

The word 'decolonisation' does not have a very long history but does have a rich and complex one.[10] Dominant early uses, mainly from the 1950s onward, meant mainly elimination of formal colonial rule (usually as exercised by European powers) from occupied lands. It was thus effectively synonymous with a transfer of political power or sovereignty. Perhaps the closest direct equivalent in twenty-first-century university systems might thus lie in the old 1960s slogan of 'Student Power!' But it was soon broadened, usually with the addition of a qualifying adjective, to involve also shifts in or claims to economic, strategic, cultural, and (our main concern here) intellectual power relations: legacies of colonialism which, it was said, remained pervasive well after the transfers of sovereignties. Terms like neo-colonialism, semi-colonialism, or informal empire were (especially the first) widely invoked. It is intriguing that none of these seems to have been much used by our post-2015 movements. Also intriguing, in the South African context, is that the now-ubiquitous term decolonisation does not have an especially important history there. Although the African National Congress, following the lead of the South African Communist Party, influentially analysed apartheid as a 'colonialism of a special type', the language of struggle against apartheid or in its immediate aftermath – in the university world as elsewhere – did not speak much of 'decolonisation' but far more of 'anti-apartheid education', 'education for liberation', and most of all simply 'transformation'. One unwelcome consequence of the current pervasiveness of the language of decolonisation may be that, as several South African critics have remarked, the specificities of the apartheid legacy are unhelpfully bundled together with those of colonialism, of racism, and of multiple sorts of 'foreign' intellectual influence.

As that last allusion implies, there is also a real danger that insufficiently critical or too indiscriminate uses of the idea of intellectual decolonisation may result in a retreat into a kind of parochialism or nativism: a rejection, in the name of intellectual independence, of all ideas originating from formerly colonising places, from Europe, from (in the South African case) anywhere outside Africa, or most crudely just from white people, simply because they are 'foreign'. The disturbing, sometimes violent, manifestations of xenophobia, victimising mostly migrants from elsewhere in Africa, not anyone who could be regarded as representing a former oppressor, may find here their intellectual equivalents. It is disconcerting to say the least to find some South African proponents of decoloniality – though certainly not all or even most of them – offering genealogies of the idea consisting only of thinkers of African descent and ignoring its Latin American and other roots. At worst, one finds in some circles (including, in this writer's observation, some current 'decolonising' student ones) all too much credulity towards the clearly unsustainable claims made for ancient African scientific knowledges by some mostly US-based Afrocentric thinkers, or the closely parallel ones advanced by certain Indian writers of the Hindutva persuasion. Sometimes, alongside this, one finds the notion that 'Western' thought not only makes false claims to be universal, rational and scientific but is inherently debilitating in its atomism, splitting knowledge into fragments, dividing reason from emotion, subject from object, body from mind and spirit, wrongly privileging a disembodied reason over emotion and bodily being. It is, in a word, cold, whereas African – or Native American, Indian, etc. – thought is warm. Here one finds some of the most sweeping and dubious early pronouncements of the *négritude* school revivified. When decolonial theorist Anibal Quijano calls for us 'to liberate the production of knowledge ... from the pitfalls of human rationality', and to achieve in pursuit of knowledge 'the liberation from all power organised as inequality, discrimination, exploitation, and as domination' we are surely moved to ask whether the first objective is at all desirable, and the second humanly attainable.[11]

Such intellectual nativism is all the more depressing, when one encounters it in light of the indisputable global entanglement of current thinking about intellectual decolonisation, in both scholarly and more agitational veins. To single out just a few names among many, one might mention current and recent work by Amy Allen, Claude Alvares, Marta Araujo, Akeel Bilgrami, Patrick Chabal, John and Jean Comaroff, Raewyn Connell, Jack Goody, Qadri Ismail, Achille Mbembe and Chela Sandoval here, as well as the whole current of decolonial thought put forward by theorists such as Anibal Quijano, Ramon Grosfoguel, Enrique Dussel, Walter Mignolo and Arturo Escobar.[12] We may, as enthusiasts urge, be witnessing indeed something of a redrawing of the global intellectual map; a shift which started during the moment of political decolonisation but is today much expanded and intensified.

For the stories from within Europe's intellectual traditions, here too rediscovery and reconnection are in the air. A few voices had for decades cried out for more attention to how Europe's intellectual history and canonical thinkers were far more heavily shaped by the colonial experience, and indeed by ideas about race, than is usually recalled. They were mainly voices from the ranks of the colonised, but have included some of European origin, as with Robert Young's pioneering if contentious *White Mythologies*.[13] Now, though, we witness a small flood of such work. Again to pluck out just a few instances, one might cite Susan Buck-Morss's *Hegel, Haiti and Universal History*, and the debates it engendered, Paige Arthur's fine study of Jean-Paul Sartre and decolonisation, Richard Wolin on French Maoism, George Steinmetz and his collaborators on colonialism and sociology, or Christoph Kalter's *Die Entdeckung der Dritten Welt*, which is perhaps the most detailed study of French or European Third Worldist thought yet to appear.[14] Very little of all this seems to be referenced in current South African, or British, controversies.

A problem which is perhaps more fundamental still is the sheer multiplicity of ways in which the discourse of decolonisation and/or decoloniality has recently been deployed in relation to education, or even specifically to university curricula. Do advocates propose the *replacement* of 'Western' knowledges by others, or rather their *supplementation* or augmentation? Is the *decentring* of 'European' thought intended, so that other centres are given due weight while also recognising and exploring that none of them is or ever was freestanding, but always entangled and cross-fertilising? Or is it rather the Africanisation, Indianisation, etc. of knowledge which is demanded, with all the attendant dangers, again, of gross intellectual parochialism? Should a main focus be on engagement with and critique of the power relations that underpin what is considered to be knowledge? And more mundanely but very practically, if the broader and more inclusive alternatives are the aim – as presumably most thoughtful participants would prefer – then how could any curriculum in any subject simply find time for it all? And where can the relevant teaching, research and curriculum design expertise be found, especially in a case like South Africa where the gross inadequacy of school-level public education, past and present, has meant that the pool of available proficiencies is uncomfortably small and, still, racially skewed?

We must take note of yet further difficulties. For instance, too often Fallist and decolonial rhetoric has misrepresented 'Western' knowledge as being in some sense a monolith; as if every question and challenge raised by the campaigners had not been hotly, often repeatedly debated within European intellectual traditions for centuries – as of course they have also been in others, though some have evidently done so in more elaborate and systematic ways than others.[15] Even in mathematics and the 'hard' natural sciences, multiple vigorous debates over their philosophy and methods have repeatedly belied the image of 'European science' as positivist and (falsely) universalist and exclusionary, though unsurprisingly these remain the fields where the very meaning or possibility of intellectual decolonisation is most often doubted.

Moreover, it is hard not to be perturbed by the extent to which relevant debates have thus far been conducted overwhelmingly in the language of negative critique, at the expense of proposing substantive, positive 'new' knowledge; or put differently, it has been about the past (too often, as we have suggested, a notably oversimplified vision of the past) and its continuing legacies, with too little to say about possible futures. No doubt these are inescapable traits of what has after all been thus far mainly a moment of protest – one which is both still very new and largely composed of students and other very young people. Yet it may also reflect more enduring deficiencies in much anti-colonial and postcolonial thought, whatever the ages either of the movements or of the individuals concerned. The problem was vigorously stated some while back by Hisham Sharabi in the very different, though far from unrelated, context of contemporary Arab thought:

> [T]he radical critics should be regarded more as *methodologists* than as *theoreticians*, for they have engaged more in promoting a critical approach than in devising an original theory. Thus the radical critique derives its effectiveness not so much from discovery as from acquired modes of analysis and interpretation. And so the Arab writers and scholars engaged in the new cultural criticism may be termed second-degree critics, for none of them can be properly regarded as a truly *creative* or *original* historian, philosopher, sociologist, or literary critic. Even their most advanced output is still largely negative ... [and therefore] represents only a first stage of autonomous self-consciousness.[16]

The litany of shortcomings thus far identified in decolonial-Fallist discourse could naturally, if ungenerously, be much further extended. Indeed, some of the most elementary faults have not yet been mentioned, though they are to be found only in some, perhaps ephemeral, parts or manifestations of the movements concerned. If debates over academic knowledge systems have, as noted, varied or been imprecise over whether what is desired is mainly supplementation, replacement, or re-contextualising reconfiguration, those over statuary, public arts and symbols have been simpler, perhaps cruder: removal of the old and tainted, *perhaps* replacement by something 'better' and more congruent with contemporary sensibilities. Another strand of Fallism has seemed to place its main emphasis on *who* should be teaching and learning, rather than, or more than, on what, how, and why. Calls for more black and minority students, teachers and researchers, especially in old and elite institutions such as Oxford or Cape Town, are of course neither unimportant nor unworthy. But they do not at all engage either with the substance of 'knowledge-regimes' or the question of how these are constituted, as the decolonial idea has always undertaken to do. It is thus no surprise that some institutional responses, up to the time of writing, have been limited, defensive, superficial or even tokenistic: draft in a few more non-white bodies, add a few new courses on non-North Atlantic history or philosophy, remove a statue or painting. When the prestigious American Historical Review, in January 2018, announced that it was 'decolonising' itself, it seemingly meant only or mainly a little more ethnic diversity in its review coverage and editorial board.[17]

In sum, then, and as Jonathan Jansen has (again) urged with particular force and clarity:

> [T]o speak about decolonisation requires one to be precise with respect to the context of usage – 'where', 'when' and 'what' questions are required. Colonialism was only one influence on knowledge and curriculum. It follows that to label every institutional problem as in need of decolonisation is to render the word impotent whether for purposes of analysis (what is going on?) or progressive action (what is to be done?). It is, moreover, to deny the complexity of power and authority that shaped, and continues to shape, what counts as knowledge.[18]

Let us now return from such very broad questions of power-knowledge to the more delimited spheres of colonial and imperial studies, and of representations of imperial pasts and their remnants. I wish here to address three main questions: the role – present and potential – of decolonial thought in relation to these, the place of moral judgement within them, and finally their relation to notions of academic freedom and of civility.

I cannot here offer either a general survey or a substantive critique of the decolonial project, which has, as we've noted, latterly been taken up (though more in rhetoric than in substance[19]) in many and diverse places. It certainly offers a bold and politically challenging alternative to a North Atlantic postcolonialism that is now widely seen as having reached a point of critical exhaustion. Yet one may register preliminary doubts over how effectively it might 'travel' beyond its Latin American points of origin, despite Mignolo's and others' strong claims for transverse relations among Latin, Muslim and other sites of (de)colonial domination. Its main intellectual points of reference seem to remain, so far, very specific to the southern Americas and – ironically – to western Europe. No reader of Edward Said will need convincing of the point that 'travelling theories' often, perhaps inevitably, become distorted and run the risk of being disarmed during their migrations. That certainly seems to me to be the case in some recent appropriations of Indian, African, Middle Eastern and other postcolonial debates by scholars in other locations. It remains to be seen whether decolonial thinking can escape that fate or move beyond the faults it shares with an earlier postcolonialism: excessive abstraction, rampant culturalism and/or textualism, and the ready propensity to indulge in sweeping global 'everything is colonial' rhetoric. There may too often already be tendencies for the notion of the coloniality of knowledge to reproduce earlier postcolonial studies' too exclusive focus on a knowledge–power nexus, deriving of course above all from Foucault and, more directly, from Said's *Orientalism* and Bernard Cohn's essays on colonialism's 'forms of knowledge', to the neglect of relations between interest and power. Equally, decolonial thought's ideas of the coloniality of power may reprise or intensify the sorts of excessively sweeping claims well encapsulated some decades back by Timothy Mitchell, whereby:

> Colonising refers not simply to the establishing of a European presence but also to the spread of a political order that inscribes in the social world a new conception of space, new forms of personhood, and a new means of manufacturing the experience of the real.[20]

On all these counts there may seem to be all too many, all too good reasons for historians of empires and colonialisms, especially those of a more empiricist or positivist bent, to wonder whether contemporary decolonial thought – or *any* of the intellectual currents I have alluded to so far – can actually speak to their concerns at all, and whether there is any common ground or basis for dialogue. There may be a readily understandable urge to dismiss the 'decolonial moment' as simply not engaging with properly historical thinking, just as was rather widely, and again often understandably, done with the earlier moment of postcolonial theory. Indeed Saul Dubow seems to imply as much when he suggests that:

> Try as one might, it is very difficult to scrutinize coloniality in the same way that historians have looked at concepts like colonialism, imperialism and decolonization, namely, as objects of investigation with more or less recognized temporal and spatial boundaries, with discernible and contestable political logics, and as discursive practices inviting rigorous textual readings ... There seems to be a profoundly existential aspect to the idea of coloniality that is unimpressed by and indeed resistant to historical analysis.[21]

To make things just a little worse still, some deployments of the idea of the decolonial have in my view been quite startlingly, even disturbingly, subject to a 'bad' politicisation. That is, they have used the rhetoric of intellectual decolonisation in a way that is crudely, even emptily, rhetorical and is, moreover, pressed into the service of some questionable political ideas. Claiming this does not, should it need saying, mean to imply some total separation or hierarchical relation between pristinely scholarly and vulgarly populist uses of decoloniality or ideas about 'decolonising the mind'. Indeed, some rather renowned scholars engaged in these debates have recently exhibited some pretty stark declarations too. The unreliably reported opening words of one such foray by Slavoj Žižek may suggest what I mean here. They were (with apologies to anyone this might offend!) 'F*** You Walter Mignolo!' Some other contributions to those particular exchanges, by holders of equally distinguished Chairs, were on a somewhat similar level.[22]

However, it is in Paris far more than in Žižek's Ljubljana, in London or New York – and at least as much as in Cape Town – that the decolonial concept has recently been brought directly, and with a fairly high profile, into the political arena. Here I have especially in mind the rhetoric and programme of the *Parti des Indigènes de la République* (PIR) and its most prominent spokespeople, Houria Bouteldja and Sadri Khiara. The PIR came to wide attention for their fierce critiques of France's, and especially the French left's, republicanism, supposed false universalism, secularism and alleged racism, especially following the Charlie Hebdo attacks in 2015. As Bouteldja, especially, has repeatedly proclaimed, those critiques are launched from a base in the decolonial idea, conceived of as radical, total emancipation from all European and Eurocentric thought. It is a stance also dependent on seeing the position of ethnic minorities in France today as being fully and directly subject to colonialism.[23] Incidentally Andrew Hussey's book *The French Intifada*, the most substantial analysis of such developments yet to have appeared in English, follows the PIR in this.[24] Once again, I cannot here offer even the beginning of a full critique of the ideas concerned. I can only, summarily and no doubt provocatively, register the view that PIR's politics involve a narrow and stark identitarianism, a crude, essentialist and ahistorical culturalism, seemingly growing complicity with anti-semitism, and also increasing complicity or alliance both with political Islamism and with the extreme right in France. This is decolonial thought reduced to the lowest common denominator of all its varied strands.

A pervasive and, in this writer's view, largely debilitating, feature of much recent debate on modern empires and their legacies is what must be described as a new moralistic tone. This was well exemplified in the arguments over Biggar's 'Ethics and Empire' project. Many of us who have taught in relevant fields have long been accustomed to urging on our students that a question such as 'Was (the British) Empire morally a Good or Bad Thing?' is neither a properly historical problem, nor one ever answerable at such a level of generality. It is thus unsatisfactory in the extreme to begin historical investigation with a presumption of empire's inherent and universal evil, and then proceed merely by deploring its villainies and celebrating the virtuous minorities, including those within Britain, who opposed these – as is done for instance by Priyamvada Gopal.[25] The impetus towards an ethical accounting of the history of the British Empire cannot, however, be dismissed entirely. Any historian, and any public intellectual, with any ambition must surely be driven in some large part by the desire to understand totality including the sources of ethical ideas – the promise to do so forms, for instance, a large part of the appeal of Marxism. And anyone with a social or political consciousness who is also a scholar must surely wish to find an ethical purpose in their work.

So, how might we seek to arrive at an analytical understanding of the British Empire which would go at least some way towards meeting the demands for comprehensiveness – in this sense of some elementary understanding of the phenomenon as a totality – and also for moral-political meaning? Even beginning to answer that question naturally depends on a belief that the empire was on some level an entity with enough coherence or unity across space and time to be discussed and perhaps evaluated as an entity. Some – in ways I have explored elsewhere – strongly doubt whether this can even in principle be done.[26] Still more doubtful in many minds is whether the empire may be said to have had a purpose, an underlying logic, whether consciously willed or otherwise. The belief that it did indeed have such a thing, some overarching meaning, is a point on which the great early, largely approving, historians of empire have found a surprising concurrence with much more recent radical, self-proclaimedly anti-racist and anti-imperialist, scholars.

Perhaps the most ambitious, and in some respects still most analytically powerful, attempts to discern such an underlying logic have been Marxist ones. But the boldest, not to say some of the most strident, recent efforts have found the coherence, the purpose, to lie not in economics and social class but in race. Can we, should we, either bring these perspectives together in some unifying analytical frame or meaningfully choose between them? Here there is an intriguing parallel with the dilemmas posed for the history of Nazi Germany by the work of Timothy Mason. It is also in some ways a disturbing parallel. Disturbing because Mason finally believed that such an achievement was beyond him, and the resulting sense of failure is widely believed among those who knew him to have contributed to his sadly early death.[27]

The dominant, and in some respects inescapable, perception of Nazi Germany – with which Mason wrestled, finding here a moral and emotional as well as intellectual challenge – is that the logic of biological racism formed its goal and meaning. Is there any plausibility in saying the same of the British Empire? Most attempts to do so thus far have been frankly little more than mere assertions, however strident, or have traced the logic of racism in very particular, often rather small, times and places. Might we however find promising starting points in the ambitious if often elliptical writings of Sylvia Wynter (who may aptly be seen as an underacknowledged precursor of much decolonial thought), or the somewhat related more recent efforts of David Marriott, Achille Mbembe or, more local in their focus, of Deborah Thomas?[28] All focus on anti-black racism, framed in wider concepts of biopolitics, necropolitics, conceptions of the human. Applications of such frameworks specifically to British imperialism and its thought may indeed be promising. Yet any comparisons with Nazi Germany surely falter or collapse unless it could be shown that a racial logic of empire was not only hugely powerful and determining but incipiently, implicitly and frequently in actual practice genocidal. Hitler's 1939–1945 Greater Germany is often, near-routinely, described as a 'racial empire'. Might the same label aptly be applied to British global power? This too has indeed sometimes been asserted, especially in some very recent writing. But, for reasons which cannot fully be explored here, I do not find it convincing.

Even wider issues also arise in all these disputes over how to study empire, or indeed whether and how that study itself requires decolonisation. They include claims to universalism as against cultural or religious particularisms; support for supposedly common (or, others say, specifically Enlightenment, Western or European-derived) values such as democracy and human rights as against support for national liberation movements or embattled subaltern identities, including religious ones other than the Judaeo-Christian; rationalism against nationalism and/or faith. Central to much of this contestation has always, but now ever more, been the 'Question of Islam', and almost startlingly often the 'Question of Israel and Palestine', which has of course recently come ever more to be discussed using the language of colonialism,

Falling Rhodes, building bridges, finding paths 307

and/or specifically settler colonialism, in both analytical, and intensely polemical ways. Often inextricably intertwined with all these have been ideas about colonial legacies, persistencies and renewals, claims about 'civilisation' and the more-than-etymologically linked notion of 'civility', and about intellectual and, more narrowly academic, freedom, and more.

A striking case in point is that of Palestinian-American scholar Steven Salaita. He came to be at the heart of a bitter, globally publicised battle over his being first offered, then ejected from, a post at the University of Illinois. The stated reason for his dismissal was all about civility: his alleged *in*civility in writing, notably in social media posts, about Israel and Palestine. His own argument was however that:

> My discourse might appear uncivil, but such a judgment can never be proffered in an ideological or rhetorical vacuum. Civility and incivility make sense only in frameworks influenced by countless social and cultural valuations ... Insofar as 'civil' is profoundly racialized and has a long history of demanding conformity to the ethos of imperialism and colonization, I frequently choose incivility as a form of communication ... In colonial landscapes, civility is inherently violent.[29]

In South Africa a little later Anthea Garman saw two crucial implications in the discursive character of Fallism and other recent protest movements. On the one hand:

> The debates that go on in the South African public domain are primarily a battle over regimes of the sayable. If one pays attention to what is said on social media – primarily, but also in the agenda-setting, mainstream media – one hears young, black activists and intellectuals directly addressing the sayable and the unsayable and setting new terms for debate by speaking overtly about the how of the debate ... In addition to powerful, new, young voices demanding space and time, we also see strong statements about what these new voices will not be doing. They will not educate those who do not work to understand the new terms of engagement and its topics. They will not reassure those who find the new style of engagement abrasive or overly angry or unsubstantiated or unreasonable. They will not respect the old rules of engagement that demand deference to certain styles embedded in another regime of truth ... This can be seen as a thoroughly good thing because such an opening up to other voices enlarges and includes, thereby making the democratic space more useful, more viable, more possible of being owned by everyone.

But more troublingly:

> [T]hese demands and behaviours also unsettle the public sphere's powerful reliance on a particular rational-critical modus operandi, with its powerful adherence to logos (the argument, the statement) over ethos (the person/positionality from which the statement comes). Some of the tactics used to unsettle the politics of the present also strike at the foundations of not only the public

sphere, but also knowledge generation and consolidation based on rational, evidential techniques in the academic sphere. What we can know in a shared, accepted way is critical to making decisions, creating community, holding to social compact (rather than using force) and deciding on the shared future.[30]

The arguments mounted by Salaita, and by Garman on the 'positive' side of her ambivalence, are undeniably powerful. In post-imperial, post-Brexit Britain – whether in its academic world or more broadly – their echoes are still comparatively faint. Yet it is hard to doubt that they have gradually become louder, as what are too glibly labelled 'culture wars' attain a new salience in politics. Almost every front in these 'wars' has more or less centrally involved ideas about imperial legacies, decolonisations, and decoloniality. They thus influence, and intertwine with, the older 'imperial history wars'. This chapter has offered some highly critical, though it is hoped also sympathetic, reflections on their character. It has been implied throughout that they badly need more conceptual clarity, more positive prescriptions for change – and yes, sometimes more civility. In addition, just as South African debates have tended to collapse together colonialism, apartheid, and racism, so the British ones, partly under US influence, elide empire, slavery, race and more.

To end, however, somewhat more affirmatively, even amid such doubts and perhaps disillusions, what all those different decolonising moments at least have in common is the aspiration, perhaps still no less important for former colonisers than for the once colonised, that in Rex Nettleford's wonderful phrase they 'be liberated from the obscurity of themselves'.[31]

Notes

1 S. Dubow, 'Rhodes Must Fall, Brexit, and Circuits of Knowledge and Influence' in S. Ward and A. Rasch (eds), *Embers of Empire in Brexit Britain* (London: Bloomsbury Academic, 2019), p. 118.
2 Y. Di-Capua, *No Exit: Arab Existentialism, Jean-Paul Sartre, and Decolonization* (Chicago: University of Chicago Press, 2018); M. Richardson (ed.), *Refusal of the Shadow: Surrealism and the Caribbean* (London: Verso, 1996).
3 Including notably J. D. Jansen (ed.), *Decolonisation in Universities: The Politics of Recognition* (Johannesburg: Wits University Press, 2019); S. Booysen (ed.), *Fees Must Fall: Student Revolt, Decolonisation and Governance in South Africa* (Johannesburg: Wits University Press, 2016); J. D. Jansen, *As by Fire: The End of the South African University* (Cape Town: Tafelberg Publishers, 2017); and several interventions by Achille Mbembe, such as 'Decolonizing the University: New Directions', *Arts & Humanities in Higher Education*, 15:1 (2016), pp. 29–45.
4 The most substantial exception thus far is a collection of essays by mainly British based scholars: G. K. Bhambra, D. Gebrial and K. Nişancıoğlu (eds), *Decolonising*

the University (London: Pluto, 2018). A book emerging from the Oxford (and other) Rhodes protests has a more activist, generally less reflective, orientation: Rhodes Must Fall Movement, *Rhodes Must Fall: The Struggle to Decolonise the Racist Heart of Empire* (London: Zed Books, 2018). The most academically significant contribution there is probably that by Patricia Daley.

5 Richard Drayton offers a sharply critical view of Biggar's career and views in 'Biggar vs Little Britain', in Ward and Rasch (eds), *Embers of Empire*, pp. 143–156. Biggar responded with considerable heat in 'The Drayton Icon and Intellectual Vice', *Quillette*, 27 August 2019.

6 www.mcdonaldcentre.org.uk/ethics-and-empire (accessed 31 August 2019).

7 This seems to the present author, who has regularly attended such seminars for forty years, to be simply and utterly untrue.

8 'Oxford Continues to Defend Colonialism at Every Opportunity – A Response from Common Ground', Facebook post, 14 December 2017.

9 'Cecil Rhodes statue row: Chris Patten tells students to embrace freedom of thought', *Guardian*, 13 January 2016. I may perhaps mischievously note that I had in fact read Popper's book as a schoolboy, before going 'up' to Oxford, and did not agree with it at all!

10 Stuart Ward traces important parts of its early employment, notably in the writings of Moritz Bonn, 'The European Provenance of Decolonization', *Past & Present*, 230:1 (2016), pp. 227–260.

11 A. Quijano, 'Coloniality and Modernity/Rationality', *Cultural Studies*, 21:2–3 (2007), pp. 168–178, at pp. 177–178.

12 Space precludes citation even of selected major works from thinkers on this already abbreviated list.

13 R. J. C. Young, *White Mythologies: Writing History and the West* (London: Routledge, 1991; 2nd edn. 2004).

14 S. Buck-Morss, *Hegel, Haiti, and Universal History University* (Pittsburg: Pittsburgh University Press, 2009); P. Arthur, *Unfinished Projects: Decolonization and the Philosophy of Jean-Paul Sartre* (London: Verso, 2010); R. Wolin, *The Wind from the East: French Intellectuals, the Cultural Revolution, and the Legacy of the 1960s* (Princeton: Princeton University Press, 2010); G. Steinmetz (ed.), *Sociology and Empire: The Imperial Entanglements of a Discipline* (Durham: Duke University Press, 2013); C. Kalter, *The Discovery of the Third World: Decolonization and the Rise of the New Left in France, c. 1950–1976*, translated by T. Dunlap (Cambridge: Cambridge University Press, 2016).

15 Here – to refer again especially to Africa – some acquaintance with the long, vigorous debates among philosophers in Africa, over what 'counts' as philosophical thought and the status of what was often called ethnophilosophy, might helpfully inform some current controversies.

16 H. Sharabi, *Neopatriarchy: A Theory of Distorted Change in Arab Society* (New York and Oxford: Oxford University Press, 1988), pp. 119–120. Emphases in original.

17 'Decolonizing the *AHR*', *The American Historical Review*, 123:1 (2018), pp. xiv–xvii.

18 J. D. Jansen, 'On the Politics of Decolonisation: Knowledge, Authority and the Settled Curriculum' in Jansen (ed.), *Decolonisation in Universities*, p. 59. In here reiterating my major debts to Jansen's work on these themes, perhaps it might be added that this does not imply *total* agreement: I feel that occasionally he has slipped from justified reservations about Fallism into an unjust tone of simple scorn.
19 There are some honourable exceptions, such as, for African studies, S. J. Ndlovu-Gatsheni, *Coloniality of Power in Postcolonial Africa: Myths of Decolonization* (Dakar: CODESRIA, 2013).
20 T. Mitchell, *Colonising Egypt* (Berkeley: University of California Press, 1988: cited from 1991 2nd edn.), p. ix.
21 Dubow, 'Rhodes Must Fall', in Ward and Rasch (eds), *Embers of Empire*, p. 113.
22 Žižek denies ever using the phrase, which was attributed to him (without a specific reference) by another eminent scholar, Columbia's Hamid Dabashi: see Dabashi, *Can Non-Europeans Think?* (London: Zed Books, 2015), p. 1; Žižek, 'Reply to My Critics', *The Philosophical Salon*, 5 August 2016.
23 PIR publications and the controversies they generate are of course mainly in French, but much of Bouteldja's writing is collected in English as *Whites, Jews, and Us: Toward a Politics of Revolutionary Love* (South Pasadena, CA: Semiotext(e), 2016).
24 A. Hussey, *The French Intifada: The Long War between France and its Arabs* (London: Granta, 2014).
25 The allusion is especially to her book: P. Gopal, *Insurgent Empire: Anticolonial Resistance and British Dissent* (London: Verso, 2019) – which however also has many strengths, and, it should be noted, offers very generous praise and acknowledgement for the present writer's own closely related early work.
26 S. Howe, 'British Worlds, Settler Worlds, World Systems, and Killing Fields', *The Journal of Imperial and Commonwealth History*, 40:4 (2012), pp. 691–725.
27 See especially T. Mason (ed. Jane Caplan), *Social Policy in the Third Reich: The Working Class and the 'National Community'* (Oxford: Berg, 1993).
28 Once again, space does not allow for even very selective citation of these writers' numerous works.
29 S. Salaita, *Uncivil Rites: Palestine and the Limits of Academic Freedom* (Chicago: Haymarket, 2015), pp. 29–30.
30 A. Garman, 'Babel Unbound', *New Frame*, 22 July 2020 – and see the book from which this is excerpted, L. Cowling and C. Hamilton (eds), *Babel Unbound: Rage, Reason and Rethinking Public Life* (Johannesburg: Wits University Press, 2020).
31 D. Scott, '"To be Liberated from the Obscurity of Themselves": An Interview with Rex Nettleford', *Small Axe*, 10:2 (2006), pp. 97–246.

Index

Abercorn, 3rd Duke (Governor of Northern Ireland) 154
Africa's Fighting Men (film) 29
African National Congress (ANC) 10, 103, 112, 113
amarespectables (Christianised Africans) 105
Amery, Leo 26, 179, 180, 185
Anatomy of Britain (Anthony Sampson) 1
Anglican Communion 192–207
Anglo–Irish treaty (1921) 175, 177
'Anglosphere' 15
Ansari, Sarah 66
ANZUS alliance 213, 214, 217, 219–221
Archer, Angelina 42, 46
Argentina 275, 284
Armitage, David 18n31
Asquith, Herbert 175
assisted/subsidised migration 35, 37, 259, 260, 261–262, 263
Association of British Civilian Internees – Far Eastern Region (ABCIFER) 55, 56, 57
Atlantic Charter (1941) 25, 34, 158
Attlee, Clement 34
Australia
 Anglican Communion 193, 195–196, 198, 199, 201, 202, 206–207
 immigration policy 34, 35, 37, 203–204, 259, 260–261
 migration from UK 256, 258, 260
 recruitment to armed forces 23–24, 33, 35–36

 republicanism 126
 security/defence policy 213–229
 US armed forces 28

Baghdadi Jews 47, 49, 50, 58
Bailkin, Jordanna 234, 236, 237
Bajpai, G. S. 70
Balfour, Arthur 176
Barbados Advocate 96
Battle of Manners Street (Wellington, New Zealand) 28
BBC 29
Beamish, Henry Hamilton 158
Belfast Newsletter 153
Belgrave, Michael 9
Belich, James 8
Bell, Duncan 8, 215
Bell, George (Bishop of Chichester) 197, 198, 199, 202
Bengal famine (1943) 27
Betta, Chiara 50
Biggar, Nigel 297, 305
Black Lives Matter movement 296, 298
Bogle, Paul 91
Bolton, Angela 27
Bone, A. N. G. 77
Bossano, Joe 281, 284, 286
Bourne, Kenneth Morison 41, 50, 51–52, 58
Bradford, Reverend Robert 162
Break-up of Britain (Tom Nairn) 1, 3
Brexit 7, 15
Bright, Rachel 7
British Board of Film Censors 31
British Israelite cult 163

British Nationality Act (1948) (BNA) 63, 64–66, 68, 76, 78–79, 275, 276, 277
Brockway, Fenner 245
Brooke, Basil (father) (Viscount Brookeborough) 161–162
Brooke, Basil (son) 165–166
Browne, Gloria 87
Butler, R. A. 162
Butterfield & Swire (company) 45

Calwell, Arthur 35, 36
Canada
   citizenship law 65, 183
   immigration policy 34, 205, 259, 264–266
   migration from UK 256, 269n16
   recruitment to armed forces 23
   republicanism 126
Canadian Nationality Act (1946) 183
Cardus, Neville 95
Carney, Dora 41, 51
Carney, John James (Jim) 41, 49, 51
Carson, Sir Edward 151
Ceylon Citizenship Act (1948) 68
Chamberlain, Mary 99n23
Chari, R. T. 70
Charlie Hebdo attacks (2015) 304
Chaudhuri, S. N. 72
Chichester-Clark, James 164
child migration 204
China Britons 41–58
China Navigation Company 45
Church of England
   see Anglican Communion
Churchill, Winston 27, 33–34
citizenship law 63–79, 183–184
Clarke, Banjo 28
Coghlan, Sir Charles 149, 150–151
Cold War 184, 216
Colley, Linda 3–4, 5, 17n20
Commonwealth citizenship 69–71, 72
Commonwealth Immigration Act (UK 1962) 58, 183
(British) Commonwealth of Nations 172–186
Commonwealth Secretariat 180
Congress Alliance (South Africa) 111
Congress of the People (South Africa 1955) 111

Constantine, Learie 95
Council for Empire Settlement 201–202
Craig, James (Lord Craigavon) 150, 152
Craig, William 163
Crapp, Errol 32
Crawley, D. J. C. 63
Cripps, Stafford 28
Crosland, Anthony 239
Curragh 'incident' (1914) 161
Curtin, John 214

Daily Gleaner (Jamaica) 96
Daily Telegraph 36
Darwin, John 297
Datar, B. N. 78–79
Davies, Ednyfed 237
Davies, Sonja 28
Davis, N. Darnell 94
Deakin, Alfred 214
Dellipiani, Frank 286
Devine, T. M. 5
Dhlamini, James 136
Dilke, Charles 8, 9, 93
Dilley, Andrew 7
'Doctors' Pact' (South Africa) 108
Dominions 31–32, 181
   see also Australia, Canada, New Zealand, South Africa
Drum newspaper (South Africa) 114
Dubow, Saul 7, 20n47, 113, 295, 304
Dunbar, Rudolph 29
Durban 103–111
Dutt, Subimal 71

Eastern Cape (South Africa) 132
Ede, James Chuter 85
'Edna' (anonymous Jamaican) 87
Elias, Diana 56–57
Elizabeth II 126, 156
Empire Windrush 84, 95, 97
European Economic Community (EEC) 172, 183, 184, 217, 277
Evening Standard 96
extraterritoriality 47–48

Falklands/Malvinas 272–273, 274–278, 284–285, 289–291
Falklands War (1982) 284–286
Falls, Cyril 155

Index

Farquhar, M. E. 96
Faulkner, Brian 164, 165
Finlay, Richard 17n23
Fisher, Geoffrey (Archbishop of Canterbury) 192, 194–195, 197–198, 205
Foster-Hall, Dick 53, 54, 55
France 304–305
Franks Commission (1966) 235
Free and Assisted Passage Agreement (UK–Australia) 260
French Intifada (Andrew Hussey) 304
Froude, J. A. 9, 93–95

Gallagher, Jack 151
Gambia 127, 142–143n12
Gamble, Andrew 4
Gandhi, Manilal 107
Gandhi, Mohandas K. (Mahatma Gandhi) 25, 105
Garcia, Joseph 290
Garman, Anthea 307–308
Garvey, Marcus 92
GATT 182–183
Gendi, Kofi 33
George V 148–149
Ghana 127
Gheewalla, J. C. 111
Gibbs, Humphrey 135, 138, 147
Gibraltar 272–273, 274, 275–284, 285–291, 293n75
Gibraltar Chronicle 287, 288
Gordon-Walker, Patrick 70–71
Gorton, John 213, 222, 224–229
Greater Britain concept 8–9, 10, 15
Griffith, Alan 226–227
Guam doctrine (Richard Nixon) 229
Guyana 87

Hall, H. Duncan 175, 176
Hall, Stuart 96
Hangings Case (Rhodesia 1968) 136
Hanham, Harry 3
Hansen, Randall 65
Hardoon, Isaac Silas 42, 52
Hasluck, Paul 220, 223
Hassan, Sir Joshua 281, 282–283, 286, 289
Hayton-Fleet, Bertie 42, 46
Hayton-Fleet, Natalia 42, 52

Hayward, Howard 53
Hayward, Jack 56, 57, 58
Hayward, Menahem 41, 47, 52, 58
Hechter, Michael 3, 16n13
Hewitt, John 165
Hinds, Donald 88–90, 97, 99n24
Holt, Harold 223, 224
Hong Kong 43–44, 49, 51, 53, 277
Hopkins, A. G. 221
Howe, Stephen 85
Hughes, Billy 216
Huxley, Elspeth 150

Immigration Act (UK 1971) 184
immigration policy (Dominions/Rhodesia) 33–35, 36–37, 93, 203–205, 253–254, 260–266
immigration policy (UK) 183–184, 253
Immigration Restriction Amendment Act (New Zealand 1920) 33–34
Importance of Being Earnest (Oscar Wilde) 57
India
   citizenship law 63–79
   violent repression 26–28
India Consequential Provision Act (UK 1949) 73
India Marches (film) 32
Indian Citizenship Act (1955) 68–72, 76, 77–78
Indian National Congress 26, 106
Indian South Africans 66–67, 103–119
Indonesia 223
intellectual decolonisation 294–308
interracial marriages 36
interracial sexual relationships 31, 36
Irish Times 163–164
Isola, Cecil A. 282
Isola, Peter 278, 281
Itote, Waruhiu 30

Jack, Ian 4
Jackson, Sir William 288
James, C. L. R. 92–93
James, Winston 101n63
Jansen, J. D. 310n18
Jardine, Sir Colin 205
Jennings, Sir Ivor 179

Jewish diaspora 60n14
John Swire & Sons (company) 45, 48
Johnson, Boris 10
Johnson, James 245
Johnson, Lyndon 213, 225–226
Joseph, Gilbert 97
Journey to an Illusion (Donald Hinds) 88
Judd, Frank 235, 243, 246

Kajee, A. S. 103, 109, 114
Katju, K. N. 67
Kennedy, John F. 219
Khama, Seretse 36
Kipling, Rudyard 166
Kiralfy, Albert 161
Kissinger, Henry 228
Koditschek, Theodore 95
Krishnan, Kathilal Sankaran 77–78
Kumar, Krishan 4
Kuper, Hilda 112

Lamming, George 88
Lardner-Burke, Desmond 135
Latham, Michael 283
Laurier, Wilfrid 175
League of Nations 177
Lee Kuan Yew 222
Lester, Alan 9
Levy, Andrea 84
Levy, Hannah 47, 50
Lipski, Sam 229
Lisbon Agreement (Spain–UK 1980) 274
'London is the Place for Me' (song) 84
Louis, Wm. Roger 220
Lovers and Strangers (Clair Wills) 85
Luthuli, Albert 111, 115, 117

MacKenzie, John M. 166
Mackenzie King, William Lyon 34
Macmillan, Harold 112
McNamara, John 246
Malaysia 221–224
Malta 159
Mandela, Nelson 103, 113
Mander, John 2
Mandler, Peter 9
Marryshow, T. A. 95

Mason, Timothy 306
Matthews, James 118
Maudling, Reginald 245
Maximum Effort (film) 25–26
Menon, Krishna 71
Menzies, Robert 172, 216
Mifsud, Michael 280
migration 201–206, 252–266
    see also immigration policy
Miller, M. S. 237, 246
Ministry of Information 25, 26
Mitchell, Robert 164
Mitchell, Timothy 303
Mlambo, Victor 136
monarchy 125–126
    see also republicanism
Moolla, A. M. 119
Morgan, Philip D. 10
Morning Post 151
Morris, Jan 3, 105
Mosaka, Paul 117
Muldoon, Andrew 27

Naicker, Monty 103, 111, 114, 115–116
Nairn, Tom 1
Natal 108, 115–118, 132
Natal Indian Congress (NIC) 103–104, 105, 107, 109, 113
Natal Indian Organisation (NIO) 103, 109, 112
National Party (NP) (South Africa) 128, 129
National Union of Students (NUS) 235, 240, 241, 247
nationality
    see citizenship law
Nazi Germany 25, 306
Nehru, Jawaharlal 67, 75, 79, 118–119, 182
Nettleford, Rex 308
New Statesman 164
New York Times 134–135
New Zealand
    American armed forces 28
    Anglican Communion 196, 198
    immigration policy 34–35, 37, 203, 259, 261–262
    migration from UK 256

recruitment to armed forces 23
security/defence policy 213, 216
News Chronicle 26
Nigerian Eastern Mail 24
Nixon, Richard 227
Noel-Baker, Philip 73
non-aligned movement 182
North-China Daily News 44–46, 49
Northern Ireland 147–148, 152–156, 162–166

O'Brien, Conor Cruise 159
Oceana, Or England and Her Colonies (J. A. Froude) 9, 93
Ogborn, Miles 7
Olley, Charles 157–159
Olusoga, David 87
O'Neill, Terence 147, 164
Open Society and Its Enemies (Karl Popper) 297
Orange Order 157, 163
Oriel College, Oxford 296, 298
Ottawa Economic Conference (1932) 179
overseas students 234–247
Oxford University 235, 239–240, 296–297, 298

Padmore, George 24
Paisley, Ian 163
Pan African Congress (PAC) 112, 113
Pant, Govind Ballabh 79
Paris 304
Parkes, Sir Henry 215
Parti des Indigènes de la République (PIR) 304, 305
Patel, Sardar 67
Pather, P. R. 109, 112, 119
Patten, Chris 297
Peliza, Robert 282
Penguin News 277
Perraton, Hilary 234, 235, 236
Perry, Kennetta Hammond 92
Pert, Lilian 30–31
Phillips, Doreen 87
Phillips, Mike 87
Phillips, Trevor 87
Picture Post 26
Pietsch, Tamson 7, 19n39, 234, 235

Plaid Cymru 3
Pohe, Porokuru Patapu 22
Pollock, Hugh 153
Poovalingham, Pat 115, 116, 118, 119
Powell, Enoch 2, 148, 180, 184–185
preferential trade 178–179, 182
Putnam, Lara 91, 97
Pym, Francis 289

Quebec 126
Queen's Proclamation (1858) 105
Quijano, Anibal 299–300
Quit India movement 26, 27, 28

race nationalism 9
Rahman, Tunku Abdul 222
Rasch, Astrid 88
Ray, A. K. 77
recruitment to armed forces 23–24, 32–33, 35–36
republicanism 111–115, 126–141
Resolution 1514 (UN General Assembly 1960) 274, 275
Reynolds, Z. Nia 86
Rhodes Must Fall campaign 296, 297
Rhodesia
  immigration policy 205, 259, 262, 263–264
  migration from UK 256–257, 268–269n15
  reactions to decolonisation 159–161
  republicanism 133–141
  self-government 147, 156–157
  see also Ulster–Rhodesia analogy
Rhodesian Front 133, 159
Richards, Eric 258
Riddell, Patrick 165
Ridley, Nicholas 276–277
Robbins, Keith 3
Robbins Committee on Higher Education 237–238
Rogers, William 227–228
Roman Catholicism 202–203, 206
Roosevelt, Franklin D. 25
Roy, Anupama 68
Royal Air Force (RAF) 22, 23, 24
royal visits 107, 108–109
Rush, Anne Spry 92, 100n45
Rusk, Dean 222, 223, 225

Salaita, Steven 307
Sampson, Anthony 1
Samuel, Raphael 3
Sangha, Karta Singh 41–42, 46, 47, 52
Sassoon, E. D. 50
Sassoon, Victor 45, 50, 58
Schwarz, Bill 9, 86, 91
Scottish National Party 3
Scottish separatism 3
Searle, Jon M. 287–288
Second World War 23–34
Seedat, Dawood 107
Seeley, J. R. 8, 9, 93
Serle, Geoffrey 218
Sexwale, Frank 33
Shadrack, Duly 136
Shanghai 44–46
Shanghai Municipal Council (SMC) 46, 48
Shanghai Race Club 44
Shanghai Volunteer Corps (SVC) 49, 55
Shanks, Michael 2
Sharabi, Hisham 301
Sharpeville massacre (1960) 112, 113
Silkin, John 283
Singapore 26, 221–224
Singh, Fateh 75
Singh, Rajah Maharaj 110
Small Island (Andrea Levy) 84
Smith, George Ivan 163
Smith, Ian 133–134, 136, 137–138
Smuts, Jan 108, 149
Soske, Jon 111
Sotelo, Leopoldo Calvo 272
South Africa
    Anglican Communion 196
    armed forces 24, 32–33
    immigration policy 205, 259, 262–263
    intellectual decolonisation 296, 307
    interracial marriages 36
    migration from UK 252, 256–257
    republicanism 111–115, 128–133
    royal visits 107, 108–109
    support for Rhodesian UDI 134
    see also Indian South Africans
Southern Rhodesia
    see Rhodesia
Statute of Westminster (1931) 176

sterling bloc 178
Stockwell, A. J. 234–235
Stockwell, Sarah 235, 244
Straw, Jack 241
Sundaram, K. V. K. 69
Sunday Telegraph 134
Sunday Times 36
Sydney Morning Herald 27, 34
Sykes, E. L. 72–73

Tambo, Oliver 117
Tawse Jollie, Ethel 151, 157, 158
Tet Offensive 224
Thatcher, Margaret 275, 285, 286, 287
Thomas, John Jacob 94
Thomas, Peter 29
Thompson, Andrew 9
Thompson, Dudley 23, 24, 33, 36
Times newspaper 17n19
Toye, Richard 148
Tredgold, Sir Robert 161
Trinidad 24
Trinidad Guardian 96

UDI (Unilateral Declaration of Independence) (Rhodesia) 133, 134, 135, 159, 161, 163
Ulster–Rhodesia analogy 147–150, 157–159, 161–166
United Nations (UN) 108, 172, 274
United Party (South Africa) 130–131
United States (US/USA)
    armed forces 28–29
    inclusion in Greater Britain 215–216
    opposition to British imperialism 28
    relationship with Australia 213–214, 215, 219–229
    trade policy 182
Utrecht, Treaty of 280

Van Straubenzee, William 245
Vernon, James 6, 19n35
Verwoerd, H. F. 112, 128, 129, 132
Victoria, Queen 10
Vietnam War 213, 224
Vucetic, Srdjan 215

Walker, Jean 75
Waller, Keith 223, 227

Wand, William (Bishop of London) 202
Watson, Neil 277
Wavell, General Archibald Percival 27
Webb, Keith 3
Welensky, Sir Roy 159
Welsh separatism 3
West Indian Britishness 84–98
West Indies Calling (film) 31, 32
Whipping Act (India 1942) 26–27
'White Australia' policy 34, 36, 203, 259, 260, 261
Whitehead, Sir Edgar 159
Whitlam, Gough 226, 261
Wickson, D. W. H. 76
Williams, Gwyn 3, 16–17n16
Williams, Henry Sylvester 91

Wills, Clair 85
Wilson, Harold 136, 147, 163, 217
'Wind of Change' speech (Harold Macmillan) 112
Windrush
  see Empire Windrush
Windrush era 84–98
Wolrige-Gordon, Patrick 243
women 25–26
Woods, Edward (Bishop of Lichfield) 197–198

Xuma, A. B. 108

Zimmerman, Valdemar 47
Zionism 50

EU authorised representative for GPSR:
Easy Access System Europe, Mustamäe tee 50,
10621 Tallinn, Estonia
gpsr.requests@easproject.com

www.ingramcontent.com/pod-product-compliance
Lightning Source LLC
Chambersburg PA
CBHW051559230426
43668CB00013B/1915